Farewell to Cricket

FAREWELL TO CRICKET

DON BRADMAN

Introduction by David Frith

THE PAVILION LIBRARY

First published in Great Britain 1950

Copyright © Don Bradman 1950
Introduction copyright © David Frith 1988

First published in the Pavilion Library in 1988 by
PAVILION BOOKS LIMITED
196 Shaftesbury Avenue, London WC2H 8JL
in association with Michael Joseph Limited
27 Wrights Lane, Kensington, London W8 5TZ

Series Editor: Steve Dobell

British Library Cataloguing in Publication Data
Bradman, *Sir* Donald
Farewell to cricket.
1. Cricket
I. Title
796.35′8′0924   GV917

ISBN 1-85145-224-9 Hbk
ISBN 1-85145-225-7 Pbk

Printed and bound in Great Britain by
Billing & Sons Limited, Worcester

Cover photograph reproduced by kind permission of
The Bradman Archives

INTRODUCTION

The little green bookseller's label states: Dymocks Book Arcade, George Street, Sydney. The marked price was twelve-and-six sterling, but this book cost a bit more in Australia. That bookshop, a high-vaulted, old-world establishment, was an Aladdin's Cave for any schoolboy looking for the rarely-afforded luxury of a brand new cricket book. There were other cricket biographies available at the time, but this one, even if two years on the market already over in the UK, was the *big* one. It was paid for, wrapped in brown paper, and taken home on the train, my little parcel of cricket history.

Farewell to Cricket is an entrancing book. I thought so in 1952 and I'm glad I've had occasion (having referred to it *en passant* many times in the interim) to re-read it 35 years later, an indulgence for one who now can barely keep up with the torrent of new cricket books which he is obliged to read.

It starts – rather like that tapped single off the first ball – at the beginning, Cootamundra, 27 August 1908, and finishes at the end of that matchless career. Much has Sir Donald Bradman contributed since then in the areas of administration and journalism, where his opinions have been sought relentlessly, and carefully dispensed. But I think we all know in our hearts that it was the years of on-field achievement that count. His razor-keen mind is reflected in every paragraph, and the mass of detail from his stupendous, wide-ranging career is recorded with characteristic precision, as if by a scientist of sport. He has always shunned small-talk, in conversation as well as in strokeplay. The reader rides ever upward with him on The Don's ascent to apparently limitless heights of accomplishment. His only weakness seems to have been seasickness.

I used to hang around for hours, like some fixated pavilion cat, outside the members' entrance of the Sydney Cricket Ground, and once, between current Australian and South African cricketers, I actually caught sight of Sir Don Bradman. Naturally, he was not clad in Australia's green-and-gold blazer and flannels, but wore a sober grey suit and pork-pie hat. Here was the administrator, the Test selector in the phase of life which followed the matchless years of active participation. Intrepid as I may have viewed myself as a seeker of autographs, I could not drum up the courage to ask for his. He seemed rarefied and completely unapproachable. How gratified, if not disbelieving, I would have been in 1952 if a voice had whispered to me that I would one day come to know him well – indeed, almost to perish alongside him late one night in Adelaide, as he drove me back to my hotel, and a speeding car almost hit us at an intersection. I'll always believe it would have been easily the most glorious way for any cricket-lover to die.

It is generally recognised that Bradman has 'mellowed' over the years, and if that is so, it could be because the distressing pressures linked to primary fame have eased in some respects just as they have intensified in others, principally in the matter of his beloved wife Jessie's health. In *Farewell to Cricket*, with the same word-economy that assures his match descriptions of a notable modesty, he conveys the grief felt in losing a child as well as the helpless anguish an athlete knows in physical adversity. Loss of feeling in his right thumb and forefinger since half a century ago is among the surprising revelations in this classic book.

It can have been no easy task to record by oneself for world consumption an absolutely unique trail of record-breaking triumphs. Others have done it on his behalf, before this volume was first published and afterwards, but nothing else matches his poise, his perpetual tone of no-nonsense intent and subsequent sense of 'Right, that's another major plan executed; now on to the next objective.'

The tightly-written, important chapter on 'Bodyline', the 'think' pieces at the end on the Laws of the game and its history, the appraisal of contemporaries, the condemnation of irresponsible Press coverage, the documentation of the cease-less struggle to preserve privacy: these passages all have an enduring significance. So too does Lord Harris's statement that cricket 'is more free from anything sordid, anything dishonourable, than any game in the world' – a postulation that has been put severely to the test in modern times. These 'beautiful words' The Don commends to all players as a 'glorious creed'. Lord Harris would never have had cause to cavil at this Australian's conduct on or off the field.

The photograph of young Bradman in the stance position remains imprinted, icon-like, on the retina of the subcon-scious: bare head (he would have worn a helmet in appropriate circumstances had it been in vogue in his time); crisp shirt, sleeves rolled up in wide laps to the elbow; rubber-nipple batting-gloves, open at the palm; bright buckskin pads; white ankle-boots with polished leather heels – none of your modern plastic trainers; and a simple, light, willow bat, half-brown and free of garish labels. But most riveting of all are the firmly determined mouth and fiercely purposeful eyes – the most famous face not only throughout Australia but much of the old Empire.

The wiry youngster from the bush captured the imagination of millions through the Depression years and beyond, his hold growing stronger with every passing year. It is a spine-tingling experience to look upon the countenance of the elderly Bradman and see in it the virile young man from the flickering greyness of the newsreels, the leathery dynamo who con-quered legions of bowlers and floundering fieldsmen, and left millions of cricket-lovers slavishly spellbound.

Here is his story, the saga recorded with the utmost authenticity. 'Dear Don,' he recalls an English lad writing upon his retirement in 1948, 'Thank goodness you've quitted. Perhaps we'll have a chance now.' He spoke for opponents everywhere. Or, as Raymond Robertson-Glasgow put it in *Wisden* in his rather more urbane manner: 'So must ancient Italy have felt when she heard of the death of Hannibal.'

Neither of these phenomena can be taken from us so long as his story glows on parchment like this.

Guildford, 1988   David Frith

FAREWELL TO CRICKET

by

Don Bradman

CONTENTS

CONTENTS

ILLUSTRATIONS

7

In the Beginning

THE FIRST TIME MY NAME APPEARED IN A NEWSPAPER WAS ABOUT 1921 when this paragraph was published in a New South Wales journal called *Smith's Weekly*:—

Bounding Ball. Saw a curious thing at a junior cricket match at Bowral (New South Wales) recently.

"Don Bradman (crack 'bat') sent a ball over the boundary fence. It struck half a brick, rebounded on to a fence post, poised there for an appreciable time, and ran along the top of the palings the whole length of a panel of fencing before descending outside the boundary.—John."

Curiously enough, the story was perfectly true, but what a coincidence that some twenty years later my own son, now at school, should be called John. His parents were not influenced in their choice of names by the writer of the paragraph.

From the first, my name was linked up with the town of Bowral and I was dubbed the "Boy from Bowral", but my birthplace was at a much more remote country town, Cootamundra, New South Wales, where I was brought into this world on 27th August, 1908. From old correspondence recently discovered, I believe the event occurred in Adam Street.

I was the baby of our family, being four years junior to my brother Victor, and my three sisters Islet, Lily and May were older than either of us.

Before I reached three years of age our family moved to Bowral, where my boyhood days were spent.

This beautiful town, about 80 miles south of Sydney, set in the midst of agricultural land, is a most popular resort for Sydney people who like to get away from their business worries and spend weekends in the balmy atmosphere 2,210 feet above sea level.

My education commenced in the normal way. I attended the Bowral Intermediate High School, and although our educational facilities were much the same as those at any other school, there was little or no organised sport for the children in the primary school.

Our headmaster, Mr. A. J. Lee, was a good sport who often amused himself by playing with the boys, but there was no coach. We were left to our own devices and had to play as nature advised, without knowing whether we were adopting orthodox methods or not.

During weekends and after school, I usually found myself without any playmates because no boy lived close to our home. For this reason I had to improvise my own amusement, and this, during the hours of daylight, almost invariably centred around the use of a ball. It was either kicking a football, playing tennis against a garage door or an unusual form of cricket which I invented for my own enjoyment.

At the back of our home was an 800-gallon water tank set on a round brick stand. From the tank to the laundry door was a distance of about eight feet. The area under-foot was cemented and, with all doors shut, this portion was enclosed on three sides and roofed over so that I could play there on wet days. Armed with a small cricket stump (which I used as a bat) I would throw a golf ball at this brick stand and try to hit the ball on the rebound. The golf ball came back at great speed and to hit it at all with the round stump was no easy task.

To make my game interesting I would organize two sides consisting of well-known international names and would bat for Taylor, Gregory, Collins and so on, in turn.

The door behind me was the wicket, and I devised a system of ways to get caught out and of boundaries. Many a time I incurred mother's displeasure because I just had to finish some important Test Match at the very moment she wanted me for a meal.

The open side of my playing area corresponded to the on-side of a cricket field, and therefore I did not have to chase the ball for any shots on the off-side.

This rather extraordinary and primitive idea was purely a matter of amusement, but looking back over the years I can understand how it must have developed the co-ordination of brain, eye and muscle which was to serve me so well in important matches later on.

Another form of amusement was to take a golf ball into the neighbouring paddock where I would stand some 10 or 15 yards from the dividing fence and throw the ball to hit a rounded rail. My main purpose was to make the ball come back at various heights and angles so that I could catch it. Obviously this also developed the ability to throw accurately, because if I missed the selected spot, it would mean a walk to retrieve the ball.

The playground of the primary school was separated from that of the high school by a fence, but we had the privilege of standing at the gateway. I was frequently to be found at that gateway watching the senior boys play cricket, and once or twice at their invitation managed to have a few hits with them.

Even in the senior school playground, there was no cricket pitch, and our practice was carried out on dirt, which resembled Nottingham marl in appearance. Our wicket was the bell post. A chalk mark indicated the height of the stumps, and many an argument ensued as to whether the post had been struck above or below the chalk mark.

Bats mainly consisted of pieces of wood from a gum tree, fashioned after the shape of a baseball bat. Pads were never worn, and the ball was of a type commonly known as a " compo ". A boy usually occupied the crease until he got out.

The first cricket match in which I played occurred when I was about eleven years of age. It was at Glebe Park, Bowral ; not on a cricket ground but on the football field. The pitch was plain dirt, and was the most level piece of earth we could find.

Bad as it was, I don't think that it equalled the Australian pitch which "W.G." described thus : " There was so much dust on the pitch that the ball sometimes stopped where it was pitched by the bowler." (Ref. *The Graces* by Powell-Canynge Caple). They must have been slow lob bowlers.

Little did I dream that later a beautiful cricket ground would exist on the same recreational area bearing the name of " The Bradman Oval ".

In this first match of mine our captain won the toss and decided to bat. For the other side a left-hand bowler obtained a wicket with his first ball, another with his second ball, and I arrived at the crease, a none too confident lad, to stand between the bowler and a hat trick. How I survived the first ball remains a mystery, but I did, and eventually carried my bat for 55 runs.

In the High School there were occasional matches on sports afternoons between scratch teams, and there were only two occasions when I played for our school team against a neighbouring school. In the first of these two matches, against Mittagong School, we played on a concrete pitch covered with coir matting, and out of our team's total of 156 runs my contribution was 115 not out. I was then twelve years of age, and that was my first century.

Naturally I was elated, but my pride was short-lived, for next day we were lined up in the playground at school and the headmaster said : " I understand that there is a certain boy among you who scored a century yesterday against Mittagong. Well, that is no reason or excuse why you should have left a bat behind." I was never guilty of a similar offence again.

In the second of these two matches, which we also won, my contribution was 72 not out, so that in competitive matches at school against outside teams I scored a total of 244 runs without losing my wicket.

Despite the lack of modern sporting facilities, these school days were completely happy. Apart from cricket, I thoroughly enjoyed all other sports, representing the school at tennis, playing for the school Rugby League Football team, and winning the 100 yards, 220 yards, quarter- and half-mile races for boys of my age.

Sparse as it may seem, that constituted the background of my sporting education at school.

At weekends I often walked for miles on shooting expeditions, and loved fishing in the nearby creek.

Swimming was an exception. Two episodes nearly ended in tragedy. They were enough.

Mathematics was my favourite subject, though science ran a close second until an accident at the school (a student caused an explosion with an unauthorised experiment) made me apprehensive.

They were normal boyhood days.

Further Education

ALTHOUGH I REVELLED IN ANY FORM OF SPORT, MY GREAT LOVE IN THOSE early days was always cricket, and nothing gave me greater pleasure than to be allowed to act as scorer for the Bowral Team.

My uncle was captain and the team played competitive matches on Saturday afternoons against neighbouring townships within a radius of about twenty-five miles.

Having to sit on a wooden kerosene box in the back of a lorry shod with hard rubber tyres, and to journey in this fashion over metal roads for many miles, was not even considered a hardship. I hate to think what such an experience would do to me now.

Apart from the joy of scoring, there was always the possibility of getting a hit with the men. Sure enough, one day the eleventh man failed to turn up, and our captain was left with the choice of playing with ten men or including me in the team, because we were at Moss Vale, some six miles from home.

I was sent in at the fall of the eighth wicket. I was still in short trousers and used a man's full-sized bat which was almost as tall as I, but was 37 not out when the last wicket fell. Thus, at the age of thirteen, I made my first appearance in senior cricket. The following Saturday when the match was continued, I was allowed to open our second innings, and had scored 29 not out at stumps.

Following these boyhood efforts, and no doubt realising my disability in having to use a man's bat, Mr. Sid. Cupitt, a member of the Bowral team, gave me one of his old bats. It was cracked, and my father sawed three inches off the bottom. Despite its imperfections I was very proud of my first cricket bat.

Unfortunately for me, the District Cricketers did not fail to turn up any more, and so I had to return to my job as scorer.

Then came an incident which fired my enthusiasm, and I think played quite a part in my future decision to make cricket my number one sport.

My father, always a great cricket enthusiast, decided that he would go to Sydney to watch the Fifth Test Match between Australia and

The author as a baby

England. It was played on the Sydney Cricket Ground from 25th February to 1st March, 1921. After much persuasion he agreed to take me with him, and so I beheld for the first time the Sydney Cricket Ground, and had my initial experience of watching first-class cricket.

It is interesting to recall that my next view of a match on the Sydney Cricket Ground was one in which I appeared, and I saw no more first-class cricket until I myself was a participant.

The vision of that magnificent ground remains with me as vividly as ever. I still feel that the Sydney Cricket Ground is the best in the whole world on which to play, and I have a peculiar affection for it which will never be supplanted.

In that memorable Test Match I was privileged to see Macartney, in all his glory, making 170 runs. I can picture his delicate leg glances, and one flashing drive—not through the covers but over the top. My great favourite was Johnny Taylor. He was my boyhood hero, though I had never met him, and I can still remember the sinking feeling which came over me when Patsy Hendren caught him out.

Other incidents such as Armstrong being caught first ball, Woolley's beautiful stroke making, the smooth rhythm of Ted McDonald and the glorious catching of Parkin by Johnny Taylor still come back to me as though they happened yesterday.

We only saw the first two days' play because my father had to return home, but it seemed as though a lifetime of dreams had been crowded into that brief period.

My father must have been amused when I said to him: " I shall never be satisfied until I play on this ground."

In the years that followed it was lovely to reflect upon the fulfilment of these early hopes, and to know that my father saw many of the wonderful matches in which I was privileged to take part on that famous ground. And he was there to see my final appearance in the Kippax-Oldfield Testimonial Match.

After leaving school, I entered the services of Mr. Percy Westbrook, who conducted a real estate business in Bowral under the title of Davis & Westbrook.

Apart from cricket, I was at that time very fond of tennis, and, probably because one of my uncles had a court upon which I was always free to play, I devoted myself to tennis for one whole summer. The following summer I again played tennis until towards the close of the season, but cricket, which was so surely implanted in my blood, lured me back to the Bowral Cricket Team.

My first innings gave the scorer no trouble. I was out first ball for a duck. My second effort was not much better.

Then we had to play in the semi-final of the competition against Wingello. Although our team was beaten, my own contribution was 66, top score for our side.

Cricket thereby ended for the season, but I had made up my mind to concentrate on it the following summer, and from that time onwards no other sport was allowed to interfere.

Competition Cricket

WITH THE BEGINNING OF THE SUMMER OF 1925, I REALLY COMMENCED my serious cricket career as a regular member of the Bowral Team. I was only seventeen. Some of my colleagues were in the forties. I deemed it quite a privilege to have the opportunity of playing with these grown-up men.

At first nothing of very great consequence occurred. Then we were drawn to play against the Wingello team which had beaten Moss Vale in the final the previous year, thanks to splendid bowling by a chap named O'Reilly.

Although I had not seen O'Reilly in action, stories of his prowess had preceded his arrival at Bowral with the Wingello team.

These matches were played during two consecutive Saturday afternoons, the first on the ground of one team and the second on the ground of the other.

The opening day's play of our match against Wingello took place at Bowral on the ground which now bears my name. Naturally I was anxious to do well because of the reputation of our opponents, and there was a great struggle for supremacy between O'Reilly and myself.

With considerable help from Dame Fortune during the early overs, I managed to get on top, and finished the day with a score of 234 not out, in the last 50 runs of which were 4 sixes and 6 fours.

Continuing my innings on the Wingello ground the following Saturday, I was bowled first ball round my legs by O'Reilly, whose ability even then to turn a leg break with speed amazed me, and kindled an admiration for his skill which the passage of time considerably deepened.

This score naturally received a certain amount of publicity, but it was a subsequent innings in the final of the competition against Moss Vale which, more than anything else, was probably responsible for getting me a chance to play in Sydney.

This final match was set down for the Moss Vale ground, and under the Competition Rules had to be played to a finish on consecutive Saturday afternoons from 2 o'clock until 6.

Rivalry between the two clubs was intense, and there was much local enthusiasm.

My uncle, George Whatman, who was captain of the Bowral team, won the toss and sent me in to bat with Mr. Prior. We were together until just before stumps when Prior was dismissed for 52. I was 80 not out.

The match was continued on the second Saturday, and at the end of this day's play Bowral had scored 475 for 1 wicket. I was then 279 not out and my uncle 119 not out. Between us we had added 323 runs in three and a half hours.

On the third Saturday our innings ended at 9 for 672. Another uncle by the name of Dick Whatman could not bat because he had broken a toe after the match had commenced, and of course he could not be replaced by a substitute, his name having been declared in the original team. My brother Vic. played in our side, but made only one run.

I think perhaps the scores of this memorable innings might be of interest, so here is how the Bowral total was made up:—

Don Bradman c. Prigg b. Ryder	..	300
O. Prior b. S. Tickner	.. ..	52
G. Whatman b. S. Tickner ..	..	227
S. Cupitt run out ..	.. ..	4
V. Bradman b. Aynsley	.. ..	1
E. Waine b. S. Tickner	.. ..	36
G. S. Bensley b. S. Tickner ..	..	1
O. Knopp b. S. Tickner	..	11
N. Sinden c. Cowley b. Soden	..	5
A. Stephens not out ..	.. ..	7
Sundries	..	28

9 for 672

You will notice I was out caught Prigg. He was a fine left-hand bat in the country. I was so pleased when he came to see me at my hotel in Sydney during the Kippax-Oldfield Testimonial in 1949. We had not met in all those years, but in keeping with the good fellowship of cricket, recognised one another at sight and had a long chat about the early days.

We dismissed Moss Vale for 134 in the first innings and 200 in the second, so that Bowral won by an innings and 338 runs. In addition to getting 300 with the bat, I took 4 wickets for 39 runs.

The match had lasted five Saturday afternoons, and brought forth the following humorous paragraph in the *Sydney Sun* :—

" At last ! Yes, it is really over. The final match in the Berrima District Cricket Competition has been brought to a conclusion——

16

It was the easiest win in the history of the Berrima District Cricket, but it took Bowral five weeks to vanquish their persevering rivals."

Before the game commenced my mother had promised me a new bat if I made a century so I suggested that she now owed me three bats, but my arguments did not prevail. The promised bat, the first I had ever selected for my own use, was duly purchased, and it is somewhat remarkable that I should have chosen a bat made by William Sykes Ltd., the make which subsequently bore my personal autograph throughout my career.

It was rather unusual for a match to last so long, and it created considerable interest not only in the district but elsewhere. A well-known Sydney cartoonist drew a humorous sketch depicting firstly " Young Don " running up and down the wicket like a rabbit, then as a fully grown man, next as an old man, rheumaticky and bent, with a beard touching the ground, and as a grand finale two of us on top of the Heavens asking St. Peter where the Moss Vale cricket pitch was so that we might finish the game.

Looking back on the season, I had very great reason to be satisfied with my performances. Not only had I created a District record score of 300 in one innings, but for the whole season had made 1,318 runs at an average of 101.3, had taken 51 wickets at an average of 7.8, and held 26 catches.

Naturally, I was already hoping that some day I might participate in cricket of a higher standard, and even that I might be selected to play in what is known as Country Week during the 1926-7 season.

Before that time arrived, however, a scheme was devised to try and find promising bowlers, and the New South Wales Cricket Association organised a cricket practice on the Sydney Cricket Ground No. 2 so that the selectors could witness the country talent. On the 5th October, 1926, the Secretary of the New South Wales Cricket Association wrote to me at Bowral. At that time he did not even know my address and the letter was sent care of the captain of the Bowral team.

The letter said, *inter alia*, " The State Selectors have had under consideration your record in cricket in the past season, and in view of such record they particularly desire to see you in action. For this purpose I would like you to attend practice at the Sydney Cricket Ground on Monday next, 11th inst. Practice commences at 4 p.m. and continues throughout the afternoon. I sincerely trust that you will give this matter the consideration its importance warrants, and hope that you will realise that this is an opportunity which should not be missed."

My expenses were of course paid by the Association, and needless to say I was very thrilled to get this opportunity and certainly did not miss it.

My father accompanied me to the trial, and although it was perhaps somewhat awe-inspiring for a lad of eighteen to be thrust before the

17

eyes of men who had been my legendary heroes, and particularly as I was unaccustomed to turf wickets, I went to the nets quite confidently.

Press comments were favourable and helpful—one in my scrap book says : " Perhaps the most surprising feature about yesterday was that the practice, which was devised primarily for the benefit of bowlers, produced a batsman and a batsman from the country too." The article went on to say that my batting was fairly correct but not polished, and my footwork exact but clumsy—a fault associated with most country players who bat on hard wickets.

In later years some writers have given considerable prominence to this early trial and claimed that I batted in white trousers with black braces. It might make a good story but it wasn't true. Do you think such a thing would have been passed over by the hawk-eyed writers of that day or the even keener-eyed camera men ? What a scoop picture it would have been if it were true ! Needless to say, no such picture exists.

The result of the trial was that I was asked whether I would be prepared to play for one of the Sydney First Grade Clubs, and finally arrangements were made for me to go to the city each Saturday and play for St. George.

Before that could take place, the New South Wales Cricket Association invited me to play in an all-day trial match on the Sydney Cricket Ground after which the New South Wales team for Queensland was selected. Thus it was I played my first innings on the Sydney Cricket Ground No. 1, and although scoring 37 not out, it was not sufficient to catch the Selectors' eyes for the State side. However, it probably assisted my selection in a further trial at Goulburn, where a match was held, after which the Southern Country Week side was chosen. In this Goulburn trial I scored 62 not out and took 4 wickets.

Although cricket was my first love, I was still playing tennis at odd times, and was chosen to represent the district in Country Week Tennis also. It meant that I had to discuss the position with my employer, Mr. Percy Westbrook, to whom I owe a deep debt of gratitude for his help and encouragement in those days. Mr. Westbrook never placed any obstacles in the way, but on this occasion he made it clear that I could have leave to play in one Country Week, but not both. Cricket won.

These Country Week matches are a grand idea. Teams are selected from the various country districts and they play against one another during the week on various Sydney grounds. The matches are played on turf and provide splendid experience. The " Week " culminates in a match between a city team and a combined country side on the Sydney Cricket Ground which is an inspiration to the players.

This was the busiest period of my cricket life up to that time. The country matches were played every day from Monday to Friday. My highest score was 46, my lowest 21, and I obtained a few wickets. Several of the country players later obtained a place in the State first or second eleven, and there were such figures as Aub. Sieler (of tennis fame) and Eric Weissel who became one of the greatest Rugby League five-eighths Australia has known. Eric's magnificent catch to dismiss me when we played South could hardly have been surpassed.

On the Saturday of this Country Week I took my place in the St. George First Grade Team against Petersham. Included in the opposition were Internationals Sam Everett and Tommy Andrews, but using the cherished bat which my mother had given me I managed to survive some anxious moments, and reached 110 before being run out. On the Monday I was one of the fortunate players to be selected for the combined country team against the city, and it was a great thrill to play for the first time against such a brilliant batsman as Charlie Macartney. Although I had to chase a number of his shots I delighted in seeing him score 126 against us.

In our innings I was caught at first slip just as the clock struck time. The score-board and press reports showed me 98, but I believe the official record has my score down as 100.

This had undoubtedly been a very happy and interesting week's cricket, and my knowledge of the game, through meeting players of a higher standard, especially on turf, had been improved.

Returning to the country, my next opportunity of any note came when I was selected to play for the New South Wales Second XI against Victoria on the Sydney Cricket Ground on New Year's Day, 1927.

We had lost 3 wickets for 47 runs, but Dudley Seddon (afterwards a New South Wales Selector) and I took the score to 105 before being separated. After making 43 (top score for New South Wales) I pulled a ball from Ebeling on to my stumps.

In our second innings I had made 8 when I hooked a ball to the leg boundary. In doing so my foot slipped and struck the leg stump, dislodging a bail. The umpire, George Borwick, ruled that I was out, much to my disappointment.

Apart from my own participation in this match, it is worthy of mention that Bill O'Reilly played for New South Wales.

I am amused to see by some old press cuttings that in those days the State Selectors were severely criticised because I was not chosen for the New South Wales Sheffield Shield Team. In recent years I have been one of the criticised Selectors because other players have been omitted. Fortunately I recognised, even then, that only eleven men can play in a cricket team.

For the remainder of this season I continued playing for St. George, but it involved a journey from Bowral to Sydney each Saturday morning. I had to rise about 5 a.m. to catch a train at approximately 6 a.m. which landed me in the metropolis before 9. After the day's play was over, the train journey back had to be undertaken, and I could not get to bed much before midnight.

This travelling was a disability, but a greater handicap was my lack of practice on turf during the week. Despite these difficulties, I had made 289 runs at an average of 48.1 when the First Grade season ended. But there was still another match to play.

Having started the season in the country and having played for Bowral in the District Competitions, I was eligible to take part in the final match of the season against our opponents, Moss Vale. In the corresponding match the previous season I had scored 300. This time the match did not last so long.

Moss Vale won the toss and, batting first, were dismissed for 73. We commenced our innings, and at stumps I was 58 not out. The match was resumed the following Saturday when the Bowral team's score was carried to 480, of which my share was 320 not out, including 6 sixes, 1 five and 43 fours.

Needless to say Bowral won the match, and as a result of my performance, the local Association subsequently passed a rule that no first-grade player would in future be eligible to participate in such competitions.

So concluded a very interesting and instructive season. I had been brought into the company of players like Alan Kippax, Archie Jackson and Charlie Kelleway, and had tried hard to absorb the knowledge which was so obviously to be gained by watching them.

One thing in particular caused me a lot of thought. I noticed that my grip, developed on the concrete wickets, was different from that of most players. It assisted me in pulling a ball, and was much safer for on-side shots, though it handicapped me somewhat in playing the ball between mid-off and point.

I experimented—worked out the pros and cons—and eventually decided not to change my natural grip.

Throughout a long career my grip caused many arguments, but I think it is sufficient to prove that any young player should be allowed to develop his own natural style, providing he is not revealing an obvious error. A player is not necessarily wrong just because he is different.

I was looking forward to the following season. There was still so much to learn.

Sheffield Shield Cricket

AS I WAS STILL LIVING AT BOWRAL, IT WAS NECESSARY FOR ME TO CONtinue my journeys to the city each Saturday at the commencement of the 1927-8 season in order to play first-grade cricket. I had been approached to see if I would play for the Northern District Cricket Club, but in view of the happy relations which existed between the St. George Club and myself, I decided to continue with the latter.

The first match of the season was against Paddington, and in the St. George total of 258 I contributed 130 not out. More important to me than my score was the experience of playing against the redoubtable Jack Gregory, one of these mercurial personalities who are such an attraction to cricket lovers the world over.

Despite early successes, I did not find a place in the New South Wales team which went to Queensland at the start of the season, nor was I chosen for the Southern Tour to South Australia and Victoria.

Then fate took a hand. Jack Gregory and H. S. Love dropped out of the New South Wales team, and Albert Scanes and I were chosen in their stead.

This was indeed an opportunity, and I was conscious of the great honour that had come my way in such a short space of time.

Apart from the thrill of being selected to represent New South Wales, there was also the prospect of journeying to Adelaide and Melbourne, quite an adventure for a young lad who had never been outside the State before.

On this particular occasion the team went via Broken Hill. It necessitated spending a night in the train, a new experience for me, and in December that train journey from Sydney to Broken Hill can be exceptionally hot and dusty.

We struck a bad trip. Sleep eluded me, and the injudicious use of the electric fan no doubt contributed towards a cold in the eye which became evident next morning. On the same journey Archie Jackson developed a boil on the knee, so that upon our arrival in the Silver City, Dr. McAdam (our manager who later met a tragic death in Macquarie Street, Sydney) insisted that Archie and I should spend the day in bed instead of enjoying a trip underground with the rest of the team.

In many respects Broken Hill is a remarkable city. I believe its silver lead mines are the richest in the world, but in those days it could not claim to possess ideal cricket facilities. Scarcely any rain had fallen for about two years. There was not a blade of grass on the oval from one end to the other. The soil was a deep red colour, with dust in some parts a couple of inches thick. The concrete wicket was very good, but the bowler had to run up on a concrete approach—something I have never seen anywhere else. Cricket boots with sprigs were quite useless. Most of our team played in sandshoes, but not having a pair with me I played in ordinary walking shoes.

Despite these difficulties, we had a most enjoyable match, and at the end of the game I managed to obtain the ball as a souvenir of my first game with a Sheffield Shield side. It is still a cherished possession, and as this ball was one of the old type (before the reduction in size came into force) the comparison with a modern ball is particularly interesting. The difference in size—just by the feel of the ball in the hand—is most noticeable.

We continued our journey to Adelaide, where in the normal way I was to have been twelfth man, but luck was with me once more. The boil on Archie Jackson's knee prevented him from playing, and I received my chance in the eleven.

The weather was extremely hot, and our captain, Alan Kippax, had to retire twice during his innings owing to a touch of sunstroke.

South Australia's attack included fast bowler Jack Scott (afterwards an International Umpire), P. K. Lee, who subsequently bowled for Australia, and the one and only Grimmett. I was naturally elated at scoring 118 in my first innings in first-class cricket. It was 17th December, 1927. Strange that on the same day Ponsford made his 437 against Queensland which remained the world's record score in first-class cricket, until I passed it.

The beautiful Adelaide Oval is a lovely setting for a match at any time, though I don't suppose it ever looked better to me than on that summer afternoon. In later years much of my cricket was played there, and not only was it the scene of my initial innings in first-class cricket, but also my last—the Arthur Richardson Benefit Match, March 4 to 8, 1949.

In our second innings against S.A., Clarrie Grimmett bowled marvellously well on a turning wicket to take 8 for 57, and in scoring 33 out of our total of 150, I faced leg-break bowling of a higher calibre than any I had met before.

The match ended in an exciting victory for S.A. by one wicket. With the last man in, a ball sent down by McNamee did not rise an inch. It missed the stumps by a coat of paint and the batsmen ran 4 byes whilst the fieldsman desperately tried to save the day. Shooters were occasionally seen on the Adelaide wicket in those days. Times have not changed.

Apart from the cricket itself, I treasured the opportunity of meeting Clarrie Grimmett and watching the way he could spin a soft rubber ball on a table. I have not seen anybody who can make the ball perform such tricks. At that time I thought Grimmett the best slow leg-break bowler I had played against. With the passing of the years I see no reason to alter my opinion. No other leg spinner since 1918 has possessed his phenomenal accuracy.

Arthur Mailey was, of course, a magnificent bowler who imparted more spin to the ball than Grimmett and bowled a far better " wrong-un ". In between he bowled many bad balls. A bad one from Grimmett was a rarity.

From Adelaide we journeyed to Victoria where my modest scores of

Don Bradman (age 8 years) and his brother Victor

31 and 5 were disappointing, but as I fielded for scores of 202 and 38 by Ponsford and 99 and 191 not out by Woodfull, there was plenty to be gained by watching those splendid batsmen. I have always maintained that watching first-class cricketers in action is a wonderful education to the young player.

Back in Sydney, I appeared for New South Wales against Queensland on the Sydney Cricket Ground, but had the mortification of being bowled first ball for a duck. What a lesson it taught me !

When I went in, Alan Kippax was batting against slow bowler Gough. The first ball Kippax gently pushed to mid-on and we ran one. It all appeared so simple to me that before the next ball was bowled I made up my mind to do the same thing. Of course I overlooked the fact that Kippax had been batting a long time and was accustomed to the conditions. Instead of the ball coming slowly and turning as I anticipated, it went straight through and fast, taking with it my middle stump. Since that day I have never made up my mind what to do with the ball before it has been bowled. I commend this advice to all players.

What a delightful innings Kippax played in that match ! His 315 not out was a gem, and although they say Victor Trumper was even more beautiful to watch, it is hard to conceive more graceful batting than our skipper produced on that occasion.

A curious incident happened during his innings. Kippax jumped out to drive a " no-ball " and played it on to the stumps, dislodging the bails. O'Connor, the wicketkeeper, seized the ball, pulled out a stump and appealed for a run-out with Kippax still out of his ground. The umpire decided " not out ", and arguments ensued on all sides as to the corrrectness or otherwise of the decision.

My next Inter-state match was also at Sydney against South Australia. I still remember being out, caught and bowled by Doug. McKay. It was a dreadful shot, for I tried to turn a full toss off a new ball (which was swinging away to the off) round to the on-side, and skied it off the edge of my bat back to the bowler. In later years when Doug. McKay became a specialist in Adelaide and ministered to my children, I thought more kindly of him than when he made me look so foolish in Sydney.

A final innings of 73 against South Australia, and then 134 not out against Victoria concluded the first-class season. It had been grand experience, but I found these Inter-state matches much more strenuous than the one-day games to which I had been accustomed. It had been necessary gradually to alter my outlook on the game because there was so much more skill in the opposing bowlers.

I had also realised for the first time how different is the behaviour of turf wickets in Adelaide, Melbourne and Sydney. Another lesson driven home to me was the necessity for a sound defence as a basis on which to develop stroke production.

Although the season had been one of fluctuating fortunes, I cherished a natural desire to gain selection in the Australian Team which was to tour New Zealand at the end of the season. However, when the Team was announced, the Selectors, Vic. Richardson, Hugh Trumble and Tom Howard, had decided I was not to get a place ahead of Jackson or Schneider, but I was named as a reserve batsman in case one dropped out. This did not happen, so I missed the tour. I shall always regret not having played in New Zealand. A tour of that lovely country somehow eluded me.

Following the completion of the first-grade matches, a cricket team under the captaincy of Vic. Richardson and composed mainly of St. George players, visited Bowral for the purpose of opening the new turf wicket at Loseby Park. A reception and dance was held one evening at which I was presented with a gold watch and chain, a lovely tribute from the citizens of the District. In later years the captain of the Bowral Team, Mr. Alf. Stephens, took a great interest in my career and journeyed to England more than once to watch the Test Matches on the other side of the world.

A further trip which brought me valuable experience, even though it consisted only of second-class matches, was that with Arthur Mailey's Bohemians to Parkes and other places including Cowra, Cootamundra and Canberra. It was disappointing for me to be run-out for 1 the only time I played in my birthplace, and also to have my stumps scattered for 0 by Rex Norman at Canowindra. But these were only further links in the chain of experience which was being forged in matches of all kinds.

It now became clear that if I was to progress and achieve my ambition of playing for Australia, I must live in Sydney where I could gain regular practice on turf wickets and avoid the journeys from Bowral to Sydney which were proving very onerous.

Test Cricket

IT DID NOT TAKE MUCH THOUGHT TO MAKE ME REALISE HOW IMPORTANT the 1928-9 season might prove to be. The English Team was coming to Australia, and clearly Australia would soon have to find young players for the Australian Eleven.

My employer, Mr. Percy Westbrook, decided to open a business in Sydney, and in order to assist me, and at the same time meet the needs of his Company, he offered me the position of Secretary. Realising what it could mean to my future career I accepted, despite the implication that it meant leaving my home and family.

During my early years at Bowral, I had formed a close friendship with Mr. G. H. Pearce who was a country traveller for a Sydney Insurance Company. To assist me, Mr. Pearce kindly offered accommodation in his home. This was a great comfort, not only to me but also to my parents who were rather reluctant to see their young and inexperienced son going off to live in the city.

Having taken this all-important step, which enabled me for the first time to get turf practice during the week, I concentrated on improving my cricket in an attempt to make the Test side.

At the commencement of the season Australia (under Bill Woodfull) played against The Rest (under Vic. Richardson) in Melbourne. I was in The Rest, but was out for 14 in the first innings and 5 in the second. Admittedly our top scorer in the first innings only made 31, but I was not conscious of the satisfaction apparently felt by a writer commenting on the début of E. M. Grace who made 1 in the first innings and 3 in the second. The writer said : " As there were no fewer than 20 ducks in the Club's two innings, this lad of 13 years did not do so badly." I felt I had done badly because Grimmett and Oxenham had bowled too well.

My disappointment was soon erased for, a week later, playing for New South Wales against Queensland, I scored 131 in the first innings and 133 not out in the second.

This gave me confidence for the match between New South Wales and the M.C.C. on the Sydney Cricket Ground. It was my first encounter with Tate, Hammond, " Tich " Freeman and Harold Larwood. I scored 87 in the first innings and 132 not out in the second.

Then came another match in Sydney between an Australian XI and the M.C.C. Newcomers to me were George Geary and Jack White, and on a wicket none too easy we had to fight desperately for every run. Although scoring 58 not out in our first innings, the runs took me 3 hours and 20 minutes. Still the educational value was enormous, for this was my first experience against a tantalizing, accurate, slow left-hander like White.

I was dismissed in the second innings for 18, but the comparative successes which had come my way in the early part of the season gave me reasonable grounds for hope that I would make the Australian XI, which was shortly to be announced.

On the night in question, the names of the chosen were to be broadcast. There was some delay so I retired to bed, but had not gone to sleep when a nearby wireless gave out the names. They were in alphabetical order and therefore mine was first on the list. So this ambition had been achieved.

The match was played in Brisbane, and what a thrashing we got !

England won by the huge margin of 675 runs, the heaviest defeat by runs ever suffered by an Australian XI.

For me it was a real grounding. I did not mind having to chase 521 runs in England's first innings, for there were lessons to be learned watching these fine English players. I did not even mind being dismissed for 18 runs in our first innings, for my form had been quite good up to the time Maurice Tate defeated me with a slower ball. But it was a great disappointment to bat on a sticky wicket in our second innings (the first time I had ever seen one) and find I knew absolutely nothing about that kind of wicket.

Charlie Kelleway developed ptomaine poisoning and could not bat in our second innings; neither did he play Test Cricket again. But the poignant memory is of Jack Gregory coming into the dressing room after his knee had given way and with tears in his eyes saying, "Boys, I'm through, I have played my last game." Thus ended the career of possibly the most magnetic personality that Australian cricket has known.

Gregory was not as fast as Larwood, and I am sure it will surprise readers to know he only took 38 wickets in Sheffield Shield Cricket, but his whole attitude towards the game was so dynamic, his slip fielding so sensational, his brilliant batting so pleasing to those spectators who love hard hitting, that thousands would flock to see Gregory play anywhere at any time.

My admiration for Gregory's attitude towards cricket was unbounded. I appreciated the modesty of his outlook, and even 20 years later he retained the same generous-hearted attitude towards the skill of other players and the same modesty in relation to his own.

These tragedies occur and the places of such men must be filled, so new faces appeared in the Australian Team for the Second Test Match.

Our Selectors were not at that time particularly imbued with the gospel of youth, for in our Team they included Jack Ryder (then aged 39), Grimmett (36), Blackie (46) and Ironmonger (41). Despite my season's total of nearly 600 runs with an average of 85 per innings, I was relegated to 12th man. This prevented me from batting, but Ponsford unfortunately suffered a broken bone when struck on the left hand by a ball from Larwood, and consequently I had to field throughout the entire match. Australia was again roundly defeated.

Before crossing swords with England once more, we met Victoria in Melbourne. My own contribution was negligible, but the match was notable for a tenth wicket stand of 307 by Kippax and Hooker after we had lost the first 9 wickets for 113 runs. In one of the most remarkable partnerships of all time these two resisted the Victorian attack for over 5 hours, during which time Kippax made 260 not out, and Hooker was finally dismissed for 62, only after New South Wales had gained a first innings lead.

27

I was brought back into the Australian Team for the Third Test Match, and managed to redeem my earlier failure with scores of 79 and 112. It was in this match that I witnessed my first exhibition of what English batsmen can do on a sticky wicket. Hobbs and Sutcliffe were caught on a really bad one, and the Melbourne sticky wicket is the worst in the world. Hobbs made 49 and Sutcliffe 135.

Even now I think Sutcliffe's exhibition that day was the nearest approach to mastery on a sticky wicket I saw throughout my career.

Hobbs, of course, was renowned for his skill under such conditions, and I also remember Hammond and Leyland in splendid exhibitions, but none of them to my mind quite equalled Sutcliffe, whose uncanny ability to let the ball go when it jumped or turned was simply amazing.

With Ponsford out of the side, Australia was having some difficulty in finding an opening batsman to partner Woodfull. Richardson had been tried in the Second and Third Test Matches. A total of 35 runs in four innings was not good enough.

Public opinion and press comment probably had a lot to do with the experiment which was tried in the following Sheffield Match between New South Wales and South Australia when I was sent in to open the innings. Tim Wall, whose prowess with the new ball is the subject of comment elsewhere, quickly put an end to this idea by dismissing me for 5 in the first innings and 2 in the second, and it was Archie Jackson with scores of 162 and 90 against South Australia who was chosen to take Richardson's place in the Fourth Test Match.

What an innings he played ! Jackson, who was then 19, opened the batting and in half an hour saw Woodfull, Hendry and Kippax back in the pavilion with the total at 19. Undaunted by this setback, Jackson proceeded to play an innings which from the point of view of stroke execution, elegance and sheer artistry held the spectators as few innings in history have done.

I was Jackson's partner when we resumed after an interval. If my memory is correct Archie's score was 96 or 97, and being so much older than he (just about a year to be precise) I had the temerity to offer him some advice. Jackson was to take strike against Larwood who had a new ball, so I suggested to him that there was no hurry. " Take your time," I said, " and the century will come."

Those who saw his next stroke will agree with me that no more glorious square drive could be played. He didn't care about Larwood or the new ball which travelled like a bullet to the pickets in front of the Members' Stand.

This youthful genius went on to make 164, and became the youngest player in history to make a Test century. The score did not matter so much. It was the manner in which he scored his runs. The English players joined in the applause, for cricketers like to see artistry even when they are on the receiving end.

To think that four years later I should be called upon to act as one of the pall-bearers when this glorious young player's remains were carried to rest, a victim of that dread scourge, tuberculosis.

On the other side of the picture Hammond, with 119 not out and 177, blasted our hopes of victory, and though his career was long and masterful, I really think Hammond was then at the peak of his form.

An exciting finish developed. In the end England won by 12 runs. When victory seemed in sight, I was run-out in a hair-splitting decision, and Blackie was caught on the long boundary to end the match.

When Blackie returned to the dressing room, one of our players said to him : " What did you think as you hit that ball ? " With typical humour, Blackie replied : " I was thinking how the boys will cheer when they see me hit him for six." So in four Test Matches Australia had been defeated, but the introduction of youth was beginning to tell.

Prior to that Fourth Test Match I had played an innings of 340 not out on the Sydney Cricket Ground—up to that time the highest score by a New South Wales player in Sheffield Shield games, and the highest in a first-class match on the Sydney Ground.

Then in the Final Test Match in Melbourne, Australia at last broke through the opposition and achieved their first victory. Younger players in Jackson, Fairfax, Wall, Hornibrook and myself contributed to this win, and thus the personnel of the 1930 Australian Team began to take shape. My own scores were 123 and 37 not out, so that I had now become established as a regular member of the Australian Team.

Our new fast bowler, Tim Wall, gave a splendid exhibition, especially in the second innings when he took 5 for 66, and Alan Fairfax, with a grand 65 in his first knock, also fully justified his selection.

After participating in our early defeats, I had the pleasure of being at the wickets with our skipper, Jack Ryder, when the winning runs were made.

Although we did not realise it at the time, that match also marked the end of Jack Ryder's Test match career. He was a member of the Australian Selection Committee in 1930 which picked the Team for England, but Ryder's name was not included amongst the chosen.

As my first Test Skipper, I pay tribute to a fine cricketer of high principles who learned the game in a hard school and who set a standard which many others would now do well to emulate. In later years I was to have the privilege of serving with him on the Australian Selection Committee.

To conclude a season which must remain memorable for me I made scores of 35 and 175 against South Australia to finish with a total of 1,690 runs in first-class cricket, which still stands as the highest aggregate for one season in Australia. Unless I am mistaken, this total will be exceeded before very long.

A World's Record

ANOTHER SEASON'S CRICKET HAD TO BE PLAYED BEFORE THE AUSTRALIAN
Team was chosen for England, and a visit from an unofficial English
Team on its way to New Zealand under the captaincy of A. H. H.
Gilligan, provided the opportunity to have a match against the renowned Frank Woolley and the rising star Duleepsinhji. The latter
with scores of 34 and 47 only showed us glimpses of his Eastern skill,
but Woolley's 219 runs were made with that fluency of style which
was so characteristic of this graceful player.

Woolley was then past his best—one could not expect him to be
otherwise for he was now in the early forties—but we saw enough to
realise why he had been classed amongst the great stylists of the world.

Another interesting feature of the New South Wales Match against
the M.C.C. Team was that Arthur Allsop, playing his initial first-class
match, scored 117 and 63 not out. I had witnessed this boy's first
match on the Sydney Cricket Ground some time before and was most
impressed by his phenomenal cover driving. Later, Allsop's form fell
away somewhat, but at that time he gave every promise of developing
into a leading Australian XI batsman.

Apart from the ordinary Sheffield Shield Matches, a Test Trial was
held on the Sydney Cricket Ground between Ryder's XI and Woodfull's XI. A wonderful match ended with Ryder's XI victorious by
one wicket, after having made 663 in the first innings.

In this game I made 124, and was the last man out in the first innings
of Woodfull's XI. As we were forced to follow on, Woodfull sent
me to open the innings at the second attempt, so that I virtually went
straight back to the wickets. At the end of the day my score was 205
not out, and the following day I was dismissed for 225. This gave me
a century in the first innings and a double century in the second, in the
one day, and some argument ensued as to whether such a feat had
been accomplished before.

Despite a comparatively good season, it is remarkable that I only
played one innings over a century in Sheffield Shield Cricket that season.
It was against Queensland. In making 452 not out, I managed to
obtain the world's record score in first-class cricket. It still stands.

Circumstances assisted me because the first portion of the innings
was played on a Saturday leaving me 205 not out at stumps. This
enabled me to have a rest over the weekend and therefore come up
fresh on the Monday morning. Fortunately my health and physical

The author's idea of the proper way to follow through after making a full blooded drive. A photo taken during Bradman's world's record score of 452 not out.

condition were good, and the great effort of making such a total did not appear to be an undue strain.

Hundreds of messages poured in, the first being a telegram from the previous record holder, Bill Ponsford, who wired—" Congratulations on your great feat—a batsman of your ability deserves the honour."

It was one of those occasions when everything went right. The wicket was true and firm, the outfield in good condition and the weather warm but not unduly hot. In the early stages of the innings I had no thought of creating a record, but once my score was over the third century I felt so well that the possibility of achieving this record became obvious. Eventually, when Alan Kippax closed our innings with the New South Wales score at 8 for 761, I felt quite fit to go on.

Apart from the satisfaction of achieving a performance of this kind, I am gratified that the runs were made at a speed and in a manner which clearly demonstrated I was attacking the bowling throughout the innings, and not playing defensive cricket for selfish reasons.

In support of this statement I quote the following sectional times :—

50 in 54 minutes	
100 in 103 ,,	
150 in 140 ,,	
200 in 185 ,,	On the second day I scored
250 in 230 ,,	105 runs before lunch and
300 in 288 ,,	142 between lunch and
350 in 333 ,,	afternoon tea.
400 in 377 ,,	
450 in 414 ,,	
452 in 415 ,,	

Ponsford, the previous record holder, took 621 minutes for his score of 437.

It will be seen that the slowest 50 in the whole innings occupied 58 minutes, a scoring rate which should be sufficient to satisfy the most exacting.

At the close of our innings a spectator jumped the fence and tried to carry me off the ground. The result was that we both finished in a heap with me on his chest. The Queensland players, tired as they must have been, very generously picked me up and carried me off.

Upon reflection, it seemed incredible that in such a short space of time I should have achieved something which was beyond my wildest dreams when I first walked on to that beautiful Sydney Ground. It was quite true that my batting still did not measure up to the canons of orthodoxy demanded by those who give style number one priority in the list of essentials of the batting art. This realisation did not worry me because I took the view that my style had been moulded under hard wicket conditions and could only be gradually modified as my experience on turf wickets was extended.

Maurice Tate, in a most friendly way, had suggested that I would need to play with a straighter bat to get runs in England. So did Woolley. Percy Fender had expressed doubts as to how I would fare overseas, and others suggested my pull shots were made with a cross bat. These things had to be considered.

One of my favourite scoring shots was to pull a short-pitched ball off the stumps to the leg side. To do this, and to keep the ball on the ground, one must use a cross bat. There is no other way the stroke can be successfully accomplished.

In making the shot, as I did quite often, I knew there was some risk, but it was bringing runs and seldom getting me out. At least I was carrying out my own theory that cricket was a test between bat and ball, and I was always prepared to try and play attacking cricket unless the situation of the game or the tactics of the opposition made it impossible. I loved every minute of my cricket and tried to play it with the zest which a boy of that age should exhibit.

There could be no reasonable doubt that I would be included in the Australian Team to visit England, but at the time of the announcement I was spending a few days with my parents in Bowral, and on the fateful day had gone shooting with my brother. When we returned the Team had been announced.

The citizens of my home town staged a Farewell in the local theatre, and it was pleasing to renew acquaintances with friends and relations who had closely followed my fortunes in the city since my boyhood days in the country.

Amongst the visitors was Mr. Frank Cush, now a member of the Australian Board of Control. To him and his wife I owe a great debt of gratitude.

After my initial transfer to Sydney it became necessary for me to live in the St. George District if I was to continue playing with that Club. Mr. and Mrs. Cush offered me the peace and comfort of their own private home in order that I might pursue my normal occupation and at the same time not lose opportunities in cricket. Their help and guidance was of enormous value to me.

Amidst all the pleasures and activities, I therefore felt more than a measure of satisfaction that Mr. Cush should openly tell my kinsfolk at Bowral of the cordial relations which existed between us and of his confidence in my ability to face the vicissitudes of life which lay ahead without succumbing to an attitude of superiority.

The breath of depression was felt in real estate circles, and during the season I deemed it prudent to accept an offer of employment by one of Sydney's leading sports firms.

Thus, with a light heart, but nevertheless a realisation of the obligations which rest upon each and every member of an Australian Eleven, I joined the party on the first stage of the journey to England, which represents probably more than any other prize in the cricket world the ambition of thousands of young Australians.

To play first-class cricket is a goal, and to reach the Australian XI in Australia, probably a higher honour than to go to England in the strict practical sense. But for many reasons it is a tour of England upon which most youngsters set their hearts.

England the First Time

ONLY FOUR MEMBERS OF THE 1930 TEAM HAD BEEN TO ENGLAND BEFORE. We were a comparatively young and inexperienced side carrying with us the hopes and fears of those for whom youth is a greater attraction than experience.

For the first time, I boarded a ship, the *Nairana*, upon which we travelled to Launceston. Very soon I discovered how poor were my qualities as a sailor. Those who have experienced seasickness will understand that my condition was not improved by the jokes with which others tried to amuse me.

I was told of the old lady who asked a seasick passenger in a deck chair, " Is the moon up yet?" He replied " Madam—if I swallowed it, it is."

There were other amusing ones, but I was completely disinterested.

In the lovely Island of Tasmania we were royally entertained. Enjoyable matches were played and Stan McCabe made his opening century in first-class cricket. I began to visualise the potentialities of this delightful island, rich in natural resources, the development of which is rapidly taking place today.

There was more seasickness on the way back from Tasmania and still more on the trip to England, but this was merely incidental compared with my first opportunity to see Western Australia, Ceylon, Suez, Cairo, Port Said, Italy, France, Switzerland and then at last England.

Cricket's great stalwart, Lord Harris, was amongst those who met us, and there were others with great names, men who in the short space of twenty years have now passed on.

The first few days in England were similar to those described at a later stage on a subsequent visit. For me there was constant bewilderment at the wonderful places which formerly had only been names.

Lord's was a great attraction, but there were other places not associated with cricket including my first sight of a Wembley Cup Tie Final. To hear upwards of 100,000 people singing " Land of Hope and Glory " to the accompaniment of massed bands is an inspiring event, the more so when it happens in the presence of our Sovereign King. Not the least interesting sight was the Graf Zeppelin which sailed majestically over the ground.

It will not be possible for me to describe in detail the English tour, but only to pick out events which impressed themselves upon my memory, commencing with the opening game on that beautiful ground at Worcester with the architectural gem of a cathedral in the background.

Opening my account with a score of 236 (thereby beating H. H. Massie's record made in 1882) and following this with 185 not out at Leicester, I discovered at once that the English wickets suited strokes of a certain kind but not others.

It was also apparent this early that English wickets change in character throughout a match far more than Australian wickets. The heavier atmosphere is more conducive to swing, and the more grassy wickets enable bowlers to get some assistance from the pitch. Nevertheless, the ball usually comes off the ground at a slower speed, and owing to my comparatively short stature and preference for shots off the back foot, I began to like batting on those slower wickets.

In the third match, our little wizard, Clarrie Grimmett, performed his great feat of taking 10 Yorkshire wickets for 37 runs, the last 7 for 16. In the same fixture I scored 78—my first sight of an English wet wicket. I found it less fearsome than the Australian variety.

My first meeting with the great Australian fast bowler, Ted McDonald, who was then playing for Lancashire, was brief. My middle stump went flying, and I am ready now to argue his place amongst the greatest of all fast bowlers. It was hard to visualise a more beautiful action which, coupled with splendid control and real pace, made him the most feared bowler in England at that time, as he had been years before with the Australian Team.

After the hard Australian wickets and our warm sunshine, the cold and damp weather of England provided unusual and often unpleasant conditions. I found it difficult for instance to adjust myself to the idea of wearing a sweater, blazer and overcoat before a roaring fire awaiting my turn to bat. Then I assure you a crack on the leg in such weather causes far more discomfort than a similar crack when the temperature is in the nineties.

During a later match at Oxford, the press referred to a heat wave, but seven of our team turned out against the University in sweaters. Perhaps this only tends to indicate the difficulties which confront English players when they visit Australia.

My first game at the Oval provided an opportunity for combating the wiles of Surrey's Captain, Percy Fender, who, you will remember, had some doubts about my ability to make runs in England. After suggesting that I might become a great player, Fender had said : " He will always be in the category of brilliant and unsound ones. He does not inspire me with any confidence that he desires to take the only course that will lead him to a fulfilment of that promise. He does not correct mistakes or look as if he were trying to." I thought it best not to make any mistakes against Surrey.

Only one day's play was possible because of rain, and Australia had to bat on a soft pitch. Rain caused stumps to be drawn before time, but Australia put together 379 for 5 wickets, of which my total was 252 not out, and undoubtedly that was one of the best innings I ever played against an English County. The second hundred was scored in 80 minutes.

Because of early successes an opportunity had occurred for me to get 1,000 runs in May, a feat which no Australian had ever accomplished, and when we went to play against Hampshire it was the last day in the month. When we lost the toss and Hampshire batted, my chances appeared remote, but Grimmett overwhelmed their batsmen and then Woodfull sent me in to open the innings with Archie Jackson, thereby enabling me to score the coveted runs just as rain drove us from the ground and ended play for the day.

I feel that there was a measure of generosity on the part of the Hampshire captain in allowing play to continue when the weather might reasonably have caused a cessation.

I was not unmindful of this when it fell to my lot in 1938 to close the Australian innings at Lord's and thereby give Bill Edrich a chance to score 1,000 runs in May.

All these were preliminaries for the Test Matches, but we went to Nottingham not without hope that this young and improved Team would emerge victorious.

We were disillusioned but not disgraced. England gained the victory by 93 runs, but Australia made 335 in the fourth innings, the highest total of the match. I contributed 131 of these, and at one stage thought we might save the game, but Robins, the mercurial Middlesex spinner, bowled me with a " wrong-un " at which I attempted no stroke.

We had the worst of the inclement weather counterbalanced by an injury to Sutcliffe and the indisposition of Larwood. The latter only served to emphasise the lion heart of Maurice Tate, who sent down no fewer than 50 overs for 69 runs.

Our Second Test at Lord's provided one of those glorious chapters in cricket which connoisseurs revel in discussing by the fireside.

In a match limited to four days England scored 425 in the first innings, of which Duleepsinhji, playing his first Test, garnered 173 by masterly batting. Facing such a score, it seemed that a win was out of the question. Woodfull and Ponsford, however, gave us a splendid start, after which I played an innings of 254—in my judgment, technically the best innings of my life. Practically without exception every ball

Bradman in 1930

went where it was intended to go, even the one from which I was dismissed, but the latter went slightly up in the air, and Percy Chapman with a miraculous piece of work held the catch.

Everybody on our side made a valuable contribution until Woodfull was able to declare at 6 for 729, by which time the Lord's scoring board was in trouble, because they had no seven to put in the total. Lord's was not expecting such a mammoth score.

England in her second innings replied with 375, which should have been less, but Richardson and Ponsford both failed to go for a simple catch. Chapman took advantage of the resultant let-off in no uncertain terms. No less than 4 sixes and 12 fours came from his bat, Grimmett in particular feeling the power of his drives and pulls.

In the end we won comfortably by 7 wickets with time to spare, and thus Australia demonstrated an axiom in cricket that fast scoring wins matches.

We were again on top in the Third Test Match at Leeds, although it ended in a draw. The match was memorable because of my own score of 334, at that time a world's record in Test Cricket, a feat later to be excelled by Leonard Hutton.

Whilst admitting that my form was excellent, I have always maintained it was not such a good innings as the previous one at Lord's. It was made at perhaps a slightly faster rate and included a century before lunch on the first day after Jackson had been dismissed for 1, but there were blemishes in stroke play of which I was well aware. An Australian philanthropist, Mr. A. E. Whitelaw, sent me a cheque for £1,000 "as a token of his admiration." I was not the only Australian to be so rewarded by this unostentatious lover of sport. It was indeed a generous token.

The unreliable Manchester weather caused the Fourth Test Match to be drawn with only one side having completed an innings. The conditions did not produce any spirited cricket, except that the new English slow bowler, Ian Peebles, gave us (but particularly myself) a very anxious time. He bowled splendidly, and we were all in great trouble against his boseys. I frankly admitted that day I could not detect them.

Woodfull let one go which went over the middle stump, and each of the first three balls bowled to Kippax hit him on the pads and brought an L.B.W. appeal. We felt a new star had arisen. I understand Peebles later suffered with shoulder trouble which contributed much towards the non-fulfilment of his early promise.

Eventually the Fifth Test Match at the Oval took place, and with a splendid innings' victory, Australia made the score two to one and thereby regained The Ashes.

Our Team had now moulded into a good combination, and although Grimmett still carried the main burden of the attack, he was getting excellent support. In this last Test, Hornibrook's 7 for 92 was the result of fine left-hand spin bowling.

History repeated itself when England rejected Percy Chapman as Captain and played in his stead Bob Wyatt. Australia welcomed the idea, for the changing of their leader at such a critical stage suggested to us that the English Selectors lacked confidence in their Team.

Jack Hobbs played his final Test Match, and I felt rather sorry when the old master pulled a ball from Alan Fairfax onto his wicket for 9 runs. I wanted to see him make a good score in his final appearance.

I didn't know in 1930 that Jack Hobbs' 9 runs would be nine more than I was going to make in my final appearance on the same ground.

We had a most exciting game against Gloucester immediately following the Test. The match took a relatively normal course until the last day. Australia were set a modest total of 118 to win, and with 59 on the board without loss the match appeared over. Then came the excitement as wickets tumbled and two runs were still required when the last man went in.

Amidst extreme tension the scores were levelled. No fewer than 14 more balls were bowled without a run being scored until Hornibrook was given out L.B.W. and the match ended in a Tie—the only one in history between Australia and an English County.

There were still a few matches to play before the Tour concluded, and in the last of these at Scarborough I enjoyed batting against none other than Wilfred Rhodes, who played Test Cricket for England long before I was born.

My own personal successes on the Tour had been beyond expectation. My total of 974 runs in the Test Matches remains the highest in a series by any player, whilst my total of 2,960 on the Tour still stands as the record aggregate in a season by an Australian, but far and away beyond these personal things, was the invaluable knowledge I had gained in many directions.

Perhaps today I realise even more than I did then what one season's experience in England can do for a player. Without being dogmatic I think it right to say that no batsman could be complete or anywhere near it without the testing which is provided under England's ever-changing wickets.

Then too, one could not help remembering the many splendid innings played by men of the calibre of Hammond, Hobbs and Sutcliffe on the English side, and Kippax, Woodfull and Ponsford among the Australians.

It was a great disappointment that Jackson failed to reveal his Australian form, due in the main no doubt to the early onslaught of the illness which later cut short his brilliant career.

The Australians had been better than they themselves anticipated, and had justified the Selectors' faith in their leavening of youth and experience. So, too, the Board's judgment in selecting Woodfull for Captain had been vindicated. He developed individual talent along sound lines and enjoyed from his fellows immense loyalty which in turn created an exceptional team spirit.

One weakness was perhaps our great dependence on Grimmett with the ball, but he never faltered and came through triumphantly with the great total of 144 wickets.

And so ended my first English Tour. The English people had been kindness personified, a fact which impressed itself upon me more deeply in later tours, and the beauty of the countryside can never be eradicated from my mind.

With all the enthusiasm of youth it had been a happy Tour, and some of its memories shall always live with me, especially our meeting with His Majesty King George V and Queen Mary at Sandringham ; my talk with the Prince of Wales at the Oval ; Harold Williams singing in *Hiawatha* at the Royal Albert Hall. There were other privileged occasions, the magnitude of which became more apparent in later years.

We even spoke to Australia on the radio-telephone, then in its infancy—today commonplace, so fast has the world moved.

The West Indians

DURING THE PROGRESS OF THE ENGLISH TOUR, EVENTS HAD OCCURRED which were to have repercussions later on. For instance, I had written a book giving my life story up to that time. This had appeared in serial form in the English Press, and our Manager felt that it was a breach of the Players' Contract with the Australian Board of Control.

I disagreed with his views for two reasons. The first was that the Board had given consent for Clarrie Grimmett to make a similar arrangement ; the second—I had made it a condition of my writings that nothing regarding the current tour could appear until we were back in Australia. However, the Manager saw fit to report the matter to the Board.

There was no need for any fuss, but the incident was seized upon to try and magnify an alleged breach between the Board and myself. For instance, here is what appeared in one paper :—

" *Don Alexander Napoleon Bradman* has hit the fussy controllers to leg. Pompous Rules and Regulations of the Board of Control have been cut, slashed, and smitten into scraps. Don has done things this Tour which no lesser player would have dared to attempt. The

Pilot Shortridge and Don Bradman just before setting out on a flight from Adelaide to Melbourne 1930

Board of Control has been simply left gasping. I am informed that he even agreed to sign a contract to appear in one of the London Halls during the Fifth Test, but this last boldness was too much for the distressed Manager, Kelly, who nipped the scheme in the bud."

I was very annoyed at this propaganda which was completely untrue. There had been no disagreement of any kind excepting the question of this book.

Matters reached such a point that the Chairman of the Board was moved to make public comment. He said, "The statements are thoroughly unfair and unjust. Indeed it looks very much as if some irresponsible persons were desirous of stirring up strife and discord in the cricket world."

On top of that I found myself in a most unenviable position because I acceded to the request of my employers to leave the boat at Adelaide and travel by air to Sydney, arriving there ahead of the rest of the Team. To me this request had no significance.

It had reached me at sea by wireless. No question of refusing entered my head because my employers had a perfect right to seek my return at the earliest possible moment. Moreover, our Contract with the Board specifically allowed all players the privilege of disembarking, if they so desired, prior to reaching their home ports.

I flew from Adelaide to Melbourne (and thence to Goulburn) with Pilot Shortridge in the Southern Cloud—a sister machine to Kingsford-Smith's famous Southern Cross. We had a bumpy journey.

Not long afterwards, flying the same machine from Sydney on a scheduled flight to Melbourne, " Shorty " (as he was called), his machine and the passengers vanished. No trace of them was ever found, and no more inexplicable tragedy has occurred in Australian aviation.

This early arrival, accompanied as it was by a blaze of publicity over which I had no control, and the presentation to me by General Motors of a sports car, caused an unfortunate impression. My action was in many quarters misconstrued as an attempt to steal the limelight.

By the time this thought was conveyed to me the damage had already been done. Thus my mind was most disturbed at the commencement of a season during which we were honoured by a visit from the West Indian Players.

Later the Board of Control withheld £50 of my allowance, ruling that my writings had been a breach of the Contract. That they only withheld one-third of the unpaid amount suggested they considered the breach to be unintentional, but I know that my concentration during that season fell away because of these extraneous matters.

Of the season itself there is not a great deal which can now be written. In Sheffield Shield Matches I played 6 innings, the best of which was undoubtedly a score of 258 against South Australia in 285 minutes, though I gained more pleasure from a score of 220 against Victoria, the reason being a partnership with Wendel-Bill of 234 in 135 minutes, a fifth wicket record for Sheffield Shield Matches, which came close to bringing victory to our State.

In the Test Matches against the West Indians my form was patchy, and I think the same may be said of practically the whole of the Australian Team.

It is common for the form of first-class players to fall away somewhat in the season immediately following a visit to England. It really becomes the third season on end, and a certain amount of staleness must arise.

Then too, Australia was much too good for the West Indian Team, and with the exception of the Fifth Test, in which we were twice caught on a sticky wicket, I only batted once in each match.

My two successes in the series were scores of 223 in the Third and 152 in the Fourth Match, but my final innings in the series brought my first duck in Test Cricket. It was a slower ball from fast bowler Griffith, out of which I made a " yorker " in trying to turn it to leg, and hit over the top.

Although the West Indians won this last Test Match, they were not, at that time, quite up to international standard.

George Headley was their star batsman—a very compact little player who would hold his own in any company.

The young batsman Sealy gave considerable promise, but had not by any means reached the zenith of his powers.

Only Constantine of the others showed any outstanding skill with the bat, but even this applied only to matches other than Tests. In the latter his aggregate for 10 innings was 72 runs. The West Indian batting must be classed as weak, and their fielding was not all that could be desired.

In the bowling line they badly lacked a top grade spinner, but in Griffith, Francis and Constantine they had a trio of fast bowlers quite up to Test standard.

Constantine became a great favourite with the crowds in Australia as he did in other countries, and without hesitation I rank him the greatest all-round fieldsman ever seen. Gregory may have been his superior in slips, Percy Chapman excelled him near the wicket in specialist positions, but the phenomenal agility and anticipation of Constantine made him a perpetual danger in any position.

One could understand why his name became first on the list of all Lancashire League Cricketers. In this class of cricket where matches are decided in one afternoon, I cannot envisage a player with better qualifications. In a quarter of an hour of terrific speed bowling or unorthodox hitting he could swing the fortunes of a match.

At the conclusion of the first-class season, I journeyed to Northern Queensland with a team led by Alan Kippax. These Tours were at one time a regular feature, and did a great deal to encourage and promote cricket in the Northern Centres.

We went by boat from Sydney to Townsville, a journey which involves travelling inside the Great Barrier Reef, that wonderful stretch of coral which attracts tourists from all parts of the world. The beauty and the richness of North Queensland must be seen to be believed. Here is a fertile land, untold wealth of timber, abundant rainfall, and it is a pity more permanent white settlers are not migrating North to enlarge the population which could safely be carried in that rich area.

Although some good cricketers were found at Townsville, it was not expected that we should meet serious opposition.

By the time we had reached Rockhampton, I had scored on the North Queensland Tour 645 runs and taken 33 wickets. But then I met with misfortune. In the first few minutes of play I badly sprained my right ankle in an attempt to run a batsman out.

This put me in the Rockhampton Hospital for 18 days, and the ankle was many weeks returning to normal. In fact, the accident probably weakened it, contributing to the more serious mishap at the Oval in 1938 and a final misfortune in my last match.

I regretted missing the opportunity to conclude the Tour in more ways than one. Amongst other things I missed seeing Stan McCabe's 173 at Gympie, a score which included 18 sixes. That must have been worth watching.

Nevertheless, the enforced convalescence may have been a blessing—it certainly gave me a rest which would not have been voluntarily taken, and provided a tonic for a constitution somewhat jaded by concentrated cricket and publicity.

The South Africans

PRIOR TO THE COMMENCEMENT OF THE 1931-2 SEASON A FURTHER UPSET occurred which disturbed my peace of mind. Australia in common with the rest of the world had been in the midst of an economic depression. Things were uncertain in the business world, and I was not satisfied with my employment, which depended to a large extent on my successes or otherwise at cricket. Under no circumstances could my work be more than of a transient character.

It was not unnatural therefore for me to give some consideration to my future in life, especially as the announcement of my engagement indicated an early acceptance of heavier responsibility.

Apparently Constantine had reported favourably regarding my ability to the Lancashire League, for in August 1931 an offer was made to me to join the Accrington Club.

Right from the outset I made it clear that I had no desire to leave Australia, but surely no sensible person could deny my right to ascertain what terms would be offered and what obligations would be incurred.

All sorts of rumours gained credence, and once more I was subjected to conflicting emotions as opinions and counter opinions were given the headlines.

I even received a letter from a member of our Federal Parliament in which the writer said : " My Dear Friend, I deeply resent the criticism that you have been subjected to. Many International Cricketers who helped to win glory for Australia suffered want in their old age, and some of them even had to pay admission to see cricket played. Under these circumstances, and using all the wisdom I have garnered in 77 years, I strongly advise you to accept the position that has been offered you."

On the other hand, Dr. Evatt wrote me a charming letter in which he expressed the hope that I would not decide to leave Australia.

These were serious letters. So was another one from an elderly lady, though I am afraid I thought it most amusing. She said : " Dear little boy, take the advice of an old woman, hit while the iron is hot, go and marry an heiress. With your face and record you can."

I am afraid I did not share her view that an heiress would be interested in my record—still less my face.

Before I had made any decision, one paper published : " We go one better this week and tell the world that Bradman will accept the offer."

I deplored all this fuss about what I was going to do. Later on, when Alan Fairfax, a member of the 1930 Australian XI, negotiated a contract and actually went to the League, nobody queried his right to do so.

In the end I remained in Australia.

Associated Newspapers Ltd., Radio 2 U.E. Ltd., and F. J. Palmer & Son Ltd. combined to offer me a contract which I felt was not only satisfactory, but would also provide me with the opportunity of continuing to play big cricket.

The contract brought difficulties later which were not foreseen at the time. It meant a financial sacrifice, but it enabled me to follow my innermost desire to continue playing for Australia.

Whilst on this subject of Lancashire League Cricket, I might express some anxiety regarding the drain on leading Australian players which has occurred in recent years. As I write these words there are sufficient Australians in the League to create an eleven of international standard. The number of front-line players in Australia at any time is limited and any defection from the ranks in this country has the same effect as retirement. Australia can ill afford to lose numbers of players.

Not for one moment can the decision of the individual be questioned. It is his inherent right to play or go wherever he wishes.

What is the remedy which will make conditions in Australia sufficiently attractive and lucrative to keep the players here? That is the query.

Frankly, I don't know the answer.

Australia is not able at this juncture to support professionalism in cricket.

Those who become Internationals are finding it increasingly difficult to give the necessary allegiance to their occupations without prejudicing their future prospects if they participate in all matches.

The advent of West Australia into the Sheffield Shield Competition, and the growing frequency of International Tours merely accentuate a grave problem.

It should be made clear that prominent League Professionals can earn really big money, apart from their ordinary fee. Subscriptions are taken up for exceptional performances (which in practice means almost every week) newspapers pay for articles, and in numerous other ways the player may increase his emolument to a figure which would be the envy of leading business executives—and all for five months of the year. No wonder it is hard to resist.

Perhaps a system of regular testimonial matches or a cricketer's superannuation fund will be the answer. Only time will tell.

The problem threatens to become worse, and must seriously exercise the minds of legislators and players in the future.

Before the important matches commenced in 1931-2 I went on a country tour of New South Wales with Alan Kippax's XI. We played matches at Lithgow, Parkes, Forbes, Grenfell, Young, Murrumburrah, Wagga, Tumut, Gundagai and Yass. New South Wales is fortunate in having such fine country centres as potential breeding grounds for players.

In the game at Parkes our skipper, Alan Kippax received a nasty injury. His nose was broken by a ball which lifted quickly.

We were to have opened a new turf wicket, but owing to rain it was decided to use a mat. After Alan had been struck, a big spike was found underneath the mat. Not much consolation to him at that stage. This accident, followed by the one in Brisbane shortly afterwards, in my opinion, sapped his confidence against fast bowling. A very great pity, because earlier in his career Kippax was a classical hooker.

During the first-grade matches I scored 246 against Randwick in 205 minutes, and 201 against Gordon in 171 minutes. The latter innings was against Kelleway, Macartney and Campbell, and the second century was made in 45 minutes.

A splendid example of the movements made by the author when cutting off the back foot

I remember it clearly because I hit a ball for six over point from a half volley and was told by a fieldsman the stroke was a mishit. For his benefit I nominated this shot and repeated it later on, but must add it could hardly be done except on a small ground like Chatswood.

My Sheffield Shield scores were peculiar—in sequence—0, 23, 167, 23, 0. The first of these ducks was in the sensational match at Brisbane when Gilbert started off by getting 3 wickets for 12 and sent down in that period the fastest " bowling " I can remember. I say " bowling " because, without wishing to castigate the umpires, the players all thought his action decidedly suspect.

Anyway, on this green top wicket the ball came through at bewildering speed which seemed to be accentuated because Gilbert only shuffled about four quick steps before delivering the ball. One delivery knocked the bat out of my hand, and I unhesitatingly class this short burst as faster than anything seen from Larwood or anyone else.

When Gilbert was rested, Kippax went to hook a ball from Thurlow, who, although reasonably fast, was so slow by comparison, that Kippax had completed his shot before the ball arrived, and received a terrific blow on the side of the head which hastened his retirement.

Soon after that we met the South Africans. Like the West Indians of the previous year, our friends from South Africa did not prove equal to the task of holding Australia's full strength at bay.

They were a most charming bunch of fellows, and certainly one of the most popular teams ever to visit our shores.

Individually they possessed excellent players, but the combination was defeated in all five Test Matches.

My successes against them in the Tests were due to fielding lapses as much as anything.

In the First Test, Neville Quinn, the medium pace left-hander, who came off the wicket so quickly, had me sorely puzzled, and I was missed off him twice in my innings, then went on to make 226. Other scores of 112, 2, 167 and 299 not out made this my most successful Test Match Season.

An incredible thing happened in the last Test of that series. Grimmett and I were both in the Australian Team. I did not bat and Grimmett did not bowl.

I had been announced as a member of the Eleven and the Team was just going out on the field, when, in jumping down from a form in the dressing room, I twisted an ankle which prevented me from batting.

Grimmett did not bowl because he was not required. South Africa made 36 in the first innings and 45 in the second, and Bert Ironmonger off 23 overs took 11 wickets for 24 runs in the match.

The outstanding South African batsman for the Tour was Jim Christy, though at times Herby Taylor gave us glimpses of the form which made him world famous many years before.

Perhaps my most outstanding impression is of their skipper-wicket-keeper, H. B. Cameron. The untimely death of this great player was a sad blow to South Africa, for he combined great batting ability with superlative wicketkeeping and shrewd captaincy.

Perhaps Cameron was inclined to be rash with his batting, and there were times when his wicketkeeping fell below the recognised standard, but on other occasions he rose to the greatest heights in both departments.

Quinn worried me more than any of their bowlers, and appeared to come off the pitch faster than any medium fast bowler I have met in this country with the possible exception of Maurice Tate. His best ball, unfortunately for him, came in towards a right-hander's legs. Had it gone the other way Quinn's figures would have been better.

Their tireless fast bowler, Sandy Bell, did an enormous amount of work, and never slackened his energies. He too bowled mostly inswingers, and although he bowled them extremely well (and I can still picture Woodfull's astonishment when attempting to play one of these to the off and having his leg stump knocked over) the lack of a good outswinger was his failing.

Under normal circumstances, McMillan might have been regarded as a first-rate slow bowler. Our standard, however, was based on Grimmett, a rather unfair comparison for any young slow bowler.

Bert Ironmonger had the astonishing figures of 31 wickets at an average of 9.67 in the Tests. Why he never went to England with an Australian Team is a mystery to me. It is said that his action was doubtful, and he was not selected because of the fear that he would be "no-balled" by English umpires. This can hardly be a reasonable excuse, seeing that the Australian umpires passed him. Anyway, in fairness to Ironmonger it should be pointed out that his peculiar delivery was caused by the loss of the first joint on the index finger of his left hand. This prevented him spinning the ball in an orthodox manner. I did not think his action questionable, and I feel sure he would have been a really outstanding success on an English Tour.

The future star, O'Reilly, came into the picture that year, playing in the last two Test Matches and achieving moderate success.

After the great showing of the South Africans against England in 1930-1, Australia had not expected these easy victories.

By way of explanation a Sydney paper revealed that the Africans had been playing against a ghost. In a Queensland newspaper, the *Cooktown Independent*, the following paragraph appeared :—

"*Don Bradman Dead*—Australia today mourns the loss of the greatest batsman the world has ever seen. During the progress of the Test Match in Brisbane (Australia v. South Africa) Don Bradman was attacked with dysentery, to which he succumbed on Saturday."

Thank goodness it was only in the *Cooktown Independent,* but it just goes to show what things can really happen in this world without our knowledge.

I believe that from the point of view of the Australian public who came to watch cricket, this was my best season.

After having settled the question of my future (at least for the time being) and having a better mental outlook following the winter's rest, I was extremely fit throughout the summer. I do not think in future seasons I again approached the same fitness, though possibly greater soundness took the place of a few risky shots.

Before concluding reference to that season I must tell of a match at Blackheath, New South Wales. It was only a second-class fixture and I was playing against a team from Lithgow on a malthoid wicket.

Included in my score of 256 were 14 sixes and 29 fours. Batting with Wendell-Bill, I at one stage scored 100 out of the 102 added in three overs. The following are the hits which made up the 102 :—

First Over	6,6,4,2,4,4,6,1.
Second Over	6,4,4,6,6,4,6,4.
Third Over	1,6,6,1,1,4,4,6.

The scoring shots made by Wendell-Bill in those three overs were the first and fifth singles in the third over. Residents of Cairns (N.Q.) claim that the fastest hundred ever scored was made there in 1910 by Lorry Quinlan—18 minutes. No time was recorded at Blackheath, though I think it must have been less than 18 minutes.

One of the bowlers who played against us was Bob Nicholson. He bore no malice, for at the end of the season Bob came to Sydney and sang at my wedding, which took place on 30th April, 1932. Nicholson subsequently rose to fame as a renowned baritone singer both in this country and in America. In fact my wife jocularly maintained that the guests took more interest in his singing than the wedding.

Thus began the best partnership of my life. Canon Hughes, who was President of the Victorian Cricket Association, came across from Melbourne to Sydney to do us the honour of performing the wedding ceremony.

The most difficult days were just around the corner, and my wife's sound judgment and wise counsel were to prove invaluable.

America, 1932

ARTHUR MAILEY IS KNOWN THROUGHOUT THE CRICKET WORLD FOR HIS slow bowling skill, but few people realise that underneath the whimsical smile there exists a visionary character, keen on adventure and anxious to promote cricket wherever possible.

This idealism caused Arthur to arrange a tour of U.S.A. and Canada in 1932 by an Australian Team. After protracted negotiations and, finally, thanks to certain guarantees from the Canadian Pacific Railway Company, the tour became a reality.

Arthur had earlier approached me and made it clear that unless I agreed to become a member of the party, he could not get the necessary financial backing.

Should I go? It was not a simple decision to make. There was my work in Australia to consider. Also I thought it unreasonable to go on a cricket tour and leave my wife behind when we had just set out to accept life's responsibilities together.

But the prospect of seeing America appealed to us both, especially as I visualised no other opportunity later on. Also there was the knowledge that if I didn't accept, the tour would not take place and my potential colleagues would be denied the chance of visiting the New World.

I agreed to go, providing my wife could accompany me. As this was a private tour, not subject to Board of Control regulations, there was no objection and my condition was accepted.

The Team contained a mixture of Test and State players, and some who were scarcely in the top-grade.

Finance was difficult. Some of the lesser lights (in the cricketing sense) paid their own expenses, whereas the leading players had their expenses paid and received a small daily allowance. Cricket tours are a costly business, and when there are small crowds—in some case no entrance money—somebody has to foot the bill.

On Thursday, 26th May, 1932, we left Sydney on the S.S. *Niagara*, little dreaming that this grand old ship would, during the next world war, find a watery grave off the coast of New Zealand and provide material for one of the most amazing salvage exploits in history—the salvaging of gold which went down with her.

So far as I know, there was no gold on board in 1932. I'm afraid I wasn't very interested in her cargo, for I had contracted influenza before leaving, went straight to bed after going on board and didn't get up until the ship berthed at Auckland.

We had a short but pleasant stay in that attractive city, and then at our next port of call, Suva, enjoyed an enthusiastic welcome from the Fijians.

There was to have been a match at Suva, but rain prevented play. We inspected the ground where Kingsford-Smith made his miraculous aeroplane landing, and, even to the inexperienced eye, it was obvious what a remarkable feat he had performed.

Cricket being out of the question, we were taken for a drive to see the beauty spots of the island, and some of the team sampled the local drink " Kava ". It is not unlike coffee in appearance, but from what I was told (not personal experience) I understand has a very different effect.

The natives staged a Rugby match in the afternoon—all in bare feet. Their kicking would have done credit to any team—boots and all.

Although there was no cricket, I was sought out by the local fast bowler, Edward Thakabou. He was accompanied by a policeman, quite an unnecessary bodyguard I thought, for Edward was 6 feet 3 inches in height and built in proportion.

Evidently Fijian people think that the prowess of a cricketer may be judged by physical standards, for there was considerable merriment when Edward felt my muscles and proudly displayed his superiority. I joined in the hilarity. It seemed good policy.

We also met in Fiji the great Chief Rapu Pope (I hope that spelling is correct) who came to Australia with a Fijian cricket team many years before.

Our next port of call was Honolulu, and here we were under the American flag. For most of us it was the first time.

Looking back on my diary entries at that time, two things are interesting. One entry said : " The number of Japanese one sees everywhere is remarkable "—shades of Pearl Harbour, had we but realised it ! Another was a prophecy that the day was not far distant when air transport would bring people from America to such holiday resorts as Honolulu and even to Australia.

The surfing at Wai-ki-ki was interesting, but in my opinion not superior to some Australian beaches. There was no sign of cricket. The young lads were making an attempt to play baseball with cocoanuts.

Continuing our journey, we reached the Port of Victoria, Vancouver Island, on June 16, where the cricket officials gave us a warm welcome in dreadfully cold weather. Our ship did not berth until nine o'clock at night, but we started our first match the next morning, so you can see the question of getting acclimatized or accustomed to local conditions didn't apply on this trip.

The cricket ground at Cowichan where we played our first game was in a superb setting—a small field perfectly grassed and entirely surrounded by lovely ornamental trees.

Some of the cricket played that day at Cowichan was rather extraordinary. The local team of 18 men made 194, to which we replied with 503 for 8 wickets. At one stage our skipper, Vic. Richardson, and I added 50 runs in 7 minutes, and Stan. McCabe hit one ball so hard in a knock of 150 that it fractured a small bone in a woman spectator's leg. By a coincidence she was the wife of one of the opposing players. Six different balls were lost during the day in the nearby bush. At one time four were in use, so that play would not be held up while a search was being made amongst the trees for the lost ones.

We were booked for a banquet that evening, but when it came to changing after the match, very few of the team were able to locate their full outfit of dress clothes—there had been so little time to sort out our luggage. One had everything but his shoes, another had everything but his suit and so on. A good deal of borrowing from locals had to take place, and there were many laughs at the result.

Our next game was against a Victorian team. In this match I had the very unusual experience of taking 6 wickets in one over (8 balls) without getting a hat trick.

From this lovely island, we went across to the mainland, where we commenced a series of matches at the Brockton Point Ground, Vancouver.

This is without question the most beautiful cricket ground in the world. No doubt the champions of other grounds will hesitate to agree, but I cannot imagine a more delightful place for cricket. The ground is on the edge of a beautiful wooded park. Sitting in a deck chair on the verandah of the rustic pavilion, one can look across the field towards the towering, snow-capped mountains, while in the foreground an arm of the harbour runs behind the sightboard, and lazy old ferries dawdle across the bowler's arm. To the right there are small clumps of ornamental trees. Then further to the right is the harbour where seaplanes come in to graceful foamy landings, and beyond is the city itself with its tall, stately buildings on the skyline.

The fielding surface of the ground is a delight, but the wicket (when we were there) consisted of cocoanut matting on grass—the only blot on this perfect setting.

We played three one-day matches at Brockton Point. There was great excitement on the second day when the local team, by sensational fielding, snatched a victory on the first innings by 18 runs.

It was in this game that I experienced for the first time the guile of Arthur Mailey. A batsman came in. Arthur sensed he might be a hitter, so offered him a cigar if he could hit a six. The batsman promptly hit a six, but without hesitation Mailey doubled the offer, and within a matter of seconds the scorer had recorded once more " caught outfield, bowled Mailey."

We were sorry to leave beautiful Vancouver, but were soon to be charmed by the journey through the Canadian Rockies. The glories of nature are scattered profusely through miles of stately fir trees, lovely swift running rivers, unsuspected waterfalls here and there, and always the snow-clad mountains in the background.

On this train journey eastwards we made the acquaintance of Benny— our porter. Benny seemed very proud of having to look after a cricket team, although he had no idea what cricket was. His interest in " Massa Don " (as he called me) was apparently brought about by hearing comparisons between me and Babe Ruth, and of course the latter was his idol.

The journey across the great Canadian Prairies was tiring but interesting. We were four nights and three and a half days reaching Toronto, and one was able to make some comparison between the wheat fields of Canada and those of Western New South Wales.

At the time of our visit, Toronto was the headquarters of American cricket. In earlier days I understand it was Philadelphia from whence came the renowned swerve bowler Bart King.

The Gentlemen of Philadelphia once put together a team strong enough to tour England and play the counties, but today their famous cricket arena is studded with tennis courts.

The Armour Heights Cricket Ground at Toronto has a splendid club house, in which members are well catered for and the social aspect of cricket plays a prominent part. There are tennis courts, a putting green, table-tennis is played and dances are held in the pavilion. I understand that the club, in addition to owning the ground, bought the land surrounding it so that they could control the types of buildings to be erected and thereby preserve the beauty of the cricket ground.

During our stay in Toronto, we played three or four matches, and found the local standard reasonably good. Some of those who played against us subsequently toured England with a Canadian cricket team.

We were all impressed with this great city and its lovely suburban areas.

During one of the functions held in our honour, we were privileged to hear a splendid address by Sir William Mulock, who was at that time Chief Justice and designated " The Grand Old Man of Canada."

Following Toronto, we played a one-day game at Guelph where a Western Ontario 18 could only muster 88 runs. McCabe had the impressive analysis of 11 wickets for 33. We lost 7 wickets for 479, and my own score of 260 is, I believe, still the highest made on Canadian soil. The game was played in the grounds of the Ontario Reformatory, and the inmates waited on us at lunch and afternoon tea.

The following day we played a match at the Ridley College School against the old boys and school boys combined. In this match " Spark " Bell made 109 not out—the only century recorded against us on the trip.

During this portion of our tour we had the opportunity of seeing the wonder and grandeur of Niagara Falls, one of the world's great show places, especially in the evenings when the natural beauty is enhanced by coloured searchlights.

There was genuine enthusiasm for cricket at Toronto and at Ridley College, but none whatever at Montreal where we played three one-day matches.

The French-Canadians have no interest in cricket. The attention of local ball-game patriots turns towards baseball.

In one of the matches Fleetwood-Smith took 8 wickets for 14, and the poor showing of the locals would have been even worse had it not been for the assistance they received from West Indian players. Even these remarkable figures were dwarfed in the next match, when, against an Ottawa team of 16 men, Fleetwood-Smith took 9 wickets for 7. This match was played in the grounds of Rideau Hall, the Governor-General's residence.

For the time being we left Canada and went to New York. There is not much cricket played in New York, and certainly the highest standard of play is produced by West Indians who are resident there. These West Indians made quite a good showing against us at Innisfail Park, and one or two incidents are worthy of mention.

In my second innings I was out for a duck. The bowler who had dismissed me immediately ran to the fence where in the space of a few seconds he collected a hat full of dollars from the jubilant spectators. Actually, I was caught by Ollivierre in the slips off Clark, and the newspaper description of the match said : " The crowd made the best of it and gave Clark and Ollivierre a rousing send off." Just what that means I still don't know.

A yorker caused more excitement than anything else, and was always the signal for much cheering.

The umpires took their job somewhat lightheartedly. One of them when officiating at square leg would go across to the boundary fence and talk to friends.

It was in this game that Australia's wonderful old wicket-keeper, Sammy Carter, was hit in the eye, a blow which eventually caused him to lose the sight of it. A ball from McCabe flew very quickly off the coir mat which was laid on a not-too-even surface. Carter had no chance of avoiding the ball when, at the last second, the batsman pulled his bat away.

In addition to playing the West Indians, we had three one-day games against a New York Team (mainly Englishmen resident there) at Staten Island. The standard of these " lilywhites " was not nearly so high as that of the West Indians.

One thing about New York—it was a great relief to walk down the street and find nobody interested in obtaining an autograph, for the population as a whole was completely disinterested.

Amongst our outstanding memories is a visit to the Empire State Building, the tallest in the world. Australians will find it hard to visualise a structure which has 102 stories above the street and enough floor space to shelter 80,000 people. The building has 63 passenger elevators and four freight elevators. The steelwork, which weighs 60,000 tons, was begun in March 1930 and completed in six months. If some of our potential home-builders of today read about this they will be very anxious to find the reason for such speed and efficiency.

Other highlights of New York were a banquet at the famous Waldorf Astoria Hotel as the guests of Frank D. Waterman of fountain pen fame. Also a visit to one of their big baseball stadiums, where the Yankees beat the White Sox.

Babe Ruth, nursing a leg injury, was sitting in the pavilion, and I had the pleasure of a conversation with him as the game was in progress.

An evening's entertainment we shall never forget, was the one we spent at the Casino Theatre, where that magnificent negro bass singer, Paul Robeson, was playing in *Show Boat*.

A night's train journey from New York took us to Detroit, where we continued our one-sided games. Whilst staying at Detroit, we played a match at Windsor, on the Kennedy Collegiate Stadium Ground.

My most vivid recollection of this game is that of the umpires. One gave 6 balls to the over, the other 8. When Vic. Richardson queried this procedure, he was told that they couldn't agree whether we were to play under M.C.C. or Australian conditions, so decided that each would go his own way. Vic. quickly put a stop to that nonsense.

After Detroit our next stop was Chicago. We had always thought of Chicago in terms of gangsters, but left it with the feeling of having seen one of the greatest and loveliest cities in the world. Its system of parks and its delightful suburban areas could well be a model for other cities.

The match at Chicago was played on Grant Park, which is open to the public, but at no time did more than 5,000 people bother to attend. There was the usual crop of incidents, starting off with the young American boy—obviously a baseballer—who came to our tent and wanted to know, in the middle of the day's play, who had won the first game.

Kippax caught and bowled one of the batsmen, and seeing the non-striker out of his ground quickly threw down the wicket at the bowler's end. More for fun than anything else (the striker obviously being out) Kippax appealed " How's that ? " The umpire answered " I don't know. It was too quick for me."

The pitch was in very poor condition, and we complained about the unevenness of the surface. Upon arriving at the ground for the last day, we found, to our amazement, that it was quite wet. In all seriousness the local authorities told us they were upset about our complaints, and therefore had watered the pitch to make it easier. I hope this sort of thing is not catching in other parts of the globe.

A twenty-hour train journey took us to Winnipeg, where we arrived early in the morning and played a combined Canadian Team the same day. In this match we experienced a sample of Canadian heat, which was about on a par with that of Adelaide.

Unfortunately, the game coincided with a grasshopper plague. The insects swarmed all over the ground, and on more than one occasion the ball, after being bowled, landed on a grasshopper and did the unexpected.

During our stay in Winnipeg we were entertained at a banquet by the famous Hudson's Bay Company. The menu was printed on a wooden maple leaf—a unique souvenir for the guests.

After leaving Winnipeg, we journeyed to Regina and thence to Moose Jaw. There was a lot of fun at Moose Jaw. One of the umpires was a traveller for the local chewing gum manufacturers. Copious supplies were handed round amongst the players, who promptly used some of it to stick the bails on (the day being rather windy).

A liberal amount was attached to one bail which fell slowly towards the ground when one of the batsmen was stumped. On appeal, the umpire refused to give him out until the bail actually reached the ground.

The local team batted 17 men, and therefore, despite Bill Ive's analysis of 11 wickets for 23 runs, there was still room for others to put up a good performance. No less than 14 of the opposition bowled against us, the greatest number of bowlers I have seen used in a match in one innings. It was almost like baseball the way the reserves came out onto the field.

From Moose Jaw to Yorkton we travelled by car, and as it is a distance of some 200 miles, most of us did not arrive until about 3 a.m., but we were on the field again the same morning playing against a team of locals.

There were other pleasant games at Saskatoon, Edmonton and Calgary. Most of the pitches in these areas were of ant-bed covered by coco-nut matting, and some of the parks in which the matches were played were most attractive.

Following this particularly strenuous part of the tour, we had a short respite, during which we visited Banff and Lake Louise, two of the renowned beauty spots of the world. Many stories have been told regarding the scenery in these regions. They are not exaggerated.

Back to Vancouver where we had a resounding victory over the local XI, which could only muster 37 runs in the first innings and 96 in the second, compared with our 337 for 3 wickets.

An experiment was made next day when Arthur Mailey captained a team of British Columbia colts against the touring side. Then the following day Alan Kippax took charge of the team of colts. The local boys did well, especially Hendry (no relation to the Australian XI player) who made 57.

We now finished our stay in Canada and journeyed down to Seattle, thence through the wonderful Oregon forests to San Francisco. This was a fascinating journey, but after approximately one and a half days' continual travelling, we had to commence cricket almost immediately upon our arrival.

The Australians playing in the Kezar Stadium at San Francisco

The San Francisco game was played in the Kezar Stadium which will seat 70,000 people, but looked a somewhat peculiar sight with only a few hundred spectators at our match.

The San Francisco players had virtually no idea of cricket. In their first innings, the Northern California All Stars Team (to give them their proper title) of 15 men, made 20 runs, of which Percival made 10. There were 3 sundries.

All Stars improved on their total in the second innings, scoring 33, but this time no batsman reached double figures. Australia replied with 2 for 268 declared.

In the field during their first innings, I touched the ball only nine times for three catches and four run-outs.

One of the opening batsmen, having watched two of his partners go for ducks, became vocally scornful about the Selectors for having chosen a lot of rabbits to support him, but when he did get a strike he was out first ball.

There were some West Indians in the team, and one of them came in for some barracking because, having played a ball to third man for a possible two runs, he refused to budge from his crease. Calling out " No " in determined tones to his partner, he shouted " Never mind them—let them do the hollerin' out there, we'll do the judgin' right here." I admired his principle more than his judgment.

The local newspaper report of the match made interesting reading. Of Sep. Carter, the writer said he was " As hawk-eyed a man as ever squatted behind the wickets." I was referred to as " The antipodean slugger." Evidence of his knowledge of the stock market was shown when the newspaper critic said " Local wickets fell like the price of stock."

It seemed funny also to read of my own batting : " He wore out four California bowlers." Keith Tolhurst and I certainly put on 168 runs in 34 minutes, but that was hardly time enough to wear them out.

Despite the low standard of cricket, the stay in San Francisco was most enjoyable, and it was with some reluctance that we moved on to Los Angeles—Hollywood. Here, in the famous world of films, it was fascinating to meet and see at work such stars as Mary Astor, Jean Harlow, Myrna Loy, Boris Karloff and Sir C. Aubrey Smith.

The film colony could not do enough for us. A memorable day was spent looking over the studios of Metro Goldwyn Mayer, though I must confess that to see behind the scenes somewhat spoils one for the finished article.

Sir Charles Aubrey Smith captained the Hollywood team, and so far as I could make out he was the very life-blood of cricket in that part of the world. I doubt if any other man of his age could have batted so well, but then he captained the English team which visited Australia in 1887—more than twenty years before I was born. Apart from his inspirational work for cricket in Hollywood, Sir Charles was recognised as one of the finest actors of his day, and I have no doubt they mourned his passing in California no less than in England.

One can say little about the cricket, for the standard of play there was not equal to putting up a show against our internationals. But then it wasn't only the cricket. Such memories as an evening spent with that lovable pair Leslie Howard and his wife, who entertained us at their home, of meeting there Maureen O'Sullivan, Norma Shearer and many others, are still green.

Now one recalls with sadness the tragic disappearance of Leslie Howard during the war. Thus passed a true gentleman and one of the world's renowned actors.

From a cricket viewpoint it had been a whirlwind tour. In ten weeks we had travelled in the region of 6,000 miles, during which time

I had no less than 51 innings, scoring 3,779 runs at an average of 102. In the same period Stan McCabe made 2,361 runs and took 189 wickets.

By our standards, cricket in America is at a very low ebb, and I fail to see any prospect of the game making headway in U.S.A. To a large extent the same is true of Canada, where baseball occupies such a prominent place, though cricket still serves to unite empire-minded people who see in their favourite sport a link with the motherland.

For my wife and me, cricket had thus provided the opportunity of seeing the New World—an opportunity unlikely to have occurred through any other medium. It had been far too strenuous, but nevertheless, it was placid compared with the storm which lay ahead, and of which at that time we had scarcely heard the rumblings.

Jardine's Men

THE SELECTION OF THE MEN TO COME TO AUSTRALIA UNDER JARDINE IN 1932 was made while we were in Canada, and it seemed obvious that we were to be subjected to a battery of fast bowling, although the precise nature of it could not, at that stage, have been foreseen.

I had been off-colour during the latter portion of the American tour, due I think to the excessive strain. An injured leg did not assist matters, and in order to prepare for the Australian season I rested on the journey from San Francisco to Sydney—that is if one with my well-known propensity towards seasickness can rest on board ship.

Upon reaching Australia I had to take up the threads of my new contract which involved broadcasting and newspaper work plus certain duties with a retail organisation.

Things went smoothly until I made what I thought to be purely a formality, namely an application to the Board of Control for permission to continue my occupation and also play in the Test Matches. To my astonishment the Chairman of the Board ruled that I could not write and play because the Board Regulations only gave that latitude to any-one whose *sole* occupation was journalism. It was not denied that journalism was the chief part of my occupation. On the other hand it was certainly not my sole means of livelihood.

You can imagine my mental state when this decision was conveyed to me. I promptly did what I thought any man of integrity would do—announced that I would honour my contract, and therefore, if the Board was adamant, I would not be available for Test Matches.

Not only did it foreshadow the prospect of no Tests for me in 1932/3, but there was the 1934 visit to England in the background.

Whilst this matter was sub-judice, I accepted an invitation to go to

Perth and play in a combined Australian XI team against the M.C.C.

Perhaps it was an unwise move as events turned out. The journey from Sydney to Perth meant five nights in the train, and when Richardson lost the toss we spent two whole days in the field, during which I had to bowl no less than 19 overs. To rub salt into the wound, it rained over the weekend and we batted twice on a sticky wicket. Verity was magnificent, taking 7 for 37 off 18 overs. The astute English Selectors left Larwood, Bowes and Voce out of their team, so that no hint was forthcoming of later developments.

The long journey back to Sydney was just completed in time for me to play in a State match against Victoria. This was my first meeting with Fleetwood-Smith, fresh from his triumph of taking 6 for 22 against Queensland.

My score of 238 in the first innings took 195 minutes, the first century in 70 minutes, and was rated by "Not-out" in the Sydney *Referee* to be the equal of any innings seen on the Sydney Cricket Ground.

In the second innings of the same match I made 52 not out, but these isolated bursts did not erase the feeling of ill-health which had intermittently affected me following the American Tour.

My disagreement with the Board of Control developed into a public wrangle. This was due to no fault of mine. The New South Wales members of the Board of Control interviewed the newspaper concerned. From London came big offers to write. All these things disturbed me tremendously when in fact I only wanted to do my duty. Finally the newspaper requested me to play cricket and forgo my writings during that summer. Thus the decision was taken out of my hands.

Meanwhile I had gone to Melbourne to play for an Australian XI against M.C.C. where Jardine turned on the full force of his body-line attack for the first time. Its purport was obvious to me. I promptly confided to responsible officials my predictions regarding the future, but found little sympathy for my views.

The match was chiefly notable for possibly the grandest exhibition of medium pace off-spin bowling I have ever seen. The giant twin, Lisle Nagel of Victoria, in 10 overs scattered the English team to take 8 for 32. In later matches he did not reproduce this superlative form, though with his tremendous height and deceptive flight, I think he might have been a big success on English wickets had he been given the opportunity.

The strain of cricket and travel and argument was beginning to tell. It was reflected in my play for New South Wales against the M.C.C. in a match which saw brilliant bowling by Tate, who had belatedly joined the team following some doubt as to his fitness. Certainly Maurice was not the Tate of former years, but he was still a fine bowler. He was bitterly opposed to Jardine's new theory, and in addition was upset because under the new scheme of things there was no room in the team for a bowler of his type.

The first Test Match was due to be played the next week. It had been established that I was available to play, and would not be expected to write for the press. An absurd anomaly was that I could adhere to my broadcasting contract—in other words I could voice my opinions over the air, but not write them. No doubt the Gilbertian aspect of the situation was responsible for the subsequent legislation which put broadcasting on the same plane as newspaper writing.

I knew that my health had deteriorated considerably, and consequently I informed the Selectors of my doubts as to my fitness. They demanded a medical examination which resulted in an order to rest completely.

Although unable to play I watched the match, and can picture even now the daring brilliance of young Stan. McCabe, who, with an innings of 187 not out, obtained his first century in Test Matches. Towards the close of the innings he flogged the bowling, and with Tim Wall as his partner dominated a 10th wicket stand of 55 runs in about half an hour, of which Tim made four. With the exception of his later innings at Trent Bridge, McCabe was never seen to better advantage, and I doubt if any other player has more completely subdued a fiery and resolute attack.

Outstanding in the match too was the magnificent bowling by Larwood, whose sustained accuracy and tremendous speed were admired on all sides. In the second innings when Larwood took 5 for 28 in 18 overs, I think he bowled faster over a longer period than I can remember seeing from him or anybody else.

Australia was overwhelmed, for not one of her batsmen except McCabe reached 50, and it was with all this background that I resumed my place in the Australian team for the Second Test Match at Melbourne, having meanwhile taken a complete rest. Before an enormous crowd, I listened to a most inspiring ovation as I walked to the wicket. Herbert Sutcliffe, whom I passed on the way, commented on this wonderful reception and I replied, " Yes, but will it be so good when I am coming back? " In a matter of seconds I was returning in deathly silence. Bowes' first ball pitched short and well outside the off-stump, but aided and abetted by a faulty pull shot, hit my leg stump.

Fortunately, I was able to make amends in the second innings by scoring 103 not out in a total of 191. It was amusing in the second innings when our last batsman, Bert Ironmonger, came in with my score in the nineties. The story is told of someone telephoning the ground to speak to him. On being informed that Bert could not come to the phone as he had just gone in to bat, the enquirer said, " Well, 'll hold on."

I walked to meet Bert, but he got in first with " Don't worry, son, I won't let you down." Hammond was bowling, and never have I seen two balls go closer to any man's stumps. But Bert did not let me down.

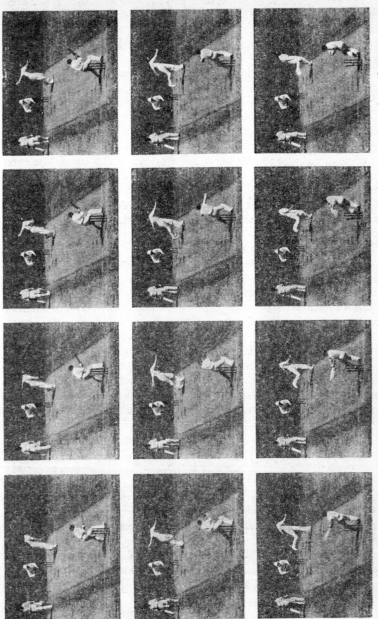

A complete slow motion film of Bradman's duck, bowled Bowes, on the Melbourne Cricket Ground in the 2nd Test, 1932

The match resulted in a win for Australia. O'Reilly took 10 wickets, thereby giving England a taste of his quality, and the highest total by either side was 228. The full force of Jardine's plan was put into operation, but the abnormally slow wicket made it less effective than in other matches.

The following Test at Adelaide was a regrettable affair. It is well known to all cricket enthusiasts that Oldfield suffered a terrific blow on the head.

Larwood was not blamed, but spectators were already incensed over other events and there was a genuine fear that someone would lead an invasion of the field of play.

It occurred once in England over such a trivial affair as this. At lunch-time Australia, in a match at the Oval, needed just a few runs to win. The onlookers were so upset because play did not proceed that they occupied the ground, tore up the stumps, and policemen had to clear them off so that the game could be continued.

The only spectator who recently braved the forbidding Adelaide Oval fence did so in order to take a photo of me. He was promptly arrested, taken to court and fined £2 with 15/- costs. Refusing to pay, he spent a few hours in jail instead. Worse still, his photo was confiscated. Somehow or other the photo found its way into the press so he may have made a profit on the deal. Who knows, he might have won a side wager. I always felt he was harshly dealt with. If a thousand people did the same thing would they all be penalised?

Speaking of jail reminds me of a story concerning an Australian aboriginal who was sentenced to imprisonment for life because of a serious crime. When the penalty was made known to the culprit's best abo. friend, he said, " Too bad—Jacky will never do it." When questioned why, he clarified the matter by adding : " He'll never see the sentence out—he's too plurry old."

Reverting to the Adelaide match I am sure the responsible authorities were relieved that no disturbance took place.

Woodfull was also injured, and altogether the atmosphere of the match was deplorable.

The famous incident between Sir Pelham Warner and Bill Woodfull occurred in the Australian dressing room, and the first of the unfortunate cables which passed between the Australian Board of Control and the M.C.C. was sent.

I cannot praise too highly the courage of Woodfull, who despite his injury and the incredible mental strain under which he laboured, carried his bat through Australia's second innings for the second time in his career.

Of the remaining Test Matches it is perhaps best that little should be written. The Australian captain, even if he could have retaliated, refused to have any truck with such ideas, and the matches proceeded in an antagonistic atmosphere. It was a relief to all concerned when, with a dramatic off-drive right over the Sydney Cricket Ground fence for six, Hammond brought the series to an end.

In the Final Test Larwood broke down, and though we did not realise it at the time, he was never again to be seen playing against Australians.

The subject of body-line bowling has been dealt with in a separate chapter. It involved a principle of such importance as to occupy a special place in the history of cricket.

Two other events that season are worth recording. In the final match between M.C.C. and Victoria a tie occurred—the only one in history between M.C.C. and an Australian State. Victoria required seven to win when the last over commenced, but could only get six of them, for in attempting to score off the last ball of the day, Rigg lost his wicket.

The other event to which I must refer was Tim Wall's sensational bowling for S.A. against New South Wales in a Sheffield Shield fixture. He took all 10 wickets for 36 runs—a feat not achieved by any other bowler in Sheffield Shield matches. The New South Wales score is of such interest that it is tabulated below :—

Fingleton b. Wall	43
Brown c. Whittington b. Wall	0
Bradman c. Ryan b. Wall	56
McCabe c. Walker b. Wall	0
Rowe b. Wall	0
Cummins c. Walker b. Wall	0
Love b. Wall	1
Hill b. Wall	0
Howell b. Wall	0
O'Reilly b. Wall	4
Stewart not out	2
Sundries	7
	113

At one stage Wall took 4 wickets for no runs. He took the last 9 wickets for 5 runs, six of them clean bowled. The wicket was normal. I have seen Tim bowl better, but for once he gained full reward for every delivery—something bowlers seldom enjoy.

Body-line

THE LAST THING I WANT TO DO AT THE CLOSE OF MY CAREER IS TO REVIVE unpleasant memories. However, I would be failing in my duty if I did not record my impressions of something which very nearly brought about a cessation of Test cricket between England and Australia, especially as I was one of the central figures.

Jardine, who captained England in that series, wrote a book defending his theory. So did Larwood. The defence could have impressed the jury not at all, for body-line is now outlawed.

Of paramount importance is the fact that body-line can no longer be bowled *because the M.C.C. has passed a law which has the effect of prohibiting it.* I make this point very strongly because even today, in parts of England, people think Australia stopped it.

The M.C.C. at first were reluctant to believe the reports emanating from Australia as to the nature of the bowling, called " body-line ". They very rightly wanted evidence, and one understands their reluctance to act without it.

Having obtained the evidence they did not hesitate.

Now what exactly was body-line bowling? It was really short-pitched fast bowling directed towards the batsman's body with a supporting leg-side field.

In his book, *Anti-Body-line,* Alan Kippax defines it fairly well in setting out the following objections to that type of bowling :—

1. That a considerable proportion of the deliveries were directed straight at the batsman's body.
2. That many of these deliveries were deliberately pitched short enough to make them fly as high as the batsman's shoulders and head.
3. That an intensive leg-side field was placed, including four and sometimes five men in the short-leg positions, supported by two (occasionally one) in the deep field at long-leg.

Kippax was an Australian batsman, so perhaps it would be more convincing to quote the definition given by an English batsman. This is how Wally Hammond defined it :—

1. Delivered by a speed merchant.
2. Bumped so as to fly high above the wicket.
3. Delivered straight at the batsman.
4. Bowled with a leg-side field of 6 to 8 men.

Of course the protagonists of body-line always claimed that it was leg theory—an entirely fallacious claim.

66

Warwick Armstrong, Fred. Root and others bowled leg theory. Nobody was in the slightest danger therefrom.

With body-line it was different. The risk of actual physical danger to the batsman became his chief consideration.

In order that we may get things in their proper perspective, I feel impelled to quote the remarks of Sir Pelham Warner, who, so far as I know, was the first man to protest in writing against body-line bowling, though at that time the term " body-line " had not been coined.

Writing in the London *Morning Post* of August 22, 1932, of a match between Yorkshire and Surrey at The Oval, he said, " Bowes must alter his tactics. Bowes bowled with five men on the on-side and sent down several very short-pitched balls which repeatedly bounced head-high and more. Now that is not bowling ; indeed it is not cricket ; and if all the fast bowlers were to adopt his methods M.C.C. would be compelled to step in and penalise the bowler who bowled the ball less than half-way up the pitch."

So Bill Bowes was evidently the first man to use this form of attack in England, and at once it was denounced. It was not leg theory.

Where did body-line originate?

Jardine in his book is very reticent on the point. He devotes several pages to details of the evolution of legitimate leg theory which is really only drawing a red-herring across the track, because, as I have pointed out, *leg theory is not body-line.*

Leary Constantine in his book *Cricket and I* says :—
" One could read Jardine's book from cover to cover and, if it were not for the general excitement about body-line bowling, never discover what the essentials of body-line bowling were."

He is not far out. However, the following points are of interest.

Jardine wrote : " Though I did not take part in the Test Match against Australia at the Oval in 1930, I have been told on all sides that Bradman's innings was far from convincing on the leg stump whilst there was any life in the wicket. I am sorry to disappoint anyone who has imagined that the leg theory was evolved with the help of midnight oil and iced towels simply and solely for the purpose of combating Bradman's effectiveness as a scoring machine. It did, however, seem a reasonable assumption that a weakness in one of Australia's premier batsmen might find more than a replica in the play of a good many of his contemporaries." Larwood in his book, was a little bit more direct, for he wrote :—
" Fast leg theory bowling was born in the Test Match at Kennington Oval in August 1930. A spot of rain had fallen. The ball was ' popping '. My great friend, the late Archie Jackson, stood up to me, getting pinked once or twice in the process and he never flinched.

67

With Bradman it was different. It was because of that difference that I determined then and there, that if I was again honoured with an invitation to go to Australia, I would not forget that difference." Let me first have a word to say *re* Jardine's statement. He quotes a 1930 match as the basis for his idea, but completely refutes his own statement by the following reference to a match in 1932 :—

" To our surprise we found an *almost totally unsuspected weakness* on the leg stump in the play of several leading players. This had been particularly apparent in the case of Bradman as early as the second match of the tour, when he came to Perth to play against us."

The thing becomes entirely ludicrous when I tell you that Jardine did not include in his team against us on that occasion any one of his three body-line bowlers, Larwood, Voce or Bowes. Furthermore, I batted twice on a badly rain-affected pitch, scoring 3 and 10.

He must have been amazingly observant to discover such a weakness in those few minutes.

Unfortunately for Jardine, F. R. Foster put the show away when he gave an interview to the press and said : " Before Jardine left England he came frequently to my flat in the St. James and secured from me my leg-theory field placings. I had no hint that these would be used for body-line bowling. I would like all my old friends in Australian cricket to know that I am sorry that my experience and my advice were put to such unworthy uses."

Walter Hammond also made no secret of the development of the theory when he wrote on the subject. According to him " body-line " was born in the grill room of the Piccadilly Hotel, London, where Jardine, Arthur Carr, Voce and Larwood worked out the idea. Hammond claims that P. G. H. Fender had suggested to Jardine that he should adopt these tactics. " Jardine," says Hammond, " spent some days painstakingly analysing all the scoring diagrams which Ferguson, the famous M.C.C. scorer, had made of the Australian batsmen's Test innings." It was after this meeting, according to Hammond, that Jardine went to see F. R. Foster.

From my own talks with members of the M.C.C. Team, I understand this theory was discussed in detail on the way out to Australia, a fact which Jardine does not deny. I think readers will be able to judge what type of bowling it was, and furthermore that I was to be the principal target, with the proviso that success against me would, so Jardine believed, automatically mean success against others.

There is a suggestion by Jardine and Larwood that the theory was justified because of alleged shortcomings disclosed by me in my innings of 232 at The Oval in 1930. The following reports of this match from the press hardly support their case :—

Bradman given out c Duckworth b Larwood, 5th Test, the Oval 1930

1. " Before lunch at The Oval was a glorious period for Australia today, and provided the most courageous batting I have ever seen. Despite the most difficult wicket, Bradman and Jackson gave the English public an exhibition of versatility, pluck and determination rarely seen on a cricket field.

2. " The dangerous wicket helped the bowlers, who made the ball fly, Larwood being particularly vicious. Frequently the lads, after being hit, writhed in pain, but bruised and battered from head to toe, they carried on. Certainly it was a wonderful display of courage to withstand such a terrific onslaught.

3. " This Bradman is lion-hearted, physically and figuratively. He made a double century despite the whirlwind rib-breaking tactics of Larwood. Don was doubled up with pain when a terrifically fast ball struck him in the chest. Shortly afterwards another Larwood ball crashed onto his fingers. It would be hard to realise the pain he was suffering as he flogged the bowling. It was real cricket courage.

4. The *Daily Mail* comments on " the courage of Bradman and Jackson when facing the fast stuff on a wicket which was distinctly unpleasant after the rain, and when they were hit repeatedly and painfully, but stuck to their task with unflinching determination."

It is worth recording that I scored 98 runs before lunch in that period when the ball was flying on a rain-damaged pitch, and also that I was given out caught behind off Larwood when I did not hit the ball. It swung away slightly as I played at it. Noticing the swing I turned my bat at the last moment, and was amazed when Larwood appealed (he was the only one who did) and more amazed still when the umpire gave me out.

I have a photo of the dismissal. Duckworth is standing with the ball in his gloves, hands in front of his chest. Anyone who has seen Duckworth make a catch will remember how he would throw the ball high in the air, one foot off the ground and emit a war-cry. In this instance he did not appeal. Neither did Hammond at first slip, who is shown in the photo standing upright with hands hung low in front of him.

I am not complaining of the decision. There have been other occasions when I have been out and given not out. My purpose in clarifying the matter is to prevent anyone thinking Larwood and Jardine justified in their claim or that they can support it by saying Larwood obtained my wicket.

Jardine has made lavish use of quotations in his book, and in the preface quotes a long interview given to the *Cape Times* by a Mr. J. H. Hotson. In that interview Mr. Hotson refers to Larwood's habit of

Woodfull c Duckworth b Peebles, 5th Test, the Oval 1930
Contrast the gleeful attitude of the wicket-keeper with that in the other picture when Bradman was given out but claims he did not hit the ball

70

reverting to leg theory (after his few opening overs) because he had lost his swing. The inference is clear that such a move was necessary to suit the type of bowling. But it hardly tallies with a photo in Jardine's book showing Bromley (a left-hander) batting to a leg field, and being caught by Verity at short-leg from a shot made purely to prevent the ball hitting him in the face. Larwood goes to great pains in an effort to prove that by 1932 he had developed amazing accuracy and quotes figures to prove it. He cites this not only as a reason for his success, but also as support for the claim that his accuracy precluded any risk to batsmen.

Nobody would dispute his accuracy. That it was newly-acquired is another story.

I imagine accuracy is gauged by runs scored per over. At least that is the basis used by Larwood, for he quotes figures for 1930, 1931 and 1932. They show for 1932 : overs bowled 866, runs scored 2,084.

However, a little research revealed that in 1928, four years earlier, he bowled 834 overs for 2,003 runs, and a short mathematical calculation will reveal slightly greater accuracy in 1928 than in 1932.

But a far more important matter is this. If body-line is allowed in first-class cricket, it must be allowed in *all* forms of cricket. One bowler cannot have a monopoly of a theory. For this reason, I again quote Larwood from his book. " If it really was body-line, bowling would be really dangerous to the batsmen."

When the personnel of the English Team to tour Australia in 1932–33 was announced, I foresaw the possibility of trouble because of the abnormal selection in England's team of four fast bowlers.

Body-line was first used against me in a match on the Melbourne Cricket Ground between the M.C.C. and an Australian XI. I reported privately to certain cricket administrators that, in my opinion, there would be serious trouble unless the matter was dealt with quickly. Then after the First Test had been played in Sydney, Dr. E. P. Barbour reviewed the game and made a very strong appeal for the elimination of this new type of bowling. He made the following comment :—

" The deliberate banging of the ball down less than half-way so that it flies up round the batsman's head is not cricket. If continued, and extended to all grades of cricket as they should be if they are fair, the end result of such tactics will be the disappearance from first-class cricket of every champion after he has put up with three or four years of assault and battery. Perhaps a more serious aspect still is the imminent danger to the good fellowship and friendly rivalry that has always been associated with cricket."

Up to this time the cricket administrators had not been sufficiently impressed with the views of players to make any move.

I always visualised the misunderstanding which would arise if exception was taken to body-line bowling at a time when we were being defeated. It was for that reason I again privately, but very forcibly, expressed my views to certain authorities, after the Melbourne Test Match which we won.

Here was the psychological moment, if any action at all was to be taken, to let M.C.C. know Australia's views.

I thought then, and I think now, that Australia's great mistake was in not dispassionately making an effort to clear up misunderstandings when the Tests were one all. It was ultimately done in the heat of battle at a much less appropriate time.

It must be admitted that although the Australian players and most ex-players strongly condemned the new type of bowling at once, this unanimity did not occur so readily amongst cricket officials, many of whom accused our players of squealing. One State Cricket Association had a motion brought before it to the effect that " The Association disassociate itself with the action of the Board in sending the first cable to England." The motion was defeated by only one vote.

The action of the Board of Control and the cables which passed at that time are now history.

The Australian Board appointed a Committee consisting of Messrs. Roger Hartigan, M. A. Noble, W. M. Woodfull and Vic. Richardson to report on what action was required to eliminate such bowling from cricket. The Committee framed a suggested new rule which was duly sent to the M.C.C. for approval, but up to that time the M.C.C. still had no evidence.

When the West Indian Team visited England in 1933, they had two excellent fast bowlers in Martindale and Constantine, who tried out Jardine's theory in the Second Test Match at Manchester. One result was that Hammond " had his chin laid open by one of many short-pitched rising balls " (*Wisden* 1934). Hammond is reported to have said then and there that either this type of bowling must be abolished or he would retire from first-class cricket.

Jack Hobbs made a similar threat after his experience against Bowes in 1932. A humorous sidelight was the reversal of opinion by players when they themselves had to face it.

George Duckworth thought body-line against Australians quite in order. On returning to England in 1933 he gave lectures and said so. That was before Lancashire met Nottingham.

Then it became a different story. Photos were taken of Duckworth's bruises and used as exhibits.

Lancashire broke off diplomatic relations with Notts. and refused to play against them in the County Championship.

Retribution if you like ! Fifty years earlier Notts. had declined to play Lancashire because the latter team had amongst its players one whose action Notts. considered unfair.

The M.C.C. took steps to investigate the position, and at a joint meeting of the Advisory County Cricket Committee and the Board of Control of Test matches at home, held at Lord's in November 1933, it was agreed that any form of bowling " which is obviously a direct attack by the bowler upon the batsman " would be an offence against the spirit of the game. It was decided to leave the matter to the captains. This principle was affirmed by the Imperial Cricket Conference in July 1934.

However, this did not suffice, for the same type of bowling still persisted. In November 1934 the M.C.C. issued a communication indicating that " as a result of their own observations and from reports received, the M.C.C. Committee consider that there is evidence that cases of the bowler making a direct attack upon the batsman have on occasions taken place during the last cricket season."

In order to eliminate this type of bowling from the game, the M.C.C. Committee ruled : " That the type of bowling regarded as a direct attack by the bowler upon the batsman, and therefore unfair, consists in persistent and systematic bowling of fast short-pitched balls at the batsman standing clear of his wicket."

I have gone to some length to detail what occurred because I want to establish the all-important point that Australia did not stop body-line bowling. Certainly the original protest came from Australia (if we exclude Sir Pelham Warner's first comment) simply because Australian batsmen were the first ones exposed to its dangers. But immediately the M.C.C. Committee were satisfied that such a type of bowling existed, they acted promptly and firmly to define it and to outline the procedure to be adopted by the umpires to stop it.

Larwood himself was very critical of Australia's attempts to legislate against this type of cricket, and he wrote : " Cricket ought to be eternally grateful that its laws are made by the M.C.C." I hope he is still of the same opinion.

Could Body-line be Mastered?

I doubt if this question can be authoritatively answered.

It was used consistently for only one season against the same players, and nobody mastered it. A batsman who played defensively would certainly get caught by one of the short-leg fieldsmen. To try to hook the ball would result sooner or later in a catch on the boundary. Neither defence nor attack could overcome it for long, unless the batsman was particularly lucky.

Playing the good length balls and dodging the others may sound all right in theory, but it would not work in practice. The batsman doing this must of necessity be hit.

In fact no Australian batsman of any note failed to get hit, some on many occasions. Players naturally began to take the view that there were other sports offering many of the attractions of cricket without the risk of serious injury.

After his retirement from Test cricket, Hammond wrote about body-line, and I greatly admired his forthright condemnation thereof. Remember that Hammond was a member of the English Team which used it, and later became Captain of England. This is what he said :—

"I condemn it absolutely. Body-line is dangerous. I believe that only good luck was responsible for the fact that no one was killed by body-line. I have had to face it, and I would have got out of the game if it had been allowed to persist !

I doubt if there was any answer to such bowling unless grave risks of injury were courted."

In that 1932-3 season I endeavoured to counter body-line by unorthodox methods which involved stepping away to cut the ball to the off, and in my view exposed me to a graver risk of injury than the orthodox type of batting. Whilst not completely successful, I did score over 50 runs in an innings 4 times in 4 Test Matches.

McCabe and Richardson both tried to counter it by orthodox methods. Both were very capable, game players and excellent hookers, yet each of them could only once exceed 50 in an innings in the same four matches. Our comparative figures in those four Tests were :—

	Inns.	Runs	N.O.	H.S.	Average
Bradman	8	396	1	103	56·57
Richardson	8	230	—	83	28·7
McCabe	8	166	—	73	20·7

In many quarters I was the subject of bitter adverse criticism for my methods. Jack Fingleton, a contemporary player, later wrote a book in which he cast very grave reflections on my tactics. It may be well to remind readers that his last 3 Test innings against Jardine's men yielded 1, 0 and 0, whereupon he was dropped from the Australian team. In the same 3 innings I scored 177 runs at an average of 88·5. These figures scarcely give Fingleton any authority to criticise my methods. Apparently I had to make a century every time and also be hit more often than anyone else to satisfy the tastes of some. May I be pardoned for again quoting Constantine, a great batsman, and one of the fast bowlers who used body-line against England at Manchester. He says :—

"Of all batsmen in the world the last two to whom body-line should ever be bowled are Bradman and McCabe."

Bradman Kangaroo shooting in the Australian bush

Furthermore, he refers to Jardine making a century against it and says that to stand up and play defensive strokes at Lord's or the Oval as he did at Old Trafford would have been quite impossible, and Jardine was over 6 feet in height. How much harder for those of short stature. It wasn't only a question of whether it could be mastered, but rather that fellows would not bother to try—they would not consider it worth the candle.

Undoubtedly body-line was a reaction against the dominance of the bat over the ball, magnified by my own fortuitous 1930 season in England. But it was the wrong remedy. Killing a patient is not the way to cure his disease.

It was also a form of protest against the inadequacy of the L.B.W. law, because bowlers get very exasperated when they beat a batsman only to be deprived of his wicket by his pads.

Body-line certainly did some good in that it caused an alteration in the L.B.W. law (which M.C.C. agreed to at the time).

In my view the L.B.W. alteration, admirable though it was, did not go far enough. Long before the advent of body-line, I was in favour of an alteration to help bowlers. I openly advocated a change in 1933 ; I again made a strong appeal in an article I wrote in *Wisden* in 1938, and I am still agitating for a further change.

Recently I read an article where the writer was uncharitable enough to contend that my suggestion is related to my retirement. He obviously was poorly informed about my past expressions on the subject.

And there I want to end my references to body-line bowling. It was a passing phase, and I sincerely trust there will never be any need for umpires to contemplate taking action as they are empowered to do.

But I think it is desirable that the facts as detailed herein should be chronicled so that the matter shall be viewed in its proper perspective. The whole thing caused great misgivings and created much feeling. The best way for any reservations in the minds of the English public to be finally swept away is for them fully to understand and appreciate the real facts.

Season 1933-4

DURING THE WINTER MONTHS FOLLOWING THE NERVE-RACKING SEASON which saw the beginning and the end of body-line in Australia, I endeavoured to get some rest and was feeling more like my normal self when the cricket season came round again. Even so I felt that something was wrong. Not being able to diagnose any basic trouble I simply put it down to over-work.

My job was very strenuous. It kept me busy in the evenings and there was the constant strain of playing, thinking and talking cricket.

At that time I made a complete study of the laws of cricket, sat for, and passed, the N.S.W. Cricket Umpires' Association test, and therefore became qualified to act as an umpire.

I had no intention of becoming an umpire though I did try out the knowledge in a match Chamber of Manufactures versus Trades Hall on the Adelaide Oval in 1949 when Tom Playford and I both officiated as umpires. At least our South Australian Premier could not produce his " Union ticket."

As a player and a captain I felt it my duty to know as much as I could about the laws under which we played. I commend this idea to all players.

I don't suggest that they should go to the extent of passing an examination, but they should at least study the rules. Discussions amongst themselves would often be helpful.

From that day onwards I can only remember one incident happening in cricket for which I did not know the correct decision. It was on the Adelaide Oval in the 1948-49 season when Geoff. Noblet, in swinging at a wide, hit his wicket and on appeal was given out " Hit wicket " under Law 38.

I was questioned as to the correctness of the decision, and frankly admitted I didn't know. Can a man be out " Hit wicket " off a wide ? Have you ever seen a man hit his wicket when playing at a wide ?

There was a hasty checking of rules. The umpire was quite right. Law 29 clearly says : " The striker may be out from a ' wide ball ' if he breaks Law 38—the law of ' hit wicket.' "

Arthur Mailey's cartoon of Bradman when he passed his Umpire's examination

Still I was not alone in my ignorance for I do not think one spectator or player on the Adelaide Oval that day knew the answer.

So far as I know, the incident has not happened anywhere else in the history of cricket, but such things *can* happen, and it is the duty of the players, no less than the umpires to know the answers.

In 1933 I regretfully had to leave the St. George Cricket Club which had made possible my entry into Sydney Grade Cricket. The district cricket system demands that a player shall appear for the club in whose district he resides and I had now made my home in North Sydney.

O'Reilly was at that time playing for North Sydney. Later he went to St. George. Strange how our two careers, starting in the country, became so intermingled in the city.

An occupation of much interest to me in association with my employment was the formation of a team of boys called the " Sun-Palmer " team.

These lads were selected from various schools. In addition to coaching them I would at times organise matches. It was most gratifying that in later years almost every one played first-grade cricket and many of them played for New South Wales.

The first-class season concluded rather earlier than usual owing to the necessity for getting the Australian Team away to England.

Apart from Sheffield Shield games, two testimonial matches were arranged, the first for Blackie and Ironmonger and the second for Collins, Andrews and Kelleway.

These matches may be designated " test trials " but they seldom produce the serious competitive cricket which features Shield matches. Players are naturally anxious to help the beneficiaries and so they try to make the cricket entertaining without being one-sided. They also have an eye to the duration of the match.

No sensational cricket was seen in the two games referred to, but the accurate medium pace bowling of Ebeling no doubt contributed to his subsequent selection for the 1934 tour of England.

Don Blackie was a cricket phenomenon who, born in 1882, was thus 46 years of age when chosen to play in his first Test match. English folk will find it hard to believe that a man of his years who had scarcely been heard of before, could suddenly show skill superior to that of his younger colleagues. Yet it was so.

There have been many off-spinners of high class. If the record book is a true guide, C. T. B. Turner, Hughie Trumble and M. A. Noble were the greatest. Each was of pre-1914 vintage. Of their skill I cannot speak though a fleeting glimpse of Noble, long after his best years had passed, left me with a feeling of admiration for him.

Without any question Blackie in 1928 was the best off-spin-bowler in Australia. His run to the wicket was long and curved, his delivery a little more round-arm than Archie MacLaren would have desired. This may have militated slightly against his accuracy, but it had the redeeming virtue of producing a tantalizing flight and exceptional spin.

To turn a ball from the leg side with the third finger is simple. The reverse spin with the index finger is much harder, and I cannot recall any player who brought the ball back from the off-side more than Blackie. He and Ironmonger (of whose virtues I have written elsewhere) were noble warriors who toiled for cricket at an age when most people are either content, or forced, to sit and watch. Public support of their testimonial was evidence of the esteem in which they were held.

It may not have been very apparent this season from the scores, but I found difficulty in concentrating. I was not wholly satisfied with my stamina as I had been in earlier years. Almost without exception my batting was hurried. I felt that the runs had to be obtained quickly before fatigue intervened.

Against Queensland in the opening match of the season my score of 200 was made in 184 minutes, and in the return match I scored 253. In the latter innings Kippax and I had a record 3rd wicket partnership of 363 in 135 minutes.

This beautiful and stylish player was unlucky to emerge on the horizon of big cricket at a time when New South Wales had virtually an international side for its State XI. When his opportunity did come, Alan proved a real stalwart. In addition, his Trumperian style must have influenced for good vast numbers of young boys.

Unquestionably, the line of Trumper and Kippax has much to do with the grace and elegance which is more frequently associated with players from New South Wales than from other States.

In the middle of the season, trouble with my back temporarily put me out of cricket, and after the New Year's Day match I played in only one more first-class fixture. That was at the end of January, when in ninety minutes I scored 128, including four sixes and 17 fours against Victoria.

In the same match Ernie Bromley, erstwhile West Australian of superb physique and splendid natural ability, scored 92 and 33 not out, efforts which must have impressed the Selectors. It looked as though another Clem Hill had been unearthed. But his judgment did not keep pace with nature's gifts. Although he afterwards turned in some good performances, the early promise was never fulfilled.

By now my three-sided contract was maturing, and again I had to think about the future.

I had proved to my own satisfaction that it was much too exacting for one to live cricket day and night, and I decided completely to divorce my business life from sport.

A most attractive offer was forthcoming from the Sydney *Sun* to write for that paper quite apart from broadcasting or any other activities. The journalistic life had its attractions, but always I came back to the absolute necessity of being able to free my mind from cricket when the day's play was over.

My career had begun in New South Wales. All my relations and the great majority of my friends were there, so naturally I had no desire to leave my native State.

At this time, however, an offer was made by Mr. H. W. Hodgetts, a member of the Board of Control, who had his own share-broking business in Adelaide. He invited me to join his staff on my return from England.

There were avenues which could be followed in New South Wales, but in no instance was I offered anything tangible except where there was the direct link between business and cricket.

So with a good deal of reluctance on my part and considerably more on the part of my wife, the change was decided upon, and in order to qualify residentially for South Australia in the 1934-5 season, I took up residence in Adelaide in February 1934.

Almost immediately I was again troubled by extremely indifferent health, and despite having passed the Board of Control's medical examination for the English tour, I went at my own expense to see two Adelaide specialists.

I made it clear to them that the tour of England would prove a great strain. It would be a little more severe by virtue of my appointment as vice-captain of the Australian team, and I was concerned as to my ability to see the job through.

A thorough check-up failed to disclose more than an extremely run-down condition, and I was passed with the proviso that I should not play again before reaching England, and also rest completely on the boat during the whole journey.

To be chosen as vice-captain ahead of Kippax, the latter my State captain in N.S.W., was a clear indication of the Board's policy. They had marked me as a future Australian XI captain.

Under Woodfull one could not help gaining valuable experience. Bill was orthodox without being completely stereotyped. He eschewed any attempt to defy the law of averages, preferring to trust the known way than providence. Consistency, not brilliance, was his theme.

In him one had a splendid mentor.

The Australian Team as selected was more or less according to forecast, unless we regard Chipperfield as a surprise choice.

Thus it was with some problems solved and others yet to be revealed, I prepared for my second journey to England.

England, 1934

OF OUR BOAT JOURNEY TO ENGLAND IN 1934 I HAVE LITTLE TO SAY, because throughout the period I was attempting to regain some of the joy of living which goes with perfect health. Unfortunately, there is no quick method of recharging the human battery when it is run down.

However, I do recall the intensely interesting time spent by our lads with the Davis Cup players who were on the same ship—Jack Crawford, Don Turnbull, Adrian Quist and Vivian McGrath. A humorous sidelight occurred when the boys organised a match between Viv.

McGrath and Clarrie Grimmett and arranged that Grimmett should be allowed to win in an exciting finish. You would have thought Clarrie had just taken 10 wickets in a Test Match. I still do not know whether he saw through the joke.

On our arrival in England there were the usual greetings and preliminary functions at which the younger players made their first acquaintance with leaders of British sport, and the older ones renewed friendships of the past besides adding new ones to the list.

Lord Hailsham was now President of the M.C.C. He was another of the long line of men who have distinguished themselves in the more serious life of the community, but who still found time to take an active interest in cricket.

The Football Cup Tie Final at Wembley was an exceptional thrill because the Conductor, leading the community singing, found out that the Australians were present and led his 93,000 voices in the singing of " For They are Jolly Good Fellows."

The Prime Minister, Mr. Ramsay MacDonald, received us cordially, and spoke in friendly terms at a luncheon given by the Institute of Journalists. (Later on we were his guests at " Chequers ").

These spontaneous expressions of goodwill helped to dispose of any doubts regarding the reception we might anticipate following the turbulent Australian summer of 1932-3.

The tour had been arranged only after an exchange of views between the Australian Board and the M.C.C., wherein the latter gave an assurance that cricket would be played in England as hitherto.

A small cloud appeared on the horizon when Jardine was reported as having said : " I have neither the intention nor the desire to play cricket against Australia this summer."

The public very obviously wished to see cricket, and there was no hint of reserve in their enthusiasm.

Bad weather interrupted our practices, but we used Alan Fairfax's Indoor Cricket School where Bert Oldfield had the misfortune to get his eyebrow cut open when a ball rebounded off an iron staunchion. Indoor schools are good for coaching, but poor substitutes for real practice.

Still feeling very much below par, I asked that I should be omitted from our team for the opening match. Woodfull persuaded me to play on the grounds that my withdrawal would lend colour to rumours about my unsatisfactory health and might prove of psychological value to England.

So I played, and under considerable strain steeled myself to see through an innings of 206. It was made in quick time and obtained a cordial press, but I was the only one aware of the drain on my resources. Indeed, it was largely as the result of this initial exertion that my cricket fell away, and I only once more exceeded 50 before the last week in

May. In that time I also registered two quick and unimpressive ducks.

It soon became obvious that Grimmett and O'Reilly were to be the spearheads of our attack, whereas our batting gave promise of being strong and sustained.

O'Reilly's 11 wickets against Leicester and Ponsford's 229 not out against Cambridge followed by his 281 not out against the M.C.C. were portents of the future.

Following my duck against Hampshire I played an innings against Middlesex at Lord's which probably ranks as the most attractive of my career from a spectators' point of view.

Middlesex had made 258 and Australia in reply had lost Woodfull and Ponsford both for none. As I had made a duck in the previous match I was not altogether in a confident frame of mind. Luck went my way in the first few minutes as big Jim Smith shaved my stumps with a beautiful outswinger. From then on things went right until off the last ball of the day I scored my 100th run made in 75 minutes with 19 fours. The Australian total was then 2 for 135. On the Monday I managed to carry on to 160 when Jack Hulme took a dream catch, rolling down the bank in front of the Lord's pavilion as he did so.

Just to add some excitement to the play, Tommy Enthoven took the hat trick. Because of my belief that here was an innings worthy or special mention, I take the liberty of giving you William Pollock's description of it :—

" An innings that thousands of us who love cricket are going to enshrine in our memories was played as the sun went down over Lord's on Saturday. For more than 40 years I have watched great batsmen, W.G., Ranji, Trumper, Frank Woolley, Macartney, Jessop, Hammond and Hobbs, and am grateful for many precious hours from them, but never have I seen a masterpiece of batting more glorious than Don Bradman's 100. It was supreme, it was epic.

Le Don came in when the Middlesex J. Smith had got both Woodfull and Ponsford out for nought with his village blacksmith fast stuff, and for a ball or two he was not quite sure of himself, but the bit of luck that all batsmen need at the start was with him, and then in five minutes the bowling was his toy. His timing was marvellous, the power he got into his strokes extraordinary, through the covers, straight past the bowlers, round to leg, down through the slips the ball raced from his almost magic bat. All the shots were his, the whole field his kingdom. Smith's quickies, Walter Robins' slows, Ian Peebles' lengthy ones including an exceptional googly, were just so much meat and drink to him.

Le Don seemed to be inspired. He danced down the pitch and hit. He flung out his left leg and drove. He lay back and pulled.

Woodfull bowled by Bowes at the Oval, August 1934

I do not believe that any bowling in the world could have stopped the torrent of his run-making.

During this wonderful hour and a quarter, it was an honour to bowl and field during such an innings. It is not more than the frame of the picture to say that he put the ball to the boundary 19 times and that he got the one run he wanted for his 100 off the last ball of the evening.

Le Don has played the great innings of the season. If there is anything better to come from him or anyone else, may I be there to see and share. The real great things of cricket are treasure."

William Pollock has passed on, but I am indebted to him for this description.

By the time the Tests arrived our Team had avoided defeat, but had not greatly impressed the critics.

Woodfull himself had been sadly out of form until just before the Test Match.

Fate played into our hands somewhat for apart from Jardine's self-expressed desire not to take the field against us, his deputy elect, Bob Wyatt, fractured a thumb in the Test Trial and could not play. Thus the leadership devolved upon Cyril Walters, appearing in a Test against Australia for the first time, rather a heavy handicap even for the most skilful of captains.

In addition, Walters was of a quiet reserved disposition, and undoubtedly felt a trifle overawed in leading old campaigners like Sutcliffe, Hammond and Hendren.

It was an exciting match, not a century being scored, but one must recall the dreadful luck of Chipperfield who, also playing in his first Test, was 99 not out at lunch time, only to succumb to a catch behind the wicket immediately afterwards without further addition to his score.

A feature of the match was the great début of Kenneth Farnes, the handsome English school teacher whose tragic death in an air crash in later years cast such a gloom over the cricket world. Farnes took 5 wickets in each innings and bowled with great fire. On the last day we achieved victory with a bare 10 minutes to go.

O'Reilly's confident appeal for L.B.W. against Mitchell was adjudicated upon by Dolphin, and my sympathy and admiration went out to this splendid umpire because he had to do his duty at such a critical moment to the detriment of his own country. Just one more piece of evidence to show how scrupulously fair and impartial umpires are! As further testimony in support of our much maligned umpires and as proof that they should not be molested in their work by critics, I must report the following paragraph which appeared in the press during the match :—

" Bradman definitely did not touch the ball from which he was given out either with his pad or his bat. The ball came off Ames' pad. Ames called out 'Wally, catch it,' bluffing Dolphin the umpire who gave the decision."

I am very pleased to say the umpire did *not* make a mistake, because the ball, after touching my bat, flew off the wicketkeeper's gloves, and it was a legitimate catch. Umpires do make mistakes, but not nearly so often as the critics sitting in the pavilion.

For some unaccountable reason there were rumours in the air that Kippax was annoyed at non-selection for the Test and I at being sent in second wicket, and there were others of a more serious character. There was not a vestige of truth in any of them.

In England the practice is frequently adopted of roping in the playing arena—something quite foreign to Australians who are accustomed to the picket fence. The Nottingham Test Match Ground was so enclosed, and in the terrific excitement following the end of the match, the crowd surged onto the field itself, completely obscuring the rope and our path of exit. Racing off the ground in an attempt to reach the sanctity of the dressing room, I inadvertently caught my foot in the rope. It not only brought me down but also the man behind me. The resultant serious thigh injury caused me to need a runner in the next match and to withdraw from the following one.

Then came the Second Test at Lord's and defeat for Australia by an innings.

England had made a comfortable score of 440 and we were at least making a respectable attempt to achieve this number, when rain put an end to whatever chance we may have had. I should say rain plus Hedley Verity, for the wonderful Yorkshire left-hander took no less than 15 wickets including 8 for 43 in our second innings.

Australians are not, generally speaking, so much at home on wet wickets as Englishmen, but I do not think any team in the world could have coped with Verity's spin and accuracy that day. In our first innings I made 36. It was a modest total, yet it moved the melodramatic Cardus to write a description thereof which I quote as a historical record of a choice morsel of memory :—

" Let us thank fortune that Bradman got out when he did, on the crest of an innings of terrible power and splendour. The moment he reached the wicket Farnes was put on. Propaganda had established beyond doubt that Bradman does not like fast bowling. He hooked Farnes' first ball for 4 catastrophically. The second was a boundary too, half pulled, half driven. A hit of genius, superb in strength and swiftness. The last ball of the over was a glorious cover drive. In the same over Bradman hit a 2 to the on, off the back foot.

No other living batsman could have forced the ball, which was excellent, more than a few yards away even if he could have stopped it at all.

Bradman struck the fire of genius out of the match's honest and rather dull rock. The atmosphere became tense and luminous. We could feel that Bradman was the creative force of the day, and while he was at the wicket the hour was enchanted, that in the forge of his batsmanship molten history was being beaten into shape. Farnes had 14 runs hit off his first over to Bradman. Geary came on in Farnes' place and Bradman drove him for a sumptuous four to the off. Another fieldsman joined the tight cordon and Bradman of course retaliated by a cut to the place from which the fieldsman had been taken. Verity bowled from Geary's end. His first ball was crashed by Bradman for 4 through the crowded covers. Every fieldsman was stone, not one of them could stir. The velocity of the strokes all along the grass thrilled the imagination. I could not take my eyes from Bradman for a second. My heart was beating as I saw his bat go back so masterfully, so grandly. Then when he drove Verity again for 4 to the off and next ball cut him forward for 4, three boundaries in three balls, a lump of pride and affection came in my throat. Bradman's innings came to an end for me with a sickening suddenness. Mischance brought down the young eagle. The critics shook their heads as Bradman departed. 'A flamboyant innings,' they said. For my part, Bradman's innings of 36 this afternoon was far greater than his 334 at Leeds. Spirit lived in every stroke. Beauty that comes out of life at the crown of manhood. It was an innings as safe and perfect in technique as any ever played by Trumper or J. T. Tyldesley.''

For once it may be noted how desperately important became the follow-on rule. If we had managed a bare 7 more runs in our first innings, England would have had to bat again on the worst of the sticky wicket, with perhaps a different result to the game. All the more credit to her bowlers for driving home their advantage in the first innings.

Further county matches followed. I was greatly amused about this time to see an advertisement in a Gloucestershire paper :—

Australians v. Somerset
If Don Bradman comes to Jones' Garage he can
have a second-hand Austin 7 for a present.
(1 dozen still in stock).

I enjoyed the proprietor's humour and advertising acumen, but I wonder whether his garage would survive the public visitation if such an advertisement had appeared in these recent years of shortages. I did not take advantage of the offer. Let me refer also to the extraordinary generosity of another Englishman who gave a second-hand car as a prize one day when our team competed at golf. Arthur Chipperfield won the car. What happened to it I can't remember.

Amongst odd souvenirs collected during the trip was a cheque payable to Dr. W. G. Grace which had been endorsed by him. It went through the bank in 1907, a year before I was born. This was sent to me by an enthusiast and is still in my possession—the only autograph I have been guilty of preserving other than those of players on official photographs.

About this time we were troubled by various things, not the least of which was a peculiar ailment designated " Wimbledon Throat ".

During the Third Test at Manchester, which to everyone's astonishment was played throughout in tremendous heat and under a blazing sun, Kippax, Chipperfield and I were all victims. Kippax was not well enough to play, whilst Chipperfield and I were obliged to go from our sick beds to the wicket thence back to bed for observation. For some time it was feared that we had diphtheria, but happily no such serious ailment developed.

I can still remember the dreadfully slow wicket for this Test, and how heartbreaking it was for the bowlers.

O'Reilly put up a marathon effort, having no fewer than 214 runs scored off him during the match, but at least he provided the one great sensation. A number of press reporters were so fatigued by the weather and the unexciting play that they decided to adjourn for some refreshment. During those few fateful minutes, O'Reilly, in four balls, obtained Sutcliffe's wicket caught in the slips, clean bowled Wyatt, had been hit for four by Hammond, and also clean bowled the Gloucester champion. By the time the reporters returned to their seats, sensations were over, and they were obliged to watch centuries by Hendren and Leyland before another wicket fell.

At one stage it seemed likely that Australia would have to follow on, but this was averted by our last pair, O'Reilly and Wall, and from then on the match could have only one ending.

Recovering from this ailment I began to feel more like cricket, and was much happier against Yorkshire when in a partnership of 189 with Bill Woodfull my own contribution was 140 made in 115 minutes. This innings, which included 22 fours and 2 sixes, at least brought some retribution, for Verity was again amongst the opposition.

In the Leeds Test rain undoubtedly saved England from defeat after much exciting cricket. Firstly, England had been dismissed on a beautiful wicket for 200. Towards the end of the day, with 37 runs on the board, Australia lost Brown. With an eye to the morrow, Woodfull sent in Bert Oldfield as a stop gap, but two runs later he was caught behind and our skipper went in himself only to have his stumps scattered by Bowes, and 3 were down for 39. Not another wicket fell until 10 minutes to six on Saturday evening when Ponsford dislodged a bail with his foot in hooking a ball from Verity to the boundary. His had been a most wonderful innings of 181, during which that broad blade seemed even broader than usual.

Cricket bats are made to a standard width and all new ones go through the gauge.

Sometimes, when a bat is used to make a goodly number of runs, it spreads until it won't satisfy the requirements of the laws which stipulate a maximum width of $4\frac{1}{4}$ inches.

Ponsford's bat was often referred to as " broad "—a tribute to his defensive powers. A Sydney umpire once took the matter to heart and tested Ponsford's bat—it failed to pass. I cannot recall any other occasion. Apparently it happened frequently in olden times if one can believe the following advertisement which appeared about 60 years ago :—

" Will you allow me to give notice through your paper that in all matches we play we shall provide our own umpire and also our opponents with a $4\frac{1}{4}$-inch gauge, and shall object to the use of any bat which is of more than the regulation width."

It was signed by the club secretary.

At last I had returned to something approaching my best form, and finally was bowled for 304. It was not in any sense an innings comparable with my 1930 effort on the same ground, but it had an enormous moral effect as far as I was concerned. The tremendous strain of such a long innings coming after a period of lean scores played havoc with my muscles. Upon returning to our dressing room I was literally undressed by my team mates and carried to the massage table. Subsequently, when fielding I tore a thigh muscle so badly that I was forced to leave the field and to enter a nursing home, not to play again for three weeks. Indeed, I did not play another first-class match prior to the Fifth Test at the Oval.

Sir Douglas Shields, to whose care I had been committed, was concerned with my condition. Even though my leg improved he insisted that I should spend a period of convalescence at his private home at Farnham Common.

Just at the back of his charming home was a small natural wood. I delighted in walking through there each morning—to see the squirrels and birds in a setting which had remained unchanged for centuries. Nothing in this world has ever appealed to me more than England as nature made her.

Bill Woodfull had been experiencing a lean time, and even advocated

Clark's body-line field against Australia at the Oval 1934. Brown c Allen

his own exclusion from the Test side, so it was a great relief to find him back in top form prior to the concluding Test which resulted in an overwhelming victory for Australia.

England suffered cruel misfortunes. First, she brought back into the side the veteran, Frank Woolley, whose lack of experience against O'Reilly proved an impossible handicap. To make matters worse, Ames suffered from lumbago and had to retire, thereby causing Woolley to appear very much out of place as a wicketkeeper. Moreover, Bowes suffered an illness during the match.

Once more Ponsford, with a grand innings of 266, and I, with 244, made the game safe in the early stages. Our partnership of 451 for the second wicket created a new world's record.

It should be mentioned that in the match against Nottinghamshire prior to the Test, the Australian Team had been subjected to " direct attack " bowling for the first time during the tour. Voce it was who used this type of bowling, and there was considerable unpleasantness.

It may not be generally known that in the Fifth Test Match the fast left-hander Clark at times adopted a full leg field which, to quote the press, was " Indistinguishable from that used by Larwood and Voce in Australia." Both Brown and Ponsford were caught in the leg trap in our second innings, but McCabe and I attacked the legside bowling with such vigour that Clark was forced to abandon his tactics.

Thus once more Australia won the rubber on the anniversary of Woodfull's birthday.

In my final two first-class innings of this tour I put together scores of 149 not out against an English XI at Folkestone and 132 against Leveson-Gower's XI at Scarborough. The former included one over in which I scored thirty (3 sixes and 3 fours) from the six balls delivered by Freeman. The total occupied 105 minutes.

The Scarborough century should, I think, be bracketed with the knock against Middlesex as the most exciting I ever played in England. Brown had been bowled by Farnes for 3, and then against an attack which consisted of Farnes, Bowes, Nicholls and Verity, I was back in the pavilion before lunch, after having made 132.

Serious cricket was at an end, and lovable Bill Woodfull had once again led his men to victory with very great credit.

In a brief analysis of the tour, one can hardly do justice to the many worthwhile performances which could be detailed. It would be only natural to stress the great dependence of the team on our spin bowlers, O'Reilly and Grimmett. Big Bill was a terror to the opposing players, except when, as at Manchester, all the life had been taken out of the pitch, and, despite his advancing years, Grimmett was not far behind him. These two took 53 wickets in the Tests, the other bowlers between them 18.

Fleetwood-Smith had to take second place to Grimmett, but emerged with an enhanced reputation, and clearly indicated that he was forcing his way to the front.

A leg injury seriously interfered with Tim Wall's efficiency, and though Ebeling was an able substitute, he lacked penetrative power. Bromley disappointed everybody, failing to adapt himself to English conditions and appendicitis caused his premature withdrawal from the field of play.

The batting successes had been mainly shared by Ponsford, McCabe and myself, Stan. scoring the most runs in first-class matches and enjoying his most successful tour.

Everybody did well on occasions, but victory must be credited to all-round performances rather than to individuals.

In some quarters we were styled the " silent sixteen ", because of our policy of refusing to comment on anything contentious, but this was a very wise and diplomatic rule on the part of Manager Bushby and Captain Woodfull which contributed to a complete healing of earlier wounds.

It had become clear that English cricket needed rejuvenation, for men such as Woolley could not go on forever.

Our team was back in London preparing to leave for home when I became ill once more. On the day in question I had kept an afternoon tea engagement with an old school chum from Bowral at our hotel. My symptoms became so acute that Dr. John Robert Lee was summoned. He called that evening and again early the next morning, but failed to reach any conclusion. Then, as he revealed to me later, Dr. Lee went for a long drive, by himself, away into the English countryside.

Returning to my bedside, the doctor said he had purposely gone for the drive to concentrate on my case and by a process of elimination try to ascertain the correct diagnosis. He had come to the decision that despite conflicting symptoms my trouble was appendicitis which demanded urgent attention.

He asked that a distinguished Australian surgeon, Sir Douglas Shields, should be called in for consultation. They were in agreement, and before some of my team mates were aware that I had been ill at all, I had been operated upon by Sir Douglas in his Park Lane nursing home.

There can be no doubt that for some time I hovered on the brink of eternity, which was not nearly so bad for me as for my wife in Australia, who had heard the general rumour of my demise. Indeed you can imagine her anxiety after hearing such news whilst awaiting a 'phone call to the London hospital. Fortunately, the rumour was exaggerated —by how much I did not really care.

The Australian air hero, Sir Charles Kingsford-Smith, at that time preparing for the Centenary Air Race, communicated with my wife and offered to fly her to London if need be. The necessity did not arise, and now with great sadness one must think back on the irreparable loss to aviation, when shortly afterwards, Sir Charles disappeared on his flight from England to Australia. Thus passed on a man who had captured the imagination of the world by his daring exploits; who helped to pave the way for today's marvels, and whose thoughtful gesture in my own illness endeared him very greatly to us.

By kind assistance of all concerned, my wife was enabled to get through, in double-quick time, the formalities attendant upon leaving Australia. By journeying overland to Perth, she was able to join the *Maloja* which had left Sydney days before. The P. & O. Company had generously placed a passage at her disposal, and it must have been a tremendous relief for her to receive better news from the hospital by the time the boat sailed.

Sir Douglas Shields, whose great skill and kindness shall ever remain amongst my foremost memories, had apparently removed at last the underlying cause of much indisposition both before and during the tour. Not content with the normal recovery period, he firmly ordered me to have a complete rest for some months. I was allowed to leave hospital only the day before my wife reached England.

Here again there was kindness on all sides. A car and a chauffeur were placed at our disposal, and whilst enjoying the opportunity to show my wife some of the beauties of England, I was at the same time enabled to rest completely.

Apart from the natural effects of such an illness, my eyes were troublesome, and for a brief period I had to resort to glasses.

Despite its attendant anxiety, my illness had brought about the only thing which could possibly restore me to reasonable health. An over-dose of cricket and the cricket atmosphere demanded, as an antidote, such things as a quiet beach, a sailing skiff, a country farm or some such uncricketing atmosphere. Like so many people, I would not have voluntarily taken these remedial measures. Now they were forced upon me.

Before setting out for Australia, my wife and I drove as far north as Edinburgh, where by now the moon had, in the shortening winter days, commenced to shed a useful as well as ornamental light round afternoon tea time.

A short holiday was spent in Perth as the guests of Mr. and Mrs. A. K. Bell, a name famous in Scotland and elsewhere in connection with whisky. Not being a connoisseur I offer no comment, but of A.K. I can speak affectionately. He was a true philanthropist and spared neither time nor money in endeavouring to advance cricket in Scotland.

A unique experience was to spend a day in London, having as a guide John Burns, the first Labour man ever to become a British Cabinet

Minister.   He showed us the unusual, unfrequented spots.   No other Londoner was better informed.

We experienced touches of an English winter before journeying on to the Continent.

A happy Christmas in the south of France, a terrific contrast to the atmosphere at the same place as we departed in 1938, and then homeward bound.

Under doctor's orders, cricket was out of the question for the remainder of the Australian summer, which I spent in the champagne air of my own home town at Bowral.

It took three more months before I was able to return to normal duties.

The 1934 English trip must remain one of conflicting emotions, and can truthfully be said from my point of view to have been sensational.

To South Australia

IT WAS ON ANZAC DAY 1935 THAT I ARRIVED IN ADELAIDE TO TAKE UP belatedly the threads of my new work.

I knew nothing of the art of stock and sharebroking.   A new field of learning lay before me.

This type of work not only appealed to me, but impressed me as being of greater importance in the community than is generally realised.

Sharebroking can be a diversified occupation.   People in general look upon it as having to do with shares in companies.   How many would know that the type of company which is largely responsible for big business in the community today was also behind the establishment of the State of South Australia ?

About 1834 the fate of the projected colony that was to become South Australia was being discussed in the English Parliament.   It was eventually decided to establish a province here, but certain monetary demands were made by the authorities as a guarantee of good faith and early development.

Land in the new Utopia was offered for sale to prospective settlers, but even 134 country acres and one city acre for £80 failed to induce enough buyers to raise the sum required as a guarantee.

In January 1836 George Fife Angas formed a joint stock company with a capital of £200,000 to back the enterprise, and this was primarily responsible for the successful overcoming of early difficulties.

The rest is well known, but I want to place emphasis on the fact that South Australia largely owes its existence to the joint stock company method of finance.   It is a fascinating elastic system enabling people all over the globe to subscribe into a common pool, whereby the carrying-on of trade and business may be facilitated.

This method has enabled development of our huge silver lead industry, steel, textiles, automobile and all types.

With such development comes progress, for large sums must be available for research in laboratories indispensable to scientific discovery.

Companies provide a large percentage of employment and a source of taxation.

It is wrong for people to think of our large companies in terms of wealthy industrialists when they are, in the main, owned by thousands of shareholders and are a vital necessity to the well-being and democratic progress of a country.

By the time summer arrived, my health had shown an enormous improvement, thanks to the long break from cricket, a complete physical rest and the clearing up of my appendix trouble. To get my muscles back into some sort of condition for cricket I indulged during the winter months in the more gentle exercise of golf. More for fun than anything else I entered in the Mount Osmond Club Championship, and to my surprise won it. The walking did me good—perhaps because I cover more ground in a round of golf than most people.

So it was with much more of my earlier enthusiasm I commenced playing in my new State.

The M.C.C. Team on its way to New Zealand called at Adelaide and played a match. My form was very ordinary, which was quite understandable.

Top score for South Australia was made by our little wicketkeeper, Charlie Walker, which reminds me of a story Charlie was very fond of telling against himself.

During the English tour of 1930 Charlie met with scant success as a batsman. In one of the concluding matches his team mates in the dressing room gave him a big round of applause when he scored a single. Thinking it must signalise Charlie's 1,000 runs for the season, the skipper of the fielding side walked up and congratulated him. "Your 1,000 I suppose?" he said. "Oh no," replied Charlie, "that is my 50."

The Australian XI was in South Africa. I had been forced to decline the trip on the doctor's advice, and as Woodfull had retired, Vic. Richardson of South Australia was chosen as Captain. In his absence I was chosen to captain S.A., and became for the first time skipper of a Sheffield Shield side.

Our opening match was against my former home State, and it was the first serious trial to which I was subjected after my illness. The score book shows that I made 117 (just one run less than in my initial game for New South Wales against South Australia), but what a

94

" My favourite portrait of my wife who has been such an inspiration throughout my career."

struggle it was ! The muscles refused to co-ordinate, and in my score was a high percentage of singles.

Still we won the match by an innings, and in my next game against Queensland, it was a pleasure to find the old co-ordination returning. With a score of 233 I was right back into form, and obtained revenge on Eddie Gilbert who had dismissed me so quickly on a former occasion. This time Gilbert's figures were 2 for 121, but he achieved destruction in another sense, for he hit Badcock on the hand, and a fracture resulted.

Playing against Victoria in Melbourne on New Year's Day, I compiled a score of 357 out of the S.A. total of 569, my highest score on the Melbourne Cricket Ground. Still it was not enough to achieve victory in the time at our disposal.

It was a pleasure this season to bat with young Jackie Badcock of Tasmania, who had also thrown in his lot with S.A. Jack was a lovable and completely unspoiled personality—a great cricketer whose failures in the Tests in England in 1938 detract somewhat from an otherwise splendid record. I tried hard to assist him, and I feel there was much similarity between our styles. In the last match of the season, Badcock made 325 against Victoria, thus putting the seal on the promise he had displayed earlier.

We finished up winners of the Sheffield Shield, having gone through the season undefeated. It was South Australia's first win for nine years.

I was naturally delighted at this result, and still treasure the following letter which I received from the President of the South Australian Cricket Association :—

" Dear Don,

Please accept my very heartiest congratulations for having in the first year of taking charge of the S.A. XI been able to annex the Sheffield Shield.

The dropping out of six players with the cricketing ability possessed by Richardson, Grimmett, Lee, Nitschke, Lonergan and Tobin in one fell swoop would be enough to dampen the ardour of any new captain. You with your co-selectors have faced the problem of building up a new side, and with the material at your disposal you have by your determination and astute generalship and the inculcation of a real team spirit, as well as your own personal accomplishments on the field, so welded the members together as to produce for us a team of which we are proud.

On my own behalf, as well as on behalf of the S.A.C.A., I warmly thank you for the efforts you have put forth, and the splendid result of those efforts.

Yours with sincerest regards,
(Sgd.) B. V. Scrimgour,
President,
S.A. Cricket Association."

It was gratifying to know that my first effort at captaincy had met with such a ready and happy response from the young players I was fortunate enough to lead.

There was one more match before the season ended—against Tasmania. I was probably in form equal to my previous best in making 369—the highest score ever made on the Adelaide Oval and the highest ever made for S.A. Incidentally it broke a record previously held by Clem Hill, and with typical humour Clem sent me a telegram : " Congratulations you little devil for breaking my record."

I think I may reasonably give the scoring rate in this 369, as it represents the fastest in any innings I played of that size :—

First	50 in 40	minutes
2nd	50 ,, 30	,,
3rd	50 ,, 36	,,
4th	50 ,, 47	,,
5th	50 ,, 21	,,
6th	50 ,, 19	,,
7th	50 ,, 29	,,
Last	19 ,, 11	,,

369 in 233 minutes

I should refer to the brilliant debut made by Ron. Hamence in this match. He made 121, and our partnership of 356 for the third wicket, created a record for South Australia.

Gubby Allen's Men

THE 1936/7 AUSTRALIAN SEASON WAS ONE OF EXTREME FLUCTUATIONS. It started with a Testimonial Match to Warren Bardsley and Jack Gregory in Sydney.

I did not have the good fortune to see Warren Bardsley play until long after his best years were past. Nobody can deny his worth to Australian cricket.

Apart from myself, Bardsley is the only Australian to have made more than 50 centuries in first-class cricket. Remember, too, they were not made going in No. 4 or 5, but as an opening batsman who had to face the bowling at its most hostile moment.

Of Gregory I have spoken elsewhere. If ever a player could be termed vital and vehement it was Gregory. His bowling in the early days was positively violent in its intensity. The way he wrecked England's hopes at Nottingham in 1921 by an inspired burst in which Knight, Tyldesley and Hendren succumbed in quick succession practically settled the rubber. In the slips he was worth two men. What he meant to Arthur Mailey's career could not be estimated.

Victor Richardson's all-conquering team which had returned from South Africa with an outstanding record was pitted against the Rest of Australia, captained by myself.

According to reports, O'Reilly and Grimmett had been almost unplayable in South Africa, and the public were anxious to see this great pair of bowlers against an Australian Team.

It was an exciting match in which Richardson's team was defeated by 6 wickets after there had been some excellent cricket displayed by both teams.

My own form was exceptionally good for such an early stage of the season, and my score of 212 in the first innings was made out of our total of 385.

The outstanding performance of the match was by slow bowler Frank Ward, who during Grimmett's absence the previous season had operated splendidly for South Australia. Frank obtained 12 wickets for 227 runs in the testimonial as compared with Grimmett's 7 wickets for 228. Very few of the tourists were comfortable against him.

Returning to South Australia, I was to have played against the M.C.C., but on the eve of the match suffered a personal bereavement which forced me to stand down.

The night before the Englishmen arrived in Adelaide, my wife presented me with our first-born—a son. It was topical news. I was the recipient of many congratulations, notably at a civic welcome tendered to our visitors.

Alas, I had to suffer my torments in silence. The congratulations were sincere, but I dare not reveal the doctor's warning. All was not well. He could not hold out much hope of the child's survival.

The following day I was hastily summoned to the hospital, where my wife and I were grief-stricken on being told the worst.

In the lives of young parents there can scarcely be a sadder moment.

The hopes and ambitions of a father for his son, fine and noble though they may be, are as nought alongside the natural love of a mother.

Perhaps this experience has something to do with my belief that the medical profession above all must bring enormous satisfaction to its practitioners who daily bring happiness into the lives of suffering humanity or at least relieve anxiety and pain.

Hammond with a century in each innings against South Australia showed superlative form. As he had already made two centuries in the West, these made four in succession.

Again Ward bowled splendidly to take 10 wickets.

This M.C.C. team under their popular Australian-born skipper, Gubby Allen, performed indifferently against the States. They only just beat a weakened S.A. XI, had the worst of a draw against Victoria, failed against N.S.W., and were behind in the first innings against Queensland.

Slow bowling seemed to hypnotise them. In S.A. Ward had taken 10 wickets, in Victoria the little known Frederick took 8 wickets, in Sydney, Mudge captured 8, Allen of Queensland 6, whilst in the game M.C.C. v. an Australian XI, Chipperfield took no less than 8 in one innings. Of these slow bowlers only Ward was rated highly, and with most of his batsmen out of form, Wyatt with a broken wrist and Robins with a damaged finger, it looked as though Allen had an insurmountable hurdle to negotiate when the First Test Match commenced.

I had been elevated to the position of an Australian Selector, due to the death of Dr. C. E. Dolling of S.A., and accepted the position with some reservations. The armchair selector who may send his unofficial team to the newspaper and find numerous reasons why the official selection is a bad one is in the fortunate position of not having to carry any responsibility.

A Selector's job is interesting, sometimes exasperating, occasionally heartbreaking. For a captain to sit on a committee which leaves one of your trusted colleagues out of an Australian team, because in their collective judgment he must give way to a better player, is not a pleasant experience. Thank goodness most cricketers understand full well that only eleven can be chosen, though occasionally a Selector finds an unfortunate repercussion from a disgruntled player. Favouritism is a luxury no Selector can afford. Sentiment must not cloud his judgment, for his job is to try and select the best possible team.

As Woodfull had retired and Richardson was not in the team, I was given the task of leading the Australian XI in the First Test Match at Brisbane.

Ward's splendid efforts had caused him to be chosen ahead of Grimmett.

On paper our chances looked bright. My bad record of tossing was started by losing this one, only to be redeemed with a sensational wicket first ball, followed by two more shortly afterwards, and England were 3 for 20.

Then our fast bowler McCormick broke down. We got caught on two sticky wickets following heavy rain, and England gained a very meritorious though unexpected victory in just over four days' play.

My own captaincy came in for a good deal of criticism. I was not surprised. My experience as a captain had been of comparatively short duration and the team was playing its first match as a unit. It takes time to weld a cricket eleven into a smooth-working machine.

I still think we would have won the Test given fine weather throughout, but in saying that I do not for one second wish to detract from England's clear-cut victory.

I omitted to mention earlier that Fleetwood-Smith was not a candidate for the First Test Match because of a damaged tendon in his left hand. He had still not recovered when the Second Test came.

We were at rather a disadvantage for this Second Test. Both McCormick and Ward had to be medically examined, and whilst both were passed fit to play, there can be little doubt neither was capable of

A rather extraordinary photograph showing Bradman pulling a short ball in front of square leg. Notice the back foot has been taken behind the stumps in a pivotal movement which has enabled the striker to gain more than the normal use of the crease area.

doing his best. McCormick's back was still troublesome. Ward, who had suffered a broken nose in the Brisbane Test, could not breathe with normal freedom, and later had to undergo an operation.

True to form, I lost the toss again, and with Hammond at his very best in an innings of 231 not out on his favourite Sydney wicket, we got into trouble. Then came the rain once more to add to our woes, plus illness of Badcock who was confined to bed.

Further, Allen and Voce who had routed us in Brisbane, bowled brilliantly, and the match was virtually over at once.

Suddenly, the English team were two up with three matches to go. Instead of being a negative, tentative side, they were on top, and it really was a huge task that we faced.

These unexpected reverses caused misgivings, and a report was published that certain members of the Australian team were not giving me the co-operation that a captain is entitled to expect. Whilst these rumours were promptly denied, both by the players and myself, there was certainly a section of the public who thought the cares of captaincy were undermining my efficiency. They advocated the inclusion of Richardson for captain, stressing the successes of his team in South Africa.

They overlooked the difference in the opposition and the cardinal point that the Selectors did not consider Richardson good enough to be in the Eleven. I knew the captain's job was not upsetting me, though my own comparatively poor scores did little to support my contention.

We were encouraged by the recovery of Fleetwood-Smith, who was back in the team for the Third Test, and by the fact that at last I won the toss. We did little to take advantage of the splendid wicket, losing 6 wickets for 181 on the opening day, but this time the rain came to benefit Australia, and we saw a sensational battle of tactics such as circumstances rarely allow.

Having batted on to see how the wicket would play, I closed at 9 for 200, thinking it would be the psychological moment.

The Englishmen batted stubbornly, particularly Hammond and Leyland, whose defence on this atrocious wicket—the worst I ever saw in my life—was beyond praise. Finally, each of their efforts was brought to an end by miraculous catches on the part of Len Darling. The one he took off Leyland could not have been bettered. It was a full length dive, the ball being held inches from the ground in his left hand from a robust pull to the leg side.

Eventually, I could see that we were getting England out too quickly, for once Hammond and Leyland had gone no other batsman looked like getting a run. I instructed our bowlers not to get wickets so that Australia could avoid batting on a sticky wicket that evening. Every moment I was afraid that Allen would see through my tactics and combat them by closing the innings. At last he did with England 9 for 76, but a most valuable half hour had been lost.

In a bad light and with rain again threatening, I countered Allen's strategy by sending Fleetwood-Smith and O'Reilly to open up. I can still picture the look of incredulity on Fleetwood's face when I told him to put the pads on. He said, " Why do you want me to open up ? " and at the risk of offending his dignity I told him the truth. " Chuck," I said, " the only way you can get out on this wicket is to hit the ball. You can't hit it on a good one, so you have no chance on this one."

My theory was so absolutely right that not only did he fail to get out that evening, but when the game was resumed on the Monday morning, he lost his wicket to the first ball which touched his bat.

My counter nearly went astray when O'Reilly got out first ball, but obstinate batting by Ward proved invaluable. Then as the wicket improved, the recognized batsmen drove home the advantage. Fingleton and I put together a sixth wicket record partnership of 346, and the rumour that cares of captaincy were upsetting my play were dissipated by my own total of 270.

For England I think Leyland's 111 the best innings of the tour, and it provided one of the most humorous incidents I can remember on a cricket field. Leyland had batted most of the day and was very tired when, at a quarter to six, leaving 15 minutes to play, Robins came in. At any time Robins was extremely fast between wickets. Now he was fresh and Leyland very tired. First ball Robins drove through the covers and raced down the pitch. They ran two and Robins turned hopefully for a third, but the burly Yorkshireman quietly sent him back with the rejoinder, " Steady up, lad, we can't get them all tonight, you know." As England still wanted over 400 runs you can understand our laughter.

At the conclusion of the match there was a most regrettable happening. Four members of the Australian Test Team, McCabe, O'Reilly, Fleetwood-Smith and O'Brien were summoned to appear before a Board of Control Sub-Committee.

To this day I am unaware of what actually took place, but it seems pretty clear that the four players were questioned concerning certain " rumours ". Where the truth is not revealed there must be conjecture. In this case it varied from charges regarding the captaincy to others that they were not taking the matches seriously.

My concern over the incident was natural. The interview was arranged without my knowledge. I was captain of the team, but had not been consulted. I was afterwards told, unofficially, that such a procedure was designed to protect me, but in actual fact I immediately felt that I was suspect of having made adverse reports on these players. Nothing could have been further from the truth for I was in complete ignorance of the whole affair. No public statement was issued as to what took place.

In the Fourth Test Match at Adelaide we at last had a match free from rain. Our team could only muster 288 on a lovely wicket. England, with 330, did little better, frittering away a golden opportunity to establish a big lead after having mastered our attack. Still it was a desperate situation. With Allen setting a deep field to me, thereby forcing me to run singles and preventing me getting more than an occasional boundary, I had to put up a marathon effort of 437 minutes batting in our second innings for a score of 212. It still left England in a good position, and when the sixth day's play commenced with Hammond still not out I feared the result.

Walking onto the field I handed the ball to Fleetwood-Smith, and endeavoured to inspire this erratic genius by telling him the result of the match was in his hands. He rose to the occasion grandly, bowling Hammond with a glorious sinuous ball which swerved away from the bat then viciously spun back between bat and pad as the flight drew the batsman forward.

In a flash I thought of dear old Sammy Carter, who had years before expressed the belief that Fleetwood-Smith might one day win a Test match for Australia. If ever the result of a Test match can be said to have been decided by a single ball, this was the occasion. That glorious off-break turned the scales, and going back to Melbourne for the Fifth Test match and winning the toss, we had no difficulty in clinching the deciding match of the series.

Just before the Fifth Test Match, England had played Victoria, the latter team including Laurie Nash, a fast bowler better known for his skill as an Australian Rules Footballer.

There had been resentment by the Englishmen at some short-pitched bowling of Nash in the State match, and when he was included in the Australian team for the Fifth Test Match, I think Gubby Allen was a little apprehensive.

I did not see the match against Victoria, and had nothing to do with whatever methods were employed, but I do know that in the Final Test no possible exception could have been taken to either McCormick or Nash, whose bowling was scrupulously fair.

Once again Dame Rumour got busy, and reports were circulated that Board Members had attempted to influence the Selectors. An ex-Australian XI captain wrote an article in the press and claimed that the usefulness of fast bowling had " been restricted this match by a ridiculous agreement which prevents fast bowlers from using the bumping ball even in the most legitimate manner."

There was no such agreement. In all matches under my captaincy, irrespective of what bowlers were at my command or at the disposal of the opposition, I have refused to encourage the bowling of bumpers as a matter of policy even without a supporting field. But I have never requested any fast bowler not to bowl an occasional and legitimate bumper, which is a totally different matter. It is only a question of adhering to the spirit of cricket, and there is no need for agreements. I would never be a party to one nor would I ever instigate tactics which I thought were detrimental to the game of cricket or likely to promote ill-feeling.

Gubby Allen was most crestfallen at the loss of the Ashes, but had every reason to feel satisfied with a grand job. Injuries and illness had beset his team, and whilst I still think he could have won the Third

Test Match by closing his innings earlier, one must be fair and point out that rain threatened and nobody could forecast the turn of the weather which gave us a lovely wicket for the Monday.

By Test standards the batting of his team was not sufficiently reliable, but Gubby himself made amazing physical efforts to redeem any shortcomings. More important still, he completely erased the unhappy memories of 1932-3.

For Australia certain ground work had been accomplished. Some of the younger players such as Gregory and Badcock had done very well.

There have been few more promising youngsters in Test match ranks than Ross Gregory, and I still feel he would have enjoyed a splendid career but for an untimely accident which temporarily retarded his advancement. Before there was time for a complete recovery he gave his life for his country.

McCabe was consistent with his scores, exceeding 50 six times in 9 hands, and making his runs with that ease and grace which always characterised his batting.

Fingleton also had a fine record, and as usual his fielding was of the highest order.

Over the five Tests, O'Reilly was again our best bowler. At times I felt that he overdid his leg-stump attack, and better results would have been achieved by concentrating on the middle and off stumps. I felt that such a move would have been more positive.

Still, it is difficult to argue with your best bowler, especially when he possesses the determination of " Big Bill ". Moreover, a departure from any time-worn practice can have an unsettling influence. O'Reilly was difficult enough to play irrespective of which theory he employed.

Taking the series as a whole, the standard of play was not high. There was much excellent cricket which would bear comparison with the highest Test standards. No one could deny, however, that the general quality of play was below some earlier encounters, and certainly the Australian standard of 1948 was vastly superior.

An intensely interesting season's cricket ended with an exciting match in Adelaide when McCormick made a determined bid to equal Tim Wall's record of 10 wickets in one innings in a Sheffield Shield Match. He had taken the first 9 and the giant Victorian, Sievers, was given the ball with strict instructions what to do and what not to do. In his first over he scattered the batsman's stumps, and thus passed for ever McCormick's chance to enter this hall of fame.

Season 1937-8

FOR A CHANGE THERE WERE NO DISTRACTIONS IN THE SHAPE OF VISITING teams and all our best players were available for the Sheffield Shield matches. There was the usual keenness which characterises the season immediately preceeding an English tour.

The opening first-class match of the season for me was on the Adelaide Oval, where a team captained by Victor Richardson played a team captained by myself, and the proceeds were equally divided between Richardson and Grimmett.

It was a fitting tribute that the services of these two players should be recognized by the State to which their cricket had meant so much.

Vic. Richardson's international career was brief. In Sheffield Shield cricket he played more innings than any other batsman, namely 148, scoring no fewer than 6,148 runs at the highly respectable average of 43·6. Only two other batsmen, Clem Hill and myself, exceeded this total.

I had the greatest admiration for Richardson's skill as an athlete. He was a representative of the State in other sports besides cricket, and it is doubtful whether Australia has produced a better all-round athlete. His physique was ideal, his courage undoubted, and I sometimes felt the only thing which prevented his figures being better was a tendency to lose concentration.

One great innings of his on the Adelaide Oval against Larwood will long be remembered. Richardson shone against fast bowling more than any other type, for his pet shots were the hook and the square cut.

As a fieldsman he was in the class of Chapman and Constantine. Some of his work at silly-point to Grimmett was brilliant in the extreme, and his nonchalant method of taking difficult catches in the slips frequently clouded the value of his efforts.

Grimmett actually played one more Sheffield Shield match than Richardson. Nobody else can approach his stupendous total of 3,558 overs which brought him 513 wickets at an average of 25·29. Figures are not entirely conclusive especially short-term figures, but it is difficult to avoid their significance if a man produces them year after year against every type of opponent and under all conceivable conditions.

It may surprise readers to know that Grimmett took more than twice as many wickets in Sheffield Shield cricket as his nearest rival. Of course he bowled ever so many more overs than his colleagues. No other bowler has reached 2,000 overs in Shield cricket.

South Australia placed great reliance upon him and used him accordingly.

Grimmett's performance, apart from being a tribute to his skill, is a monument to his phenomenal stamina. He was a small wiry, unobtrusive little figure, whose fielding was once described by a writer as reminding him of a cat walking on a wet pavement.

Clarrie was a theorist. He liked to adopt a stereotyped field and stick to it, basing his success upon the law of averages. The field he set was sound, and he bowled to it as no other slow bowler in history could do. I have seen Grimmett take the ball, and immediately drop into a perfect length to bowl three or four maidens in succession. He rarely sent down a truly bad ball, and thus could be used for long periods without being inordinately expensive.

The consistency and perseverance of Grimmett could well be an object lesson to aspiring young bowlers.

Regrettably, the weather restricted the Testimonial Match to Friday and Saturday, thereby reducing the reward which would have otherwise gone to these two recipients.

The Sheffield Shield competition saw New South Wales victorious after a lapse of five years, with South Australia second.

No extraordinary performances were recorded by the younger players, but successes came mainly to those well tried. If there was an exception one could mention Sid. Barnes, whose batting for N.S.W., especially in the last match against Victoria, earned him a place in the touring side.

South Australia possessed on paper an excellent team, and would normally have stood a good chance of taking the season's honours. Our hopes were frustrated by O'Reilly, who, in our very first match, turned in an amazing performance against us. He bowled 33·6 overs (8-ball) to take 9 wickets for 41.

Our first batsman fell L.B.W. to O'Brien so there was never any chance of O'Reilly getting the 10, which was his misfortune, for he bowled well enough.

In this particular game my own scores were 91 and 62, so that I had plenty of time to battle against my old antagonist.

My best performances during the season were 246 and 39 not out against Queensland, followed by 107 and 113 in the return match.

When we played New South Wales on the Sydney Cricket Ground in January, we had the misfortune to strike, I fancy, the hottest day on record in that city. Trusting to memory, I think it was 113·5 with hot westerly winds, made worse by smoke from the country bush fires. I cannot recollect another day so trying.

Charlie Walker, keeping wickets for us, broke a finger, and in this stifling heat I became saddled with the wicketkeeper's job including the trappings. Although getting three of the next four wickets which fell, it did not lessen my discomfort.

The Trials over, places were filled for the 1938 tour of England, and I was honoured with the position of captain.

It was good to look forward to another visit amongst overseas friends. Naturally, I hoped for better fortune than befell me in 1934. To some extent my hopes were fulfilled. Nevertheless, once again the trip ended on a tragic personal note.

England, 1938

THE MEMBERS OF THIS 1938 AUSTRALIAN TEAM ASSEMBLED IN MELBOURNE on February 25th to commence the Australian portion of the tour.

As usual, there were matches in Tasmania and Western Australia.

There had been perhaps a little more criticism than usual of the selected team. The omission of Grimmett and Oldfield had been seized upon, whilst the inclusion of Brown had been questioned.

Irrespective of the arguments advanced, it was potentially a strong side, the oldest member being only 32.

Our Manager was Mr. W. H. Jeanes, Secretary of the Australian Board of Control, who was honoured during the tour with the Order of the British Empire.

Quite apart from the merits of individual persons, there can be no doubt that the policy of sending the Secretary of the Board as Manager was highly beneficial to Australian cricket. Those people who have not accompanied a modern international touring team have no conception of the multi-sided issues to be faced. I am sure in later years the Australian Board has been very grateful for the useful knowledge brought back by their Secretary.

The initial portion of the tour is always rather exciting, especially for the young player making his first trip. Farewell functions are arranged, and there is much hurry and bustle.

It is quite a rest to board the ocean liner and spend a few days away from the atmosphere of cricket. At least this is so for most of the team, but the captain immediately commences to think of the various duties which lie ahead. I knew that in 1938 I was very tired upon leaving Australia, and spent the first portion of the journey in bed with a sore throat and a bout of influenza. At the same time it enabled me to do some reading and make valuable notes which proved useful once we arrived in England.

Our first contact with the grim reality of forthcoming events was when we reached Naples. I wrote back to a friend in Adelaide and said : " From the deck of our ship we counted 36 destroyers, 8 cruisers and 72 submarines. I guess they were not built to rust." Marines were being drilled on the water-front. On all sides there were obvious signs that Europe was contemplating a grim future.

During our day in port we visited the ruins of Pompeii, the ghastly remains of a previous civilization. Our Manager was stricken with lumbago and could only accompany us on this Pompeii visit with the aid of a walking stick. Whilst the party were surveying a particularly battered part of the ruins, McCormick, the humourist of the team, brought roars of laughter by suddenly exclaiming : " Bill, old boy, I can hardly tell you from the ruins."

This fellow McCormick had the sharpest wit and the keenest humour of any tourist I know. No matter what the situation, he invariably found a fitting remark to cause a smile.

One day on the Sydney Cricket Ground when Ernie was receiving a severe pasting from a batsman, he turned to a nearby fieldsman and said : " Have you heard the latest cricketer's song ? " When the answer was in the negative he said, " You're Driving Me Crazy."

The team suffered a great misfortune at Gibraltar when its baby, Sid. Barnes, had a nasty fall in the early morning on a slippery deck. At the time we thought it was only a sprained wrist, but after reaching England a fracture was discovered. This left us short of reserves. We thought it necessary to have another player. A cable was sent to the Australian Board to this effect, but the Board refused.

This decision threw a much greater strain on the remaining players, especially as we had more than a normal share of injuries and mishaps. Barnes did not play until the end of June, by which time the Second Test Match had already been decided. Some Australian was unlucky, for had the Board agreed to our request, probably Ross Gregory or Keith Rigg would have been flown to England.

The first night I was in London, Dr. R. J. Pope and I paid a call on Sir Douglas Shields, who, you will remember, had played such a part in my anxious moments of 1934.

I wonder how many Australians realise what a friend to cricket Dr. Roland Pope has been. No man loved the game more. At his own expense he travelled with Australian teams to England and elsewhere on numerous occasions. With him he always took valuable medical equipment, together with an incredible array of books and other items which he considered might be useful. More than these things was the remarkably wise counsel which this highly cultured and delightful gentleman gave to anyone in need. It was his custom to send boxes of fruit into the players' dressing rooms in Sydney, and by innumerable acts of kindness he endeared himself to everyone with whom he came in contact. The world would be a happier place if we had more men with the spirit of Dr. Pope, whose services to cricket and to mankind have never been appropriately recognized.

At the commencement of our tour there were the usual functions, one of which, the Lord Mayor's dinner in the Mansion House, had a really South Australian flavour. The Lord Mayor was none other than Sir Harry Twyford, whose wife came from that State as also did our Manager and I. The outstanding artist who had been engaged to provide the entertainment was another South Australian, Peter Dawson.

The opening cricket match was our customary engagement at Worcester, where I was fortunate enough to compile my third consecutive double century on this attractive ground. In my own view that was the best of my three innings at Worcester.

To commemorate these performances, the Directors of the Royal Worcester Porcelain Works made a special vase. On one side was reproduced a painting which was a replica of a most attractive photo taken during the Worcester game by *The Times* photographer. It showed the field of play, the spectators, the lovely trees along the river bank, and dominating the whole scene the architectural masterpiece which is the Worcester Cathedral. On the back was a suitable inscription. This souvenir is one of my most cherished possessions.

The Worcester captain won the toss and sent us in, a fact which brought the following satirical comment from a writer who changed the dialogue of the old comic picture by Phil. May to read :—

INMATE. What are you all doing here ?
COUNTY CAPTAIN. Playing Bradman and the other Australians.
INMATE. Whose batting ?
COUNTY CAPTAIN. They are. I won the toss and asked them to bat first.
INMATE. Come inside.

It is so easy to be critical when a gamble fails, but if we could all foresee the future there would be little point and certainly no spice in having the right to make our own decisions.

I must refer to the extraordinary mishap, if such it may be termed, to McCormick. This tall Victorian at his best was a really hostile fast bowler, and whether it was the desire to do exceptionally well in his first game, or whether it was due to the English conditions, I cannot say. The fact is that his first over comprised 14 balls and the second over 15.

During his first three overs he was " no-balled " 19 times by umpire Baldwin. I went to the umpire and asked was McCormick dragging over the line, and he replied, " Is he dragging over the line ? He is jumping two feet over it." Ernie shortened his run, lengthened his run, changed his pace and did everything except rectify the trouble.

At one stage he was marking out his run afresh, and I might add that he ran about 20 yards. By the time he got to the 19th step, a spectator near the sight-board called out : " Quick, shut the gate—he'll be out on the road." To make matters worse his first delivery hit Charlie Bull a terrible blow over the right eye. Momentarily I thought we had a fatality on our hands. Bull retired, later to pluckily resume his innings, and then when the match was over discovered that he had batted with a broken finger injured at practice just before the match commenced.

McCormick never completely recovered from this early setback, and with one or two exceptions did not at any stage reveal his best form.

The tour progressed in normal fashion, and apart from cricket we were privileged in many directions.

I have vivid memories of that truly great artist, Gracie Fields, who seemed to capture an audience by her personality more than anyone else. There was a treat for the musically minded to hear Richard Tauber singing at the Queen's Hall, and on one of my rare free evenings I enjoyed a game of snooker with Joe Davis, who reigned supreme as the world's greatest exponent of snooker. Cricketers on tour love to get away from cricket. I was no exception to the rule.

During the Middlesex match we were the guests of the M.C.C. at a dinner at Lord's.

Mr. Stanley Baldwin, former Prime Minister of England, was also President of the M.C.C. and made a most delightful speech, in which he referred to the fact that as a youth his ambition had been to become a blacksmith.

In my reply I referred to this remark, and added that my own boyhood ambition was to become an ordinary house painter.

"You see, Sir, we have both been thwarted in our ambitions," was my summing up. I hardly think either of us would care to retrace our steps.

Australia's R. G. Menzies, Attorney-General at the time, upheld an already glowing reputation by one of his very best speeches.

In the first few matches our batting showed itself to be very strong. In four games, centuries were scored by Fingleton, McCabe, Hassett, Badcock, Chipperfield and myself.

Then came a fine performance at which we had easily the best of a drawn game against M.C.C. at Lord's. In this match I scored 278, my highest total at Headquarters. The M.C.C. attack included Ken. Farnes, Jim Smith, R. W. V. Robins, Compton, Edrich and Captain Stephenson, the latter, a most volatile medium pace bowler who was a strong candidate for the Test side.

In our matches against English Counties it is not customary for any reception to be held upon arrival at the town concerned. Against Northampton this arrangement was changed, for we were met at the station by the Lord Mayor and a woman's Scotch band. The " Lassies " piped us all the way from the railway station to our hotel, something we did not experience even in Scotland.

Bill Brown must have been inspired by the pipes, for against the County he made 194 not out. Bill had been out of form and had lost his confidence, but luck was with him. He was dropped six times and survived numerous L.B.W. appeals. Bill never looked back, and from that moment became his own classical self and one of our most valuable players.

Luck plays such a big part in cricket. The greatest of players will experience a lean period, then a missed chance will enable form to be recovered in a match. One decent innings is better than all the net practice in the world.

In the following game against Surrey, I ran into some criticism because I did not enforce the follow-on. The old conflict arose as to whether one should treat each individual match strictly on its merits or allow the tour as a whole and the Test Matches in particular to be the primary responsibility. My view supports the latter theory. It would be absurd to wreck one's best bowler against Surrey for instance, and thereby win the match, only to reduce the said bowler's efficiency for the rest of the tour.

McCabe had been selected to play against Surrey, but had to drop out with neuritis. Fleetwood-Smith, McCormick and Waite all had minor injuries, O'Reilly an abscess on a tooth and White a slightly poisoned toe. In the interests of the team I did not think it fair to aggravate these complaints, but the spectators disagreed with me. At least it enabled them to see an extraordinary batting performance by Laurie Fishlock, who put together 93 runs out of a total of 1 wicket for 104 in 70 minutes.

My early batting successes once more gave me an opportunity to score 1,000 runs before the end of May. No other Australian has done it and as no Englishman has accomplished the feat more than once, I was keen to achieve the honour.

I succeeded in doing so against Hampshire at Southampton, a repetition of 1930. Once more rain threatened to defeat one's prospects. It was a race against man and the elements combined.

Up to this stage our tour prospects appeared very bright, despite the over dependence upon O'Reilly. The first setback to our confidence came when Middlesex headed us on the first innings.

Once again I was the subject of the crowd's displeasure, but this time their wrath quickly turned to cheering. They thought I had agreed with the opposing skipper to terminate the match early, and resented the closure. When it became apparent that I had merely closed the nnings so that Edrich would have an opportunity to obtain his 1,000 runs before the end of May, they wildly cheered his every stroke, and there was great enthusiasm when Bill finally obtained the runs. Although giving him the chance, our bowlers tried hard to keep him quiet. They did not make him a present of the runs.

In this game I suffered further trouble with my back, and was compelled to seek medical attention. My adviser happened to be an Australian, Dr. Isaac Jones, who ordered me to rest until the First Test Match.

It is remarkable how many Australians of accomplishment are to be found in England in the field of medicine and art as well as other spheres. One is constantly meeting distinguished personalities who have left their native land because of the opportunities awaiting them in the mother country. Almost invariably they are extremely popular, and leaders in their respective occupations.

By the time the First Test Match arrived, we felt that the chances were fifty-fifty. In a short while we were struggling to avoid defeat.

I do not think I have ever seen a better wicket than that upon which England batted after Hammond had won the toss. The spinners could not spin (and when Fleetwood-Smith could not turn the ball nobody could). The fast bowlers could get no life out of it, and lunch time came without an English wicket having fallen.

Charlie Barnett of Gloucester gave us the most scintillating display of stroke-making seen in Test cricket from an Englishman by scoring 99 not out before lunch. We were jealous of Australia's record in this direction, and hard though Barnett tried he could not steal the extra run. Only Australians have claimed the magic century before lunch. Nothing can detract from the brilliance of his driving and cutting. Even O'Reilly failed to curb his stroke play.

Leonard Hutton and Denis Compton each made a century, each was playing in his first Test Match. Then just to uphold the proud position of Lancashire Eddie Paynter came along with 216 not out.

England declared at 8 for 658, and quickly had us in trouble until McCabe, with what I firmly believe to be the greatest innings ever played, held us all spellbound with a display which is described in detail elsewhere. Even so, it could not prevent the follow-on, and throughout the whole of Tuesday, Australia was compelled to defend for dear life on a pitch now showing considerable signs of wear. It could not have been attractive from the spectators' point of view. Defensive cricket seldom is. We, however, had no option. Victory was impossible, and it was our plain duty to save the match if we could.

Bill Brown and I were together most of the day, Bill making 133 whilst I remained 144 not out. I do not think either of us ever played a more valuable innings for the side.

In the first innings of the match, I was given out caught Ames bowled Sinfield by Frank Chester, and consider it the cleverest decision ever made against me. The ball turned from the off, very faintly touched the inside edge of the bat, then hit my pad, went over the stumps and was caught by Ames. Whilst all this was happening amidst a jumble of feet, pads and bat, I slightly overbalanced and Ames whipped the bails off for a possible stumping. There was an instant appeal to the square leg umpire who gave me not out, whereupon Ames appealed to Chester at the bowler's end, and very calmly, as though it was quite obvious to all, Chester simply said, " Out, caught," and turned his back on the scene.

It was one of those miraculous pieces of judgment upon which I base my opinion that Chester was the greatest of all umpires.

This Nottingham Test setback, which revealed more than ever the weakness in our opening attack, reduced some of our early confidence.

Two more hard matches against the Gentlemen of England and Lancashire did nothing to improve it.

In the Lancashire game there was little to choose in the first innings— Australia 303, Lancashire 289. I had failed again, as was customary for me on the Old Trafford Ground.

In our second innings, Brown and Fingleton were so unenterprising that I felt impelled to do something about it. At lunch time I told them to hurry things along. Then when Brown got out I proceeded to put this policy into effect by scoring 100 in 73 minutes, the fastest 100 of the season to that date.

The Second Test at Lord's was again drawn in England's favour. Two performances stood out. Hammond's 240 for England, Brown's 206 not out for Australia.

McCormick, revealing his Australian form for the first time on the tour, took 3 quick wickets, and England were 31 for 3.

Hammond and Paynter took the total to 253 before Paynter was given out L.B.W. for 99.

I have always held the greatest admiration for Hammond's cricket, but can recall no instance when his superb artistry shone so brilliantly. There was the bad start to retrieve. He suffered a painful blow on the elbow and also pulled a leg muscle, yet surmounted all difficulties with apparent ease and nonchalance. He displayed a more versatile range of shots than usual, though once again it was his driving which caught the eye. Chipperfield will testify to the power behind the shots, for in trying to stop one of them he split a finger and could not field again.

Les Ames suffered a fractured finger, thus giving Paynter an opportunity to display his very creditable prowess as a wicketkeeper.

Bill Brown joined the select band who have opened the innings in a Test Match and batted right through. We would have been in a sorry plight without him.

Fortunes fluctuated rapidly in the second innings, and when England was 7 for 142 I thought we might win. It was young Denis Compton and Wellard who thought differently.

Bradman in action against a slow bowler

The Somerset all-rounder did not worry about the artistic. He offended every principle in cricket by hitting an outswinger with the new ball over long-on for six. But the runs counted.

The Second Test Match at Lord's coincides as a rule with the tennis at Wimbledon. We had a lovely television set on loan to the team, and for the first time were able to witness this new scientific marvel. Television was then in its infancy, but even so the tennis came through quite distinctly.

We had spoken on the radio telephone to Australia in 1930 when that service first came into being, and it is interesting to contemplate our participation in the early development of modern wonders which are destined to become commonplace in the future.

You may remember how I described the tremendous heat at Manchester in 1934. By way of contrast, in 1938 not a ball was bowled and Hammond and I did not even bother to toss. That at least saved me the indignity of losing all five on the tour.

When it came to Leeds I had a feeling that it was now or never. Australian teams had done notoriously well on this Yorkshire Ground and my own happy experiences there caused me to be optimistic. The wicket appeared good for a large score. My spirits dropped when England earned the right to bat first. Then for no apparent reason other than excellent bowling, wickets fell until the team had been dismissed for 223. The pre-lunch figures of O'Reilly are worth repeat-

ing.   14 over 11 maidens 1 wicket for 4 runs, of which two came from
" no-balls ".   Three catches were missed off him too.

We set out to chase this total, but we also found ourselves in difficulty,
not only because of the wicket, but heavy rain clouds appeared over-
head, and it seemed certain that we would be deluged.

I thought we would make more runs in that light on a dry pitch
than in a good light on a wet one, so instructed our batsmen not to
appeal.   The fielding captain of course had the right so to do.   This
prerogative was exercised once in a Test Match in South Africa, but
obviously it would be unusual because a bad light normally benefits
the fielding side.   On this occasion it was the darkest in which I have
ever batted.   One press reporter told a confrere that if I did not soon
appeal he would, because he could not see to write his copy.   Matches
being lit in the grandstand were plainly visible from the centre.

We managed to get a first innings lead, but a very slender one.

Then Big Bill O'Reilly, at his most hostile best, turned on bowling
which only he could produce, ably supported by Fleetwood-Smith.

I can picture now the unplayable ball which bewildered Hardstaff
and made a shambles of his stumps, and the one following from which
Brown at short-leg snapped up a low one-handed catch off Hammond.

On a wicket receptive to spin, but not unduly difficult, England
could only muster 123 runs.   It looked all over, until Australia's second
innings wickets also began to fall, and again the rain clouds banked up.

Fearing the storm I told our boys to force the pace.   Wickets began
to tumble.   The match became so exciting that for the only time in
my life I could not bear to watch the play.   The scene in our dressing
room could hardly be imagined.   O'Reilly with the pads on, hoping
and praying he would not be needed, was walking up and down on
one side of the centre table.   On the other side I was doing the same,
but, to prevent my teeth chattering in the excitement, was consuming
copious supplies of bread and jam augmented by a liberal quantity of
tea.   We relied upon our colleagues to give us a running commentary
of the play.

Our manager was even worse.   He could not bear to stay in the
dressing room, and had gone outside the ground for a walk, where
thousands of people were lined up in queues unable to gain admittance.

This was the sort of cricket which made the spectator's blood course
through his veins.   Nobody could take his eyes from the centre for
fear of missing a sensation.

In that electric atmosphere, it was Hassett who forced the issue.   The
imperturbable Victorian midget, who in a crisis has always been such
a masterful player, lofted his drives and threw caution to the winds in
a race to beat the weather.

A glorious victory was achieved and we could no longer lose the
rubber.   More important still, we had seen (or heard) what I fondly

believe to be the greatest Test Match of modern times. I have argued many times since that if groundsmen could produce wickets similar to that one we would have less complaints about the necessity to alter the rules of cricket.

We could not resist the temptation to hold a private Team Dinner at our Harrogate Hotel to celebrate this amazing match.

It was hard to concentrate after the excitement of Leeds. The matches between this and the Fourth Test Match were relatively unimportant.

Our team was now to suffer in the Fifth Test the most humiliating defeat of all.

We took some risk in leaving McCormick out of our side. He had not been very well, suffering from neuritis in the shoulder, and in a long and gruelling match it was felt he might break down. Our resultant opening attack of McCabe and Waite was insufficient to break through, and on a feather-bed wicket England quickly got away to a winning start. She piled up runs and runs and more runs, until the stupendous total was reached of 903 for 7 wickets.

In some quarters it was said that the Englishmen were playing the Australians at their own game. In others that they were out to kill once and for all Test Matches played to a finish, because England preferred matches of a limited duration. I did not care about these side issues.

Our attack had become so exhausted that, attempting to ease the burden by taking a turn myself, I went over on my ankle in one of the holes which had by now become worn by the bowlers. An x-ray revealed a slight fracture of the bone, and that was the end of my cricket for the tour. My misfortune brought me a charming letter from England's former Prime Minister. It read :—

" I can't tell you how grieved I was when the news came through. I know you will bear this infliction with that cheerful courage that is part of you, but it is cruel hard.

I was very sorry not to see you and your companions again.

In saying good-bye for the present I hope you won't think it impertinent of me to say with what pleasure I have made your acquaintance.

Bradman the cricketer is known to all the English-speaking world, but Bradman the man I hope I may call my friend.
Yours very sincerely,
Baldwin of Bewdley

Fingleton too had retired from the contest with a badly torn leg muscle.

Throughout this gruelling period we saw a truly remarkable display of temperament and concentration by Leonard Hutton, who batted for no less than 13 hours 20 minutes to compile the world's record score in Test cricket of 364. There was scarcely a flaw. During the first century a ball from Fleetwood-Smith left him stranded, but it went so close to the top of the off-stump that Barnett failed to gather it and Hutton regained his crease. Other than that I cannot remember a definite chance.

Throughout the long innings his defence remained utterly impregnable, whilst all shots were correctly made and every ball played on its merits.

I was fielding at short-leg when Hutton passed my own previous record of 334 and was the first one to shake him by the hand.

Others to contribute towards England's massive total were Leyland who was run out for 187 (he seemed unlikely to get out any other way) and Joe Hardstaff 169 not out.

As a contest the match was dead long before Australia even went in to bat, and thus the series ended one all with Australia retaining the Ashes because she previously held them.

Being unable to take any further part in the tour, I did not see the remaining matches.

By now our team was suffering the after-effects of a gruelling season, and was again defeated, this time by H. D. G. Leveson Gower's XI at Scarborough.

I spent the remainder of the tour recuperating at the home of my great friend, R. W. V. Robins, at Burnham, and fortunately the ankle duly made a complete recovery.

A minor disappointment over my ankle injury was that it prevented the fulfilment of an engagement with Amr Bey to play squash. He was the undisputed champion of the world, and as a comparatively modest exponent of the art, I was anxious to pick up a few points. We had lunch together, the occasion upon which the engagement was made, and seeing his small, almost frail-looking physique, one marvelled how he could so excel at a game which makes tremendous inroads upon one's stamina.

Looking back on the tour one must admit that our great weakness was the lack of a virile opening attack. When we left Australia, McCormick gave promise of great things, but right from that fatal day at Worcester could not seem to get properly going. There was no other bowler of pace in the team, and thus we were unduly forced back onto the spinners.

Normally it may have succeeded. In 1938 we ran into wickets upon which you could not turn the ball an inch for at least two days, and under the circumstances our spin bowlers could not be expected to get quick results. As mentioned earlier, there was so much dependence upon O'Reilly and, to a lesser extent, Fleetwood-Smith.

Frank Ward performed extremely well despite his heartbreaking experience in the First Test Match.

On an English tour the speed with which a bowler captures wickets is terribly important. This applies more particularly in the county matches which are limited to three days.

Alec Hurwood's lack of success in 1930 could be directly traced to such a consideration. He bowled excellently, but Woodfull could not afford to keep him on. It would have meant more time in the field.

To dismiss a team for 150 in 2 hours is far more valuable than to get them out for 130 in 3 hours, i.e. providing your batsmen can score the necessary runs.

Ward had an outstanding record in this direction. In all matches he captured his wickets at an average of 1 for approximately every 33 balls bowled.

It was a higher ratio of wickets per over than either Grimmett or Mailey ever achieved in England.

Those who know the skill of these great spinners will readily recognise Ward's value in county games.

I think this method of assessing the merit of a bowler is too often overlooked.

Our batting was sound though we sadly missed Barnes, who was expected to be one of our mainstays, and instead was mostly an onlooker. His subsequent successes under English conditions indicate how much his loss meant to us.

An inexplicable thing was Badcock's failure in the Test Matches. Against the counties he displayed excellent form, yet somehow could not get a start in the Tests, scoring a mere 32 runs in 8 innings. He thrashed similar bowling in county matches, and nobody could ever say Badcock suffered from nerves in big cricket.

Having experienced the job of captaincy for the first time, I was better able to appreciate how exacting, even exhausting the job was. There had been times when I found it difficult to keep going, and although still not old in the cricket sense I did not feel capable of standing the strain on another occasion. Whilst not making any decision public this was how I really felt, and I visualized the possibility of perhaps one more Test season in Australia before retirement.

The course of events was changed by circumstances, but I am still convinced that in the normal sense, without any break in the continuity of play, 1938 would have been my last tour of England.

After the final Test Match, the wives of our Manager, Stan. McCabe, Fleetwood-Smith and myself joined us in England, and this delightful journey no doubt compensated them somewhat for our long absence.

We were all perturbed by the trend of events in Europe. Air raid trenches were being dug in London, and it seemed that we might be engulfed in Hitler's dream of world domination.

A breathing space came, and even though my wife and I acted against the advice of our travel agents, we journeyed across Europe before rejoining our ship for the homeward voyage.

1938-9

RETURNING TO DOMESTIC CRICKET, FOLLOWING OUR TOUR OF ENGLAND, I once more had the pleasure of leading South Australia to victory in the Sheffield Shield Competition.

We snatched the honour from Victoria by one point.

Our opening match was against New South Wales in Adelaide, where I was in good form with a score of 143, but my innings was completely overshadowed by a wonderful knock of 271 not out by Jack Badcock.

On this occasion O'Reilly, possibly still feeling the strain of his great exertions overseas, was not so effective.

On the other hand, Clarrie Grimmett showed much of his former skill and cunning in taking 11 wickets for the match.

Against Queensland, Badcock and I again shared the runs, Jack getting 100, my own total being 225.

My next score was 107 against Victoria followed by 186 in the return match against Queensland.

Returning to Sydney I made 135 not out against N.S.W. and thus, including 118 made in the Melbourne Cricket Club Centenary Match at the start of the season, I had equalled C. B. Fry's world record of six successive centuries.

There was great interest in our final game to see whether I could add one more to the sequence. Luck did not favour me for Fleetwood-Smith, never a brilliant field, held a sizzling catch right on his toes with my score at 5.

This ended my most successful season in domestic cricket.

Generally, there seems to be a falling away in skill and enthusiasm immediately following an English tour. One must remember that the season actually becomes the third on end, by which time the bowlers in particular badly need a rest.

Cricketers are often highly-strung individuals, and to keep them playing under tension for long periods is equivalent to racing a horse without occasionally turning him out to grass. In the player's own interests it should not be done. Other sports can provide a form of mental relaxation.

Partly for this reason, after migrating to South Australia, I took an interest in squash.

Sitting at an office desk all day is not the best method of keeping one's muscles fit for cricket. Squash offers concentrated exercise. The game is far more popular in England than Australia, for which I imagine climatic conditions are largely responsible.

Eventually my squash playing took me into the final of the South Australian Championship, where I met Don Turnbull, of Davis Cup fame, in the winter of 1939. What a tussle we had. I finally won— 0/9, 4/9, 10/8, 9/3, 10/8. In both the third and fifth sets I was well down. The game lasted an hour. It was more exhausting than a full day's batting.

When starting squash I had been advised by Harry Hopman not to play longer than 30 minutes. His words came back to me. I never played competitive squash again.

The summer of 1939-40 saw the Sheffield Shield return to New South Wales.

South Australia made an excellent start and looked like retaining her position when an unexpected reverse at the hands of Queensland turned the scales.

The outbreak of war in September 1939 cast a shadow over the play.

At the instigation of high Government officials, the season was continued, and surely this was a fine tribute to the morale building value of cricket. Furthermore, patriotic matches were held, one of which benefited the Fund concerned by approximately £1,500.

O'Reilly performed wonderfully well during the season, taking 52 wickets at an average of 13·5. He absolutely dominated match after match.

I think also that in this season I gave my best Sheffield Shield performance.

It was in a match between South Australia and New South Wales on the Adelaide Oval.

The visitors had made 336 and when O'Reilly got on top we were fighting hard.

First with Ward and then with Grimmett as a partner, I kept all the strike I possibly could from O'Reilly. This enabled us to obtain a useful lead.

My first innings score was 251 not out, and of the last wicket partnership of 113 I made 87.

In the second innings I was 90 not out in a score of 3 for 156.

The reason I place this performance so high is that O'Reilly was in his most devastating form, and therefore the quality of the opposition was undoubted.

During the remainder of the season I made some useful scores, finishing up with a total of 1,062 runs for 8 times out, including an innings of 267 against Victoria.

With the worsening of events in Europe I felt the urge of all patriotic

Bill Johnston loosens up at the nets

citizens to do my duty in a sterner sphere, and enlisted as a member of air crew for the R.A.A.F.

At that time the supply of manpower far exceeded the number of aircraft available and training facilities. I could not be called up for some months but was placed on the reserve. My age was approaching the air crew limit, so the Army authorities sought my assistance for special work on which I could be used right away.

Into camp I went, and there did my utmost to cope with the rigorous work only to experience muscular trouble which had bothered me on and off before.

An eye specialist, hearing I was there, sought leave to test my eyes. He was engaged in special research regarding eyesight, reflexes and so on for pilots, and thought I should be an ideal subject for testing.

Unfortunately, the tests revealed something of an entirely different character—something I suspected but had fought against—the first signs of further illness.

Despite this knowledge, I agreed to play in two first-class matches for which leave was obtained. They merely confirmed the doctor's evidence for I could register but 18 runs in 4 innings, including two ducks. I just couldn't see the ball at all.

My 1934 troubles (minus appendicitis) recurred with greater severity. The onset of fibrositis sent me to hospital. After three spells in hospital I had to undergo an examination by a medical board which passed sentence. The only hope of cure was a long convalescence and complete rest.

It was indeed a hard decision. At the crucial moment I had been given out and the umpire's decision was final.

For some months I had once more to return to my 1935 convalescent camp near Bowral, there to try and rebuild the destruction of earlier years.

Anyone who has suffered the excruciating pain of muscular ailments will understand how utterly immobilising it can be. At one period I found myself quite incapable of even lifting my right arm. It was impossible even to do my own hair.

I lost all feeling in the thumb and index finger of my right hand. It never returned—even when I again played Test cricket.

My wife, of necessity, had to become skilled in the art of using a razor and, as she had been on other occasions, was a constant source of comfort and encouragement.

It was some months before I was able to resume civilian work, whereupon I endeavoured to perform whatever useful services were open to me though compelled to work sparingly.

They were dark days. Cricket, then or in the future, never crossed my mind.

I am quite certain that the over-exertion of my earlier cricketing days was exacting retribution in full measure.

The job of rebuilding my health was toilsome. I often despaired of the outcome, but gradually an improvement was manifest.

Amongst my community interests, I held a position on the Committee of the Commonwealth Club of Adelaide. In 1944 I was elected President.

This organisation has over one thousand members of whom the great majority are prominent citizens and leading Adelaide business men. It entertains, and is addressed by, distinguished people of all ranks, both local residents as well as visitors. Lord Montgomery and Mr. Anthony Eden were two outstanding guests of recent years.

The first function during my term of office was held in honour of Dame Enid Lyons, wife of Australia's former Prime Minister, Rt. Hon. J. A. Lyons. No member of the female sex had been so honoured since Amy Johnson.

Dame Enid's warm, vivid personality and the logical commonsense of her arguments have won her a place of great esteem amongst Australians.

I also had the pleasure of voicing our appreciation of an address by the Rt. Hon. John Curtin (who was then Prime Minister of Australia) and expressing the hope that he would live to see the " twin rewards of victory and peace."

Overwork and strain prevented this, for " Honest John "—to give him the title by which he was widely known—collapsed and passed away before the moment of triumph had arrived.

In my position of Commonwealth Club President, as in other walks of life, I found the qualities of English gentlemen were a never-ending source of delight. It was emphasised by one experience in which the present Governor of South Australia was concerned.

A luncheon had been arranged for Lord Keyes. It was to be held on a given date in the Adelaide Town Hall. Invitations had been issued. Nothing could be retracted. As principal host I was as usual anxious for everything to proceed smoothly.

Imagine my dismay when on the appointed day I read in the morning paper that Lord Keyes had been taken ill and under doctor's orders had cancelled all engagements.

I rang Government House (where Lord Keyes was staying) with some trepidation, hoping to ascertain better news from the Private Secretary. The time was not yet 8 a.m., so when the phone was answered I inquired most apologetically for the Secretary or one of the Aides.

To my astonishment I was informed that these people were not yet available but it was the Governor speaking—could he be of assistance ?

After obtaining confirmation of the unfortunate news, I diffidently suggested that His Excellency might step into the breach. Instantly came the answer, " I was thinking perhaps I could help you." This courteous action of substituting for Lord Keyes brought forth from an appreciative gathering a spontaneous tribute which must have warmed the Governor's heart.

Since that date Sir Willoughby Norrie has continually earned the admiration of South Australian citizens who regard him with the same veneration as they did the Earl of Gowrie, possibly the best-loved Governor of this State.

So high was public esteem for Lord Gowrie (as he was at the time) that a fund was organised called the Gowrie Scholarship Trust Fund. I acted as Honorary Secretary and Organiser in South Australia. Altogether a sum of about £140,000 was subscribed. From this amount and the interest thereon, scholarships are awarded every year to members of the Services or children of members of the Services.

The scholarships are keenly sought. It would be hard to conceive a more fitting manner to identify the name of Gowrie with the growing generation, and to perpetuate his memory.

The allied world was uplifted in 1945 by the end of hostilities in Europe.

For me personally there suddenly came a disaster. Overnight the firm by which I was employed went bankrupt.

My whole purpose in moving to South Australia in 1934 was to try and obtain a position in business whereby my work would have nothing to do with cricket and would offer security. Now, in the midst of a long struggle to regain my health, and through no fault of mine, I became the victim of another's misfortune.

There was no time for reflection. I had to make an immediate decision as affecting my whole life. Despite the unprecedented difficulties there were trustworthy friends whose loyalty was responsible for my decision to commence my own business.

I wasn't really fit to carry the strain of the next few months. It would be idle to try to explain the numerous troubles which had to be surmounted. They called for long hours and little rest. Again my wife by her faith and actual physical assistance was of incalculable help.

Ever so slowly it seemed another summer came round.

I had no thought of playing cricket, though the prospect of witnessing some inter-state matches offered some hope of passing a pleasant hour.

There were to be no Sheffield Shield matches but ordinary State matches were to be supplemented by games against the Australian Services' Team, returning after brilliant displays in England.

These boys had performed splendidly in the Victory Tests and also in India, though I rather fancy the latter portion of the tour unduly tired them.

It was arranged that the proceeds of all these matches should be devoted to charity.

When December came I was approached to see whether I would play against the Services' Team.

South Australia's resources appeared thin on paper and the authorities were anxious to achieve some worthwhile result for charity.

I was not playing Saturday afternoon cricket or practising in any way so it seemed most unlikely that I would be of much use. However, if my presence was going to assist charity I wanted to play my part, and therefore agreed to assist South Australia in the match.

Just prior to the Services match, S.A. were to play Queensland on the Adelaide Oval. As this was to be during the Christmas holiday period I offered to participate rather than go straight into the Services game without even a hit at the nets. My scores against Queensland were 68 and 52 not out, though both were of a somewhat painstaking character.

I was not much better against the Services. Certainly the score book says I made 112, but it doesn't record the reflex nature of my strokes.

The Services lads were stale after a surfeit of cricket and did not reproduce their best form. Even so one noticed a great improvement in Hassett.

Another who showed every sign of being a great player was Cecil Pepper. Unfortunately for Australia, his skill was lost to this country when he decided to throw in his lot with the Lancashire League.

The Australian Board of Control had agreed to send a team to New Zealand at the end of the 1946 summer.

Much as I would have enjoyed a trip to that inviting country I was quite unfit to consider it and was compelled to announce that I was unavailable. Just as well I did. About that time I suffered a recurrence of fibrositis in its most severe form, and all hope of ever again taking the field seemed to vanish. Treatment brought temporary relief only.

My colleague on the Australian Selection Committee, Mr. E. A. Dwyer, persuaded me to pay a visit to Ern. Saunders, a Melbourne masseur, whose name was a household word in that city for his amazing work, especially among injured athletes. I was sceptical. With more faith than hope I agreed. As his steel-like fingers ran over my muscles and my spine they seemed miraculously to locate the sources of trouble.

Saunders believes in nature. His manipulation is done without anaesthetic. I did not know that before I saw him. In later years I saw other people gladly suffer the agonies of his first treatment, such was their faith.

After my first visit the relief from searing muscle pain was like a draught of ice cold water in a heat wave.

Saunders claimed that he could remove the cause of the trouble and restore my muscles to the standard required for cricket.

He proved to be right even though the road was still uphill.

Post-War Tests Resumed

THE WINTER OF 1946 WAS DEVOTED TO BUILDING UP MY HEALTH. Gradually hope returned that I might be fit to play against England the following summer. Still there is a vast gap between reasonable health and the muscular tone required for international cricket. Under no circumstances did I desire to make an attempt which would end in failure.

On the other hand, cricket badly needed a good start in the post-war era, and I was anxious to assist in that direction if it lay within my compass.

My wife strongly encouraged me, and with a woman's sentiment said it would be a pity if my son John grew up without having seen me play in Test cricket.

At this time the only thought was whether I could do justice to the Australian team for one season, and not for a moment did I contemplate the future beyond.

Before the season's cricket was due to commence, I went to Sydney for an Australian Board of Control meeting. I had been far from well beforehand and the anxious inquiries from my friends and relatives merely accentuated my own fears of still more trouble.

On returning to Adelaide, my condition became worse and I was obliged to enter hospital for an operation. The fates seemed to be working against me.

The English cricketers were shortly due in Adelaide and the press were violently agitating for a definite answer as to my intentions regarding the Test Matches. They resented my refusal to satisfy their query.

The truth was that I couldn't. It was impossible.

I asked my own doctor what he thought, and the answer was not encouraging.

He told me quite plainly I should not play for South Australia against England, and as for the future, suggested a conference with two specialists. This was arranged.

Their verdict was simple but clear.

In their opinion I was not in sufficiently robust health to attempt big cricket and would be wise to give up any idea of playing in the Tests.

I had a premonition that this would be their answer.

Then came the all-important question.

Being pig-headed and wanting to play, I asked, " Will I be risking permanent injury to my health if I try ? "

They replied no—subject to the reservation that I must not over-exert myself. Furthermore, they definitely indicated their views that I could not hope to attain more than a fraction of my former standard of play.

So there I was placed in a dilemma.

The evidence had been given. I was the judge.

My wife and I discussed it fully. On the one hand was a big press contract and no worry, backed by medical testimony that I would be foolish to play.

On the other my own eagerness to play—and the tiny ray of sunshine—it would not damage my health if I was careful. Contrary to the doctor's advice I decided to play in the preliminary matches, and if these were safely negotiated, to place once more my services to Australian cricket as my No. 1 duty.

The first game was for South Australia v. England at Adelaide. It was with considerable anxiety and diffidence I took the field against Hammond's men.

Things were not improved by my usual luck in losing the toss. We chased 506 runs for 5 wickets before Hammond decided to close the innings.

It was a very subdued effort which brought me 76 runs, whilst the second attempt found me back in the pavilion for 3.

I was a shadow of myself, physically, mentally and in cricket form.

One journalist wrote of my play : " I have today seen the ghost of a great cricketer and ghosts seldom come back to life."

Such comments were scarcely helpful. I knew the pitfalls ahead better than any journalist and I was the one taking the risk.

Encouragement was what I needed, not doubts.

My second match of the season was for an Australian XI in Melbourne where I showed slightly improved form to score a century, but tore a leg muscle and found it hard to keep going.

Then a State match against Victoria brought another century and returning confidence that after all I might be able to see it through.

The moment for my decision was imminent.

O'Reilly had announced his intention to retire and write for the press. Bill had shown great form after the war, especially in New Zealand at the end of the previous season where, in 19 overs, he had taken 8 wickets for 33 runs in the only Test played.

Apparently he felt that his doubtful knee would not stand a hard season on Australian wickets.

I thought Australia might be sorely pressed without her number one bowler.

With due modesty I felt the need was greater than ever for me to play.

Some experienced players were required to re-start Australian cricket on a sound course.

Putting aside all other considerations excepting what I believed to be

127

my duty to Australian cricket, I allowed my name to be included amongst the players chosen for the First Test in Brisbane.

The ghost had come back to life, and now that the years have rolled by I can reflect upon those crucial weeks and with pride upon my decision to follow my conscience and risk the consequences.

In the Australian team were three men only with pre-war Test Match experience against England—Barnes, Hassett and myself. Of these, Barnes had played but once. England had six, and on paper it was an open match.

Winning the toss from Hammond for the first time enabled us to have first use of a splendid wicket. In a flash Morris had been caught in the slips by Hammond with the same facile confidence which made him the greatest of all England's slip fieldsmen. For some time Barnes and I battled against excellent bowling until the latter was out to a catch by Bedser on the leg side which only Bedser's 6 foot 4 enabled him to reach.

Then came perhaps the most debated incident of the series. Voce bowled me a ball which was near enough to a yorker. I attempted to chop down on top of it in order to guide the ball wide of the slip fieldsmen. Instead it flew to Ikin at second slip.

In my opinion, the ball touched the bottom of my bat just before hitting the ground and therefore it was not a catch. Accordingly I stood my ground waiting for the game to proceed.

Somewhat belatedly there was an appeal. Without the slightest hesitation umpire Borwick at the bowler's end said, " Not out." He was not even sufficiently doubtful to consult his colleague at square leg. Had he done so the result would have been the same, for Scott wrote an article after the tour in which he said, " It was a bump ball. It hit the ground a few inches from Bradman's bat."

I am well aware that some of the English players thought it was a catch, and they explained the " belated " appeal by claiming that they did not think an appeal was necessary.

The broadcasters were quite unanimous in their view that it was not a catch. The newspaper writers were divided.

The truth is that nobody outside the fence could possibly give an authoritative opinion.

The incident assumed major importance simply because I went on to score 187, and thus on paper it was claimed that England had been largely penalized.

I want to make it clear that the sole point at issue was whether the ball had finished its downward course before making contact with the bat. The question of whether Ikin caught it did not arise.

This type of decision is never easy for an umpire. I can still recall Frank Chester giving Hammond not-out at Lord's when I thought he had been clearly caught and bowled by Grimmett.

The women who attend Test Matches, and squeal every time a bump ball is held, would give them all out.

I think it important to record that at the end of the match Hammond agreed to the reappointment of the two same umpires, and completely clarified his position by saying, " I thought it was a catch, but the umpire may have been right and I may have been wrong."

Under extremely trying conditions, Bedser in particular put up a grand exhibition of bowling. Seldom can any man have bowled so well to have finished with such poor figures, or have seen so many possible chances go astray. Even a touch of the sun (which caused Bedser to leave the ground) did not subdue his spirit. He returned to the field and caused us to defend with all the skill we could muster.

With Hassett, Miller and McCool all taking toll of the English attack, Australia put together an unbeatable total of 645.

England's innings had scarcely commenced when a thunderstorm broke, and she was faced with an Australian sticky.

We had a potential match winner under such conditions in Toshack, but he had never bowled on a mud patch, and made the mistake of wasting deliveries outside the stumps. His analysis of 3 for 17 off 16·5 overs looked impressive, but on wet wickets the need is to attack the stumps and get men out quickly. From our point of view his 6 for 82 in the second innings off 20 overs was much more valuable.

Miller successfully reverted to off-spinners part of the time, and courageously though the Englishmen batted, the handicap was too great.

Apparently one wet wicket was not enough, for a second stupendous downpour flooded the ground, and in half an hour one could have sailed a boat across the oval. Water was half-way up the boundary fence. The stumps which had been left in the middle floated away. One sight-screen had been blown over onto the fence by the cyclonic wind, and the hailstones on the roof sounded like machine-gun fire. We were marooned in our dressing room.

When the fury of the storm had abated and we were able to get a taxi to our hotel, we discovered the driver was wet through. Hail-stones had broken the driving door window and left him exposed to the elements.

It seemed impossible that play could take place for days, yet such are the recuperative powers of the Woolloongabba Ground that the match was resumed punctually on time next day.

It had been cruel luck for England, and there was little consolation in the knowledge that Australia had suffered a similar fate against Gubby Allen 10 years before.

Our fast bowler, Ray Lindwall, developed chickenpox during the game and was removed to hospital. His type of bowling would not have been much use under the conditions, but he did not recover in time to play in the Second Test Match at Sydney.

There could be little value to the Selectors of either team watching the Brisbane Test excepting that it enabled England to rectify an obvious mistake by replacing Gibb with Evans at Sydney. Gibb had been played in Brisbane to try and strengthen the English batting. Not only did he fail in this direction but he also displayed poor form with the gloves, and the change became inevitable.

It is perhaps interesting to recall that one English writer, seeing the ball fly on the sticky wicket, accused the Australians of bowling body-line. It would have been impossible to do so had we tried. Arthur Gilligan succinctly disposed of it in unequivocal terms. He reported, " Utter nonsense, utter rubbish. The man who wrote it should be in a lunatic asylum." All other writers supported Gilligan.

My own performance could not by any stretch of imagination have been related to the standard of eight years before. It was an innings made possible by experience and nothing else. Still, I had surmounted the major hurdle and now felt more confident of being able to get through the season.

In Sydney, where the Second Test was held, England gained an early advantage by winning the toss, only to throw the initiative away by unenterprising batting.

It is true that our bowlers performed wonderfully well, but so long as international batsmen will consistently play back to half volleys from slow bowlers they will continue to lose Test Matches no matter which side they are on.

I was even allowed the luxury of playing two short-legs with no outfield to a slow off-spin bowler, Ian Johnson. With such a field on a plumb wicket in his initial spell Johnson delivered 11 overs and took 1 wicket for 3 runs. This meant that 85 balls out of 88 were not scored from. It was incredible. Johnson finished with 4 for 31 off 25 overs— a splendid beginning in his Test career.

A catch by Tallon in this innings was a gem. The ball flew to Johnson at first slip, bounced off his chest and Tallon, diving towards slips, caught it on the rebound. A wonderful piece of anticipation.

I temporarily forgot my age and tried to move quickly in the field to cut off a four. The result was a torn thigh muscle which kept me out of the field on the Saturday.

More rain came, though not enough to affect the conditions. Still, the light was bad and there was considerable heckling of Barnes when he made several appeals. The cause of the trouble was largely an electric light which glowed just over the top of the sight-screen at the Paddington end. It must have been reasonably dark for the electric bulb to have shone so prominently, but that is a matter for the umpires.

On this question of appeals against the light, I am on the side of those who would rather have the old rule than the new. The whole thing hinges around the umpire's interpretation. What causes ill feeling amongst the public is not the appealing, but the repeated conferences between the umpires.

No conference would be necessary where the umpire to whom the appeal was addressed thought the light good enough for play to proceed.

When umpires disagree, the law makes it crystal clear that the existing state of things shall continue. Therefore, if one umpire thought the light good enough it would not matter what the other umpire thought. Under those circumstances a firm pronouncement to get on with the game would settle the matter. Despite this fact I can hardly recall a single occasion when umpires have failed to confer following an appeal.

There was heavy rain over the weekend, but brilliant sunshine greeted us again on the Monday.

Once more I was the centre of an argument. One of the fieldsmen at short-leg caught a bump ball and Bedser, the bowler, half-heartedly appealed, by saying, " That's not out, is it ? " Umpire Scott said, " Are you appealing ? " Bedser replied, " Yes," so Scott said, " Not out," and later expressed his surprise that there should have been an appeal at all.

Still, it was sufficient for the accusation to be made in some quarters that I had been fortunate to gain the decision.

Barnes and I put together a long partnership, and each man was dismissed with his score at 234. In the meantime we had established a new fifth-wicket world's record for first-class cricket.

I was fortunate to bat at all. On the Friday I tore a leg muscle which prevented me fielding on Saturday. This was followed by an attack of gastritis which kept me in bed most of the weekend, and I felt far below par on the Monday. Even then my leg was heavily strapped and the whole innings was played off the back foot. I scarcely made one forward shot the whole day.

Although the Englishmen recovered some of their confidence in the second innings, it was too late to avert defeat.

The Australians had pulled together as a unit, and now looked a formidable team.

Australia did not receive much credit for the win. Critics generally blamed the English batsmen for their lack of aggression. It certainly contributed to their defeat. Be that as it may, our bowlers did everything that could have been expected of them. The old adage, " You can only play as well as your opponent will allow," is true in cricket no less than other sports.

I cannot omit reference to the debut of Godfrey Evans who kept wickets magnificently and did not concede a single bye.

One of the things which the Australian Selectors had to keep prominently before them at this time was to create a proper balance between immediate requirements of the Test team and the future of Australian cricket.

A beautiful study of Ray Lindwall delivering the ball

Selectors are very conscientious people who are in the unenviable position of not being able to make public their views or policy.

It seemed quite clear that we were building the nucleus of a strong touring side for 1948. Lindwall, having recovered from his illness, automatically came back into the team for the Third Test, and Dooland, the young South Australian leg spinner, replaced Tribe who had bowled reasonably well in Sydney but without success.

With Australia two up and three matches to go, England had to win the Third Test Match to keep the rubber alive. We, on the other hand, realised that a draw would make the position safe. The final result of the match was a draw very much in Australia's favour. Despite this fact, England went closer to winning the Third Test than any other of the series.

The visitors had all the worst of the luck. Langridge strained a groin muscle at practice and had to be omitted from the team. Voce suffered a similar injury during the game and was not much use, while Edrich fielding at short-leg stopped the full force of a hook shot by Barnes on the knee. How he ever resumed bowling the next day I do not know. But he did ; and what is more, took a wicket first ball.

Our innings did not produce any sensational cricket. In fact, when one considers the circumstances we did poorly to get only 365. Even this total would have been considerably less but for the grand fighting knock of McCool, who put together his initial Test century in fine style.

First with Tallon and next with Dooland he was responsible for two valuable partnerships at critical moments.

England batted stubbornly in reply to secure 351.

There occurred in this English innings a most unfortunate dispute regarding the umpiring.

It is a great pity at any time when people outside the fence start questioning umpires' decisions and claiming some definite knowledge. The main trouble seemed to be caused by an English writer, who sent a despatch home to England and made a very plain statement that Edrich was not-out and Compton was not-out.

This may be an appropriate time to comment upon the umpiring throughout the season.

In my opinion, it was the best umpiring of any Test series in which I participated in Australia.

So far as I could tell, only one definitely wrong decision was made, namely the L.B.W. against Edrich in Melbourne when the ball touched his bat. When Compton was given out I was fielding at mid-on almost directly behind the bowler's wicket. He misjudged the ball entirely and in my view was clearly out. I also believe that Compton knew he was out, for in a flash he drew his right foot away to the leg side. This movement was the reason why photographs of the decision which appeared in the press showed Compton's leg clear of the stumps. It was equivalent to showing the finish of a horse race some yards after the post had been reached.

Washbrook, who was batting with Compton at the time, supported my view entirely and said that Compton was definitely out.

Another decision which caused some heartburning in Melbourne was an L.B.W. against me which was disallowed. Great stress was placed upon the fact that I was right in front of my stumps. This was true, but it was an excellent decision, for the ball would have gone some inches over the top.

Umpires must adjudicate upon the height of the ball as well as the direction, a fact often overlooked by those who do not make a close study of such matters.

These rumblings about umpiring did no good to the game of cricket, and I think were resented by some of the English players, who felt that their sportsmanship had been questioned. As far as I know, the players did not in any way authorise the publication of any alleged complaints, and took all decisions in the proper spirit.

If there had been any definite evidence to work on, Hammond could have sought the appointment of different umpires for the remaining Test Matches. The rules under which these matches are played give the visiting captain the right to make a protest.

The Australian Board would be bound to listen to such a protest, providing tangible evidence was produced in support.

I am in a position to say that Hammond, whilst unhappy about the umpiring, did not and could not produce the tangible evidence required. The same two umpires officiated in all five Test Matches.

There were perhaps half a dozen decisions during the season upon which a difference of opinion was expressed. Some favoured one side and some another. As indicated earlier, I only know of one wrong decision. Umpires would be more than human if they did not occasionally make mistakes.

Australia's position was made reasonably safe on the fourth day of this Third Test, when in our second innings Arthur Morris revealed his true form during a knock lasting six hours and totalling 155. We were not completely out of the wood until Tallon and Lindwall became associated in a partnership which put on 154 runs in 87 minutes.

Australians knew Tallon to be an attractive batsman. They also knew Lindwall to be a fine player, but they were not prepared for the valiance of this onslaught and the power and brilliance of his stroke-making. Tallon's cricket centres around the drive (especially through the covers) the square cut and the hook. Lindwall seldom hooks and prefers to drive straight rather than at an angle.

This day each player gave full rein to his strokes, and a stream of powerful shots flew from their bats. Even though the field was gradually deepened, the ball still went through to the fence.

When Lindwall was 96 and taking strike to Bedser, I surveyed the field and could not see any prospect of a four, but he drove the ball back along the ground past the bowler with such velocity that the fieldsmen on each side of the sight-screen were as stone. They had no time to start before the ball had reached the fence.

It is seldom our privilege to witness two such attractive stroke players making a big stand in Test cricket, and I am sure the public went home thrilled with the display they had seen.

After this partnership, there was no possibility of Australia being defeated. It was only a question of whether we could get England out in time.

A fine century by Washbrook, his first against Australia, and excellent support from Yardley (who thus completed a splendid double) held the match to a draw.

This was the first drawn Test in Australia for 65 years.

We in this country had for so long adhered to the principle of playing Test Matches to a finish.

In 1946-7 a compromise had been reached with the M.C.C. providing for a time limit. Englishmen are accustomed to drawn games. Australians like to see a finish. Even so I am inclined to think the experiment of limiting tests in Australia to six days was a success. There is a great advantage in being able to plan an itinerary with certainty, and at times an exciting finish can develop owing to the limit placed upon the duration of the match. There are sound arguments both ways.

My own scores in this game were 79 and 49. It was the one and only Test Match of my career, played on the Melbourne Cricket Ground, during which I was dismissed without making a century.

I can offer no explanation for my successes on this ground, unless it is that the ball comes higher off the pitch, thereby taking me back a little closer to the concrete wickets of boyhood days.

My eight Test Matches there produced 1,671 runs at an average of 119·3.

Another peculiar feature in relation to the Melbourne Ground is the comparative failure there of Charlie Macartney.

Here are Macartney's scores against England at Melbourne : 37, 54, 12, 29, and against the South Africans, 7 and 5.

Reverting again to the Test Match, one must pay tribute to Godfrey Evans who failed to concede a bye in Australia's first innings, the third consecutive innings in which he had done so.

The position had now become rather desperate for England when the Fourth Test Match commenced at Adelaide. She could not win the rubber, but at least she could tie with Australia by winning the last two matches. All her efforts should have been bent in that direction. This was definitely an occasion for tactics, and under such circumstances it would have been better for England to lose the match than make a draw of it.

We were handicapped by the loss of Sid. Barnes. Illness prevented him taking his place in the Australian side.

England won the toss and had every conceivable opportunity, but once again her team was not quite the equal of the Australian.

Throughout the match there was intense heat, the temperature reaching 105, and for Adelaide we experienced an unusually high humidity. One expects the latter in Brisbane, but Adelaide heat is, as a rule, associated with dryness.

The conditions must have been exceptionally trying for the Englishmen.

Hutton and Washbrook gave England a century start in each innings. The way was paved for a big score which was not forthcoming.

Denis Compton and Arthur Morris took the honours in the match, both players getting a century in each innings.

This was the first time an Australian had performed the feat in his own country, and both players were the recipients of handsome presents from the South Australian Cricket Association to recognise their performances.

Another exceptional effort was that of Lindwall who took the last 3 English wickets in their first innings (all bowled) in 4 balls.

It could not be said that this match produced thrilling cricket, yet it did provide outstanding moments. There could be no doubting the charm of Keith Miller's batting in our first innings. He was not-out over night on the Monday, and when he resumed the next morning hit the first ball of the day, a no-ball from Wright, over the fence for six.

As far as I have been able to ascertain, this has never been done elsewhere in Test cricket.

Towards the end of Miller's innings, Yardley pinned him down with a leg-side field, but it did not take away the lustre of perhaps the most attractive batting in the series.

There was not much between our first innings scores, and this was the stage for England to go for runs quickly. It was her only chance to get Australia at the wickets again so that time would be available to dismiss us.

To offset this possibility I unsparingly used Toshack, who is notoriously hard to force. Mainly through his efforts, ably supported by Ian Johnson, the scoring rate was kept within bounds, and Toshack's bowling that day was described by O'Reilly as the best of his career.

Coming to the last day, everything hung upon the initial partnership between Evans and Compton.

I was roundly condemned in most quarters because of the deep field which I set during this portion of the match, a point upon which I think some comment is necessary.

Cricket is a game of skill and of tactics. One is entitled to his own opinion on what policy to follow. I was willing, and have been so throughout my career, to meet a reasonable challenge from any other captain. If he was agreeable to take a tolerable risk so was I. But I have never been one to so betray the interests of my own side and country as to give the match away just to please the opposition.

On this particular morning when play commenced I set the normal field and the game would have taken its ordinary course.

The change came when Compton played a ball down to a fieldsman on the boundary and refused to run because by so doing he would have lost the strike. Compton was entirely within his rights.

However, it indicated clearly England's policy. She had taken the initiative and shown her hand, so I promptly countered this move by employing a deep field so that if Compton did not run singles he would not be made a present of fours.

I know it produced dull cricket. But it wasn't the field which produced the dull cricket. It was the refusal of the batsmen to run unless they could get two or unless it would enable Compton to get the strike.

Evans batted for 95 minutes to break his duck. This could scarcely be attributed to our bowlers or to me. As I saw it, England, by adopting such non-aggressive tactics, was virtually making a certainty of a draw which would give us the rubber.

I considered my fundamental duty was to win the series, not any particular match, and therefore I was satisfied to allow these English tactics to be pursued.

At lunch time on the last day Evans and Compton were still batting. On the resumption one ball only was bowled when Hammond closed the innings—the most inexplicable decision I have ever known. It simply deprived the spectators of an additional ten minutes play and served no useful purpose.

When we batted in our second innings Australia was set the task of making 314 runs in 195 minutes. It was not impossible but it was difficult and would have involved Australia taking considerable risks. I would still have been prepared to take the chance had not England shown her policy in Bedser's opening over with the new ball by placing five men on the leg-side.

This was an unreasonably defensive field, and persistence in these tactics would have made it quite impossible to get the runs.

I was roasted in some quarters. One writer blamed me entirely and instanced another match between the Australian Services Team and India where the Australians attempted to get 113 runs in 20 minutes. They got exactly 31 runs which the writer said was because Merchant bowled exaggerated leg theory. That was precisely what Bedser commenced in the first over against us in Adelaide.

Even so, it is worth pointing out that Morris made his century in the extraordinarily fast time of 124 minutes, whilst my own 50 in that innings was the fastest of the match.

Earlier in this same season the positions had been reversed. Victoria were playing South Australia in Adelaide and had to get 79 runs in half an hour to win the match.

I was then the fielding captain and with a perfectly orthodox field accepted the challenge and gave the batsmen an opportunity. They obtained the runs with two minutes to spare.

I could quite easily have prevented this by adopting negative tactics, but I would never start that sort of thing or go beyond what I considered to be the normal and reasonable requirements.

The Ashes had been decided, but it did not seem to lessen public interest in the Final Test Match on the Sydney Cricket Ground.

Once again the Englishmen won the toss and therefore could not complain, for Hammond had called correctly in three out of the five matches.

There was good and exciting cricket until on the last day the air became electrical at one brief period, when Australia, with only five wickets left and with Wright and Bedser bowling like demons, still wanted more than 30 runs to win.

In England's first innings we saw one of the finest displays of fast bowling ever given in this country.

Ray Lindwall took 7 for 63 off 22 overs. He was very hostile throughout, holding his pace and continually moving the ball in the air. It was an outstanding effort by a young bowler who had not enjoyed the best of health throughout the series and was never one hundred per cent. physically fit.

Only Hutton, and to a lesser extent Edrich, stayed long. The gallant Yorkshireman recorded his only century in the series under adverse circumstances, for he was troubled all the time by a bad throat, and at the end of the first day's play was ordered to bed. He took no further part in the game.

After a comparatively normal opening on the Friday, it rained all day Saturday. The wicket was saturated, but dried out on the Sunday, and as there had not been any rolling in the meantime, the surface of the pitch tended to lift when the game was resumed.

This produced sporting cricket, and also enabled Doug. Wright to give the Australians a glimpse of his very best bowling form. He took 7 wickets in one innings, and was chiefly responsible for England gaining a first innings lead.

The last day was full of drama. We lost both our opening batsmen quickly, and then with my score at two, Edrich dropped a catch off Wright. Had it been accepted the whole course of the match might have been changed, for I helped to steer the side through a difficult period.

When Miller and McCool were together in that last sensational half hour, Bedser was right on the spot. Three balls in succession pitched on a perfect length, turned just sufficiently from the leg side to beat Miller's bat and also the stumps.

I could see that the crisis of the match was here, and sent a message to Miller that the only hope was to attack. In a flash the whole complexion of the match was changed, for Miller lifted Bedser over mid-off for 4, then drove him back over the bowler's head for 4, and almost in a twinkling victory was ours.

It had been touch and go. One of the most interesting Tests I can remember, and one which could have been lost just as easily as it was won.

We had every reason to be satisfied with the performances of the Australian team.

Not only had the more experienced players shown good form, but the new ones had exceeded our expectations.

I had been privileged for the first time to lead an international team which, in my opinion, possessed the necessary theoretical combination of bowlers to take advantage of all conditions.

We could be excused a wry smile when Warwick Armstrong, writing of the series said : " The Australian bowlers particularly are extremely weak. Australia will have to find new bowlers if she is to succeed in England in 1948."

Not only was he utterly wrong, but the 1948 combination proved to be one of the strongest in history.

One must admit that Hammond was very greatly handicapped by the lack of a really fast opening attack. Bedser did magnificent work at one end. At the other Edrich nobly tried to fill the gap, but was not quite up to that standard.

I still feel that Pollard could have been used in these Tests with advantage to England. Every time I met him on the tour, he bowled uncommonly well, and at least from a personal angle, I was continually relieved to see his name omitted from the Test XI.

Alec Bedser performed a prodigious amount of work, especially in the First Test at Brisbane. I doubt whether he completely recovered from the terrible gruelling he took in that stifling heat.

In later matches he bowled well at times, only to lapse into periods of comparative innocuity.

The ball with which he bowled me in the Adelaide Test Match was, I think, the finest ever to take my wicket. It must have come three quarters of the way straight on the off stump then suddenly dipped to pitch on the leg stump, only to turn off the pitch and hit the middle and off stumps. It was Bedser's misfortune to bowl quite a few more of this type which grazed the off-stump.

There was one outstanding point in regard to the season's cricket. It was the wisdom of resuming Test Matches so soon and not waiting another year.

The Australian Board of Control had pressed for an early resumption of international cricket, but understandably the M.C.C. was hesitant. Her country had been so ravished by war, and her future in the cricket sense was so uncertain that she desired a little time to take stock and gather her resources.

Had the resumption been delayed a year it could scarcely have affected the result. This could be a reasonable deduction from the 1948 series. The main thing was to start international cricket moving again, and in that connection the tour had nothing but the happiest results.

Nearly 850,000 people witnessed the five Test Matches ; surely that is the best testimony one can give as to the popularity of the game. In addition, it can never be properly estimated what a favourable effect the M.C.C. tour of Australia had upon the attendances in England in 1948. The people were literally hungry for sport and entertainment.

In the highest political quarters great stress was laid upon the " morale building " value of cricket. It was almost essential in England at the earliest possible moment, and of course the quick resumption of games in Australia gave the English public an opportunity of seeing Anglo-Australian Tests a year earlier than would otherwise have been the case.

I greatly valued two messages which came to me at the conclusion of the Fifth Test Match. The first was from Dr. Evatt, Deputy Prime

Minister of Australia, whose telegram read : " Please accept my sincere congratulations on excellent performance of yourself and your team. Your own personal achievement adds another series to an imperishable record."

The second was the following letter from the Rt. Hon. R. G. Menzies, Leader of the Opposition :—

> " I would not like the 1946-7 Test Season to pass into limbo without dropping you a line to say how much I admired your unique contribution to Victory.
>
> As a highly interested onlooker I was constantly fascinated by the skill with which you controlled the game at all stages. There are very many of us who think we have never seen a better or more subtle exhibition of captaincy.
>
> You no doubt have your critics, and I suppose like the rest of us you occasionally deserve them, but you can certainly look back over these Test Matches with unadulterated pride."

Dr. Evatt had played a leading part in bringing about the earliest possible resumption of Test cricket, and had every reason to feel delighted with the confirmation of his belief that 1946 was not too soon.

Immediately the final Test Match concluded, I publicly announced that I would be available to play against the Indians the following season.

I had come through the matches against the Englishmen better than anticipated. It had been a very great physical strain at times.

I, more than all the spectators and critics, knew the enormous gulf which existed between my 1946-7 play and that of earlier years.

For me it was not a matter of disappointment. I was fortunate to get through the season at all, but I felt that the effort had been worth while in the interests of cricket.

Believing that the season against India in 1947–8 would be less exacting and that I was now better able to stand up to it, I again felt it my duty to play this one season, especially as it was to be the first tour of Australia by an Indian Team.

At that time I was still very dubious about attempting a final tour of England.

The Indians

BEFORE GETTING DOWN TO THE PLAYING SIDE OF 1947-8 I WAS THE recipient of an honour from the South Australian Cricket Association which I greatly valued.

It came to me in the form of a letter dated 4th September, 1947, which said :—

" Dear Mr. Bradman,

We have pleasure in advising that at the 76th Annual General Meeting of members held this day you were unanimously elected a Life Member of the Association in appreciation of the services rendered by you in the advancement of the game of cricket.

A gold medallion in token of such membership is enclosed herewith.

May we express the hope that you will long be spared good health to enjoy the privilege which this election bestows upon you.

Yours sincerely,

(Sgd.) H. Blinman

President

(Sgd.) W. H. Jeanes,

Secretary "

It was indeed a privilege for one who had not entirely passed across the playing stage and gave me added encouragement to do my utmost against our friends from India.

By sterling performances in their own country against visiting teams, the Indian cricketers obviously possessed considerable skill.

In tours of England they had shown likewise, but the variable weather and the lack of sunshine probably caused them to be unreliable.

Vijay Merchant had earned a place amongst the leading batsmen of the day with others not so far behind.

Australia was looking forward keenly to the visit of their northern neighbours, who were to make their first appearance in this country.

At the outset there was great disappointment when Merchant had to withdraw because of an injury which rendered him medically unfit to make the trip.

There were other withdrawals, too, of prominent players which must have affected the overall strength of the team. But it was the loss of Merchant that I think was mainly responsible for India's relatively poor performances in the Test Matches.

There had been correspondence between the Australian Board of Control and the Indian Board regarding the playing conditions in Australia. There were no differences of opinion excepting that Australia felt it would be more advantageous to the Indians if wickets remained covered.

Surprisingly the Indians decided they would prefer the M.C.C. idea of uncovered wickets.

I thought India was making a grave mistake. We do not see many wet wickets in this country, but we see more than the Indians do in theirs.

Our players do not possess quite the same skill as Englishmen under such conditions, but it seemed clear they would have more than the Indians.

I felt that we would prove superior on dry wickets. Knowing the merits of the players who would be at our disposal, I felt that on wet wickets India would be overwhelmed.

For this reason I strongly pressed for the Indians to agree to covered wickets, and spent considerable time trying to pursuade Amarnath, the Indian Captain, of the soundness of my views. It was all to no avail.

I think probably Amarnath saw the wisdom of my suggestion, but was willing to trust the favouritism of the weather gods.

On the contrary the Indians suffered grievously through being caught on wet wickets. The result of the matches may not have been affected, though most certainly the end was expedited.

In addition to the effect it had on the results, the financial aspect of cricket cannot be ignored. I do not suggest the interests of cricket should be subservient to finance, but it must have been obvious to experienced observers that the Indian tour would make very little if any profit. The shortening of matches and the one-sided nature of victories could not do otherwise than have a detrimental effect on the gate receipts.

The Indian team had as its Manager, Peter Gupta, a famous personality who has probably created a world's record for the number of times he has acted in a managerial capacity.

Peter did not confine his activities to cricket. He loved hockey, and wherever an Indian hockey team went he was almost sure to be found.

Amongst his other qualifications was journalism. Perhaps this accounted for the extremely forthright attitude he took towards the Australian Press the moment he set foot on Australian soil. Being of the same ilk probably made the journalists respect his attitude.

Amarnath took over the captaincy when Merchant dropped out. This picturesque player had been a member of the Indian team which toured England in 1936 under the captaincy of Maharaj Kumar of Vizianagram. The tour was in progress and Amarnath had scored 613 runs (more than anyone else at the time) and taken 32 wickets, when dissension developed among the party and he was sent back to India as a disciplinary measure. It seemed a very stern punishment, especially as no convincing explanation was given at the time by the authorities.

Throughout the whole of the Australian tour I found Amarnath and Peter Gupta absolutely charming in every respect. They co-operated in all conceivable ways to try and make the games enjoyable, and the most wonderful spirit of cameraderie existed between the Australian and Indian players.

We, of course, had to play the best cricket of which we were capable. We proved too strong for them. I believe we played the most attractive cricket possible, and the public who saw the matches found them just as enjoyable as the closer and more serious contests against England.

Amarnath was such a splendid ambassador that it makes it all the more difficult to understand his recent suspension by the Indian Board of Control.

Lala, as he was called, certainly believed in speaking his mind at all times and was not averse to expressing his opinion in regard to a controlling authority or an individual, but in Australia he always did it with the utmost courtesy and tact.

I look back on the season with him as my opposite number, as one of my most pleasant cricket years.

I first saw them play in Adelaide when South Australia were their opponents. I made a century in this match, and in doing so formed the conclusion that our Test team would make a lot of runs against them, for two reasons. Firstly, their bowling, whilst reasonably steady and sound, lacked a really fast bowler, and what is probably more important, a really high-class spinner. Secondly, to my surprise they were weak in the field.

Remembering the amazing agility of men like Constantine, I rather expected that fielding would be our visitors' strongest department. It probably proved to be their weakest.

Came a match between an Australian XI and India on the Sydney Cricket Ground. For me personally it held more than usual significance.

I had scored 99 centuries in first-class cricket, and in addition to the natural desire to score another one had set my heart on making that century on the Sydney Cricket Ground. Throughout the years no cricket ground in the world had supplanted Sydney in my affections. I always felt that the crowds there were sympathetic towards me, with the result that I wanted to achieve this record at the Sydney Cricket Ground.

The setting was perfect.

The Indians had batted first, and their innings closed at 326 before lunch on the Saturday. We lost an early wicket and I was forced to defend rather grimly in the pre-lunch session to hold my wicket intact. At lunch my score was only 11. The press had featured the possibility of my getting this 100th century, and a big crowd was present in the afternoon to see play resumed.

Keith Miller was my companion and between the resumption of play and the afternoon tea adjournment it was orthodox cricket of a standard which should have satisfied the most exacting. Both Miller and I were in good form against an excellent and accurate attack. The Indians played with great zest.

Gradually my score mounted until it reached 90. I became perhaps a little too anxious. Slowly the extra runs were added. I turned a ball to square leg, ran one and then went for what the crowd thought was a risky second. One could literally feel them rise in their seats as they thought I might not make good my ground. Even in the most exciting Test Match I can never remember a more emotional crowd nor a more electric atmosphere.

Finally, with my total at 99, Amarnath called up Kishenchand who was fielding on the boundary. He had not bowled before and I had no idea what type of bowler he was. It was a shrewd move, as one could have so easily been deceived, but I treated him with the greatest respect until eventually came a single to mid-on and the great moment had arrived.

I think of all my experiences in cricket that was my most exhilarating moment on the field. The huge crowd gave me a reception which was moving in its spontaneous warmth.

All this time Miller had played a grand innings, willingly sacrificing himself for an occasion, and he was the first to shake my hand. That was the last over before tea. I felt the crowd were glad of a respite to break the tension. Most certainly I was. It came as a tremendous relief.

Resuming after the adjournment I was determined to give that wonderful crowd some reward if it lay within my power. The Indians had a new ball, but I set about the making of strokes in the way I would always have loved to do had circumstances permitted.

One can so often make an early mistake to defeat the best intentions, but fate was kind this day for I was able to add another 71 runs before being dismissed. These runs were scored in 45 minutes, and I class that particular section of my innings as about the most satisfying of my career.

Just before getting out I was torn between two minds—I so dearly wanted to entertain the public, yet it was no pleasure to take heavy toll of the Indian attack in a match of relative unimportance.

Suddenly the way was clear, for I tore a muscle in my leg, and instantly took it as a cue to give my innings away.

I cannot tell you why there was any special significance about getting 100 centuries. It was just a magic milestone. No other Australian had reached this goal though 10 Englishmen had.

My centuries were scored in 295 innings, which I understand is the highest ratio yet recorded.

Jack Hobbs leads the list with 197. To do this he batted 1,315 times. Jack was desperately keen to get the remaining 3 thus to become the first man to score 200 centuries. He played on after realising he should give up. The strain became too great and eventually he had to quit the stage just short of this unique total.

The New South Wales and South Australian Cricket Associations and the Sydney Cricket Ground Trust very generously rewarded me with handsome presentations to mark the performance.

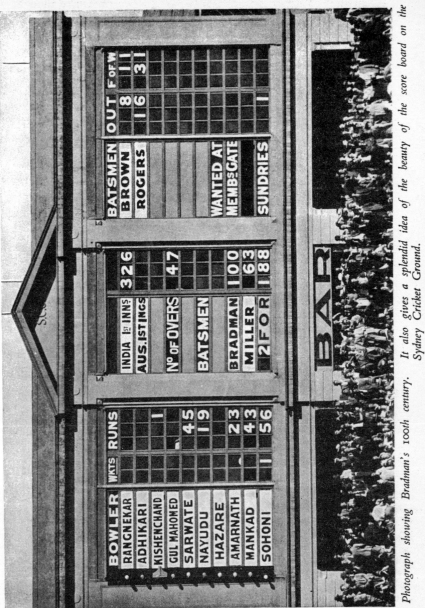

Photograph showing Bradman's 100th century. It also gives a splendid idea of the beauty of the score board on the Sydney Cricket Ground.

The first real trial of strength between our Test teams came at Brisbane. It turned out to be rather a tragedy for the Indians.

I won the toss, and at the end of the first day we had scored 273 for 3 wickets, of which I had made 160 not out.

My form was immeasurably superior to anything I had shown against the Englishmen the previous year, simply because of further improvement in my health during the winter months.

Rain came at the end of the first day's play and from that moment India's chances were hopeless.

There were the usual wicket inspections. I wanted to play—Amarnath did not. The crowd for some unaccountable reason thought I was objecting to a resumption, and I was roundly hooted. So were the umpires when they came out. It was just one of those regrettable occasions when the weather intervenes and nothing can be done about it.

True to my forecast as to what would happen on a wet wicket, the Indians could only make 58 runs.

Toshack had the astounding analysis of 5 for 2 in the first innings and 6 for 29 in the second, really phenomenal performances under any circumstances.

Only twelve months before, Toshack had seen his first wet wicket. One could scarcely have expected better figures from Rhodes or Verity, and it augured well for his chances in England.

Towards the close, Toshack's foot slipped in the wet ground, causing him to twist a knee. He had to leave the field. This injury was the one which ultimately caused his withdrawal from active participation in the Australian tour of England and a cartilage operation.

It was hoped that the Indians would enjoy better fortune in the Second Test, and when Amarnath won the toss it seemed that these hopes would materialize. They did not. It was a lively wicket upon which Miller and Lindwall produced most hostile bowling.

Rain came after about an hour, and when play was resumed, Hazare was bowled by a ball at which he did not attempt a stroke. Also, Amarnath turned his back on one which was deflected off the back of his leg on to the stumps. They could only total 188.

An early sensation came in Australia's innings when Brown was once more run out by Mankad, who, in the act of delivering the ball, held on to it and whipped the bails off with Brown well out of his crease. This had happened in the Indian match against Queensland, and immediately in some quarters Mankad's sportsmanship was questioned.

For the life of me I cannot understand why. The laws of cricket make it quite clear that the non-striker must keep within his ground until the ball has been delivered. If not, why is the provision there which enables the bowler to run him out?

By backing up too far or too early the non-striker is very obviously gaining an unfair advantage. On numerous occasions he may avoid being run out at the opposite end by gaining this false start.

I am well aware that few bowlers ever seek to take advantage of such an opportunity. It would be well nigh impossible for some of them to do so.

Imagine, for instance, Lindwall stopping himself right at the bowling crease. He could not do it. Only the slower types of bowlers have a chance.

Mankad was an ideal type, and he was so scrupulously fair that he first of all warned Brown before taking any action. There was absolutely no feeling in the matter as far as we were concerned, for we considered it quite a legitimate part of the game.

I always make it a practice when occupying the position of a non-striker to keep my bat behind the crease until I see the ball in the air. In that way one cannot possibly be run out, and I commend this practice to other players.

The Indians caught us on a very badly rain-affected pitch, and took full advantage of their opportunity. We were all out for 107, Hamence top scoring with a plucky 25.

The Indians dismissed us too quickly for their own good. They in turn had now to face the unpleasant wicket and were immediately in trouble, losing 7 wickets for 61 before stumps.

Further rain caused the abandonment of the match. Out of the 30 hours set down for play, less than 10 were completed. Three complete days were lost, an unprecedented happening in Test cricket in Australia.

The Third Test Match brought forth some interesting cricket, but further disaster for India.

I again won the toss, and although we put together only a moderate total of 394, India was 103 short of this total with 9 wickets down when the rain came once more.

It reminded me of the match against Gubby Allen's team in 1936. I had to adopt the same tactics of sending in tail-end batsmen to hold the fort until the wicket improved. As on the previous occasion the move succeeded.

Arthur Morris and I each got centuries after we had lost 4 wickets for 32 runs.

The Indians were once more caught on a glue pot and could only total 125.

In scoring a century in each innings I joined the small band of cricketers who have achieved this feat. Once again I had been in good form, scoring the last 77 runs of my century in 70 minutes.

When the rain came to give us a bad wicket, I took advantage of the situation to close our innings and send the Indians in to bat.

There were some who felt I should have allowed the Australians to continue batting and the argument was advanced that it would give our men practice of great value in view of the forthcoming English tour.

A captain's prime function is to win the match for his country, not to use a Test Match for experimental purposes. Any other outlook would be a violation of the trust imposed in the skipper.

I doubt whether people in this country generally appreciate the vast difference between an Australian sticky wicket and the English variety. Quite frankly, the Australian ones are so bad that one gets little experience by batting on them.

It is just the opposite in England. It is possible on English wet wickets to really bat with skill and quite a measure of confidence. The ball comes off much more slowly and does not kick so viciously.

One of the secrets of making runs on a wet wicket is to survive the first few balls. In our country the ball does such fantastic things that frequently one gets out before there is any chance of really finding out what the wicket is doing.

If we had enough wet wickets in Australia, then perhaps our batsmen would develop more knowledge of how to bat on them. As it is, they generally feel the necessity of getting runs as quickly as possible before the inevitable end arrives.

No such pessimistic view is taken by English players who are accustomed to their own conditions, where quite often a wet wicket may be an easier proposition than a dry one.

The Adelaide Test Match was more to the liking of our Indian friends in the sense that it produced hot sunny weather and made them feel at home.

The change was not sufficient to produce victory. Once again I was lucky with the coin, and we put together a total of 674 in which there were 3 centuries. Barnes 112, Hassett 198 not out and myself 201. This double century enabled me to achieve the distinction of having scored more double centuries than any other cricketer—one more than Hammond who made 36.

The Indians, despite a gallant fight, were beaten by an innings, but not before Hazare had added his name to the scroll of fame by becoming the first Indian to score a century in each innings of a Test Match.

When we foregathered for the First Test Match, I had a lengthy argument with one of my compatriots as to the relative merits of Hazare and Amarnath as batsmen. The skipper had performed brilliantly in one or two State matches, but I had been very impressed by the soundness of Hazare and the correctness of his stroke production. I have no wish to be dogmatic on the point at this stage. I merely want to call attention to Hazare's skill and his right to be classed as a great player.

We know Amarnath to be a brilliant run-getter, and those who saw his innings against Victoria earlier in the season rate it amongst the best ever seen on the Melbourne Cricket Ground.

In the Tests he was overshadowed by Hazare. Maybe the responsibility of being captain weighed heavily on Amarnath's shoulders. Whether it did or not one must be accurate and point out that Amarnath trusted his eyesight and natural ability to such an extent that he allowed himself the discretion of hitting against the break and otherwise taking unnecessary risks. This brought about his downfall on numerous occasions.

Hazare denied himself any such luxury. The latter's principal weakness was a lack of aggression which prevented him taking charge of an attack and tearing it to pieces, which is an attribute of such value to a match-winning batsman.

Lindwall finished off the Adelaide match with 7 wickets for 38; a remarkable performance in a total of 277 runs. It is somewhat strange that he should have performed so well against both England and India at Adelaide, where the wicket is notoriously unkind to fast bowlers.

The Adelaide Ground is the only one in Australia where the press sit directly at right angles to the bowling crease. Being on the short boundary they get an excellent view of the bowler's feet. It was here the great controversy started about Lindwall dragging over the line as he delivers the ball.

I do not wish to revive that controversy, but at the same time I desire to express a word on the no-ball rule.

It has been reasonably satisfactory, though at odd times arguments have arisen, such as in the case of Lindwall, where moving pictures showed his foot to be across the line before the ball left his hand.

No umpire can possibly watch the bowler's hand and foot at the same time. It thus becomes difficult to give an accurate decision.

To make a fast bowler keep his back foot well behind the crease, thereby allowing for a drag, is satisfactory up to a point.

I am prepared to say, however, that if a slow motion picture of all fast and medium pace bowlers was taken it would be found that the majority at times drag the back foot across the line.

I therefore feel some sympathy for the view put forward by the editor of *Wisden* 1948, that we might reasonably consider a change in the law to provide that the front foot must be " grounded " between the two creases. At least an experiment along these lines would be valuable.

It should make the umpire's task easier and eliminate any uncertainty about the present rule. On the surface of things I do not visualize any compensating disadvantages.

We assembled in Melbourne for the Fifth Test Match. I had naturally given tremendous thought to the forthcoming tour of England. All my impulses spurred me to go. I am a great lover of England and the English people. Their kindness to me, especially in 1934 and 1938, knew no bounds.

I felt that I understood what the next Australian tour would mean to their cricket and to the people in general, and if it was possible for me to make a contribution I was anxious to discharge my duty in that direction.

There were, of course, difficulties in the way. One cannot just simply walk out of a strictly personal business for an absence of about 8 months without a good deal of consideration. I would have been foolish to go if I felt that my health would not stand the strain. Remembering previous experiences, this factor was a constant worry.

Finally I weighed all these considerations in the balance, and decided it was my duty to make one last effort for the sake of cricket.

I do not think such a statement is egotistical.

Of those who played Test cricket with me in 1928 not one remained on the active list. Surely my experience would be of value.

So it was that I called press representatives together the night before the Fifth Test Match against India commenced, and gave them this statement : " I have today advised my co-selectors that I am available for the Australian tour of England. At the same time I wish to say that the game against India will be my last first-class match in Australia, as I shall retire from cricket at the conclusion of the English tour."

I did play three matches in 1948-9 on my return, but they did not constitute a breach of my statement as they were all testimonial or benefit matches arranged after the English tour had commenced. I could scarcely do otherwise than play in my own, and regarded it as right and proper that I should make my contribution to the Kippax-Oldfield Match in Sydney and the Arthur Richardson Benefit in Adelaide.

Having made the decision I was more than a little anxious as to whether it had been wise. My fears were made the worse when in the Fifth Test Match I broke down so badly that I had to retire in the middle of my innings and could not resume. It may have been a touch of the old fibrositis or it may have been a rib cartilege which gave way. Without doubt it was one of those prevalent signs which come to men who continue to play vigorous sports when the time has arrived to make way for younger players.

The Indian players seemed to lose heart in the final game. They fought well in the opening innings then collapsed badly on a perfectly dry wicket to be out for 67, and another innings victory went to Australia.

From our point of view, the dashing performance of young Neil Harvey, who scored 153 and made his first Test century, was worth going a long way to see. It was an exhilarating knock for a 19-year-old boy to play.

Reviewing the tour one is not being ungenerous to say the Indians were not quite equal to the task. Had their full strength been available it might have been a different story.

If Australia or England should lose four or five of their best players it would seriously prejudice their efficiency. How much more so with India whose resources were much thinner.

In the batting line, Amarnath and Hazare were outstanding. They were fit to be classed with any company.

Mankad did surprisingly well with the bat if one takes into account the enormous work he was called upon to do with the ball. Without being on the same plane as the two already mentioned, he was very good except against fast bowling, which was his Achilles heel. Ray Lindwall almost invariably got Mankad's wicket.

A player who definitely improved during the tour and did really well towards the close was Phadkar. He bowled fast medium with good control and quite a lot of variation in pace. Lacking the style of other batsmen he, nevertheless, showed splendid courage and the virtue of a straight bat. He always took digging out.

Amarnath bowled very well at times, though his leg theory was inclined to be a little too negative, and Mankad who had to share the burden of the donkey work in so many matches was such a tired player by the end that his form fell right away.

My injury prevented me from playing again until after the Australian team set out for England.

Throughout the season I had tried in various ways to assist the Indian players because I felt that it was part of our responsibility to encourage and improve their standard.

Test cricket between England and Australia is still supreme, but it cannot remain in isolation, and will be materially strengthened if other countries can match their skill.

That day undoubtedly will come, and as the mother country founded and nurtured her colonies, so should we assist the less mature cricketing countries to the highest standard of play.

England, the Last Time

AND SO THE DIE WAS CAST. I HAD PUBLICLY COMMITTED MYSELF TO another tour of England.

It was a foregone conclusion that I would be selected (although the team had not at that time been chosen) and although the appointment of Captain was in the hands of the Australian Board of Control, I did not anticipate any competition for leadership.

My immediate reaction to what was for me a matter of great moment, was an inward fear that my health would not stand the strain of another tour.

I began to meditate upon the possibility of failure. Was I taking on too much?

Ten years before, in 1938, I had found the job of captaining an Australian team in England so exacting that I had resolved not to undertake another trip four years later. Did it not appear a reasonable assumption that I would now be less capable of standing the strains and stresses—ten years older and much illness in the meantime?

Temporarily at least these fears haunted me, but as the day for departure approached they began to recede into the background. Instead I became fired with a zeal I had not previously experienced, a burning desire to utilize my brain and my body to the utmost in the interests of cricket and the team I was to lead.

Knowing the personnel, I was confident that here at last was the great opportunity which I had longed for. A team of cricketers whose respect and loyalty were unquestioned, who would regard me in a fatherly sense and listen to my advice, follow my guidance and not question my handling of affairs.

What a difference between the mental outlook of a captain who is 40 years of age and easily the senior member, and that of one who is several years junior to some of the men playing under him. There are no longer any fears that they will query the wisdom of what you do. The result is a sense of freedom to give full reign to your own creative ability and personal judgment.

From the moment we assembled I did my utmost to make it plain that I had the welfare of the tour and the players at heart. I gave them to understand I was purely the figurehead—the medium of expression; tried to make them see how essential it was for the team to pull together as a unit—free of all internal bickering and strife. I instilled into them the doctrine that "happiness comes from within."

I said to them, "External influences can be important, but if we all resolve to be a happy and contented party, nothing can prevent it."

Little did I then understand how true it would prove and how faithfully they would follow such a creed.

On the cricket side I was confident of our ability. Nobody knew our weaknesses as I did, but there were certain characteristics about the team which inspired confidence.

Individual ability had to be tested in some cases in the crucible of hard experience—in others it was already known.

But I knew we were better equipped in the technical sense than any other touring team with which I had travelled.

Firstly we had selected Barnes and Morris as opening batsmen—one already known to be in world class in either England or Australia—the other a potential star whose skill under Australian conditions was beyond doubt. We had implicit confidence in his ability to overcome English conditions and thus give us the ideal left-right opening pair.

As reserve opener—solid as a rock—Bill Brown always a great player in England. Better there than in Australia.

Then came an array of batsmen who could scarcely fail. There were myself (and subject to those physical doubts, I knew English wickets would suit me better), Hassett and Hamence, all right-handers and Neil Harvey, a young left-hander with the brilliance and daring of youth and the likelihood of rapid improvement.

All-rounders in Miller and Loxton, the former a hostile fast bowler as well as a brilliant field and match-winning batsman—the latter a bulldog fighter who would be at his best when others were showing signs of wear and tear and the most dangerous field in the world when the chance occurred of a run-out.

Perhaps I should include Ian Johnson, McCool and Lindwall in the class of all-rounders because their ability warranted it—but they were chosen rather for their bowling to give us respectively right-hand off spin, right-hand leg spin and right-hand fast.

Doug. Ring was bracketed with McCool as a right-hand leg spinner.

Then we had Bill Johnston who bowled either fast left-hand or slow left-hand spinners (according to the need) and Toshack whose medium left-hand deliveries were of a unique type, likely to be very successful under English conditions.

To complete the party, two brilliant wicket-keepers, Tallon and Saggers, both of whom were competent batsmen.

I have detailed these particulars for the special purpose of emphasizing the theoretical qualifications, which supported my belief in the ability of the side and which largely contributed to my enthusiasm.

Thus an important element of success was established before we started.

My unswerving belief in their skill and their potential ability as a team caused me to devote every care to the gradual moulding of the combination.

I talked to them about tactics, pointed out elementary faults that should not be found in internationals, instilled into them the important part played by the humblest member of the side, and kindled in their minds the thought that here was a team capable of going through undefeated. We would need luck—maybe the toss—maybe the weather—but firstly faith in ourselves was born.

All this did not happen on the first day of the tour—it was a gradual process, sometimes unobserved by members of the team who did not always realise the significance of some move I might make. But in my mind these things were unfolding before I left home on the eventful day of March 3rd, 1948.

Much as I dislike flying (because of resultant air-sickness) I decided it was my duty to accompany the team on the early stages of the tour which involved air travel to Hobart and subsequently to Perth.

So on the 4th March, 1948, we officially set off by air for Hobart where, on the following day, we played our first match.

For me, personally, it was disturbing in that my side, injured against India, still troubled me. Rather than aggravate the injury, I deliberately gave my innings away, and then rested from the following game v. Launceston.

The matches in Tasmania are not of a serious character, but they play a useful part in the pattern of developing cricket. One never knows where a good player will be discovered. Jack Badcock for instance was a Tasmanian product.

Returning to Melbourne, we were tendered a farewell dinner at the M.C.C. by the Victorian Cricket Association where His Excellency, Sir Winston Dugan, Governor of Victoria, proposed the toast of the Australian XI.

Most of the next day was spent in the air and we arrived in Perth about 7 p.m., marvelling at the wonders of modern air travel, but very tired.

Our final game before leaving was against West Australia, winners of the Sheffield Shield in their first year of probationary entry—a great achievement about which they were justifiably elated.

The patriotism of the Perth crowd surprised me. Cricket had very obviously gripped their imagination, and if this enthusiasm persists, it augurs well for the ultimate production of Australian XI players.

As an intended compliment to them I decided to play even though my injured side was still worrying me.

This was to be, I thought, my last first-class match in Australia. Anyway it can be recorded that I scored a century in my last serious appearance in first-class cricket in my own country, and in so doing made 8 centuries for the season, which at the time of writing, is the highest number ever made in an Australian season by any batsman.

I don't expect the record to stand long. Within a very short space of time this number will probably be exceeded.

An incident occurred in the match which is worth recording because a principle is involved, and I would like my views to be known on matters of this kind.

This was ostensibly my last Australian match—an educational game of a non-competitive nature. On the final day the local batsmen appealed against the light at 4.40 p.m. when McCool and Johnson (two slow bowlers) were operating. There could only be two reasons, to save their own wickets, or to save West Australia from defeat. Stumps were drawn early—an opportunity for the W.A. players to learn more about the game was lost—and the public were deprived of some interesting cricket. It would have been understandable had there been any danger to the players, but I refrained from using my fast bowlers for this very reason.

Contrast this with what happened in our last match of the English tour against Scotland at Aberdeen. The light was extremely bad on the last day and justified an appeal. One of the batsmen spoke to an umpire who then conferred with the Scottish Captain. The latter said his team was obviously beaten, nobody was in any danger, they wanted to learn, and the public had come to watch Australia play and he wished to continue to the end.

I mention the matter to point out how things should be viewed in their proper perspective. It is better at all times that circumstances should be carefully weighed, the comparative seriousness and importance of the match considered, and decisions arrived at in the broad interests of the game.

I want it to be clearly understood that I am not referring to matches of a competitive nature where perhaps the interests of another team may be affected or some element intervenes such as the points scored in a championship.

My final two acts in Perth were firstly to visit the Crippled Children's Hospital where I tried to cheer up the lives of those poor unfortunate inmates, and the less pleasant task of visiting the dentist to have a wisdom tooth removed.

It was Friday the 19th March when we boarded the good ship *Strathaird* for England. As we pulled out I can recall meeting on board Arthur Mailey—who said, " This will be my last trip "—Neville Cardus who said, " This will be my last trip "—I wonder—and seeing the usual cosmopolitan crowd of travellers—overhearing a woman violently arguing with, I presume, her husband, and saying with great vehemence, " What more could I do ? "

For me I knew this was definitely my last trip as a player. Her words came back to me : " What more could I do ? " I had returned to cricket in 1946/7 against the advice of my doctors, and now I was going to England against my own judgment—risking personal failure and other possibilities.

But my conscience was clear that I was discharging what I believed to be my final obligation as a player to the game of cricket and its myriads of supporters. Had I but known it, fate was going to be kind.

There is little to record of the journey, but I should make mention of our match in Colombo where some 25,000 people paid about £3,000 to watch a one-day game between our side and the locals.

Rain put an early end to the match, but not before we had become very suspicious about the length of the pitch which on subsequently being measured was found to be some two yards short. No wonder they found trouble in handling Miller, and we thought their bowlers came off the pitch rather quickly. It has no doubt happened elsewhere, but not in any match in which I have played.

Worthy of mention is the Colombo score-board which in some

respects gives more information than any board in the world—a tribute to local enthusiasm.

This Colombo game is always played in great heat—sometimes dangerous to us. Sid. Barnes in the current match became violently ill whilst at the wickets and had to retire. That evening I, too, became ill and had to call the doctor. I had to remain in bed until our arrival at Bombay, but there got up to attend a small function at which Mr. De Mello, President of the Indian Board of Control, made a presentation to the members of our team and to certain other people. He made a speech (as also did Peter Gupta and Vijay Merchant) to which hasty replies were made as the boat was about to leave.

Port Said offered the usual interest to the new travellers and provided a wonderful topic of conversation on the night of April 7th. I can still picture the player who boasted loud and long about having made the best purchase of the day—a.pair of shoes—but when the proud moment arrived to display them he discovered one was size 8 and the other size 9. You've got to be smart to beat the salesmen at Port Said.

I was initiated into the marvels of radar whilst we were making a detour near Gibraltar where advance films of the Australian players were specially sent ashore in a launch and flown to London. Such is the spotlight on modern cricketers—their features must be known to the public per medium of the screen at tremendous cost before the players themselves reach the scene of action.

Friday, 16th April, was the day we arrived at our destination, to be met, amongst others, by that outstanding figure, beloved of English and Australian people alike, the Earl of Gowrie—President of M.C.C., and so began in earnest what was to prove the greatest tour, up to that time anyway, in Australian cricket history.

England, 1948

THE MEN WHO INVENTED THE CAMERA, BOTH STILL AND MOVIE, WIRELESS and television, doubtless did a great service to mankind and made a contribution of untold value to science. But they also created weapons of publicity which are almost frightening to a team of international cricketers.

No doubt movie stars take this sort of thing complacently, but cricketers never do. We were besieged by a terrific battery at Tilbury in order that the world, but mainly England, should know what sort of people were these men from the land of the kangaroo who had come so far to test their skill against the players of the Mother Country.

Would it be more gloom in the life of a ravaged country, or sunshine to a people tired and weary of more serious aspects and who wanted healthy sporting rivalry to entertain their minds ?

I know that for me, as Captain, the next few days were a nightmare. I knew they would be before I left Australia, but I rather doubt whether the public as a whole has any real conception of the ordeal which faces the visiting skipper.

In ordinary life he is usually, like myself, a man engaged in peaceful pursuits which do not call for making speeches or public appearances. Suddenly he has to rub shoulders with leaders of the Empire, has to be the principal guest and speaker when all around him are the most brilliant orators in the land. It is a frightening prospect which I want to emphasize because it may earn my successor a degree of sympathy and understanding which I'm sure he will value.

Our first function was the following morning when the members of the team were entertained by the High Commissioner at Australia House. Along with the Right Hon. J. A. Beasley, I had to receive some 200 guests and after shaking hands with them I suddenly acquired a new-found respect for the duties of royalty, together with a fear that my right hand would not recover prior to the first match at Worcester.

The movie cameras discovered that their appetites had only been whetted the day before—also that " takes " usually have to be repeated.

Practice at Lord's in the afternoon restored some semblance of physical feeling and gave the new players their first glimpse of an English wicket.

The Australian Board of Control's liaison officer, R. W. V. Robins, organised a game of golf over the weekend at Burnham Beeches Golf Club. Most of the cricketers played and took the opportunity to get the feeling of being back on land into their legs.

These occasional golfing jaunts throughout the summer are one of the cricketer's joys. It is such a relief to get away from the incessant strain—to become an ordinary mortal—to be envious of some other fellow's ability, but above all to get the mental relaxation which golf so peculiarly affords.

I cannot explain this latter phenomenon, but all sportsmen (except no doubt golfers) will confirm that no other game seems to provide the same degree of mental rest.

We are continually plied with the question : " Doesn't golf affect your cricket ? " The answer is definitely no. But conversely cricket seriously affects golf. There is the tendency to bend the left arm and slice the golf ball over the " covers " which is a splendid method of getting in the rough.

That reminds me of a story. We were the guests one weekend on a former tour at a famous English course. Just prior to our visit, Henry Cotton had given a superb exhibition there in a competition.

For our visit, caddies, etc., were generously provided. One of our lads, who was scarcely good enough to warrant a handicap, had zig-zagged from side to side until about the 15th, where he was lost in the rough.

During the search, his nerves having become a little on edge by his poor display, he chided his caddy by saying, " You're not much good at finding the ball in the rough, you know." Quick as a flash came the answer, " No, sir. You see, I'm not usually out here. I mostly caddy for Henry Cotton."

Fortunately the rough at Burnham Beeches was not of such a fear-some variety.

We tried to get down to really serious cricket practice next morning, but my most vivid recollection of the practice was my meeting with Field Marshal Lord Alexander who had come down to watch his son at the nets. The Field Marshal was returning to Canada shortly after-wards and expressed regret at his inability to watch the Tests. He was obviously keen on the game and was anxious that his son should become proficient.

Our team were the guests for luncheon of the Royal Empire Society. The Earl of Clarendon was in the Chair and made a charming speech of welcome, ably supported by that famous ex-England Captain, C. B. Fry.

In the evening we paid an official visit to the Coliseum Theatre where we were guests of the management to see *Annie Get Your Gun*, and following the show we were entertained at supper. Here, to our very great surprise and pleasure, we met the Foreign Secretary (Mr. Ernest Bevin) and the First Lord of The Admiralty (Mr. A. V. Alexander), whilst among the guests was Lord McGowan (Chairman of Imperial Chemical Industries Ltd.) who had also been at the show.

A few speeches of welcome followed and we were delighted with Mr. Bevin's good humour. One amusing story comes to mind. He related the tale of the capitalist, communist, fascist and trades unionist, all out in a boat. It sank. They swam for the shore but the capitalist, having loaded himself with goods as the ship went down, soon sank under his load. The communist shouted so much he swallowed big gulps of water, which spelt his doom and he sank. The fascist, keeping one arm up in the attitude of salute, couldn't make the grade and he went down. Meanwhile, the trades unionist swam strongly and steadily for the shore and all appeared to be well with him when suddenly the hooter went and he sank. The knowledge of Mr. Bevin's political background helped us to enjoy the joke.

Next day our team were entertained by the British Sportsman's Club at the Savoy Hotel. A brilliant function it was. Some 430 guests attended under the Chairmanship of Lord Aberdare and heard Lt.-Col. R. Stanyforth propose the toast of the Australian Team. The luncheon lasted three hours—a grand show, but an ordeal for the skipper.

Each day practice was sandwiched in either morning or afternoon as was most convenient.

Our next function was lunch the following day when the Institute of Journalists entertained us at Grosvenor House.

There was for me quite a coincidence about the lunch. Before leaving Australia, my family doctor had given me a letter of introduction to a very great friend of his—one John Gordon—and I was wondering how and when I would be able to carry out my promise to contact this gentleman. He was the John Gordon who presided over the Institute luncheon and so a very simple answer was provided to that problem.

I would not belabour my readers with details of all luncheons but a summarised report of this one appeared in the *Journal* of the Institute of Journalists which I feel justified in quoting. Here it is :—

" The luncheon given by the London District of the Institute to welcome the Australian Test Cricket Team was an unqualified success.

Nothing of the goodly fellowship and friendliness which characterised the four previous occasions was lacking. All the guests obviously felt that they were joining in a grand reunion, as indeed they were.

Don Bradman, in his reply for the team, struck an impressive opening note when he reminded those assembled at Grosvenor House that ten long years had passed since the Australian cricketers had last been received in London by the Institute of Journalists.

The realisation that such an interval had really elapsed conjured up many thoughts and memories of the other gatherings, in particular that of 1938, the year of Munich, when the gallant Don, with a twinkle in his eye, surprised and delighted his audience with his skill as a speaker. And now here he was again, with the same merry twinkle, scoring oratorically all round the wicket as if nothing had happened, and impishly challenging the 1998 prophecy of the admirable cartoon by Giles which decorated the menu card.

John Gordon, in the Chair, beamed benignly.

Having betrayed in his introductory remarks his own colossal ignorance of cricket—a confession shared by not a few Scots reared mainly on porridge and football, or golf—he settled back to watch, wonderingly, the intrepid Don pile up fours and sixes by quip and jest with the same easy grace that he wields his bat at Lord's or the Oval.

Two places away that doyen of cricketing giants, Captain C. B. Fry, enjoyed himself hugely, especially when the rich store of reminiscences was being mined—now with a hearty nod of approval, and then with a gesture of the hand as if signalling a boundary hit.

Of course Mr. Bradman could not go on jesting all the time. He chose the moment well to make what he described as an earnest appeal to the Press of Great Britain to treat the tour as a matter of sport in which there was no place for unfortunate incidents or sensations. Most of these incidents he declared, did not originally occur in the minds of the players themselves. They were friendly and wanted to remain friendly.

He refuted robustly a suggestion made in some quarters that the Australians took cricket too seriously. In his view, that boot, or rather, that pad, was on the English leg, in support of which argument he cited the fact that in the history of cricket there were only three batsmen who had made a century before lunch in a Test Match and they were all Australians. Naturally, modesty forbade him to add that he was one of these three record breakers at Leeds in 1930.

I was glad that C. B. Fry subsequently corrected a cricket correspondent who had stated in his newspaper that Mr. Bradman had become a good speaker. Cricket correspondents, like dramatic critics, and other experts, are capable sometimes of making belated discoveries. Don Bradman has long been an accomplished speaker, but I would say he is now so accomplished that he deserves to be described as a first-class ambassador of the Empire.

Mr. Oliver Lyttleton, M.P., in a lively and amusing speech, had proposed the health of the Australian team. Among other things, he recalled that his father, the great Alfred Lyttleton, was the hero of a Test Match feat without parallel. It was at the Oval in 1884, when he was England's wicketkeeper, and, at the end of a long innings, took off his pads, went on to bowl, and dismissed the last four Australian batsmen for 19 runs, thus heading the bowling averages for the match.

When Mr. Bradman had replied, and had been presented by Mr. Giles with the original of the cartoon which decorated the menu card, the members of the Australian team, from Lindsay Hassett, the Vice-captain, to Neil Harvey, the 19-year-old baby, stalwart fellows all—were introduced individually, and hands were linked for the singing of " Auld Lang Syne ".

By way of a change we went from luncheon to dinner next day when the Cricket Writer's Club provided a really memorable evening at the Public Schools' Club, Piccadilly.

Of all the great and magnificent functions, I have been privileged to attend, this one stands out in my memory for the excellence and wit of the speeches.

Chairman " Jim " Swanton set the standard, ably supported by his co-author of that splendid *History of Cricket*, H. S. Altham, but I thought it was to Canon Gillingham and Sir Norman Birkett the honours were due.

The Canon is, of course, renowned for his after-dinner speeches, but this was my first experience of his witticisms. We laughed loud and long at his reference to some legendary Australian aboriginal who allegedly went in to bat, beard down to his waist, bat bound with barbed wire and made 60 off his knuckles.

Then he produced a copy of a London afternoon paper, published the day we arrived, and read the front page headlines: " Australian Cricketers Arrive "—" Murderers Reprieved."

But it savoured of conjuring when, following my remarks that no English county had beaten an Australian Team for about 50 years, he produced from some hidden source an old score card to prove that his beloved county Essex had soundly beaten Australia 43 years ago.

Before leaving this scene I must recall Sir Norman's great story. After referring to the excellence of the fare provided by the Cricket Writer's Club, he said it reminded him of a party he once attended in America.

During the function the speaker was paying testimony to the perfection of the menu, when an interjector got up and said, " Sir—this is nothing—in the State of Oklahoma where I come from we have drinks between drinks." He was immediately followed by another interjector, who said, " Sir—that is nothing—in the State of Arizona where I come from we know no such interval."

A memorable evening was immensely enjoyed by the most distinguished guest, H.R.H. The Duke of Edinburgh.

During my remarks, I referred to the fact that I had seen photos of the Duke playing cricket and was of the opinion he had a splendid action for a right-hand off-spin bowler. I recommended the English Selectors to bear this fact in mind. I believe the Duke is really a very keen and enthusiastic cricketer.

Before the week was out a great thrill awaited the team, for on the Saturday they were entertained at Wembley to see the Cup-Tie Final in which Manchester United beat Blackpool 4—2. We were sitting alongside the Royal Box. Their Majesties showed great interest in the game.

Of the four Cup-Tie Finals I have seen, this one provided, I thought, easily the highest standard of play, and thus we were very privileged to witness not only this thrilling spectacle, but also play of the very highest calibre. An English fan who accompanied us insisted that Stanley Matthews is the greatest footballer England has ever produced. I cannot comment on that, but I do know he impressed us that day with his wonderful ball control.

A further event to make the day memorable for me, was my introduction to Admiral Sir Bruce Fraser.

The following Monday was a day crammed with incident. Early in the morning the Australian Manager, Mr. Keith Johnson and I went to Montague House where Keith presented to Food Minister Strachey a

Her Majesty the Queen greets Bradman at Lords, 1948. *His Majesty looks on.*

consignment of food with the compliments of the Australian Board of Control for International Cricket. This was warmly received.

Our next mission was to attend the Silver Jubilee in St. Paul's Cathedral to commemorate the wedding anniversary of the King and Queen. We had tickets, and Mr. Strachey kindly offered to take us along in his car.

However, by the time we approached the scene, tremendous crowds lined the processional route and it was impossible to get the car anywhere near the Cathedral. Mr. Strachey sought the help of a policeman with the result that Mr. and Mrs. Strachey, Keith Johnson and I found ourselves in the middle of the road on Ludgate Hill with rows of fixed bayonets on either side, the only pedestrians in sight, walking in a procession of glittering cars containing famous people.

It was somewhat embarrassing, especially as here and there a small coterie of people would recognise us, but at least we got there in time and were rewarded by seeing and hearing that never-to-be-forgotten service.

No matter to what age I may be privileged to live, I shall always remember the conclusion of the service and the playing of " God Save the King " in which the Cathedral Grand Organ and the trumpets of the Heralders joined to produce music of indescribable beauty. It made one's heart swell with pride.

It was difficult to practise that afternoon—one's thoughts were still in St. Paul's—but there was another dinner at night, the Lord Mayor of London had invited us to be his guests at the Mansion House. Apart from the honour of the function, members of our team were enthralled by the sight of some of London's gold treasures which were proudly aired for the occasion.

During the evening I found myself engaged in conversation with three or four guests when one of them said, "Mr. Bradman, if you will kindly sign this menu card for me I will give £25 to any charity you name." I am so accustomed to people expecting autographs by way of right, that I took his remarks to be of a jocular nature. However, just in case, I said I would accept his offer and remembering the good work they had performed for my own daughter, I nominated the Spastic Centre of the Adelaide Crippled Children's Hospital.

My astonishment was complete next day when I received a confirmatory letter and the money was duly forwarded.

Another philanthropist may here be mentioned. Later in the season I played at Lord's, and after the match received £10 in an envelope with a short memo. to say, "Thank you for the pleasure you've given me—kindly send the enclosed to any charity you wish." That money also went to the Adelaide Crippled Children's Hospital, and so by the kind and generous nature of two men, who doubtless would prefer to remain anonymous, cricket in England was not completely divorced from the humane job of doing something, even in a small way, for the less fortunate youth of Australia.

In the midst of all this entertainment, I wonder if the public gave any thought to what was happening behind the scenes.

For instance, did they think I never contemplated having to make a speech at the Savoy before over 400 distinguished guests ? Did they imagine I just got up and spoke *ad lib* ? If so, they were wrong. People do that sort of thing occasionally, but mostly in story books.

I knew when I left Australia what the future held in store and for weeks in advance I worried about each and every function. Would I make an unholy mess of my speech—say the wrong thing—repeat myself ?

That may not happen to accomplished speakers. I make no claim in that direction and would prefer to face almost any ordeal on this earth than make a speech. But having accepted the responsibility of Australian XI Captain, I knew what it entailed, and was prepared to face the facts. Hence I made little jottings at all sorts of queer hours and places, hoping they might be useful somewhere or other and in the end I think I have no reason to be ashamed of my efforts.

Then the practices at Lord's were important, as I had to watch over the form and potential form of each man—in some cases offer advice and encouragement—change the bowling to give the batsmen practice against the type they disliked, and in numerous little ways unseen attend to matters of general welfare besides hosts of personal items.

Over and above all this was the question of the eternal mail.

Normally it was heavy enough, but the long period between our arrival in England in 1948 and the start of the first match, plus the intense publicity and broadcasting of speeches seemed to aggravate the position. Anyway, whatever the cause, my mail was terrific.

I tried hard to cope with it, even to the extent of staying up until 2 and 3 o'clock in the morning. Even so, I left London for Worcester with a large suitcase full of unopened letters.

All the way from London to Worcester, three hours in the train, I opened letters. I spent another hour before dinner, assisted by a team mate, and two hours after dinner. All that just to open and read the letters—not answer them.

The great bulk of it was of no urgency, consisting mainly of autograph requests, but the letters had to be opened because here and there was an invitation of such a nature that it demanded an early reply.

As for autographs, we signed 5,000 sheets on the boat. They lasted just about a week. Requests poured in—books—bats—photos—all kinds of items were sent, very often without return postage.

My own personal mail averaged roughly 100 letters per day throughout the tour and this will give you some idea of what it was like as a whole.

At Worcester we were met at the station by local officials and driven by car to our hotel. On the way up the street our car was stopped whilst a young lady from a nearby florists shop pushed a glorious looking flower cricket bat through the window. It was made of marigolds and green leaves (roughly Australia's colours) with the word "Don" woven as a pattern on the blade.

The preliminaries were over—we were actually at Worcester, and the cricket was about to begin.

Play

During the English tour of 1938, I called tails in all matches except the Test Matches. It probably sounds very silly now, but the reason I changed in the Tests was because I had been so successful calling tails in the county games I thought the law of averages must operate in the end.

As it happened, I lost the toss in every Test Match in 1938.

Because of this experience, I resolved to call heads again in all the 1948 Tests, thinking the luck must break, and to be consistent I decided to call heads in the other games too.

So for the opening game v. Worcester I duly put this theory into operation, promptly lost the toss, and became a little apprehensive when Charlie Palmer batted so well that he threatened at one stage to get 100 before lunch.

At that time I had no idea how highly he was regarded. How close he must have been to selection in the Test Matches was shown when, at the end of the season, he was invited to tour South Africa with the M.C.C. team.

There were some good knocks played against us at various times, but apart from batsmen who played in the Tests, none better than this splendid exhibition of stroke play by the diminutive school teacher.

In this opening match, I commenced a plan of campaign which probably played a large part in Ray Lindwall's ultimate success.

During the English tour of Australia in 1946-7, a sort of whispering campaign was started about Lindwall dragging over the line—the critics claiming that he should be no-balled.

I don't know who started it. I am sure the English players did not suppress the idea. Some of them had clearly shown that they disliked very fast bowling, and anything to curb his extra speed would naturally be to their advantage.

Anyway, a movie film of Lindwall's bowling was taken and shown in Australia not very long before our departure for England. I was present at a private screening in Adelaide.

The film revealed deliveries where Lindwall's back foot was well over the bowling crease before the ball was actually delivered. This was caused by his excessive drag. Fortunately, in the same film, an old shot of Larwood was revived which indicated that he, too, was an offender— even if not to the same extent.

Now this film was obviously going to England in advance of us and would be seen there. It could be used as propaganda amongst English umpires whose views were not known to me.

The movie camera is not a fair test because it sees the whole action from a distance, side on. It reproduces the co-ordination of foot and hand clearly visible in exact focus, whereas the umpire, standing close to the bowler, cannot possibly watch hand and foot together.

I don't think one fast bowler in ten would bowl fairly (according to the camera) if he were to put his back foot just behind the bowling crease in the act of delivery. The momentum of his run and body-swing must drag him across the line before the ball leaves the hand. Nevertheless, I maintain that the spirit of the law is being observed providing the foot is placed clearly behind the line.

In Lindwall's case I feared the effect on his morale if he were no-balled

165

early in the tour. More than that I feared the effect it would have on umpires throughout the country who had not yet seen him, but who would read about it and subconsciously perhaps become prejudiced in advance. Accordingly, I impressed upon him the absolute necessity for :—

(a) Keeping his back foot a long way behind the bowling crease, and

(b) not trying to bowl really fast until he had got through several matches and in particular had passed the close scrutiny of Frank Chester.

In the first match we had as umpires Fred. Root (ex-international player and good umpire) and D. Davies (who officiated in some of the Tests). They both had a good look at Lindwall and were well satisfied. Thus an early hurdle was overcome.

As the season progressed and Lindwall began to liven up, the umpires adopted what appeared to be a very sensible attitude.

They knew he dragged a long way, but they also knew their own limitations as regards watching hand and foot simultaneously. So they gave him a margin of about 12 inches—some umpires may have required 18 inches—and so long as Lindwall kept back to this extent, they passed his deliveries as fair.

I must admit there were times when individual instances of no-ball calls met with our disapproval—not only in Lindwall's case. We gained the impression that occasionally, if an umpire missed a no-ball call, he would place a far stricter interpretation on the law next ball. The same thing had been noticed in Australia.

Maybe this was imagination, but I don't think so.

There should not be any question of " evening up " and if an umpire does miss a no-ball, and realises it, that should be the end of the matter.

Anyway this long-range plan for Lindwall worked out very well. It was designed to help Ray and to give the umpires time and opportunity to study his particular delivery and form their own opinions.

That was fair to all parties and I must compliment the English umpires for deciding the issue on their own judgment. They were not swayed by films or critics.

I thought it rather a pity that Fred. Root lost his qualifications as a potential Test umpire because of his contributions to the press. He struck me as being most efficient.

There was the traditional dinner at Worcester in the evening of the first day's play, but Lord Cobham, who presided, very wisely and generously paid regard to our heavy programme by deciding on no speeches.

During the remainder of the match it became obvious that our players were short of practice. Still, they showed signs of adaptability and Arthur Morris, who opened and made a century, left those who saw his innings in no doubt about his capacity to handle English wickets.

It was at Worcester that I had made a double century in the first match of our 1930, 1934 and 1938 tours. On all sides there was the query—would I do it again ? Well, frankly, I think I could have done so, but having made a century, I threw my innings away. We had an unusually large number of new players and I wanted them to have batting experience under English conditions. My own form was obviously all right, but my injured side was still troubling me and I felt it unwise to carry on beyond a certain point.

Eventually the match was won comfortably, but not before we had seen some impressive off-spin bowling by Jackson, who showed our lads how much more responsive to spin are the English wickets. I'm sure Colin McCool still remembers seeing his leg stump knocked back by a ball at which he did not even attempt a stroke.

Our next encounter was against Leicester where the bitterly cold, damp weather was even more unkind to us than it had been at Worcester. The people braved the elements just the same and were rewarded by an outstanding innings of over 200 not out by Keith Miller, who had been promoted to first wicket down so that he could run into form.

Considering the conditions, our bowlers, notably Ring and Ian Johnson, did splendidly to give us an easy victory.

An interesting feature of the Leicester match was the performances of Walsh and Jackson, both Sydney boys who are now regular players for Leicester. Jackson does very well with his off-spinners and makes a lot of runs, but Walsh, with his Fleetwood-Smith type of left-hand googly bowling is much more to be feared. He is right up with the leading wicket-takers, and the very best English batsmen have the greatest respect for his bowling.

Things were now swinging along quite smoothly, so I decided to rest for the Yorkshire match at Bradford. We were to play them again later.

Not being present, I must rely on second-hand evidence, but it seems pretty clear that this was the closest to defeat our team came on tour.

Apparently the damp wicket took spin from the start. Miller and Bill Johnston bowled extremely well, the latter demonstrating for the first time how valuable his spinners (as distinct from his fast medium stuff) would become when conditions suited them.

Our team suffered a big loss when Loxton strained a leg muscle and could not bat. This left Australia a batsman and a bowler short—a fact not to be overlooked when the closeness of the match is being analysed.

The baby of our side, Neil Harvey, must have made the tough Yorkshiremen gasp when he finished the match with a glorious six. They are not accustomed to such cavalier cricket in a tight finish, or for that matter at any time.

Yorkshire were not, at that stage, regarded as likely contenders for the County Championship, but somehow or other this team is always hard to beat, especially up North. It has a wonderful capacity to rise to the occasion—to fight back, and it has not always been an idle boast by the Yorkshire supporters that their county could match the skill of the All-England side.

The Australians came back from that match very much richer in experience. It was probably a good thing to have been so hard pressed by a County early in the tour. Such lessons are a valuable brake on complacency which can so easily arise when the opposition isn't too strong.

I stayed in London whilst the team was away up North and enjoyed, in particular, one evening which was for me a great thrill. A friend invited me to dine with his family at the Savoy. By accident or design my chair was only a few feet from Carroll Gibbons who was personally conducting his Savoy Orpheans.

Carroll Gibbons had been one of my favourite pianists for years, and I revelled in this opportunity to see and hear him at close quarters. Moreover, he took me down to the dressing room, introduced me to his boys and we did some duo-playing which, though it couldn't have been very interesting to him, was a compliment to me and one which I valued very highly. Such happy personal, non-cricket experiences occur all too briefly, for there is little rest. I was back on the field again for the next match v. Surrey.

The Oval still showed scars from the ravages of war, though the wicket seemed less heartbreaking to the bowlers than in that nightmare game of 1938. Workmen were painting the big gasometer green, which I thought a decided improvement on the previous colour scheme.

We were delighted to meet Brian Castor, Secretary of Surrey, showing no physical or mental sign that he had a few years earlier been a victim of Japanese cruelty in a prison camp. Incidentally, one of his best mates whilst enduring that dreadful experience was our former wicket-keeper Ben Barnett, who, I am delighted to say, also returned safe and sound to his loved ones. Charming personality Ben—the best amateur conjurer I ever saw.

I was anxious to see how Alec Bedser would bowl under English conditions. He had impressed me tremendously in Australia and I always felt he would be better still in England. Despite the fact that I made a century, he finally bowled me with a glorious ball which pitched on the leg stump and hit the off—the same type of ball as that with which he bowled me for 0 in Adelaide in 1947.

Later in the innings, after Hassett had made a century and was seeing the ball splendidly, he too was bowled by one of the same type. There and then I instinctively knew Bedser would be the bowler we would have to fear most in the Tests.

We were lucky in that the wicket began to wear rather quickly and the Surrey batsmen were unable to cope with our spinners. Laurie Fishlock was a notable exception, for he carried his bat through the first innings and batted extremely well. Some of his drives to mid-off were terrific.

We were not at all sorry that Fishlock was passed over by the Selectors throughout the season.

In the end Australia won the match with 20 minutes to spare, but not before we had seen Neil Harvey take an outfield catch which I unhesitatingly rate as the greatest of its kind I've ever seen. A towering drive seemed certain to go for 6, but Neil, running flat out to the left, took the catch high above his head and wide on his left side as he jumped feet into the air. The ball would have gone well over the ropes, and it was some seconds before even the players realised he had made the catch—it seemed an impossibility that he could even reach it.

During this match we had to attend two more official dinners. The first was given by the Surrey County C.C. in the lovely Armourers and Braziers Hall. Lord Rosebery presided.

The dinner coincided with the 75th birthday of Mr. H. D. G. Leveson-Gower who has been identified for so long with the Surrey Club. He was the recipient of birthday greetings on all sides and cut a beautiful cake specially made for the occasion.

I clearly remember his speech in which he very charmingly made appropriate reference to the Supreme Umpire to whom he was so thankful for having given him the benefit of the doubt for 75 years.

One other dinner was held, this time under the Chairmanship of Sir Stanley Holmes in the Harcourt Room at the House of Commons. The Rt. Hon. C. Attlee, Prime Minister of England, did us the honour of attending and proposing the toast of the Australians.

After the Surrey game a relatively easy part of the programme ensued, and I decided to take a rest from the two University games. Their standard has declined from the halcyon days when an Australian XI could not count on the result as a foregone conclusion. Why, I don't know. I do know it is a bad thing for English cricket.

During the Cambridge match I again stayed in London and attended to many things which could not be fitted in during matches.

One such engagement was to dine as the guest of Lord McGowan and the Board of Directors of Imperial Chemical Industries Ltd. There were numerous other guests and some brief witty speeches. I recall one by Mr. A. V. Alexander who wove into the pattern of his address the story of a nervous suitor who was asked by his prospective father-in-law, " Young man, are your intentions honourable or dishonourable ? " and before having time to reflect upon the consequences of his answer, the young man blurted out, " Sir, I didn't know I had the choice."

Another engagement was to dine with the Chairman and Committee of the London Stock Exchange and to go over that great institution.

True to tradition, I was greeted on the floor by an enthusiastic audience. They had left a small space in the middle where a cricket pitch had been rigged up—all implements provided and one of the members bedecked as W. G. to do battle with me.

Perhaps the most amusing thing was the whisky and soda provided at the bowler's end. That may have been in accordance with the tradition of the Grace era—I don't know—it certainly doesn't exist today.

Anyway, I entered into the spirit of the occasion and the match ended when I hit the ball into some far corner of the building from which, so far as I know, neither the bulls nor the bears returned it.

Another visit worth mentioning was a brief one to the British Industries Fair. My one regret was that after having travelled so far, so little time was available to explore this exhibition of Britsh skill and craftsmanship.

During my sojourn in London, the Cambridge team was disposed of and our next encounter was against Essex at Southend. We were greeted by a balmy day, blue sky, good wicket and fast outfield.

A picnic atmosphere pervaded the crowd and must also have affected our batsmen, for in one day's batting Australia put together, by super-lative play, a total of 721 runs. This is, I believe, a world's record for one day in first-class cricket. It was simply fantastic.

Man after man scored at breath-taking speed by beautiful strokes which left the fieldsmen helpless. Strange to say, right in the middle of it all, the one man who might have really created a riot of runs, Keith Miller, was bowled first ball for 0.

No doubt there will be people who will say the Essex attack must have been poor or something must have been very much in Australia's favour.

Well, apart from the good wicket and the fast outfield already referred to, I would like these facts to be recorded.

The ground was of average size and most certainly larger than some we played on.

The opposing captain was Tom Pearce, a man of wide experience. His four main bowlers were Trevor Bailey, rated the best bowler at Cambridge and one of the most promising fast-medium boys in Eng-land—later in the year to be selected for the Gentlemen v. Australia and to play for England in 1949—Ray Smith, a very useful fast-medium who bowled in-swingers to a leg field, a type of bowling hard to score from, Peter Smith (one of Wisdens 5 Cricketers of the year in 1946) who was brought to Australia in 1946-7 as understudy to Doug. Wright and rated then as the second best slow in England, and Price, a left-hander, formerly of Lancashire, who had in 1946 headed that County's bowling averages and who was selected as a member of one of England's Test Trial teams in the same year.

Here, it seemed to me, was the first really tangible sign that we possessed a team of exceptional batting strength, one which would scourge any but the very best bowling.

It was a meritorious achievement and all credit must go to the Australians who maintained throughout the opening day of the match a scoring rate of over two runs a minute.

On the Monday, just for full measure and as evidence that the pitch was not altogether a batsman's paradise, our bowlers dismissed the Essex team twice in one day and thus gave us a colossal victory.

Upon returning to London, I accepted an invitation to dine at Grosvenor House as the guest of Sir Norman and Lady Brookes.

A distinguished company was present and we were travelling in the lift to the dining-room when for some reason it got out of control and crashed to the bottom.

The Rt. Hon. J. A. Beasley (Australia's High Commissioner) and his wife were in the party and were rather distressed, although most of us were quite unhurt.

Still, I can assure you it is a somewhat terrifying experience and one which I don't recommend for pleasure.

Our team had a kind of final work-out against Oxford and then came what might reasonably be regarded as the first major trial of the tour—our match versus a strong M.C.C. XI at Lord's.

If we benefited unduly on the tour by winning any toss it was prob- ably this one. The wicket was good and despite Yardley's efforts to keep runs down we scored all day at a steady pace. Miller made a fine century, I managed 98, whilst Barnes and Hassett also made good scores.

Rain came during the weekend and although it did not at once make the wicket difficult, luck was with us because the pitch gradually deteriorated.

On the Monday morning I instructed our boys to go for the runs. Seldom can the spectators at Lord's have been treated to a better exhibi- tion of hitting than that by Miller, Lindwall and Johnson. No less than twelve sixes went sailing up into the crowd before lunch—not just over the fence but high into the stands.

In the afternoon Ern Toshack gave what I regard as his best bowling performance of the tour. He kept one end going from 2-15 to 5-20 p.m.—27 overs, and took 6 for 51. Not one batsman faced him with any confidence, and the struggle between Compton and Toshack was worth going a long way to see. It ended in a victory for Toshack. An excellent ball which went away towards slips, was deflected and Tallon, who ran into his finest form in this game, held a wonderful catch.

We enforced the follow-on, got them out again before lunch next day, and I began to have confidence that we could more than hold our own with any team England could pit against us.

Our next encounter was with Lancashire where it was our turn to suffer the worst end of the conditions.

Rain on the opening day made play out of the question, and on the second day when Ken Cranston beat me to the toss he unhesitatingly sent us in. We struggled pretty hard to make 204 on a wicket made very uncertain by the rain.

Eventually we dismissed our opponents for a smaller figure and the match ended in a draw.

A notable incident was my dismissal in each innings by young Hilton, a 19-year-old left-hand spin bowler, who was playing his first match. This boy bowled very accurately and intelligently. He spun the ball and altogether put up what I thought to be quite an impressive performance.

Unfortunately the press made a terrific song about my being dismissed twice. It was, of course, a fact, and all credit to the boy who thoroughly deserved my wicket on each occasion, but in emphasising this aspect, I think the general excellence of his bowling was pushed into the background.

Some papers immediately advocated his inclusion in the Tests, and the lad received a vast amount of publicity.

In cases such as this, I believe the press should be careful to treat things in their proper perspective.

Hilton is a bowler of the Hedley Verity type and could hardly be expected to meet with abnormal success unless the wicket was all in favour of the bowlers. He was too young and inexperienced to be thrown against Australia when the pressure was really on and batting conditions good. But nevertheless he is a boy of undoubted talent who should be fostered and encouraged as a future hope.

I must admit I am still mystified as to why he was later in the season dropped from the Lancashire side.

I'm afraid it is characteristic of England that the young player must really win his spurs the hard way.

Before leaving the Lancashire match I should record how pleased I was to see Neil Harvey and Sam Loxton reveal evidence of better form. Sam had been troubled by his leg and therefore was denied opportunities, but Neil had been rather slow to find his feet on the turning wickets. He was destined to make amends before long in no uncertain manner.

Our next game was against Nottingham where as usual we found a typical Trent Bridge wicket awaiting us.

The local county made an excellent start, and with Hardstaff and Simpson batting, a large score seemed in prospect. Joe rather unluckily touched on the leg side the first ball he received after lunch to give the wicket-keeper an easy catch.

This started a collapse and in the end Lindwall had the extraordinary analysis of 15·1 overs, 6 wickets, 14 runs. Ray was gradually working up into good condition.

A letter I received at this stage of the tour gives some idea of the diverse and ridiculous queries which reached me from time to time. The writer told me how his uncle, named Brown, had left for Australia about 1907 bound for Sydney or Melbourne—he was not sure which. He wanted to settle down on a farm. The query was : could I tell him whether the Browns had their farm and were they prospering ? There are incredible people on this earth.

The Sunday of the Nottingham match was full of interest as we were entertained for the day at Welbeck Abbey by the Duke and Duchess of Portland. I had a special interest in this visit because in 1934, my wife and I had stayed at the Abbey as guests of the Duke, father of the present Duke.

During a discussion at that time he had told me quite frankly that upon his death, the expense of keeping up the big Abbey would be too much for his son. Therefore, he had already built a smaller home on the property in order that his son may become accustomed to such a reality.

Here in 1948 was the evidence before my own eyes. The old Abbey was now occupied by the military authorities. The lovely dining-room, the walls of which had been decorated by glorious Rembrandts, was now an officers' mess—coco-nut matting on the floor. Where picturesque lawns and flower gardens formerly existed was now to a large extent natural growth. Only one portion remained unchanged—the wing in which the Dowager still resided. She proudly showed me round and once again I admired those visions of loveliness—portraits of her by De Lazlo and Sargent, painted when she was young.

Despite her advancing years, the Dowager was still a beautiful woman, and her intellect razor-keen.

I must admit this visual evidence of a change in the social structure brought about by modern economic conditions caused me to think deeply. If the people as a whole are benefiting one cannot complain, though I could not escape the feeling that I had witnessed the passing of a traditional element of English life. It left a deep pang of remorse.

In the afternoon we were taken for a drive through Sherwood Forest, the face of which had also been defiled during the war years where the woodman's axe had cleared millions of feet of timber.

One humorous incident occurred during the drive. We came to a gate and despite repeated tooting no sign of life emerged from the nearby lodge. Eventually the Duke got out and went inside. Our players in the bus speculated as to how the Duke would deal with his negligent servant and predicted at least severe admonishment.

After a few moments, a dear old pensioner, legs and back bent with age and walking by the aid of a stick, sallied forth to open the gate. As the Duke re-entered the bus we questioned him as to what occurred. The boys were convulsed with laughter at the reply.

Said the Duke : " I went in and asked, ' What about opening the gates,' and the retort came back, ' And what about you puttin' in a pane of glass in my window like you promised.' " Sure enough the Duke had forgotten a request received from the old man some days earlier.

Altogether a memorable day. The Duke and Duchess proved themselves delightful people, and we were indeed grateful for their warmhearted hospitality.

We concluded our match v. Notts on the Tuesday.

Joe Hardstaff made a splendid century—the first against us on the tour—whilst young Simpson, who batted extremely well in each innings and fielded brilliantly, caused us to think, " Here is one of England's future batsmen."

From the Australian point of view a disaster occurred.

I gave Colin McCool an extended trial as we were approaching the Tests. It was necessary to run him into form and also to work out our prospective test combination. To my dismay, Colin's finger, third one on the right hand, gave way.

It was a peculiar injury. This finger is the one which imparts spin to the ball and the constant friction had set up a small callus or corn which in turn appeared to tear away, thus exposing the raw flesh. The wound would heal quickly, but that was not much compensation, as we obviously couldn't risk it happening in the middle of a Test.

Unless he found some cure it seemed beyond doubt that Colin could not be expected to play the part of a stock bowler, and he was downcast at the prospect.

The injury did improve during the tour, but even at the close would still reveal itself after a hard spell of bowling.

Colin deserves great praise for the fortitude he displayed and the light-hearted way in which he cloaked his own disappointment in order not to disturb the general harmony of the team.

His problem was not an isolated case. Other spin bowlers suffer in a similar way, though the exact position of the callus varies.

This may be a fruitful field for experiment by a skin specialist or whoever would be best qualified to advise on such a subject.

We could never make up our minds whether the cure was to harden the skin so that it would stand the strain or to soften the skin and thereby prevent the hard callus forming.

Our next encounter was versus Hampshire, and once more I took an opportunity to rest.

I was staying with friends just outside London, and as Hampshire were not regarded as formidable opponents, I did not trouble to get progress scores until the end of the first day's play.

To my surprise, the team was meeting strong opposition. My mind went back to the match against Yorkshire.

Eventually, when it became obvious that there were prospects of an Australian defeat, I felt impelled to despatch an urgent wire to Lindsay Hassett saying, "Bradford was bad enough but this is unbearable, heads up and chins down."

The latter part of my telegram may have presented a problem, but my meaning was clear.

When at lunch time on the final day I heard the score—Australia second innings, 1 wicket for 3, Barnes out, I became very apprehensive, but my fears were unnecessary for the lads rose to the occasion and won by a handsome margin.

Reports indicated that Ian Johnson, promoted in the batting order, played a splendid innings and further demonstrated how valuable it is to have bowlers who can do their share with the bat when the recognised batsmen are fighting hard.

We had only one more county fixture before the First Test—Sussex at Hove. It turned out to be an easy game. The Sussex attack was never hostile and our batsmen, now running along in top form handled them somewhat roughly.

Arthur Morris started the century habit. I also notched one and then Neil Harvey brilliantly completed the trio.

Evidence was accumulating that Harvey would be knocking very hard at the door for Test selection.

Ray Lindwall bowled magnificently. He was not at his fastest, but had a nice breeze which enabled him to swing the ball rather late. The Sussex players were all at sea to him.

Sam Loxton also bowled well but once more his leg gave way, so he was out of the running for the First Test.

The unlucky player of the match was Ron Hamence. I had decided to close Australia's innings at the end of the over and was actually standing up on the balcony in readiness to give the signal to the opposing captain, when Ron was given out L.B.W. to the last ball of the over.

Then to Nottingham, where once more the cream of England and Australia met—the first Test there for ten long years.

No wonder the cricket lovers of England looked forward so expectantly to the game.

The First Test

GREAT CARE WAS TAKEN OVER THE SELECTION OF AUSTRALIA'S TEAM. We discussed at length the tactics likely to bring us victory and the possible counter measures.

McCool and Loxton were unfit, a wicket-keeper had to be omitted.

Hamence was not in good enough form and Harvey scarcely ready, so the final choice was Bill Johnston or Ring.

The rain clouds were ominous, the wicket greasy, and after considering the matter from all angles, we decided to stake our hopes on speed rather than spin, knowing that Johnston could revert to spinners if the conditions so warranted.

What a fortunate decision it was !

Norman Yardley won the toss and thus carried on where Hammond left off, but it was a mixed blessing.

On returning to the Australian dressing room, not sure whether I was pleased or sorry, I remarked to the team, " That might be the luckiest toss I've ever lost."   Yardley just simply had to bat.   The wicket was a beauty and rain was in the air.

The English collapse which followed was dramatic.   First blood came when Miller clean bowled Hutton, middle stump, with a ball of beautiful length and venomous speed which crashed through Hutton's defences before he could bring his body to obey the impulses of his brain.

Bill Johnston did the same to Edrich and continued to bowl superbly, but again it was Miller who struck the heavy blow—this time by knocking Compton's leg stump over.   Denis had moved too far across and to his great astonishment was bowled round his legs.

Memories were revived of another great player, Bill Ponsford, who in his efforts to overcome a fallibility against fast bowling, committed the same error on more than one occasion and paid the penalty.

Despite Brown's brilliant catching of Washbrook on the leg boundary, our fielding was not without blemish.   Ian Johnson dropped a comparatively easy slip catch, whilst I was the worst offender, dropping two catches at cover in one over off Godfrey Evans.   Fortunately, the mistakes were soon rectified.   I was grateful to Arthur Morris who atoned for my lapses by brilliantly catching Evans at short-leg off a powerful drive.

We had, of course, hoped that Lindwall would be the destroyer but as events turned out he suffered from fielding errors and later on strained a leg muscle.   The ground surface was not exactly wet but it was greasy and in delivering a ball, Ray's foot slipped and he could bowl no more.

Hence the tremendous value of Miller's and Johnston's efforts.   They bowled with great courage on other occasions, but I doubt whether either man will ever be able to recall an occasion where his bowling so directly contributed to that break-through so vital to victory.

This was the one match on the tour when, owing to Lindwall's breakdown, I was compelled to use Miller rather severely.   He stood the test splendidly.

When, in 1949, Miller was omitted from the South African tour, I was in some quarters accused of being responsible. It was said that I had over-bowled him in England, thereby spoiling his chances.

That was utter nonsense.

Miller in 1948 bowled 429 overs (of which a goodly percentage were slow off-breaks) and batted 26 times, making 1,088 runs.

Compare that with such efforts as Ted McDonald (854 overs) or Ernie Jones (868 overs), both much faster than Miller. C. T. B. Turner on one tour bowled the equivalent of 1,295 overs (8-ball).

Jack Gregory in 1921 bowled 681 overs and batted 35 times for 1,171 runs.

For his three tours Armstrong averaged 881 overs, 47 innings and 1,523 runs. Armstrong, admittedly, was not a fast bowler, but his vast bulk was in direct contrast to Miller's athletic figure.

I applaud Miller for a fine job but the critics must be honest. He was not overworked in 1948. Indeed he was very carefully nursed throughout, except for this Nottingham Test.

After all the recognised batsmen had been dismissed, it was left to Laker and Bedser to hold us at bay. They did it with great pluck and no mean skill, even though our bowlers had prodigally spent their energy in the early part of the day in a super-effort to go through the side.

When Australia batted at 6-15 p.m., I was most anxious, but no disaster came.

So my tentative prophecy about the loss of the toss was more than fulfilled.

I must, in fairness to England, say that the failure of her batsmen was largely due to the lack of a sightboard at the pavilion end. The light may be good enough to continue play and yet bad enough to make it mighty difficult to pick up the flight of the ball. Add to this both the mental and physical handicap of suddenly playing under these conditions against bowling much faster than anything you normally encounter. And remember you've only got to miss one ball—that's enough.

At Nottingham, even when the weather was good, we all found some difficulty in sighting the ball at the pavilion end.

English authorities are very casual about such details. They don't always appear to regard the player's requirements as Priority No. 1.

This question of sightboards is a problem at Nottingham, Leeds (where there are none at all), the Oval and Lord's. It may enable a few more spectators to see the game—in other words it may add a few pounds to the gate money—but that won't compensate for somebody getting cracked on the head one day.

And where the lack of a sightboard concerns the members' pavilion it is a clear-cut issue as to whether the players or the members shall receive priority. Frankly, it should be the players.

Unfortunately, the people responsible for these decisions are generally men who are not current players and the view-point of the man actually providing the entertainment is often relegated to the background.

No first-class match is played in Australia without sightboards being provided at both ends, and I strongly recommend this practice to all English ground authorities.

I have been diverted somewhat from the Test Match, but I thought this a suitable moment to make my point.

The second day's play developed into a battle of tactics.

At first the bowlers attacked and met with moderate success, Evans' catching of Barnes being one of the most miraculous feats of recovery as well as acrobatics one would see in a long time.

Later on, when Hassett and I were making a stand, Yardley gave up all idea of offensive play. For instance, when Bedser was bowling to me, fine-leg, third-man, mid-wicket and cover were all stationed on the fence. Most certainly my batting did not demand such a field.

Then Charlie Barnett, a medium-pace right-hander, proceeded to bowl with 6 men on the leg-side. Most of his deliveries were allowed to pass 6 inches to a foot outside the leg stump.

Laker and Young also operated for some time to this field placing.

It was purely negative cricket. We were not going to be stupid enough to throw our wickets away, but neither could we score more than an occasional run.

Although it seemed a bit early for England to decide that she could do no better than make a draw of the match, Yardley was in command of his own forces and could do as he pleased. I had no quarrel with that, but his tactics ruined the game as a spectacle, and the crowd, quite openly pro-English, vigorously barracked the Australian batsmen for the slow play.

This was not very pleasant when we were in no way responsible, but I am prepared to give the public the benefit of the doubt. They were possibly voicing disappointment as much as anything.

On the third day, England had a new ball to start with and almost at once Bedser accidentally had me caught at leg slip. I say accidentally because, firstly, I need not have played at the ball. But I strongly dislike this modern habit of bowling medium pace in-swingers to a modified leg field (not for any personal reason but simply because I think its general effect on the game itself is bad), and therefore I tried to drive the ball through this field. Secondly, the ball travelled very fast and hit Hutton on the chest, after which his hands closed over it. Had the ball gone a few inches either side it would never have been caught as he would not have had time to pick up its flight.

Accident or not, this catch had a profound effect on the tactics employed by the English bowlers against me in future matches. I shall refer to them later on.

Some very fine batting by Hassett ably supported by Lindwall took our total to respectable dimensions.

Lindwall's leg was still troublesome and I sought Yardley's permission to have a runner for him. This was readily forthcoming.

It provided an Australian writer with an opportunity to attack me for seeking a runner and for claiming that one should not be allowed under the circumstances.

It is indeed difficult to follow the reasoning of some writers.

The laws of cricket provide that under certain conditions a substitute runner may be asked for, and places the onus on the captain for deciding the legitimacy of the request which, I should add, is not likely to be frivolously made nor lightly granted in Test cricket. By the same token, no player is expected to make such exertions on the field of sport that he may cause himself great physical pain and risk possible permanent injury.

In the case under review, Lindwall was not gravely handicapped when making strokes, but he was unable to run and did not bowl again in the match.

I refer to the criticism in the hope that my remarks may put things in a clearer light for those who were inclined to accept the views of the writer at a time when no corrective statement could be forthcoming.

Towards the close of the third day's play, and after England had lost a couple of early wickets, Hutton and Compton made a stand. In an effort to force a catch off a hook shot, Miller sent down a few short-pitched balls.

Now Miller was, on this occasion, not above fast medium, the wicket was easy paced with no lift in it, and there were never more than three men on the leg side. The batsmen were not in any danger. Hutton certainly got hit on the arm, but it was by a ball to which he ducked but which he could have comfortably played, scarcely more than waist high, by standing erect.

His mannerisms caused the crowd to think he resented it. The result was one of the most hostile demonstrations against a bowler that I've ever heard. Even the members' pavilion was the scene of vigorous booing of our team but especially Miller, as we left the field.

It was a senseless and embarrassing demonstration on the part of the people who allowed their feelings to be swayed by sentiment not judgment.

There is still a prevalent feeling at Nottingham that Australia, in some way or other, was responsible for Larwood's exit from cricket. This is, of course, quite untrue, as I hope I've made clear elsewhere in my book when dealing with body-line.

The fact remains that one bumper bowled at Nottingham in 1948 was still sufficient to raise hostile shouts of, " You wouldn't do that if we had Larwood." Would Larwood have done it in 1932 if we had possessed Lindwall, and so on *ad infinitum*—the argument is senseless.

To the everlasting credit of the Notts County Club, their President called on me and apologised for the unseemly behaviour of the crowd.

Before play started on the Monday, the Secretary (over the amplifier) severely reprimanded the public for Saturday's outburst and appealed for the exercise of a more rational outlook.

Monday was a day of interruptions caused by bad light and rain. Our players were not at their best under these typically English conditions, especially in the field where errors crept in. Even so, they fought on splendidly, one bowler short, and only the grand innings of Compton, who remained undefeated at stumps, kept the English flag aloft.

Denis was not quite at his top. He was missed in slips, twice behind the wicket, survived a perilously close L.B.W. and a stumping, but he stuck grimly to his task.

The occasion did not allow him to revel in playing shots or the type of game he enjoys. Indeed I thought this capacity to subjugate his personal feelings in the interests of the side revealed a more mature Compton—the one historians will write about rather than the gay debonair lad of 1938.

The game concluded just before tea on the fifth and final day. There were many anxious moments before the end.

Compton's lone hand terminated when he was in sight of his 200. A really vicious bumper from Miller caught him unawares, and in trying to make a reflex hook he trod on his wicket.

This ball caused a further mild outburst from the crowd, but let me record that in an innings which extended over some 6½ hours, only two real bumpers were sent down at him, one of which got him out. If that is transgressing the spirit of cricket, I am a very poor judge.

Despite valuable help from Evans, England set us a mere 98 to win.

The only thing that could save England was rain, which threatened and caused me to wave anxiously to Barnes and Hassett, who handled the situation with great skill and wisdom.

Prior to that I had again fallen a victim to what now became known as Bedser's leg trap. I refused to be chained down into inactivity by an obvious plan, and paid the penalty with my eyes open, to the delight of some partisan spectators who thought they saw in this old-fashioned device some new theory which would save England.

My own duck did not even register against my delight at our success. One up in England means much more than one up in Australia. We now had to lose two out of four matches for England to win the rubber, and, even with my calculatingly pessimistic outlook, I would not concede it as a likely possibility, all things being equal.

Further Progress

ONCE AGAIN I DECIDED TO HAVE A REST DURING THE COMPARATIVELY easy game against Northampton. Physically, I was standing the strain well, but there is always a nerve-racking "something" about the opening Test of a series which is not apparent in the remaining games unless it so happens that one match becomes the decider.

It was not that we were ever near defeat at Nottingham, but the suspense persisted right to the end as to whether we could force a win against time and elements combined.

Our team did not run into any difficulty at Northampton, but we were all extremely keen to put up a good show in the next game, which was the return match against Yorkshire.

There was the immediate memory of that hectic game at Bradford—the long distance one of 1938 at Bramall Lane when undoubtedly the honours were with Yorkshire.

Our team rather held the view that Bradford was more a question of bad cricket by Australia than good cricket by Yorkshire. True or not, we were taking no chances this time and played a strong side.

I have always contended that Yorkshire crowds really understand cricket better than the people elsewhere in England—further that the Bramall Lane crowd is the best Yorkshire crowd.

On this day, despite threatening clouds, the people were out in force. Long before the first ball was bowled one could sense the "atmosphere." It was like a Test Match but more intimate and concentrated.

My luck was in, for I beat Yardley to the toss, and the appearance of the wicket suggested I had already gained a substantial advantage.

This proved to be correct but it was quickly off-set, for a tremendous roar announced the dismissal of Sid Barnes whose middle stump was uprooted by Aspinall's third ball—a yorker.

As I walked out to bat, the air was electrical. The Yorkshire crowd was right on its toes, sensing something sensational, and if it were possible to capture the feeling of a gladiator entering a bull-ring, I'm sure this was the nearest I'll ever get to it.

Despite showers and periods of extreme gloom due to heavy storm clouds, we had practically a full day's cricket—full of incident. Yorkshire's fielding was keen, captaincy aggressive, bowling hostile, and we had to fight every inch of the way for a modest total of 249. The crowd must have inspired the Yorkshire players, who had from all accounts been transformed since Bradford.

In the early stages it seemed that we might be dismissed for less than 200, but finally we did better, due largely to courageous knocks by Hamence and Harvey.

This was my first encounter with Verity's successor—Wardle. I studied him closely and must say he bowled impressively. There was the usual immaculate length, direction perhaps astray at times, good spin and a deceptiveness of flight more reminiscent of Rhodes than of Verity.

Eventually I was caught at cover in attempting to drive a ball which dropped shorter than I had anticipated. Throughout the tour no other bowler of this type worried us with flight to anything like the same extent as Wardle.

On the second day of the match, the wicket was wet following the weekend rain. Conditions were such that I had to use our two left-handers Johnston and Toshack almost throughout. They did a lion-hearted job despite a lack of support in the field. For once, our lads started to drop catches. Instead of predominating in the field, our showing compared unfavourably with Yorkshire's.

Even so, we dismissed the opposition for just over 200, thus giving us roughly a 20 per cent margin on the first innings.

When the wicket is taken into account, I think the Yorkshire total certainly merits being considered equal to ours and they deserve great credit for a fine showing.

Ernie Toshack's seven wickets were his reward for a marathon effort.

In our second innings we again lost Barnes early. Then at the critical stage, when the result of the match might still have been in the balance, the Yorkshiremen themselves dropped catches.

The game finally ended in a draw very much in Australia's favour, but I'm sure all who witnessed it—including ourselves—came away with a firm conviction that Yorkshire cricket is again on the up-grade. The places of Leyland, Sutcliffe, Verity and others may not yet have been filled by men of the same skill, but at least the same pugnacious fighting spirit is there.

Without it, and the temperament which lifts one's performances to the highest degree when the opposition is strongest, skill is not always the dominating factor.

Having come through this trial with the colours still nailed to the masthead, even if not exactly flying in the breeze, we returned to Lord's for the Second Test.

Yardley and I inspected the wicket at length before tossing. We did not convey our thoughts to one another for tactical reasons, but I have no doubt we felt the same apprehension.

This wicket was green. It had not thoroughly dried out. Yet the winner of the toss could not risk sending the other side in.

When the coin did spin, I called correctly—the one and only time I was to achieve it in Test Matches in England. I don't think any other captain has lost such a proportion of tosses in two series as I did in 1938 and 1948. Moreover, I'm sure *no* captain has won the only toss he wanted to lose.

Reluctantly then, I decided to bat.

My fears were quickly translated into the realm of fact when Coxon, the new Yorkshire Test recruit, had Barnes caught for 0.

Once more I found myself in the midst of a grim struggle, for such it was. The ball came off at different heights and paces—the seamsters used the heavy atmosphere and green pitch superbly.

At lunch time Arthur Morris and I were still there, but it could scarcely be said we were entirely responsible.

I was missed by Hutton, and Evans had the mortification of missing Arthur Morris, then (later in the day) catching him, only to find the umpire's decision go in favour of the batsman.

My own innings ended soon after lunch, and we had to thank Morris and Hassett for saving Australia from what might easily have been disaster.

I would like to dwell for a moment on Arthur Morris's innings.

Prior to the Lord's Test, Arthur had displayed good form under easy batting conditions, but had been in great difficulties when he encountered a turning wicket or a green-top. I was just a little concerned in my mind, for Arthur has a peculiar style. It is not orthodox and demands exceptional skill to surmount what might be construed as technical faults.

As his innings at Lord's progressed, so did his cricketing brain absorb the lessons. His batting visibly improved before our eyes. The measure of his superiority became more evident when a great batsman like Miller found the conditions beyond him while, at the same time, Morris was giving a superb display. Only the supreme combination of eyesight and natural genius could have done it.

From that day onwards Arthur Morris was a far greater player than ever before, and no longer could anyone doubt him, no matter what conditions were encountered.

At the close of play one had to admit England were on top. The local supporters had cause to be jubilant.

Not so the next evening, for Friday was Australia's day with a vengeance. First, our tail wagged in a manner quite unexpected under these conditions, Tallon, Lindwall and even Johnston and Toshack all performed grandly.

When it came our turn to field, we were under the dual handicap of not having Miller to bowl at all owing to a back injury and Lindwall still carrying the leg which had gone on him at Nottingham. We only played Lindwall after much serious discussion and a severe trial at the nets, and when it became obvious he was gravely handicapped, I had visions of another breakdown. But Ray Lindwall has never lacked fighting spirit and despite this trouble it was his bowling more than anything else which again broke the morale of the opposition.

Bill Johnston found the wicket suited his faster type of bowling, and gave grand support.

I can still picture the unlucky Dollery. He had not that season faced a bowler anything like as fast as Lindwall and had to play him immediately he arrived at the crease. The first ball found Dollery much too late. Fortunately for him, it was not straight, but Lindwall doesn't waste opportunities, and one more ball was enough.

Without wishing to detract from Dollery's ability, for he is a good sound batsman, I thought the Selectors were asking too much of a new man whose eyesight and reflexes were possibly on the decline, to handle Lindwall first up in a Test. Simpson was much younger and had already played our fast attack with considerable success. Theoretically, he looked to be a better selection.

Despite gallant stands by Compton and Yardley, we retrieved our lost ground before stumps. Once again it seemed we had prised the door open.

Saturday's play consolidated our position. No longer could the bowlers find those green grassy spots, with the result that our early batsmen achieved their function of getting on top. We were able to spend the weekend contemplating victory.

Actually we spent the Sunday afternoon at Windsor Castle, where we had been invited by the Earl of Gowrie. It was a most absorbing experience to go over the Castle and see the relics of former years—the priceless treasures—the authentic documents and other evidence by which one can trace historic events in British history.

An amusing interlude was provided by a close study of the suits of armour worn by earlier kings. Our boys were agreed that they would have been the ideal answer to body-line except for one important proviso—you couldn't very well play cricket mounted on a horse.

Queen Mary very graciously received us at Frogmore, chatted to the members of the team, and gratified their desire to take movie films.

Later, we were entertained by the Earl of Gowrie to afternoon tea.

I recall the pleasure of meeting there amongst the numerous guests Lord and Lady Tedder. We greatly admired Lord Tedder's sense of humour. He put a towel across his arm and proceeded to serve tea and generally wait on the guests.

Upon handing a cup of tea to one of the players (who had during the war occupied a very junior air force rank) Lord Tedder suddenly found himself (the great Air Marshal) being offered a tip. He laughed with great glee at this typical Australian humour and enjoyed the joke more than anyone.

Before returning to London we were driven across to Eton College where the headmaster and his wife dispensed further hospitality, and we had a brief look around the old school buildings.

Showery weather greeted us at Lord's for the continuation of the Test on Monday.

With things in our favour, we forced the pace until I was able to close in the middle of the afternoon, leaving England about 9 hours batting time to get some 600 runs. It was not impossible—not in theory—but it had never been done before. This was to be no exception.

Sensing the opportunity, we displayed in general, a belligerent attacking spirit which was quickly translated into results by brilliant fielding.

First, Ian Johnson in the slips took a real beauty to send Edrich pavilionwards. Then Tallon dismissed Washbrook from one of the most remarkable catches ever made behind the wicket. Toshack bowled a full toss wide of the off-stump. Washbrook swung fiercely to try and square cut it for 4, but in his attempt to hit it extremely hard, was a fraction late and just touched the ball. Miraculously, Tallon got his gloves under what was to him practically a yorker. I cannot remember a similar catch. Wicket-keepers are not expected to perform miracles.

Miller continued the good work next morning when he, too, took a brilliant slip catch second ball, to dispose of Compton.

With Lindwall and Toshack bowling well, nothing could stop us. By great determination, Wright and Evans were still together at lunch, and even though rain poured down soon after lunch, the match was by then all over.

No excuses could be made or were offered. The better side had won and now we only needed to draw one of the remaining three Tests to hold the Ashes. Only a miracle could prevent us doing that.

It may be appropriate at this stage to bring in a word about umpiring.

I have always been a great supporter of English umpires, and in the past have not hesitated to say so. In addition, I've given reasons why I thought their general standard better than that of the Australians.

But in 1946-7 I took very strong exception to the criticism (in my opinion, unjustifiable criticism) levelled at Australia's Test umpires, especially when it emanated from English journalists who did not disguise their views as to its effect on the result of the games.

In 1948 I took very special care to try and see that this type of unsavoury criticism should be discouraged at every possible turn. With great pleasure I record that it was, from such an angle, one of the most delightful seasons one could wish for.

I must now be truthful and say the umpiring in the first two Tests produced at least two positive mistakes and several other decisions which were highly suspect. I merely do so to stress the following point : umpiring should not be dealt with by press propaganda nor should errors be the cause of recrimination.

A proper channel exists whereby the players and legislators can take whatever action is necessary to try and ensure the appointment of competent umpires. Let us leave it at that. May the 1948 example suffice to show how teams can accept wrong decisions without complaint so long as the press won't magnify the incidents. The trouble can be caused by undue prominence being given to matters which are very often highly debateable.

There has never been any suggestion that umpires are not completely impartial. They have a most difficult job. Seldom are they thanked for perhaps a splendid exhibition simply because it is regarded as their duty. But many times are they subject to criticism for excusable lapses.

Umpires need to be helped and encouraged in all countries—for they are an integral part of the game. The greater the importance of the match, the more quickly can an error upset the balance of power.

It is a duty of the players, no less than anyone else, to help them, not confuse them by displays of feeling or attempts to bluff them and upset their judgment.

To Manchester—The Rubber is Safe

BEFORE ENTERING UPON MORE TEST BUSINESS, WE HAD TO TRY CONCLUSIONS again with Surrey and then Gloucestershire.

In the Surrey game I thought there would be an opportunity for batting practice on what is normally a lovely wicket. The weather man didn't quite agree for there had been heavy rain and we were greeted by a damp, though firmish, wicket.

I won the toss and, with some hesitation, decided to let Surrey have first use of the pitch.

My decision was a lucky one—more luck than judgment. Not only did the dampish wicket misbehave, but there was a prominent ridge at one end, just short of a good length, from which Loxton in particular made the ball fly dangerously. Laurie Fishlock received a nasty blow on the head and several other batsmen had lucky escapes.

This business of finding occasionally a prepared pitch which is not level is something I can't understand. Admittedly we were playing well over to the side of the centre patch. Also, one must allow for the use to which the Oval had been put in war time, but this ridge was obvious to the naked eye and was inevitably dangerous when a reasonably fast bowler was in action. I was thankful we did not play Lindwall—probably the Surrey batsmen were too—for I strongly dislike seeing anyone seriously hurt. Even at Loxton's pace it became a real possibility.

The first duty of groundsmen and ground authorities is to provide a pitch which is dead level. Otherwise batsmen cannot play shots with any certainty or confidence and the game becomes one of chance as much as skill.

We dismissed Surrey for a little over 200, and mention should be made of Parker, who batted very solidly and gave me the impression that he might be worth higher honours, especially as he is also a useful bowler and good slip.

By nightfall we had played ourselves into a safe position. The wicket got easier as it dried out and Surrey did not have a man to take advantage of its imperfections.

The following day both Hassett and I completed centuries and threw our hands away in order that the other players could have some practice.

With 6 wickets down in the second innings, Surrey were only 2 ahead at stumps.

On the Friday we were anxious to get the match over quickly because the authorities at Wimbledon had kindly issued an invitation for us to witness the tennis, and our own John Bromwich was to meet Falkenburg in the men's singles final.

Our progress was delayed by the rare event of Miller missing two easy slip catches right at the start.

Profiting by these errors, Parker again displayed a broad blade to everything, and Errol Holmes gave us a taste of some lovely driving of the old vintage—the type that made him one of England's most attractive bats in pre-war days.

We were left with 122 runs to get. These were knocked off by brilliant, almost violent, cricket on the part of Loxton and Harvey, who made them in the remarkable time of 58 minutes.

So after all we saw the Wimbledon final.

I was seated in the Royal Box, the Duchess of Kent in front of me, Sir Norman Brookes behind.

One could sense how the sympathy of the crowd was with Bromwich. This may have been sentiment, Australia v. America, or it may have been a reaction to the tactics of Falkenburg in earlier games, tactics which had incurred the wrath of spectators and writers.

It was a tense struggle. When John had played himself into a winning position in the 5th set and had 3 match points, Sir Norman and I agreed that he couldn't possibly miss all three. We were wrong.

He not only missed those, but two more as well, and the coveted title slipped from his grasp.

The despair on his face was so reflective of his mind. I know how a sportsman feels when he has given everything he has only to see the prize get away.

Later on, when in the broadcasting box near-by, John acknowledged my sympathetic wave by a gesture which seemed to indicate that some-body always has to lose.

How many men would have willingly given much to be even the runner-up !

Before departing, we saw another Australian, Harper (partnered by Bergelin of Sweden) go down with his colours flying to Brown and Mulloy of America.

We came away wondering how men could be so proficient with a tennis racquet. They, no doubt, felt the same when they watched us play cricket, for sportsmen as a whole are notoriously modest about their own ability.

Another rest being due to me, I spent the following day at the home of my friend, R. W. V. Robins, whilst the boys went off to play Gloucester.

At lunch time the scores came through. Australia were batting and Morris was already a century not out.

The county scores were also given, and as result after result was announced I reflected upon yet another impressive example of the speed of Australian scoring.

Here was one man scoring runs off his own bat, against bowlers like Cook and Goddard, at a faster rate than is often achieved by county teams.

It is no use denying the fact, and I'll remind readers again later, that the legend of dour grim Australians and timeless Tests is a myth.

Neville Cardus is an outstanding exception to those English writers who have relentlessly cultivated the idea of Australian batsmen wearing down the attack by defensive play. He once wrote on the subject as follows :—

" Since the war (1914-18) a curious school of criticism has emerged in this country, from nobody knows where, which has told the public that the Australian batsman is almost invariably joyless and miserly. And nowadays, when certain English Test Match players are accused of slow play, in and out of season they reply, ' Ah ! we are playing the Australians at their own game ' ; which is the reason why, pre-sumably, the same game is played not infrequently between Warwick-shire and Leicestershire.

There never has been a great Australian batsman who declined to hit the loose ball ! ! "

I believe that our batsmen are generally more free, play a wider range of shots and score faster than Englishmen. Moreover, fast scoring wins matches and I'll shortly give you a good example.

I understand that in the match at Bristol, Goddard was handled so roughly he had to retire with a bruised hand and seriously questioned one of our players as to whether they had been instructed to hit him out of the firing line. He was disillusioned when told the answer was in the negative and that things were merely taking their natural course.

A humorous sidelight was my telling our off-spin bowler, Ian Johnson, to watch Goddard and his methods closely, for here was a chance to get some education from a really great English bowler. Goddard probably couldn't remember when he had a worse match—Ian Johnson has seldom had a more successful one. You see one has to take into account the quality of the opposing batsmen.

When he finally got out at 290 on that opening day, Morris had made what proved to be the highest score by any Australian on the tour. He was now in irresistible form and held it right to the end.

The match proved little more than a practice gallop, even though Crapp made a century and found a place in England's Test team for Manchester, where we soon assembled for the Third Test of this series.

I liked playing at Manchester but was notoriously unsuccessful on the Old Trafford Ground.

My personal realisation of this fact largely contributed to a feeling of doubt about the Third Test. I was quite convinced long before we started that here was a match which would test our skill to the utmost.

There was a minor sensation when England's selection was made known, and the name of Hutton missing. Nobody questioned Hutton's ability even if arguments may have arisen regarding his claim to be No. 1, 2 or 3.

People assumed that the Selectors had dropped him as a disciplinary measure following his display at Lord's when in many quarters his batting against our fast bowling had been severely criticised.

It is not for me to interpret the minds of Selectors but in this instance one had to accept the popular assumption as being the only logical one.

Immediately it raises a point of interest. Are Selectors entitled to drop a player even though they believe he is good enough to play?

My answer is unhesitatingly yes.

Not only was Hutton brought back for the Fourth and Fifth Tests, but he then played with far more assurance than he had done earlier in the season.

Certainly it was a bold move on the part of the Selectors but they must take into account, firstly, the interests of the side, secondly the success of the player himself. In the present case they did both.

If Hutton was not opening the English innings in a manner calculated to inspire confidence in the less gifted batsmen who were to follow, he could conceivably have been upsetting their morale. Numbers 5, 6 and 7 do certainly re-act quickly to the way numbers 1, 2 and 3 handle the attack unless they are blessed with iron nerves.

This dropping of Hutton gave Emmett his big chance to achieve fame. He started very promisingly and was unlucky to lose his wicket.

In the second innings he provided Tallon with an opportunity, almost avariciously accepted, of taking one of the grandest low and wide right-hand catches ever seen in Test cricket.

True to form, I lost the toss, and when the wicket rolled out slow and easy on a cold and cloudy day, I visualised the possible realisation of my worst fears.

The day was crammed with interesting cricket. Australia's bowlers did a grand job. We should have been in a comfortable position at stumps but a couple of vital chances went begging.

Of all people, it was Tallon who twice missed Compton, including a comparatively easy one (as wicket-keeping chances go) off the last ball of the day.

Some local feeling was roused by an accident to Compton. He tried to hook a no-ball which was only waist high. As so often happens when " no-ball " is called, Denis took his eyes off it in his haste to despatch it to the boundary.

The ball struck the top edge of his bat and flew straight up, hitting him on the forehead between the eyes. Blood poured from the gash and Denis was assisted from the field. A couple of stitches, a bit of plaster, and he was back again showing little outward sign of his misfortune.

During the day I had an experience with the English system of recording the number of overs bowled which I feel bound to relate in order to expose its weaknesses.

As an experiment we were playing under a rule which provided that the fielding side could demand a new ball after the bowling of 55 overs (6-ball). To assist the fielding captain and umpires, the scorers were instructed to display a white disc after 45 overs, a yellow disc after 50 overs, both discs after 55 overs.

According to my calculations more than 50 overs had been bowled but no disc had appeared.

I drew the umpire's attention to this state of affairs and Frank Chester went across to the scorer's box to query the matter. Immediately a white disc was put out.

One more over was bowled and a yellow disc appeared. Two overs later both discs were showing and I was utterly bewildered.

It is getting ahead of my story a little, but in the next Test at Leeds, the scorer's box was on the opposite side of the ground to the score-board. I was constantly watching the board for the discs, when one of my team mates called my attention to the yellow disc very unobtrusively appearing on the scorer's box.

The matter is important to the fielding captain, who naturally works his bowlers in relation to the new ball as well as the state of the match.

In Australia we adopt a very sound and practical method—namely, we put up on the score-board, over No. 1, 2, 3 and so on. A captain can always tell at a glance just exactly how many overs have been bowled—a distinct advantage over the less informative English method —and there is never a mistake. I wish England would follow Australia's example.

The second day's play in the Manchester Test was indeed a black one for us. The fielding lapses continued. Tallon missed Compton twice more before the latter reached 100, and then, when the keeper made a confident appeal for stumping which was disallowed, he was probably justified in thinking there was a hoodoo on him.

Despite these strokes of good fortune, Compton played a class innings of enormous value. It was all the more commendable following his injury.

Just by way of rubbing it in, Alec Bedser refused to get out. I think he would still have been batting (for I saw no way of shifting him) had not Loxton and I been associated in a piece of tomfoolery in the field.

Purely in fun we both ran for a ball, went past it, and when the batsmen thought an opportunity had occurred to steal another run, Loxton recovered quickly and ran Bedser out. There was no intent on our part—it was just one of those things.

But the great misfortune of the day was when Pollard made a mighty swipe at a ball from Ian Johnson. He connected perfectly and this fullblooded shot caught Sid Barnes in the ribs under the left arm. At the time, Sid was not fielding right up near the bat—he was about 8 yards away.

Down he went in terrible pain, and it was obvious at once we had a serious injury on our hands.

He was taken off.

I deeply regret having to record how a small number of spectators cheered this misfortune, and I do so purely to bring into prominence the need for intelligent and truthful reporting of cricket.

Early in the tour, Barnes' magnificent fielding at short-leg (especially to Toshack) had aroused the ire of a particular newspaper reporter who proceeded to publish what he called an " Open letter to Bradman." The following are extracts from what he wrote :—

" This letter is in no sense an attempt to start anything that will cloud the pleasant atmosphere of the Australian goodwill tour.

But I cannot let pass unchallenged a practice that experienced observers believe to be contrary to the spirit of cricket.

Almost throughout both M.C.C. innings in the Lord's match just ended a ring of fieldsmen was placed unusually near to the batsmen. Sidney Barnes stood repeatedly on the actual playing area. There can be no dispute about this—one foot was clearly placed across the edge of the prepared wicket . . . often he was moving—unintentionally, no doubt—after the bowler started his run.

Before the umpires are called upon to make a ruling under the heading of what constitutes fair or unfair play, I suggest that you remove the necessity for such a decision."

This article brought forth comment from other journalists, one of whom wrote :—

" Bradman will continue to get English wickets in any way that is within the rules. They, not the higher ethics, are his guide to conduct in cricket."

Such a statement at least questioned my observance of the spirit of the game and obviously was annoying.

Being of the opinion that the reporter was trying to draw me into a public controversy for his own benefit, I refrained from answering.

His accusations were not in accordance with facts and were a grave reflection on the ability of England's leading umpires as well as the sportsmanship of Barnes and myself.

It seems pretty clear that the writer also revealed his ignorance of the laws of cricket.

If he refers to the notes thereon he will find under the heading of *Fair and Unfair Play*:—

4 (1)

The umpires are entitled to intervene *without appeal* in the case of unfair play—they do not have to wait until they are called upon.

Obviously, therefore, the umpires were clearly of the opinion no unfair play had occurred.

Barnes *never* stood with one foot on the prepared wicket—he never distracted batsmen by moving as the bowler came up.

But the damage was done. The public who read the article believed there was a case against Barnes.

Here was the greatest short-leg fieldsman in the world badly injured because he was capable of doing what nobody else could do (and few would have been brave enough to do) and being the victim of admittedly slight, but nevertheless definite, hostility from a section of people who had been misinformed by an irresponsible statement.

I'm glad to say the great majority of the people recognised the true position and made amends by a generous reception to Barnes when he gallantly batted later in the game.

This injury completely upset our plans. I had to rearrange our batting order and entrusted Barnes' opening place to Ian Johnson. It was too much. Before the new ball was over he and I, too, were back in the pavilion, and the day ended with Australia struggling.

Things continued to go badly on the Saturday. Our sheet anchor, Morris, mistimed a hook and was caught on the boundary—Barnes bravely insisted on batting only to collapse in the middle of the pitch. Once more he had to be assisted from the field and taken to hospital.

An extraordinary phenomenon was, that although the injury was in the ribs below the left arm, one of the alarming consequences was a semi-paralysed and blackened left eye. I am thankful to know Sid made a complete recovery and today shows no after-effects whatever.

We had eventually a most exciting period when our tail-enders were battling to save the follow-on. I'm not sure Yardley would have enforced it but at least it was much better not to give him the opportunity.

When England batted again our run of fielding lapses continued, but in order to distribute her favours, Dame Fortune frowned this time on Hassett.

The diminutive Victorian is a great field and safe catch, but when Cyril Washbrook hooked one from Lindwall straight to him on the leg boundary, we were mortified to see it jump out of his hands.

Later in the innings, the shot was repeated right to the identical spot. As it sailed through the air I heard Lindwall say, " Catch this one." Hassett failed to carry out the instruction and promptly dropped the second chance.

Revealing that deep sense of humour which is always so close to the surface in Hassett's nature, he immediately turned to a nearby policeman and borrowed his helmet, indicating his need for it should another catch come along.

What strange thoughts can arise from simple happenings. I was actually told afterwards that a prominent Lancastrian refused to attend the rest of the match because he believed Hassett had dropped the catches on purpose. He claimed they were too easy to miss and Australia were playing " dead " for the sake of the gate.

If only he knew the chagrin felt by our whole team as they saw those catches cropped. Test Matches are not rigged. Thank goodness cricket is above suspicion in that regard. The game is too complex—events cannot be ordered even if so willed and the public need never doubt the genuineness of a match.

These lapses may have been important to Washbrook. Had the first catch been held, we speculated on whether he would have been dropped from the Leeds Test. As it was, he played, made a glorious century and doubtless his benefit match profited largely thereby.

Our resources were sorely tried. Keith Miller, who had not bowled at Lord's or this game, volunteered to try out his back and did so. Everybody worked hard.

There was a momentary ray of hope when Edrich was run out and Compton caught for o. Crapp missed a duck by a coat of paint, but we finished the day in a bad position and had much to reflect upon over the weekend.

Rain prevented play on the Monday and delayed the start on Tuesday until after lunch. Yardley closed at once and, though the wicket was wet and Johnson got out early, Morris and I played out time in between stoppages for rain.

Once again Morris played superbly against a very hostile Bedser. The value of his innings was not fully appreciated by those outside the arena and the public never knew what skill was being shown simply because we made no real effort to score, runs being of no consequence.

I made no secret about our joy that rain considerably assisted us to make a draw of the match. Indeed there was great fun in our dressing room at the constant trek of one member of the team to a rear window to report on the potential rain situation. Throughout the whole proceedings Sam Loxton kept saying, " You needn't worry, boys, she's coming up from Burnley. It's pouring out there."

To say we had the worst of a drawn match is true. To say the rain saved Australia is pure conjecture, and I must remind you of what happened in the following Test at Leeds.

That clinched the Ashes. Two up and two to go meant we could not be beaten. Moreover, I had a quiet confidence, born of past experience, about Leeds. This confidence was soon to be justified in no uncertain manner.

Leeds—A Great Victory

THE NEXT TRIAL OF STRENGTH CAME AT LORD'S WHERE WE HAD TO PLAY Middlesex.

On paper they impressed as being a strong side with, of course, Compton and Edrich the stars. In addition, there were the Test bowler Young, schoolboy Ian Bedford of whose slow leg-spinners we had heard a good deal, Robertson, the opening bat, who was in many quarters regarded as a likely Test choice, and the promising amateur bowler Whitcombe.

The team was under the leadership of George Mann, later invited to captain the M.C.C. team to South Africa.

Of the actual play there is little to tell. Once more our team completely outplayed the opposition to win by 10 wickets.

Middlesex won the toss and so had the advantage of batting first on a good wicket, but against excellent bowling and brilliant fielding could only muster the moderate total of 203. This was easily passed—in fact, Loxton and Morris alone registered more—each getting a century.

We were becoming accustomed to Morris scoring heavily, but the pleasing thing about Loxton was, firstly, the great improvement shown in his batting, and secondly, the indication that his injured leg was now better. For weeks it had hampered him, and it was a considerable relief to know that he was fit.

Middlesex had to bat for the second time at roughly 5-45 on the Monday. At stumps 4 men (including Compton and Edrich) were out and Robertson was *hors-de-combat*, having been struck on the jaw when he missed an attempted hook off Lindwall.

When this accident occurred we immediately rushed to Robertson's aid, to the accompaniment of some hostile remarks from the crowd. His first words were, " Don't take any notice of those people. It was entirely my own fault." From a man whose jaw was fractured and who felt very groggy, I regarded his words as an impressive example of courage and presence of mind.

The match ended quickly on the last day.

Whitcombe's bowling throughout was worthy of commendation. This tall fast-medium bowler took full advantage of his great height and used the wicket most intelligently. Whilst there was any moisture and greenness in it he made the ball move towards slips and to the leg side. One of the latter deliveries found the inside edge of my bat and brought about my dismissal.

Whether he will go on to higher spheres I don't know. During the game he suffered an ankle injury and was also nursing a troublesome shoulder. Sometimes these extremely tall athletes find the strain of bowling too severe and do not stand up to the work like the small and chunky individuals. Whitcombe has much ability, and it will be interesting to watch his future.

Of course we were all anxious to have a look at Ian Bedford. In the early stages he bowled very accurately and flighted the ball splendidly. Later in the match he came in for some rough treatment by Arthur Morris—a common experience for bowlers.

Bedford has been carefully handled so far. This policy should be followed yet awhile, for he is young and his time has not quite arrived.

There is good control—signs of a splendid temperament—and providing he can cultivate more spin whilst gaining experience, his name may yet figure in the list of those who have played for England.

So to Leeds where for Yardley's men it was a case of do or die.

The frigid reception accorded us by the weather belied the hot sun which was to follow, to say nothing of the warmth of the Yorkshire hearts.

The English team once again included Hutton, and looked a good side except for the absence of a leg-break bowler. The effect of this was to be emphasised later.

We were in a quandary over our selection for by now practically the whole 17 men had to be considered.

Tallon had an injured finger. Rather than risk him we decided to play Saggers, who was little behind Tallon, either in his wicket-keeping or batting, and who had thoroughly earned a Test.

Then the baby of the team, Neil Harvey, was simply forcing his way into the side by his brilliant cricket. To keep him out any longer would be unfair to him and to Australian cricket.

The problem finally settled itself.

Barnes was not completely recovered from that terrific blow at Manchester, so we decided to let him have a further rest, play Harvey and let Hassett open the innings with Morris.

Surely it was my turn to win the toss, but no—the elusive spin of the coin favoured Yardley, who fairly leapt at the chance of batting on that feather bed pitch. It turned out to be easily the best of the series.

Hutton at once gave evidence that he was not going to risk further censure at the hands of the Selectors, though it was Washbrook who really attacked the bowling and played what I consider to be his finest innings of the season.

Try as they would, our bowlers could get nothing out of the wicket, and it was not until Lindwall uprooted Hutton's off-stump with the second new ball that we achieved any success at all. Even then we had to wait until the last over of the day for another wicket.

Our bowlers had done their best and our fielding was absolutely superb, but for once the batting—allied to that easy paced wicket—was just too good, and all credit must be given the openers.

I thought England made a tactical error by not forcing the pace towards the end. We were tired and here was a golden opportunity, but England seemed more anxious to preserve wickets than get runs, even to the extent of sending in Bedser just before stumps.

This opening day's play brought forth an example of the regrettable and much too-frequent tendency of some ex-cricketers who become newspaper writers to lose all sense of proportion and values when they see an unusual performance.

Next morning we read in the press under the name of W. J. O'Reilly, the following comment :—

" It is the custom to decry the bowling when the bat happens to assume authority. Today's Australian effort does not deserve to become an exception to the rule. From the first few desultory overs the attack functioned without object—hopelessly and meaninglessly. Not one bowler can be excused from what must be classed as the poorest Australian out-cricket of the tour. Some of the so-called attack was blatantly inaccurate both in direction and length."

That it was unsuccessful—yes—meaningless—no.

As a matter of principle, I think it desirable that I should express myself on that statement.

In regard to " out-cricket "—this includes fielding as well as bowling, and by general consent Leeds has never seen a finer day's fielding.

Despite the gradual deterioration of the pitch, the following days produced respectively 291, 394, 363 and 407 runs, so (compared with 268
on the opening day) the out-cricket for the rest of the match must have
gone completely haywire.

England were dismissed in that first innings for 496. My mind goes
back to the series of Tests against England in 1938.

O'Reilly was then credited with being the greatest bowler in the
world, and he certainly had the support of other very able bowlers.

Even so, Hutton, Compton and Co. managed to compile a few useful
scores which are worth repeating :—

> 8 wickets for 658 at Nottingham
> 494 at Lord's
> 7 wickets for 903 at the Oval

In 1934 England scored 627 for 9 and 123 for 0 at Manchester against
O'Reilly and Co.

I don't know whether our attack could then have been classed as
hopeless or meaningless. I do know that O'Reilly in those days quickly
reacted to criticism in the press, and gave full play to his very eloquent
vocal chords in explaining what he thought of the wickets he had to
bowl on.

I wish cricket writers would drop the modern idea that destructive
criticism is the only worthwhile form of expression.

The great game of cricket is best served by critics who look for
virtues in others, and players need encouragement most when the going
is hardest.

O'Reilly is a writer with more than average ability. Indeed he has
all the attributes necessary to make him one of the really outstanding
writers of the day.

Players look for helpful guidance in his comments, and I hope he
won't make a permanent feature of carping criticism every time the
bat assumes the ascendency.

When the game was resumed on the Friday, we saw a remarkable
partnership between Edrich and Bedser. It produced 155 runs. Bedser had been sent in as night-watchman and now proceeded to grasp
this heaven-sent opportunity to show he could bat as well as bowl.

There were certainly no fireworks.

On that glorious wicket, 24 hours old, only 3 runs were scored in the
first half-hour.

On the last day, when I joined Morris, and we were chasing over 400
runs on a wicket 5 days old, the first half-hour produced over 60 runs.

These grim, dour Australians !

But then, I warned you earlier of my intention to try and squash for
ever that ridiculous legend.

Just for good measure, may I repeat here that only 3 men in the whole history of cricket have scored a century before lunch in Test cricket: Trumper, Macartney and myself—all Australians.

The score had reached 423 for 2 before that partnership between Edrich and Bedser was broken.

By this time one could reasonably have expected the Australian attack to falter. It had been working hard for a day and a half.

Instead, the Yorkshire crowd were treated to one of the grandest shows of out-cricket that can be found in the annals of Test Matches. From 423 for 2 England were all out 496. In other words, 8 wickets fell for 73 runs to our bowlers, all on a batsman's paradise with a fast outfield.

No praise can be too high for the spirit of our men. I can still picture Sam Loxton after a lengthy bowling spell chasing a ball down-hill to the boundary with such energy that he could not stop at the crowd and nearly caused several casualties. His clear expression of disgust at the failure of his hopeless chase, indicated by the well-known method of throwing his cap on the ground, greatly amused the spectators.

Having to bat that evening, we suffered an early blow in the loss of Morris. I took his place, and here let me record my grateful thanks to that Headingley crowd for the most terrific and spontaneous welcome ever accorded to me in my long career.

As I walked on to the ground the applause was amazing. It died slightly, and then as I approached the wicket, rose in a crescendo to a deafening roar which caused me to make a special acknowledgment and certainly raised a lump in my throat.

My luck had admittedly been in at Leeds for I had made over 300 there both in 1930 and 1934, whilst I rate my Leeds century in 1938 as one of my best. Even so, one doesn't expect such ovations away from home. This is a memory nothing can ever efface.

How I managed to survive at first I don't know, but I did, and no more wickets fell that day.

Next morning I was amused at one of my " fan " letters which I think worth quoting.

After wishing me good luck and referring to the match, the letter went on :—

" My friends and I gambled on our English weather, three doubtful cycles and the fortune of the road, and cycled to Leeds to see the second day of the Test. My friend broke a gear on the way back, I broke a mudguard and we both had to push our exhausted friend back over the moors, but it was well worth it.

Yours very sincerely,
From One hopeful cricketer,
One not so hopeful,
and
One who cannot play at all."

During the night and early next morning it rained—not a great deal—just enough to put a bit of early life in the wicket.

Taking the long view, a few showers were helpful to us, as they assisted to bind the wicket and prevent it crumbling quite so early. But the rain gave England an advantage for that first half-hour on Saturday.

It became apparent at once that we would need all our resources, for several balls misbehaved. One of these from Bedser gave me a nasty crack in a place which, had I been a boxer, would have enabled me to claim a foul. In cricket, the injured party gets nothing but sympathy, sometimes not even that.

Lindsay Hassett had all this time been doing a splendid job as substitute opener for Barnes. I thought he was set for a score when suddenly a ball from Pollard lifted sharply off a good length, hit the shoulder of Lindsay's bat and flew into the waiting hands of gully.

Miller filled the breach to score 3 off the first ball. No doubt thinking of Hassett's fate, I was looking for something of the kind to happen to me. Instead, the next ball, pitched on my middle stump, turned slightly from leg and kept very low to knock my off-stump clean out of the ground.

The crowd had every right to be jubilant. England were on top with a vengeance, and most of our experienced players disposed of.

Into such a situation strode 19-year-old Neil Harvey, playing his first Test Match against England, and a silent prayer from me went with him.

I knew he was a good player—had the strokes—had the temperament—but surely it was asking too much of him to succeed where we had failed.

There wasn't a man in that vast audience prepared for what followed.

Harvey and Miller proceeded to unwind a veritable avalanche of beautiful scoring shots.

Miller's game is based on driving.

He hits the ball with a lissom grace and rhythm despite the tremendous power he puts into his shots. He drove that day hard and often, swung Laker high into the crowd over square leg, and was sailing along merrily when in attempting to swing Laker once more he was the victim of sheer rotten luck. The ball touched the back of Miller's bat. Evans, behind the stumps, had no chance of seeing it but the ball hit him and flew up in the air to short leg where Edrich dived full length to hold a splendid catch.

With his bosom pal Loxton as his partner, Harvey serenely continued his way. Seldom has anyone seen more beautiful square cutting. Anything short was mercilessly pulled and his cover driving was a delight to watch. Yardley couldn't stop the flow of fours and inevitably the score rose until the magic three figures were posted against his name.

Sam Loxton was so excited about Neil's century that he almost got run out leaving his crease too early to go down and shake the lad's hand.

Surely the pace couldn't last ! So it proved, for he tried to pull one from Laker which was much too far up and over went the stumps.

I wish I could have been batting with him at the time to curb that little extra bit of youthful exuberance, for he could have made a very big score.

Still I have no criticism. It was a natural end to one of the greatest innings any batsman, old or young, has ever played.

In the dim dark ages (or so it seems) of 1928-9, I had been Archie Jackson's partner when that talented boy made a century in Adelaide. It still stands as a record, for he was the youngest player ever to score a century in a Test—some months younger than Harvey.

That day as I watched every ball bowled to Harvey, I was in a unique position to make a comparison. Remarkable as it seems, Harvey was less than two months old when I batted with Jackson at his memorable debut.

Jackson, of course, was a right-hander ; Harvey is left.

The former was tall and slim, rather lethargic and graceful in his movements. To him cricket was a game of finesse not brutality, and his whole repertoire of shots reflected this mental outlook.

There was the lovely fine-leg glance, the late cut, but seldom the pull. Even the full-blooded drive was eschewed in favour of the cover and square drive where the glance of the bat made it a thing of beauty as compared with the straight-out power required for a forward drive.

Not so with Harvey. His physique is smallish and compact but very strong, and that type of build does not allow quite the same grace of movement. He believes in force—drives strongly but loves above all to pull the short one with all the power he can command.

I don't think Jackson could have taken charge of the situation as Harvey did. His physical resources were too thin (as his untimely death revealed), and he required a hard fast wicket to impart the power he himself lacked.

In their way each was a gem of the first water. I am indeed a lucky man to have seen both.

The question is whether this wonderful promise of Harvey will, over the years, be translated into deeds. Providing health and strength remain, and he is now a very robust and healthy lad, no apparent reason exists why he shall not continue to delight cricket lovers for many years to come.

Meanwhile, in our elation over Harvey, we must not lose sight of another innings which, in some ways, was even more remarkable. I refer, of course, to Loxton's 93.

There could not possibly be a greater contrast than Jackson and Loxton. The Victorian all-rounder is the very essence of belligerence.

His whole attitude suggests defiance and when he hits the ball it is the music of a sledge hammer, not a dinner gong.

In the early part of his innings, Loxton was reasonably sedate. Gradually he warmed to the task and, with Harvey out, seemed to exude a spirit of revenge.

First one bowler, then the other, felt the lash. Ken Cranston bowled a ball the merest fraction over-pitched. I can picture now the arc of Loxton's bat as he swung up under it. The ball sailed over the bowler's head and must have landed twenty rows up amongst the crowd.

Cardus wrote that he got a crick in his neck watching it go up.

That particular shot was the most glorious six I ever saw hit. On the balcony standing next to me was R. W. V. Robins, an English Selector. I can see his face now—a look of incredulity—could this be true in a Test Match where a side was fighting to save defeat ?

When Ian Johnson tried to swing one from Laker into the crowd in front of square leg, he too was unlucky enough to sky it up in the air. The batsmen crossed before the catch was held so that Loxton had strike.

Almost as though to say, " You dare get my cobbers out," Loxton smote the next ball over mid-off for 6 and for good measure the one after went in the same place, away over Hutton's head.

This, too, could not last. Five sixes were chalked up against him, but in trying for the sixth against Yardley, the end came.

Nobody can ever quite assess the value of that innings. It simply demoralised the bowlers who would not have expected such treatment in a village green charity match.

The speed of the scoring rapidly nullified the advantage England had gained, for runs scored quickly are almost invariably more valuable than runs scored slowly. There are times when runs don't matter at all but given equal conditions the team scoring 400 runs in 5 hours has a big pull over the one which takes 7 hours.

Even with Loxton's dismissal, we were not done. Into the breach came Lindwall, also a powerful hitter but more than that—a talented batsman and classy stroke player. He took over the dominant role very ably supported by first one, then the other.

A note of hilarity entered the proceedings towards the end of the day. Toshack's knee had given way whilst bowling. It was badly swollen and I had obtained Yardley's permission to have a substitute runner.

When Bill Johnston got out he stayed at the wickets (under my instructions) to run for Toshack.

Before Toshack appeared, there was naturally a time lag. It was amazing to watch the reaction of the crowd and even the pressmen, who were completely bewildered.

This fellow Johnston is a great humorist and as he walked about out there, waving his arms and bat, and talking to umpires and fieldsmen, the populace all got the impression he was disputing the fact of being out. Some of the people had even begun to become vocal on the subject, when Toshack's tall figure became visible coming out from the pavilion.

Meanwhile we had spent a couple of minutes roaring with laughter.

By now the English bowlers could not penetrate even Toshack's defence and nightfall came with Australia 39 behind and still one wicket to fall. At least we were not out of the fight.

It may be interesting to mention here that our tail-enders, Johnston and Toshack, had more than once done a grand job with the bat by staying in at a critical time. Both are very tall—over 6 feet. Neither was regarded as having any pretensions to batsmanship when the tour began.

I made it my job to have a serious talk with them on this subject quite early and persuaded them to follow my doctrine.

So many tail-enders go in, try to play a back defensive shot and get out L.B.W. or attempt a difficult stroke which is altogether beyond them.

I said : "You fellows both have a long reach. Unless the ball is very short, play straight down the line. Let the drive be the basis of your shots." It took a little time but they got into the way of it and within reasonable limits carried out the idea.

The record books tell us Toshack's batting average in this series of Tests was 51, Johnston's was 20·6. Seeing that our opponents on the whole tour averaged less than 20 runs per innings, you have one of the secrets of the success of the 1948 Australian team.

The weekend press gave Yardley and me plenty of advice about what we should do for the rest of the match. I'm afraid it didn't influence us. We had to do what we thought best.

I could, for instance, see nothing but stupidity in a suggestion that I should close our innings when we were still 39 runs behind. The suggestion didn't appear quite so stupid when Lindwall got out after adding 1 run, although a valuable 10 minutes or so had been gained.

It may truthfully be argued that England had the better of the fourth day's play. Even so she frittered away in the early part precious minutes which the later batsmen tried desperately to retrieve.

From our point of view, once the early batsmen got set, the main purpose was to keep the runs down. Generally speaking, we succeeded fairly well.

That night my diary entry read, "We are set 400 to win and I fear we may be defeated."

Frankly, I expected Yardley to declare at once simply because I reckoned 400 was beyond us. He may have had a more healthy respect for our batting or less confidence in his bowling.

Whatever the reason, he batted on, and immediately everybody jumped to the conclusion his sole purpose was to use the heavy roller on the pitch.

It may have been nothing of the kind. A very legitimate and sensible reason would have been to chop another 15 minutes off our batting time if he was fearful of our getting the runs.

As captains don't discuss such matters, I'll probably never know, but I do want to air my views on this question of using the heavy roller to break up the pitch.

Critics have a wonderful way of knowing what goes on in somebody else's mind. Almost to a man they said Yardley was justified on the ground that I had on some occasion or other in Australia done the same.

Throughout my career I have had the opportunity of discussing wickets and rollers with groundsmen on every leading ground in Australia and England.

I have never yet met one who thought the use of the heavy roller would break up the pitch.

Theoretically it could. A ten-ton roller, two feet wide on ordinary earth would smash it up. But cricket pitches are hard, prepared strips— the weight of the roller is limited (usually a maximum of 30 cwt.) and the weight distributed in some cases over the full width of the pitch.

No doubt writers will go on writing about the heavy roller being used to break up the pitch and about the innermost thoughts of Test captains, but if ever a Test wicket is damaged by a heavy roller I would like to be called post-haste to see the damage. It will be a novel sight for me.

The roller " incident " over and Yardley having closed, Australia had to face up to this colossal task of getting 404 runs in 345 minutes, on the last day of a Test Match.

Nothing approaching it had ever been done before in Test Match history.

The previous highest score to win a Test Match in England in the fourth innings was 263 in 1902. In Australia it was 332.

With a very anxious heart I wished our openers, Morris and Hassett, good luck as they set out on the mission.

Both played extremely well until most unexpectedly Yardley brought Denis Compton into the attack. At once he got spin and life from the pitch and quickly met with success by following up very smartly and taking a low one-handed catch off his own bowling. Hassett played a trifle carelessly and was very crestfallen.

To another magnificent ovation from an excited crowd, I made my way for the last time on to that famous arena.

My thoughts weren't altogether clear. We wanted to win. We didn't want to lose. What should I do ?

The answer was provided for me. Yardley brought on Hutton and in half an hour before lunch, Morris and I had gathered a useful 62 runs, which put us roughly up with the clock.

In the afternoon it was a battle of wits.

The wicket was badly worn and demanded every care and vigilance.

Don't take any notice of those who say the wicket was still good. Jim Laker bowled me more than one ball which pitched well outside the off stump and clearly passed outside the leg stump.

Cricketers will understand what that means on a dry and dusty pitch.

We had to keep out the good ones somehow—score off everything loose and keep pace with the clock.

The struggle went on hour after hour—full of life and incident.

Great stress was afterwards placed upon our luck in having " lives ".

It is true that Evans missed a stumping off Morris, but the wicket-keeper was never born who could have done it. A vicious yorker which pitched in the rough outside the off stump spinning away with Morris obscuring the keeper's view by hitting over it.

I might have been caught twice in slips—once by an acrobat and once from a fairly difficult chance.

On each occasion I was attempting to score but lost the flight of the ball in the glare of the background. No sightboards are provided at Leeds. It was a hot sunny day and all the time we had difficulty in seeing the ball for the spectators had discarded their coats, leaving a motley array of white and coloured shirts in the sun. It was like looking at a draughts board.

I take my hat off to Arthur Morris.

He showed that day every quality demanded of the real champion. A rock-like defence, powerful but studied aggression and a perfect temperament.

Considering the situation and the state of the wicket, I doubt if a more valuable innings was ever played, and Arthur was unfortunate, in a way, to get out with victory in sight.

I had the knowledge of what to do under such conditions and steeled myself to the physical effort about which I wasn't so confident.

In the early afternoon I was suddenly caught with a stabbing pain in the side. At first I thought my rib cartilege had gone again as it had against India. Instead, it turned out to be a recurrence of fibrositis, and painful though it was I managed to hang on until the spasm eased—meanwhile giving Arthur all the strike I could.

After Morris got out, Miller stayed until only two more boundary shots were needed when he was adjudged L.B.W. ; so fittingly perhaps it was left to Neil Harvey to make the winning hit.

Post mortems there were in plenty, but even the most rabid English supporters freely acknowledged the magnitude of our win.

I dislike being critical if it means being destructive, and I think little criticism is warranted here, but the one great error England made was in not having a leg-spinner like Wright or Hollies in the side.

I still think we would not have made 250.

No ball bowled is as difficult to handle as the one which leaves the bat and goes towards slips.

The off-spin bowler may be very good but technically he starts under a big handicap. By intelligent use of bat and pads one is able to counter a great deal of the effectiveness of an off-break bowler. The really good leg-break beats them all.

It was in an effort to overcome this deficiency that Yardley used Hutton as a bowler—gave us most valuable runs—and was roundly condemned for having done it.

The rubber was lost and won in a glorious match which even inspired such a hardened critic as Charles Bray to write, " This was the finest Test Match it has been my privilege to watch."

To the Oval and Farewell to Tests

OF THE VAST CONCOURSE OF PEOPLE WHO WITNESSED THE THRILLING Leeds Test and the very much vaster audience which followed the game by means of radio and newspaper, I wonder how many gave a thought to what happened immediately afterwards to that victorious Australian team.

Very few, I should think. Of those who did—how close were they to the mark ?

Probably they envisaged a wild celebration or at least a celebration of some sort plus some relaxation.

How far would they be from the truth.

What actually happened was this.

We had to catch a train for Derby within about 45 minutes of the end of the match. Take my own case.

After batting practically all day and being well nigh exhausted both physically and mentally from that big ordeal, I had to shower, change, pack my bags and get to the station in time.

Once on board the train there was no dining car but only a cold hamper meal, and apart from the few bottles of soft drinks we took with us, nothing else was procurable.

It is not a very pleasant cross-country journey at any time. On this particular night it was frightfully hot and the train was late, so that we did not reach our destination until around 11 p.m.

The hotel manager was extremely good in supplying a repast on our arrival. We must have drunk quarts of tea, and by the time our trunks had arrived and been placed in the rooms it couldn't have been far short of midnight.

Not such an exciting evening as the world at large probably imagined !

My side was painful, and I had to have treatment in the early hours of the morning. It was with considerable misgivings I took the field against Derbyshire.

Now one of the hardest things for any athlete to do, is to put up a big performance or do something involving great strain and then come up and give of his best next day. Cricketers are no exception to the rule.

After playing a very big innings one day, I can scarcely remember an occasion when I followed it up successfully on the next. The muscles are slower and a bit taut, but somehow or other I imagine the mental effort is what really counts. The long concentration tells its tale and the reaction is slower and sluggish.

We were just such a team against Derbyshire. Fortunately for us, George Pope and Copson were unavailable through injuries, but as events turned out we had no cause for alarm.

Our batsmen, headed by Bill Brown, who, after a hesitant start, made a splendid century, gave us a winning total.

My own 62 was a reflex innings. On the other hand, Miller played a brief hard-hitting knock containing five fours and a six.

Having the runs to spare, I was able to use McCool and Ring without much thought other than to get wickets. Victory by an innings was achieved with time to spare.

Gladwin bowled very well and so did a new fast-medium lad, Jackson.

He was spoken of as a good England prospect, so I watched him closely. Though he bowled well, I would like to see him cultivate a much more upright delivery (or, if you like, less round arm).

On the second night of the game, our team had a " victory " dinner to celebrate the winning of " The Ashes ".

No guests were invited—it was just a domestic affair. You couldn't have seen a happier band of chaps.

From Derbyshire to Swansea was a long and tiresome night-train journey via London.

Despite the fact that we were to meet the prospective champion county Glamorgan, I felt the need of a rest and stayed in London, leaving Lindsay Hassett to deal with Wilf Wooller & Coy.

Rain interfered with the game and washed out the last day altogether.

Our team were loud in their praises of Welsh hospitality, and the enthusiasm of the Swansea folk was reflected in the keenness of the county players.

Throughout England I noticed a distinct desire for Glamorgan to win the County Championship, not because anybody had a special regard for Glamorgan or disregard for anybody else, but just that natural instincts decreed it was a good thing for the Championship to go round and not always be the prerogative of Yorkshire or Middlesex.

The public do like to see victory go to what they term the " underdog ".

Our next clash was against Warwickshire.

Any side which includes the New Zealander Pritchard (best fast bowler in England in 1948), Hollies, New Zealander Donnelly (fine left-hand bat), Dollery and Kardar (the Indian all-rounder) must be taken seriously.

The match was played throughout on a wet pitch—not dangerous but most responsive to spin and hardly anybody batted with confidence.

Our team played solid cricket as a combination and won comfortably.

I recall a phenomenal slip catch by McCool and also that our two opening batsmen, Brown and Morris, were out " hit wicket " in the first innings. I've not heard of such an occurrence elsewhere.

Outstanding feature of the match was the bowling of Eric Hollies who delivered 43·5 consecutive overs and took 8 for 107. He bowled beautifully.

The pitch gave him just that little bit of assistance he needs but even so his control of length and direction were admirable.

His performance must have earned him a place in the Fifth Test.

Then came our return match with Lancashire—notable because it was Cyril Washbrook's benefit.

As a compliment to Cyril and to try and help his benefit along, we played a strong attractive side.

The only doubts were Barnes (who was having a dress rehearsal try-out for the Fifth Test) and Toshack, about whose knee we had to be certain.

Barnes came through it splendidly, but unfortunately Toshack found his leg would not stand the strain. He broke down completely, did not play again on the tour, and had to have a cartilage operation before returning to Australia.

For financial reasons the wicket was covered. Whether this had anything to do with it or not, I don't know, but it behaved in a most peculiar manner right from the start, and on the last day became positively dangerous.

Winning the toss we batted only to find the going mighty hard against left-hand spinner Roberts, who, at one stage, had 5 for 26.

Still, a score of 321 was ample. Lancashire could only muster 130.

Worse still, Cyril Washbrook was hit so often on the right hand that he could not bat in the second innings and I don't think he played again that season. This was a result of the ball lifting sharply from a good length.

Almost every batsman was struck. I got hit on the back of the left hand.

To the best of my recollection, it was the only time such a thing happened in my career—on the right hand, yes, but never on the left.

I could have enforced the follow-on, but did not do so because it may have eliminated the third day's gate, and we certainly didn't want to deprive Washbrook of a substantial sum of money. He had been a tower of strength to Lancashire over a long period and deserved to be rewarded.

On the final day I had the pleasure of making 133 not out in my last appearance at Old Trafford—108 of them before lunch.

To make a century before lunch is a rare achievement, and so I was a little surprised to find in one of the newspaper descriptions of the match, a long one of over 80 lines, my own performance dismissed with the comment, " Bradman hit his highest ever on the ground with an unbeaten 133."

Another paper referred to it as " a dullish affair enlivened by rare spurts of off-drives and leg-pushes of the old vintage."

Some critics are pretty hard to please.

In the Oxford-Cambridge University match at Lord's in 1948, Oxford scored as a team 57 runs before lunch. That in a match where the cream of young English amateur talent—the brilliant kind—is supposed to be found.

If I could get 108 before lunch on a difficult wicket against Pollard, Greenwood, Ikin, Roberts and Cranston, it couldn't have been so very dull. If it was, then my retirement from big cricket was certainly overdue.

Closing the innings at lunch time scarcely gave us a chance to win, though only Ikin with a dashing and courageous 99, prevented us doing so.

In the final stages of the match I consider Ray Lindwall bowled tremendously fast. There was a strong wind behind, he was ambitious to get wickets and a new ball came on. His speed was terrific.

Don Tallon, standing yards farther back than usual, wrung his hands every time he stopped one. A catch went to a slip fieldsman who was almost half-way to the fence, and it just simply crashed through his hands and went to the boundary.

My thoughts went to Eddie Gilbert in Queensland in 1932 and Larwood's bowling the same season.

Dick Pollard never saw the ball which bowled him.

We left Lancashire happy in the knowledge of our contribution to the greatest benefit any cricketer has so far enjoyed.

From Manchester to Sunderland, where a second-class fixture against Durham was scheduled. Rain caused the early abandonment of this game, and so it was back to London for the final Test Match of the series.

I spent one Sunday afternoon about this time listening to a glorious recital in the Albert Hall by that brilliant Australian artist Eileen Joyce.

It was a hot day, and the pianist, having fallen from a horse during the week, was not feeling at her best. Five seconds after playing the final chord of the concerto she sensationally collapsed on the stage and had to be carried to her dressing room.

I reflected that perhaps I understood better than most people in the audience the mental strain she had endured to get through. The human nervous system is so marvellous in its ability to produce untold reserves of energy until the moment of the climax is reached.

There was a lot of rain in London before the last Test and we knew the match would be played on a wet wicket. So many people had the idea England would thereby gain an advantage.

They were quickly, very quickly, disillusioned.

Washbrook being out through injury, young Dewes came in to the English side as opener and Hollies got his belated opportunity in place of Laker.

We included a leg-spinner ourselves for the first time in the series.

Our preliminary inspection disclosed a reasonably firm pitch, but one which had been absolutely soaked through and through. The outfield was damp and heavy so that scoring would be slow.

Once again my call of heads proved wrong and my career in England as Australia's captain ended by my losing my eighth toss out of nine in Test Matches, calling heads every time. Surely this must be a warning for my successor to call heads. The law of averages did not work in my case but in the long run it must.

I did not envy Yardley having to make the decision.

He elected to bat. I would have sent England in.

In case I am accused of being wise after the event or of saying this because of England's failure, may I stress that my reason would have been mainly the condition of the outfield. It had to be slow—couldn't have been slower—and must quicken up during the game.

The wicket, too, whilst not indicating difficulty would obviously not be one on which much liberty could be taken.

Anyway, what followed Yardley's decision will be talked about long after I am dead and gone.

The first time I captained an Australian Test team at the Oval, I was carried off the field with a broken bone in the ankle and England made her highest Test Match score of 903 for 7 wickets. Now in my last match at the Oval, as captain of Australia, England made 52, the lowest score ever recorded by her Test team in the Mother Country.

It was one of those dream days for a fielding skipper.

Events opened slowly but soon a lovely ball from Miller penetrated Dewes' defence. Edrich came and made a half-hearted pull stroke off

Johnston, but Hassett pounced on the ball near the square-leg umpire and held a fine catch.

With the advent of Compton, I took very special care in the placing of Arthur Morris behind square-leg.

Ten years before I had seen Compton hook a ball at Lord's. My mind registered the exact spot to which it travelled, and hopefully I thought he might do it again. It was a question of whether he would try the shot.

He did and Morris gathered in a lovely catch, swift and sure, without time for reflection.

Next it was Tallon's opportunity, and he made no mistake when he held a tickle from Crapp.

Then for a while we did not need the fieldsmen. Lindwall, four times in succession, sent the stumps flying and at last, Hutton, who had defied our attack right through, touched one on the leg-side. He may reasonably have looked for a boundary. Instead he saw Tallon move across with uncanny anticipation, scoop the ball in his outstretched left glove as it sped towards earth, turning a somersault but serenely holding the ball aloft. No greater catch has been seen behind the wickets.

The innings lasted two hours ten minutes.

Of the 52 runs, 9 batsmen had contributed 9 runs. Hutton had made 30—never made a loose stroke—was completely untroubled. Not one man lost his wicket because of the state of the pitch.

One must give full marks to the superb, faultless out-cricket of Australia.

Lindwall from 16·1 overs got 6 for 20, of which 5 for 8 were taken after lunch. He set the seal on a grand season and caused enthusiasts to start wondering where he stood in relation to his great predecessors.

What was wrong with England?

For once, let us be content to say the bowling and fielding were too good.

The English batting lacked spirit, and even though Hutton played a fine defensive innings he did not attempt to take the initiative.

Sometimes desperate measures are necessary to combat a desperate situation and, after the early disasters, to whom could they look but Hutton?

He hit only one boundary in 130 minutes—his last scoring shot. Hutton possesses the most complete defensive technique of all the moderns. He has the shots, too, but the will to use them seems to be more a matter of mood than direction.

By way of contrast, Barnes and Morris opened Australia's innings by confident, purposeful batting and without being ruffled passed England's total in less than an hour.

In faultless, copybook Test Match style they went on to 117 before Barnes touched one from Hollies and Evans snapped it up.

As I walked out to another wonderful ovation, my mind went back 18 years to Jack Hobbs' final Test on the same ground.

The scene was re-enacted. The fieldsmen gathered round, gave three cheers, wished me good luck (for after-years, of course) and the play was resumed.

I dearly wanted to do well.

It was not to be. That reception had stirred my emotions very deeply and made me anxious—a dangerous state of mind for any batsman to be in. I played the first ball from Hollies though not sure I really saw it.

The second was a perfect length googly which deceived me. I just touched it with the inside edge of the bat and the off bail was dislodged.

So in the midst of my great jubilation at our team's success, I had a rather sad heart about my own farewell as I wended my way pavilionwards.

In my final matches at Nottingham, Leeds, Manchester and Lord's, I scored centuries, so maybe the Oval was just one of those great reminders which are continually being sent to cricketers to keep their feet, metaphorically speaking, on the ground.

Here may I quote the following extract from a London newspaper :—

" All yesterday was a day of Test drama.

When . . . reached the wicket to play what was generally regarded as his last innings in Test cricket, the opposing players paid him a magnificent tribute.

They gathered round him and at the call of their captain, took off their caps and gave him three cheers. The crowd joined in a tornado of cheering. Seldom, if ever, can any cricketer have received such an ovation.

It seemed out of keeping with the occasion that the greatest of all Test Match careers should have such an ending. But the crowd cheered him all the way back to the pavilion.

It was a saddened man who walked into the pavilion.

Emotion, it was obvious, had seized him.

He dropped his glove as he went and stooped like a man in a dream to pick it up.

The Oval spectators, disappointed as they were, cheered affectionately—an old friend was saying good-bye.

The little wicket gate swung, . . . passed through and disappeared for ever from the Test Match scene."

Maybe you are thinking that the quotation refers to my farewell innings at the Oval.

If so, you are wrong. It describes Jack Hobbs' last appearance in 1930 (my first Test at the Oval).

However, the similarity is so marked that I felt it was worth repeating. Yet so distinguished a person as Professor Walter Murdoch says that history never repeats itself.

In this instance it went very close.

The match was already over as England faced a hopeless task.

She fought back well and might still have had some chance, but for another magnificent innings by Arthur Morris, who appeared rather unlucky to lose the umpire's decision in a close run-out call. This 196 was the innings of a young master who had steadily gone from strength to strength until he stood that day firmly entrenched as not only the greatest contemporary left-hand bat, but in my opinion, the greatest left-hander I have ever seen.

There is little point in describing the rest of the game. Australia again bowled and fielded splendidly, the ubiquitous Lindwall taking a catch in the gully off Compton so quickly that it must have been instinct not eyesight. Hutton again batted for a long time, always on the defensive, but there was no hope and only a storm delayed the end.

There was a personal interest in the last three wickets.

Ray Lindwall, by taking 27 wickets in the Tests had equalled Ted McDonald's record for one series against England.

Could he get more? He tried hard but the odd one eluded him as Bill Johnston spun out the last three men also to claim 27 wickets in the series.

Before leaving the scene, tributes to my own career were kindly spoken by H. D. G. Leveson-Gower and Norman Yardley, to which I replied.

The Oval crowd gave generous applause to our team and to me personally as we left with the cricket supremacy of the world securely tucked away.

If England will only take heed of the lessons so obvious to all throughout the season's play, it may be a very different story at the Oval in 1953.

Mopping-up Operations

HAVING CONCLUDED THE REALLY SERIOUS BUSINESS AND THE PRIME PURpose of the tour—five Tests—we still had five first-class and two second-class matches on the programme.

Kent was next on the list and a record crowd thronged the picturesque Canterbury Ground, many of them hoping to see tangible signs of Fagg's claims to Test selection. The match provided further evidence of Australia's superiority.

Yardley calls for three cheers as Bradman bids farewell to Test Cricket. The Oval, 1948

Winning the toss, we batted. Brown led off with 106 and there were several other useful scores in a total of 361.

The Kent team could only muster 51 and, in the follow-on, 124. Again it was Lindwall and Johnston who started the debacle.

There was some excitement in a 71 partnership in 32 minutes between Pawson and Evans, whilst J. G. W. Davies gave a brilliant exhibition of fielding at cover—equal to anything we saw on the trip.

Our match against the Gentlemen of England at Lord's was to mark my farewell appearance on that historic ground. Naturally, I was anxious to do well.

The English team, although it included Yardley, was under the captaincy of R. W. V. Robins.

There had, throughout the season, been an agitation in certain quarters for Robins to captain England. His supporters pointed to his great year as Captain of Middlesex when undoubtedly he played a big part in the winning of the Championship. They also claimed he had a flair for doing the unexpected and disrupting the opposition.

By now I was sensing the possibility of an unbeaten record and was on the look out for any moves.

I need not have worried. I won the toss and at stumps we were unbeatable, having scored 478 for 3.

Brown got 120, Hassett was 119 not out, and my own desire to depart from Lord's on a merry and successful note was gratified by one of my best knocks of the tour for 150, after which I threw my hand away.

Incidentally, in doing so I passed my 2,000 runs for the tour to become the only Australian ever to score 2,000 runs on each of four tours of England.

The match coincided with my 40th birthday and on the second last day, one day before my birthday, I was presented at lunch with a beautiful copy of *Lord's* (by Sir Pelham Warner) and a big cake made in the form of an open book. The cake was about 18 inches square. On one leaf was the wording :—

> " To Don Bradman.
>   Many Happy Returns of the Day
>   From all at Lord's."

On the other leaf was a sweet bouquet of roses and a photo of myself inset in the right-hand corner, whilst on each corner of the base was a marzipan kangaroo.

These presentations were made by the Earl of Gowrie, President of M.C.C., who in a short but delightful address conveyed greetings from everyone and explained they were making the presentation a day early because they were fearful the match may not go on until the third day.

Prior to that small ceremony, I had closed our innings at 5 for 610, Hassett having played a great hand for 200 not out.

Bradman says farewell to the Earl of Gowrie, President of M.C.C., 1948

Nobody stayed very long for the Gentlemen except Simpson, who again had a good double and confirmed the fine impression formed of him earlier at Nottingham.

Bill Edrich in the second innings scored a century by attacking cricket of a kind he might have successfully employed in the Tests. He delayed the end, but we won by an innings and 81 runs, with 35 minutes to spare.

On the final day, the Australian players gathered around me as we entered the field and sang "Happy Birthday", probably an unprecedented happening at Lord's and one which touched me very greatly.

Then at the conclusion of the match the public converged on to the playing field in front of the pavilion and sang "Happy Birthday" and "Auld Lang Syne". Several of us went out on the dressing room balcony to wave good-bye.

So it was on my 40th birthday I left forever the headquarters of cricket, happy in the knowledge of a great win, a century, a host of wonderful friends and an abiding conviction that I must have played the game as it should be played to earn these warm-hearted tributes.

No man could have ordered his cricket life better than to end at headquarters on such a congenial note, and it was with mixed feelings of pride and sadness I drove through the Grace Gates that evening.

This sentimental angle which had crept into the final matches was proving a great strain. I felt physically and mentally tired. Moreover, my emotions had been stirred and I found great difficulty in keeping myself up to concert pitch.

A rest for the Somerset match helped.

Here an overwhelming victory came to Australia, who made 560 for 5 declared, to Somerset's 115 and 71. Harvey and Hassett made centuries. So did Ian Johnson—the first one of his career. It shouldn't be the last—Ian is too good a bat for that.

Unlucky Ron Hamence got 99. All the boys were trying so hard to help Ronnie get a century. He got to 99 and hit 2 balls with terrific speed only to see them gathered by a fieldsman, then fell to what everyone said was the best ball all day.

McCool's 8 for 44 in the match was a reminder of our strength, seeing that he had not played in a Test.

About that time I received through the post a copy of the *Portsmouth Evening News* dated September 1st.

There was a little note inside : " I know your team is good but I didn't know it was *that* good. See Stop Press." I looked in the Stop Press and found : " Cricket—Australians 1229 for two." He was right—we weren't quite that good.

The penultimate first-class fixture was a festival game against the South of England at Hastings where Brian Valentine led a composite team against us.

I'm afraid it was much the same story all over again. Australia batted and made 522 for 7, of which Hassett, Harvey and I all made centuries. Loxton appeared to be well on the way when I closed.

There was a real picnic atmosphere about the game. Players went for shots—nearly everyone had a bowl, Bill Brown getting the surprising figures of 4 for 16 in the South's total of 298.

Rain and much boisterous wind interfered with the game so that a draw was the only possible result.

We were pleased before leaving to take part in a charming ceremony at which Sir Pelham Warner, on behalf of the festival committee, presented Denis Compton with a silver salver to commemorate his great feat of 1947 in scoring more centuries in a season (and also more runs) than any other batsman.

Hastings had been the scene of Denis' triumph and this modest cricketer was obviously nervous in replying.

One to go—Scarborough—where more than one great Australian team, including Armstrong's 1921 side and the 1938 tourists, have bitten the dust.

There has always been a certain amount of feeling about the Scarborough game. Australia takes the view that if it is to be a festival match, the English team should be of a festival nature and play cricket as such.

In actual fact, Mr. Leveson-Gower has consistently selected what is commonly referred to as the 6th Test team and by their actions the Englishmen have left the opposition in no doubt about their intention to win, even to the extent of declaring and sending Australia in just before stumps, as was done in 1938.

On this present tour, I had made it plain to " Shrimp " that we would not relish a " Test " at Scarborough and would fight every inch of the way to preserve our reputation.

The Scarborough team was a strong one—just about the strongest available side, seeing that Compton and Washbrook could not play.

Robins won the toss and batted. In a twinkling we were on top, for Lindwall shattered Hutton's stumps right away.

Fishlock's 38 was top score in a total of 177 and again Lindwall had taken 6 wickets in an innings, albeit bowling at only three-quarter pace.

The issue was put beyond doubt by our batsmen, who strung together 489 for 8 before I closed.

Of these, Barnes made 151, the last 51 being made in 25 minutes and including 3 sixes and 7 fours.

I made 153 in 190 minutes, 2 sixes and 19 fours, and gave my wicket away.

A sad incident in the play was the injury to Loxton who sustained a fractured nose when a ball which he tried to sweep to leg curled off the edge of the bat into his face.

I did not attempt to force a win, for the simple reason my bowlers were now completely tired out—Lindwall and Johnston especially.

They had stuck grimly to their task right to the end and I was not going to risk physical injury by pushing them beyond the limits of reasonable endurance.

There was criticism of my action but I have no apology to make. I would do the same again.

Only those who have toured know the great strain upon Australian players after the last Test is over. Reaction sets in—there is no longer any great incentive—the job is done.

During one luncheon interval I was the recipient of a wonderful tribute from the Yorkshire County Cricket Club.

Their President, Mr. T. L. Taylor, made a speech and announced that the Club had made me an honorary Life Member. This was the first time anyone but an Englishman had been so honoured.

They also presented me with a silver tray, white rose inset, with the following inscription :—

Presented by The Yorkshire County
Cricket Club
to
D. G. Bradman
to commemorate his outstanding performances
in Test Matches at Headingly, Leeds.
1930, 334 ; 1934, 304 ; 1938, 103 and 16 ;
1948, 33 and 173 not out.

Later, I was to receive Honorary Life Membership of the Manchester
and Lancashire C.C.C.   I quote the letter I received from them, as I
value so much the sentiments therein :—

" May I say on behalf of my Committee how deeply we appreciate
your willingness to agree to our desire for you to become an Honorary
Life Member of this Club.

My Committee direct me to say that they are not only appreciative
of all you have done for Australian, English and International Cricket,
but also wish to put on record that your personal charm, courtesy,
good fellowship and complete efficiency and modesty in everything
you have undertaken, have done much to make cricket the vital force
it is today, and also to bind together our British Commonwealth
wherever cricket is played.

Yours very sincerely,
R. Howard,
Secretary

Hampshire County Cricket Club similarly honoured me, and to all
these Counties I am deeply grateful and sensitive of the honour.

Finis had been written to the last chapter of my English first-class
cricket career.   I bowled the last over of the day.   The sun went down
just as usual.

Apart from the feeling of personal satisfaction, I freely admit to the
great pleasure of achieving one ambition—to lead an Australian team
through an English tour undefeated.

No other Australian side in history had been able to avoid defeat.

We made more centuries than any previous team.   No side made
300 against us outside the Tests.   The only batsmen to make centuries
against us were those who played in the Tests.

Our record was 31 matches played, 23 won (15 by an innings), 8
drawn, the finest record of any touring team.

Prior to 1948, Armstrong's great team of 1921 and Darling's of 1902
were usually regarded as the two strongest teams to visit England.

Here are some comparative figures.

Armstrong's team won 58 per cent. of their matches.   Darling's
team 59 per cent.   The 1948 side won 72 per cent.

A direct comparison between batting and bowling averages would be unfair. One team may have been exceptionally strong in bowling but correspondingly weaker in batting.

The seasons may have been different.

It is fair, however, to quote the margin between batting and bowling figures, for this takes care of both sides of the picture.

The margin in 1902 was 8, in 1921 it was 16, but in 1948 it was no less than 30, fractions being omitted in each case.

This comparison is overwhelmingly in favour of the 1948 side.

Throughout the season the team displayed brilliant forceful batsmanship, glorious fielding supported by bowling of variety, purpose and great penetrative power.

No one could cavil at the type of cricket played; indeed it was a revelation to most English crowds.

We had our share of misfortunes.

McCool's injury put him out of the running for the Tests before we started.

Lindwall bravely carried on whilst his leg mended, so did Loxton. We had no Miller to bowl at Lord's, Toshack broke down at Leeds, and Barnes was out of a few matches.

These things more than counter-balanced England's own misfortunes in the loss of Wright, Washbrook, etc.

Yet we were never really in danger of defeat unless it was at Bradford, and there Australia batted a man short.

History may decide whether it was the greatest Australian team ever. I can't. For me, I'm satisfied to say it was a really great team, whose strength lay in its all-round ability, versatility and brilliance allied to bulldog courage.

You can often get some of these things; to get the lot is a rarity.

Seven players scored over 1,000 runs. It should have been 8, for Loxton was a mere 27 short when he broke his nose in the last game and had to retire.

Everyone of those players at times threw his innings away, the leading ones on several occasions. Figures were not made for the sake of making them.

Arthur Morris's average was the highest of any player (excepting myself) making his first tour of England.

Only Bill Johnston achieved the coveted 100 wickets. The others all pulled their weight and this wide distribution of wickets tells its own story of strength.

The team which depends on two bowlers can't hope to match, over a period, the team which has adequate resources to meet all situations.

I must, of course, make some special reference to Ray Lindwall.

Was he the best Australian fast bowler of all time? I don't know.

My era in cricket extends from the Gregory-McDonald combination because I played against these men.

I rate Lindwall and McDonald the two finest Australian fast bowlers of the period.

McDonald had a higher delivery than Lindwall and marvellous stamina. Purely as a bowler there can be little between them. Lindwall must rank far ahead of McDonald as a cricketer by virtue of his great fielding and at times high-class batting.

What a pair would Gregory and Lindwall have been in one side.

Two second-class fixtures were played in Scotland before the tour ended. Both were outright victories for us.

Scottish cricket is only about the level of a weak English county and so did not provide much opposition.

They did provide, however, in Scotland marvellous hospitality. Nothing was a trouble, and the Australians did appreciate their break in the North.

My own final innings of the tour was at Aberdeen, where I gratified not only my own wish but that of the people too by finishing with 123 not out in 89 minutes. As a spectacle it must have been my best effort of the trip.

Before going south we were the guests of the King and Queen at Balmoral on the Sunday afternoon. Blue skies and light clouds made a lovely canopy as we strolled around the gardens with their Majesties.

The two Princesses and the Duke of Edinburgh also attended, and we all cherished their friendly homely manner in meeting and chatting to us in the garden and at tea.

It was a red letter day for everyone of us.

So far as I knew, nothing happened to mar the enjoyment of the day, but I reckoned without the ubiquitous press photographer who took numerous photos at all sorts of times.

One of them, subsequently published in the press, showed me with my hands in my pockets, and this provided a glorious opportunity for certain people publicly to express their views on the question.

The same sort of thing happened on a previous occasion with King George V. Bill Woodfull and the rest of the team were then accused of bad manners because of a photo showing them wearing hats. The fact that His Majesty had requested them to keep their hats on was apparently not taken into account.

Anyway, what is one to do with one's hands on an informal occasion ? I am indebted to the editor of a country paper who expressed himself thereon as follows :—

" *IDLE HANDS.* The vexed question of what to do with one's hands when they are not actively engaged in furthering the ends of their owner has been raised once again as a result of criticism of the

Australian cricketer, Don Bradman, who is said to have had his hands in the Bradman pockets while strolling with the King in the grounds of Balmoral Castle.

Without entering into the controversy regarding what Don should have done with his hands on this occasion, it is only fair to point out that even had he wished he could not have left them behind at Lord's, and since there was apparently no bat nearby to occupy them he may have felt that in the interests of tidiness they should be put away while not in use.

From time to time various alternative methods of disposing of hands have been suggested. They range from the Ned Kelly tradition, which required that the bushranger's customers should ' put those hands up ' to the thoughtful habit of the householder standing before the open fireplace easily adjusting his coat tails to ensure a proper distribution of beneficent warmth over the largest possible expanse. Schoolmasters often are to be observed in apparently earnest consultation with their fellows with their hands resting easily beneath the bustle-like protrusions of the gathered hinder parts of their academic robes, while those of us who lack the academic robe may clasp our hands beneath our coat tails to expose a benign rotundity to the world that deplores our pockets.

But whatever may be the outcome of the social question of what exactly Bradman should have done with his hands when he took them with him to Balmoral, it is at least clear that no serious harm can come to those who keep their hands in their own pockets, and that only the income tax collector is permitted by law to put his hands in someone else's."

Subsequent events rather tend to indicate that at least His Majesty was not displeased.

I couldn't say the same for the press reporter who wanted to know what His Majesty and I had discussed, and received an answer which left him in no doubt that his interview with me was at an end.

We travelled that night to London and on the Monday were the guests of *The People*, which had arranged a big farewell luncheon in my honour at the Savoy Hotel.

Some weeks previously this newspaper had announced the inauguration of what they called " The Bradman Fund ".

Subscriptions were limited to 1/-, and from the proceeds they decided to give me a replica of the famous Warwick Vase. The history of this vase may, I think, be interpolated here :—

" The original vase now rests in safe keeping at Warwick Castle, England.

Sir William Hamilton found the vase in 1770 when he was English Ambassador at the Court of Naples.

Being something of an archaeologist, he employed his spare time draining a small lake called Pantanello and digging in the ruins of the villa at Tiber (about 12 miles from Rome) which had been held in high delight by the Roman Emperor Hadrian.

Sir William had no difficulty in finding the villa, or at least part of it, for in its original state Hadrian had a cosy little place about seven miles long, with innumerable halls, courts and libraries.

He found many rich treasures there, including the vase, complete except for one missing head. How the vase came there is not known.

Hadrian's villa was occupied by the Ostro-Gothic King, Totila, A.D. 540, when he laid siege to Rome, and the vase may have been cast into the lake to save it from the invaders.

The villa was finished about A.D. 138, but this artistic work is of an earlier date, and is attributed to Lysippus of Sicyon, a Greek artist of the close of the 4th Century B.C., when the beautiful or elegant style began to replace the noble severity of Phidias and his school.

The original vase is of white marble and is circular in form. It is 5 ft. 6 in. high and is 5 ft. 8 in. in diameter at the lip, and is placed on a square pedestal of modern construction.

The handles are formed of pairs of vine stems, the smaller branches of which twine around the upper lip, and with drooping bunches of grapes form a symmetrical freeze.

The lower rim is covered by two tiger or panther skins, of which the heads and forepaws adorn the sides of the vase, while the hind legs interlace and hang down between the handles.

Arranged along the tiger skins are several heads, all except one being those of Sileni, or male attendants of Bacchus and the single exception being a female head.

Sir William Hamilton was responsible for restoring the vase, and had the bright idea of substituting his wife's head for that of the missing satyr.

He engaged an Italian sculptor (name unknown) and persuaded Lady Hamilton to sit for him. She was one of the most striking beauties of the 18th Century—famous the world over as the mistress of the one and only Nelson.

The artist was tempermental and Lady Hamilton even more so. Sitting after sitting ended in fierce quarrels.

Then the day came when the great work was done.

Sir William found himself gazing at a striking resemblance of his wife, but for one thing. The vengeful sculptor had concentrated on milady's ears. They were wonderful ears. They were the long delicate ears of a Greek faun.

Naturally Lady Hamilton did not like her new ears, and it may have been to preserve the domestic peace of his household that Sir William parted with this precious relic.

The Warwick Vase presented to Bradman by Cricket lovers of England, 1948

He presented it to his maternal nephew, George, Earl of Warwick. It now stands, a dream of white marble, in the special conservatory built for it at Warwick Castle.

It stands on a marble pedestal bearing the Latin inscription :—

' This monument of ancient Roman art and magnificence was dug out of the ruins of Tiber which was held in high delight by the Emperor Hadrian. The Knight, William Hamilton, envoy from George III, the great British King to the Sicilian King Ferdinand IV, caused it to be restored, and dispatching it to this country, dedicated it to the father of genius of fine arts in the year of our Lord 1774.'

Between the heads of the Sileni already referred to, are thyrsi or bacchi staves twined round with ivy and vine shoots and litui, or laugural wands, used in taking omens.

The uses of the vase, which holds 163 gallons, have been the theme of speculation.

Many suppose it to have been a vessel designed to contain wine mixed with water, and intended for the centre of a chamber devoted to festive uses, but it was more probably constructed solely for decorative purposes, and may have formed the ornament of a temple of Bacchus."

So much for the history of the original. The replica, which was presented to me, is a magnificent work in solid silver, standing 21 in. high, including the base, on which is the following inscription :—

Presented to
Don Bradman
by cricket lovers of Britain.
This trophy, a tribute to a great Australian
Sportsman, was subscribed for by people
through *The People* Newspaper, London
1948

To me this trophy will always convey a special memory of the kindness of the common folk of England, and will serve to remind me of four wonderful cricket seasons in their midst which I am delighted to think brought some pleasure and enjoyment to their lives.

The balance of the fund was at my request to be employed in the laying down of concrete cricket pitches in park lands throughout England in an effort to encourage and help the budding cricketers.

Many old players attended the luncheon, amongst them 7 former Captains of England (not including Yardley) and 9 County Captains. Harold Larwood came and sat next to Ray Lindwall. What a pity we can't see them bowling in the same match, both at their top, to get a comparison.

Arthur Cousens, Chairman of Odhams Press Ltd., proprietors of *The People*, presided. The Earl of Gowrie made the presentation and Norman Yardley supported the toast.

I was very deeply sensitive of the great honour paid me, and also of the significance of the occasion, for it represented the very spirit of cricket.

At one table sat ten young lads selected to come as representatives of thousands who had subscribed to the fund. Many of the subscribers were youngsters who wrote humorous letters with their subscriptions. Here is one :—

" Dear Don,
    Thank goodness you've quitted. Perhaps we'll have a chance now. I'm sending my shilling in thankfulness.
                              Yours sincerely "

My remarks were necessarily serious. One cannot very well fail to understand the significance of retiring after such a long period of service, and I endeavoured to strike the right chord by enunciating the principles which I had followed throughout my career and which I felt I could commend to my successor.

I do think it a grand tribute that over 200 people should have come from many parts of England to say farewell.

Their deep love of the game and simple devotion to it made one very conscious how much cricket really touches the heart strings of the British people.

The rest of our stay in London, all too brief, was taken up in getting our things ready for the return journey and in saying *au revoir* to the many friends, old and new, we were to leave behind.

For me there was considerable conflict.

I love England and its people very dearly.

I could live there happily, and have always felt that I see my English friends all too seldom.

This time it was an indefinite good-bye for I could not say when or if I would return.

Norman Yardley (England's Skipper), R. W. V. Robins (Australian Board's liaison officer) and Ronnie Aird (Assistant Secretary, M.C.C.) all came on the boat train to Tilbury and saw us off. There was a short broadcast to the people, a few formalities and we were homeward bound.

As I watched the pier gradually recede, the handkerchiefs waving— not all of them dry—I really felt here was the end of a mission.

It had been without doubt in every sense the grandest tour of all.

Cricket had benefited and prospered this summer for the spirit of the game and everything associated with it had been kept on the highest level.

Whatever inspired me to go, I felt it had been ordained for a greater purpose than the pleasure or success of individuals—it had been my destiny to do what I could for cricket and in my heart I knew I could not have done more.

I am certain the early resumption of post-war Tests was welcomed by cricket lovers everywhere but particularly in England.

Our team had brought a measure of entertainment to the English workmen, appreciation of which was expressed in a simple but sincere letter which I received from one of them. It read :—

" Dear Don,

I am no sentimentalist but I feel I must convey to you and your side my thanks and appreciation for the wonderful cricket both in skill and sportsmanship your side and you have given the English public this season.

Myself, I write as an ordinary English workman who has been privileged to witness the displays of your team and you at Trent Bridge and Lord's, and what a feast of enjoyment and a tonic they have been to me in these rather exacting times.

Also on returning home from a hard day's work the radio commentaries have been so full of interest that we (and I know I speak for other workers) have forgotten about the little less sugar we now have in our tea and the shortage of meat on our plate ! ! "

The final compliment came to us in a letter I received from the British Minister of State, Philip Noel-Baker, who wrote me from the Commonwealth Relations Office in Downing Street on 25th September.

After referring to the work which the team and I had done for Commonwealth relations during the tour, he concluded by saying :—

" No team from Australia has had such an unbroken and astonishing measure of cricket success.

But your success has not only lain in victories on the field. No visiting team at any game has ever been so popular as yours this year.

No team has ever done so much to stimulate and to create good feeling.

Both the United Kingdom and Australia owe you a real debt of gratitude, and I hope you are very proud of what you have done."

Perhaps I may say, " Yes we are," but our abiding thought is one of thankfulness that we were given the opportunity and the ability to attempt it.

Summing Up

In years to come, the 1948 tour will provide a topic of conversation amongst young and old.

There will be arguments and counter-arguments as to whether it was the equal of earlier combinations. Nothing can alter the figures which will appear in black and white in the record books, but they cannot record the spirit which permeated the side, the courage and fighting qualities of the players, for these intangible things cannot be measured. They were on a very high plane.

Before long, 1948 will become a memory even to those of this generation. The youngsters will have to rely on books for their knowledge of this tour. It seems to me, therefore, that a short impression of each player by me, their skipper, might be appreciated.

The following short sketches of their 1948 form are intended to serve this purpose and not to represent a critical analysis. It will be of absorbing interest to look back on them even twenty years hence.

Don Bradman. It may appear presumptuous that I should include myself. Well, I think the world, which reads newspaper articles about the Bradman of 1948 compared with the Bradman of 1930, will be interested in what I think.

Firstly as Captain, I was conscious of far greater knowledge than in former years—purely a matter of experience. I made bowling or fielding changes more quickly, on impulse if you like, and felt no qualms about doing what I thought was right irrespective of whether it agreed with the text book or not.

Having such a loyal team and great fielding side assisted me to an enormous degree.

As a fieldsman I was a good deal slower than in former years. It was all right if the ball came to me but I couldn't risk tearing muscles by attempting an impossible save. Years before, in the exuberance of youth I did it—often suffering the consequences—such as at Leeds 1934 when a torn thigh muscle put me out for nearly a month.

In 1948 I tore no muscles. I did what I thought was more important at 40 years of age—saw the tour through.

As batsman I was more sedate—relied more on placing than power, and could not maintain for very long a period of solid aggression. Moreover, on numerous occasions, I threw my innings away rather than take the risk of breaking down, which happens more easily when muscles get tired. But I think my defence was a little sounder than before—also my judgment of what to do, and there was less unorthodoxy.

Not such a change—with one factor off-setting another—but sufficient for me to realise the best days were over and it was time I should make way for a younger man.

Lindsay Hassett. Was a great player and valuable lieutenant as Vice-captain. His knowledge of the game and views on tactics extremely sound. Beautiful stroke maker when in the mood ; capable of taking charge at critical moments and always willing to risk his wicket in the interests of the match.

A sound defence made him at home under almost any conditions. Loved the drive and the cut, but his forcing shot off the toes in front of square-leg was the one I liked best.

Also a splendid field—mostly used on the fence except when the new ball was called for when he was second only to Barnes as a brilliant specialist at short-leg.

Arthur Morris. I think Arthur, towards the close of the 1948 tour, was playing the finest cricket of any left-hand bat I've seen.

He had that wonderful quality so noticeable in good players—plenty of time to make his shots. All strokes came alike—hooks, drives, cuts, glances. Powerful wrists and forearms.

Unorthodox at times ; bat not always straight in defence—merely a sign of genius, for in actual play it did not let him down. Always forceful and aggressive in outlook with an ideal temperament.

Splendid reliable and versatile field. Took some brilliant catches near the wicket. Bowled left-hand googly with no mean skill, but his batting pushed his bowling into the background. Great team man ; studious and intelligent observer.

Bill Brown. Was still the perfect copy-book model in cricket. All his shots were made with delightful orthodoxy and he played every one in the book when the right ball came along.

Not aggressive enough to suit all tastes, but being an opening batsman was always keen on giving the side a good start.

Excellent team man. Took a great pride in his physical fitness, and on this, his third tour, fielded brilliantly throughout on the boundary—probably catching better than ever.

Nobody in my time leg-glanced the ball so beautifully. Anything on the leg stump was gracefully glided away just like a true artist.

Sam Loxton. Did a magnificent job as utility player. Very strong physically. Extremely powerful driver and the best player of the

Don Bradman (Captain) and Lindsay Hassett (Vice-Captain) of the undefeated Australian Team, 1948

lofted drive amongst the moderns. Tremendous fighter, always throwing every ounce into the game. Fast medium bowler who could keep going for long spells—on occasions bowled really fast and worried the best batsmen.

The most dangerous field in the team. Did some stupendous things to get run-outs. I have never seen anyone who had such a powerful throw when off balance.

Keith Miller. One of the most volatile cricketers of any age.

Long rangy athletic type—drove the ball with tremendous power— tried to hit sixes with abandon. Many of them were prodigious.

Would have been a far better player had he curbed this propensity and showed more judgment in his hitting. Dangerous bowler with the new ball, swinging it both ways not much short of Lindwall's pace. Also bowled off-spinners on a turning wicket.

In 1948 was the best slip field in the world.

Altogether a crowd-pleasing personality of the Jack Gregory type, whose limitations were caused mainly by his own failure to concentrate.

Sid Barnes. Remarkably solid and efficient opening bat. Seldom beaten and dismissed by a good ball but mostly lost his wicket when set and attempting a shot. Had one outstanding stroke—the square cut which he would make even from a ball pitched on the stumps.

Tremendous power in his wrists and forearms. Great fighter, as he showed at Manchester, where, despite injury, he insisted on batting, only to collapse in the middle of the pitch.

Very useful, accurate leg-spin bowler and the best short-leg fieldsman in the world.

Neil Harvey. This 19-year-old left-hander was a powerfully built lad in a compact frame. The possessor of lovely wrists, very flexible and strong.

Failed at first when the ball was turning but gradually absorbed the lessons and played brilliantly towards the end under all conditions.

Capable of tearing the best bowling to shreds and altering the whole outlook of a match in no time. Played all the shots, with the pull and the square cut predominating. Some of his audacity in stroke play astounded the bowlers. Very many critics and players too, rated him the finest outfield ever seen in England. His catching and throwing were sensational.

Ron Hamence. A fine batsman of the strictly orthodox type. Very sound and reliable with his game based on driving.

Because of the strong array of batsmen ahead of him, seldom had an opportunity to make big scores but always batted well and often at a critical moment made valuable runs.

An extremely useful reserve who could have been played in the Tests with confidence.

Very safe fieldsman in the country—good throw—and at times bowled well with the new ball—medium right hand. Above all, a great tourist who did wonders for the morale of the side.

Don Tallon. Performed some astonishing feats behind the stumps. Taking his performance as a whole, I rated his wicket-keeping better than that of any predecessor. Without having quite the grace of Old-field, nevertheless had a pleasing style for a tallish man, was like lightning in his stumpings and was abnormally safe excepting for odd days when his concentration seemed to slacken.

Was at his best when "keeping" to fast bowling.

Les Ames was a sounder bat—no other wicket-keeper I know could bat as well and none was as brilliant in stroke play. When given the opportunity (and he liked nothing better) Don bowled slow leg-breaks so well that he might easily have made his mark in that direction.

Ron Saggers. Brought over as Tallon's understudy, Saggers did a splendid job. When Tallon had to be left out of the Leeds Test through injury, it was generally conceded that we did not suffer, because Saggers performed so ably.

Had not quite the speed or agility of Tallon but could always be relied upon for a solid performance. A most polished and unostentatious player.

Batting opportunities were limited. His century against Essex showed his ability, which was far above that of the average wicket-keeper.

Ernie Toshack. A player unique in every way. I cannot remember another of the same type.

His normal delivery was medium pace left arm over the wicket, and he would cut the ball from, say, a right-hander's off stump to his leg stump. Then he would spin one from leg to off, bowl a faster one straight through and occasionally just drift one either to off or leg.

Mostly bowled to one slip, three more on the off and five on the leg side. Often had a leg slip and a short forward leg.

He worried and got out all the best bats, was amazingly accurate and must have turned in fine figures had not his cartilage given way. This necessitated rest early in the trip and finally caused an operation.

Toshack was a safe field but not very mobile, his batting not highly regarded. Nevertheless, he made 51 runs in Tests for once out and took a lot of shifting if he made up his mind to stay there.

Ian Johnson. Slow right-hand off-spinner who really turned the ball and had a beautiful control of flight.

At his best on dry crumbling wickets—the wet ones made him too slow. It always looked as though he could be hit by a fast-footed batsman. That he wasn't may be put down to his straight ball, which was hard to detect and often left the striker down the wicket.

A most intelligent bowler, always scheming.

Splendid batsman—most valuable about number 7 and quite capable of a Test Match century. Also a very good slip field and completely devoted at all times to the welfare of the team as a whole.

Ray Lindwall. The man who so often broke the back of England's batting was this fine athlete. He went on from strength to strength until it became a question whether Australia ever had a better fast bowler. He wasn't always express, for he bowled intelligently both in regard to the team and himself. On one occasion he clean bowled Hutton with a slower ball—yet it was only the fourth ball of the match.

Lovely graceful rhythm in his action. Delivery not quite so high as to be ideal—lower, for instance, than Ted McDonald.

His outstanding attribute, to my mind, was control of direction. It was better than in any bowler (of comparative speed) and his length, too, left little to be desired.

Stamina also very good, if not outstanding.

A dashing field in any position—took many glorious catches.

Hard-hitting stroke player who might easily have been good enough to play in Tests for his batting had he been able to concentrate on this phase of cricket alone.

Bill Johnston. Tall, lithe left-hander who bowled fast-medium, or slow spinners according to the need. Clean bowled some of the best, and throughout the tour was constantly getting good wickets when perhaps a little more glamour was attaching to his faster colleague, Lindwall.

They finished with 27 wickets each in the Tests.

Johnston was faster than he looked, for he had a remarkably free arm. I believe Fagg of Kent thought him much harder to face with the new ball than Lindwall. Mailey rates him above Bill Whitty.

When bowling spinners he was quicker than the normal type and had a difficult curving flight. Quite a good field and as a batsman it was noticeable how often he held up the opposition when the end seemed near. With it all, a most amusing personality who saw the lighter side of everything he did.

Colin McCool. This player was without doubt the unlucky member of the side. After his fine performances in Australia against Hammond's men, Colin was naturally expected to do well in England.

He started splendidly. Then the third finger on his right hand (the one that spins the ball) caused trouble.

A small callus or wart would pull off after he had bowled some 15 overs, exposing the red raw flesh, and the wound would bleed freely. This would necessitate over a week's rest.

We were compelled to leave him out of consideration for the Tests because in them he might have been called upon to bowl far more overs than his finger would stand. He still performed well in county matches and played his part nobly.

As a batsman, Colin's style was obviously more suited to Australian conditions, but most of his low scores were caused by miraculous catches.

Doug. Ring. Bowled consistently well—always better than his figures indicated. Forced his way into the last Test. Only took one wicket but bowled excellently.

May have tried at times to bowl too fast. He would often beat bat and stumps but did not lure batsmen out of the crease sufficiently. Very safe field. Took some splendid catches near the wicket and also a stubborn batsman when asked for an effort. Normally, he was a light-hearted cricketer who liked having a bit of a go. Test cricket to him was a game. His spirits remained high under all circumstances.

Keith Johnson. In making brief sketches of the players, I cannot very well include our Manager, but I cannot leave him out as a member of the party, for he contributed an enormous amount towards the success of the tour.

Keith worked like a slave night and day. He never stopped answering the 'phone and writing letters.

Half-way through the tour he was so obviously fatigued I feared his health would break down. That it didn't was a tribute to a bulldog determination to see the job through.

He created friends and goodwill everywhere both for himself and the team, and no side could have wished for a better Manager.

On the boat journey home the players, at a special dinner, presented him with a solid silver Georgian salver. On it were engraved all their signatures, and never did more genuine sentiment accompany a gift.

Arthur James. Our masseur must be included, for he also contributed in no small measure to our success.

Arthur was never off the job. Midnight or anytime he was at one's side if required to tend an injury. Bowlers and batsmen had massage whenever they wanted it. Their slightest ailment was quickly dealt with.

In addition Arthur did myriads of things that weren't his job. For instance, he opened all my mail at cricket grounds—did most of the incessant autographs. I've seen him with an enormous basket of letters ready for posting.

Always a keen sense of unobtrusive humour which was valuable in the dressing room.

Bill Ferguson. This evergreen scorer and baggage man still had the secret of not losing a bag. How he did the various jobs, never ruffled, never hurried, scored, attended to laundry and so on, I don't know.

Bill was a wizard at his job. There will never be another to compare with him. He produced porters, lorries, railway carriages and everything almost by magic, and I never once heard him utter a word of complaint.

Testimonial Matches

IT WAS A VERY TIRED BUT HAPPY AUSTRALIAN TEAM WHICH EMBARKED at Tilbury on the Orient liner bound for Australia. When leaving England there is considerable mental conflict. Players cannot but feel a touch of sadness at their departure from the Mother Country and the many friends which naturally are made on tour. Conversely, Australia is home, and this is a magnet, drawing them back.

Playing cricket for several months on end, and trying to cope with the attendant round of hospitality and publicity, even in an England of austerity, is a tiring business.

For the first few days most of us were content to rest. We had the most wonderful, calm, sunny weather all the way from Tilbury to Port Said, and I constantly reflected upon what was, for me, my last visit to the Old Country as a player.

I have always proudly admitted my great love for England and her people. On this occasion there was a touch of pathos in the thought that I might be leaving both for the last time.

I always think a homeward journey passes more slowly because one's mission is accomplished. It seems as though the time is being put to no purpose.

Dr. Roland Pope consoled me in 1930 with the thought that people usually grow out of seasickness after about twenty years. There must be something in the theory, for at least I was much better on this voyage than ever before. It was a very happy and uneventful journey.

Nearing Australia's shores, I received a cable asking whether it was true that I had decided to enter Australian politics.

Although I had not indicated any interest in such a proposal, the matter evidently received prominence both in the Australian press and on the wireless.

I had not been consulted by anybody and had expressed no views.

Bradman greeted by his family upon arrival at Adelaide, 1948

Yet such is the force of "rumour" that the matter gave rise to a question in Parliament. Details of the question asked and the reply are recorded in Hansard.

There was a humorous side to it.

One of the first remarks passed to me when I disembarked on Australian soil came from a wharf labourer who, in front of a crowd of people, called out in a stentorian voice, "If you're going into Parliament, Don, you'd better stand for the Labour Party."

Soon afterwards my wife received a telegram from a well-known senator. It read :—

"Please use all your influence to keep your distinguished husband out of politics stop Winston Churchill has been reduced from the status of a world idol to a political stooge by the same people who would exploit the affection and respect that is held by all Australians for your husband kindest regards."

It would scarcely be "cricket" to reveal the identity of the sender. I have always been intrigued as to the purpose of this telegram.

For a politician to try and dissuade me from entering his own chosen profession seemed at least incongruous.

During my absence from Australia, the S.A. Cricket Association had very generously sponsored a move for a testimonial match to be held in my honour. All State Associations supported the project, and accordingly the match was arranged.

The Melbourne Cricket Ground was selected as the venue, because the organisers felt that the accommodation at Melbourne was more likely to guarantee the success of the match.

All members of the touring side agreed to play except, of course, Ernie Toshack, whose injured knee had not sufficiently recovered after his operation.

Quite naturally, I regarded the match as a wonderful compliment, but at the same time I was most anxious that it should provide spectators with bright and entertaining cricket.

Everything went like clockwork.

Twenty-four hours before the game was due to commence, heavy rain fell. On the morning of the match there was a perfectly blue and cloudless sky, and the ground after the rain looked an absolute picture.

Lindsay Hassett, who was captaining one side, won the toss and decided to bat. In the first day's play his team put together 383 for 9 wickets. Included in this total was a whirlwind innings of 104 by Ray Lindwall, whose score included 5 sixes and 9 fours.

Ray is not a big man physically, yet puts tremendous power into his shots.

The innings closed on Saturday at 406, and we had made 6 for 364 at stumps.

Although the match was not of a competitive nature, I was never so anxious in my life to make a score.

The Melbourne crowd of over 50,000 people gave me a heart-warming reception, and only those who have experienced these things can fully appreciate the emotions aroused.

Not only was I anxious to make a score, but I wanted to play good cricket without any suggestion of being helped along by the opposition.

My wish came true up to the time I had scored 97 runs. In that period the cricket had been keen, no chances given, and I saw in prospect the magic three figures. Then I tried to hook a short ball from Bill Johnston and skied it wide of mid-on.

As Colin McCool chased the ball, I was running down the pitch, fearing that after all my hopes would not come true. Colin got to the ball, juggled it and finally it fell to the ground, and we were able to run three for the shot to bring up my century.

Whether Colin could have held that catch or not is something I did not ask nor shall I ever do so, but I have never been more grateful to see a catch grassed.

The match was resumed on the Monday, when the cricket lost some of its seriousness. Our team were all out for 434, then, when Hassett's XI batted again, Barnes electrified the spectators with a truly magnificent six off Noblet's first ball.

Shortly afterwards he produced a toy cricket bat from under his sweater, and caused tremendous amusement by attempting to play the next ball with this bat. It was a slow delivery which curled off the bat into his face, whereupon Barnes threw the bat towards the square-leg umpire in mock disgust and picked up his full-sized one.

There was some criticism of Barnes' levity, but I think it was one of the most humorous incidents I have ever seen, and I am sure the spectators revelled in this departure from the ordinary course of events. Anyway, Barnes proceeded to make 89 runs in an innings which for powerful and attractive stroke play could scarcely have been surpassed.

Lindsay Hassett also played a delightful knock of 102, and his team put together a total of 430. This left my XI 403 runs to win.

Wickets fell early, including my own. Bill Johnston spun a good one which just caught the edge of my bat and was snapped up by the wicket-keeper. Our team appeared to be in a bad way when 7 wickets had fallen for 210, and of this total, Arthur Morris with an innings of 108, had been predominant.

It seemed that the match would end in the middle of the afternoon, when suddenly a dramatic change came over the play. First, Doug. Ring and then Noblet partnered Don Tallon, who began to stroke the ball with that effortless timing he had displayed on the same ground against the Englishmen in 1946-7.

Hassett's team tried very hard to end the match. The bowling was purposeful and the fielding keen, but Tallon was not to be denied. Members of my team in the dressing room were clustered round the window, and there was enough excitement for a Test Match.

Finally, when Dooland began the last over of the day, my team required 13 runs to win with the last two batsmen at the wickets. Runs came until there was one ball to go and three runs required. Tallon pulled it hard to square leg and two runs were taken. The third was impossible, and so the match ended in a tie.

It was a completely unpremeditated and genuine finish to a match remarkable for its brilliant and high quality cricket, and was the finest innings I ever saw Don Tallon play.

When he came into the dressing room Don was so excited that he honestly did not know whether we had won or not. In the last few fateful minutes, he had concentrated so hard on the play that he had misjudged the number of runs required in that concluding over.

I was deeply grateful to all those who had helped to make the match such a grand success. The players and the administrators had done everything possible, whilst the spectators turned out in greater numbers than had previously been seen in any Australian Testimonial. The financial return was more than I could have expected.

My services to Australian cricket had been given without thought of any such reward, and I certainly felt more than recompensed for anything I had done for cricket. Perhaps in the years to come I may be able to make up the leeway.

I had intended to retire completely from first-class cricket at the conclusion of the English tour, but this resolution had to go by the board in view of my testimonial match, in which obviously I had to play.

A Knighthood

Then came January 1st, 1949. It was announced on the front page of the morning papers that my name was included amongst the list of Australians who had been honoured with a knighthood by His Majesty the King.

These things do not happen at once. The recipient is advised beforehand.

No man ever had less ambitions in that direction. I neither desired nor anticipated any recognition of my services. They had been spontaneously given. There was no thought of reward. However, it was clear that I was the medium through which was to be expressed England's appreciation of what Australian cricket has meant to the British Empire. In that way it was a compliment to Australia and to the game of cricket.

I had for some time carried the knowledge of the impending announcement, but obviously could not give the slightest indication one way or another to embarrassing newspaper queries.

On 31st December I attended the Melbourne Cricket Ground to watch Victoria play South Australia, and was completely taken back when numerous people came to me and offered their congratulations. When I enquired, " What for ? " they would usually say, " On to-morrow's announcement," or answer in some evasive fashion.

This was a difficult day, for under no circumstances could I give any clue as to the correctness of the rumour which had obviously leaked out.

That evening I deliberately spent with friends out of the city to dodge further awkward situations.

The wireless was playing when midnight struck and then the National Anthem was played. I immediately told my host and hostess that I was now at liberty to reveal a secret which would be disclosed in the morning paper.

They could scarcely comprehend my waiting until the midnight hour had struck before saying anything.

Shortly afterwards they drove me home. On the way we bought an early edition of the morning paper and there was the announcement.

I had little or no sleep that night, and on the fateful morning my 'phone rang very early. It was a call from my wife, who was with her parents at Mittagong, N.S.W., to say she had heard it on the wireless.

Shortly afterwards, the whole S.A. team came round to see me and congratulate me—a little gesture which I thought very fine indeed.

Rain washed out all cricket that day. However, the V.C.A. held a delightful luncheon party at the Ground, at which both competing teams, umpires, the press and officials attended. A lovely and unex-pected event was the arrival of the English Women's Cricket Team, the members of which were invited to the lunch.

The President of the V.C.A., Mr. J. A. Seitz, made a charming speech. He was supported by Dr. Robertson, Chairman of the Aus-tralian Board of Control.

In my reply I said, " The President, with his usual modesty, has not mentioned that he, too, has been this same day, honoured by His Majesty the King, he having been awarded a C.M.G."

It certainly was a remarkable coincidence that we two had been honoured on the one day.

A quiet afternoon was spent with cricket officials, and that night I caught the train for Adelaide.

Within the next few days my mail was terrific and covered an amazingly wide range. Such notable figures as The Earl of Gowrie and Lord Bruce sent their congratulations, and so did an eight-year-old cricket enthusiast from Assam.

One of the glories of cricket is its appeal to old and young. This lad wrote :—

" To Sir Don Bradman, Esq.,
    Australia.
    Dear Sir,
    I am a little boy of Assam of India.   My age is 8 years.   I do
not know if I should write this letter to you.   Please excuse me if
I am wrong.   I am so glad at your knighthood that I could not
help writing this.   Please accept my heartiest congratulations."

Of course he asked me for an autographed photograph, and needless to
say his wish was gratified.

I could not help thinking that this knighthood was a sporting example
to the world of true democracy.   Therein lay my greatest satisfaction.

Born in the country, with no influence whatsoever, I had been able
to rise to Australian XI Captaincy and to achieve this distinction.

The same opportunity exists for every Australian boy.   I believe it
was this aspect more than any other which appealed to the vast majority
of Australian people who regarded me as a symbol through whom
these thoughts were expressed.

The New South Wales Cricket Association had decided some years
previously to hold a testimonial for Alan Kippax and Bert Oldfield.
It had been postponed on account of the war, but the match was
arranged for February 1949.

It was listed as a trial match for the South African tour, and as I was
not a candidate for South Africa, I was not a potential player in this
match.

However, the New South Wales Cricket Association made a special
request that I should play, and I readily agreed to do what part I could
to help make the match a success.

These two great players had rendered sterling service to New South
Wales over a long period, and thoroughly deserved recognition.   They
were unfortunate that the weather interfered with the progress of the
match, but the financial result was still very good.

The outstanding performance amongst the players was an innings of
217 by the New South Wales opening batsman Jack Moroney, who
subsequently gained selection in the Australian team for South Africa.

Not having had any practice since my own testimonial match in
November, I was not in good shape, but satisfied my conscience and,
I hope, the Sydney spectators, with an innings of 53 runs made in 65
minutes.

There was a good deal of satisfaction in knowing that my final innings
on the ground I loved so well contained a few strokes of the old vintage.
I do not think I could have stood the physical strain of making a century, although the desire was there, but Ken Meuleman settled the issue
when he took a remarkable one-handed catch whilst running at full
speed, and so ended my final appearance on my favourite ground.

There was another Testimonial Match, for the South Australian Cricket Association had also decided to honour one of their former players in the person of Arthur Richardson. I flew back for the game.

It ended in an overwhelming victory for Victoria.

In our first innings I had scored 30 runs somewhat laboriously when I pulled one from Bill Johnston on to the stumps. There was still another innings to go, and I was hopeful of putting up a reasonable performance in what was obviously to be my last innings in first-class cricket.

Fate decided otherwise. In attempting to field a ball, I inadvertently trod on it and suffered a badly sprained ankle, the same one which had been damaged at the Oval in 1938.

There was no possibility of taking any further part in the match, and so I had to spend the final hours of this farewell game sitting in the dressing room.

The History of Cricket

DON'T BE MISLED BY THE ABOVE HEADING. I AM NOT GOING TO WEARY you with a long treatise on the development of the game. My purpose in giving some space to the subject is to give a brief outline to what I consider items of significance and interest.

There are some excellent works devoted entirely to the evolution of cricket. Not one of them has been able to establish beyond doubt how, when or where cricket originated.

Some evidence exists, sketchy though it is, that cricket (or its equivalent) was played in 1180. Other references at a later date suggest the existence of the game in the 14th century.

The writings of John Derrick, Gentleman and Queen's Coroner for the County of Kent, establish with some degree of certainty the playing of cricket about 1550.

In those very early days it seems the game was not highly regarded. There was much gambling associated with it, and some doubt appears as to its legality. It is on record that in 1654 the Churchwardens of Eltham fined seven parishioners two shillings each for playing cricket on the Sabbath. I have been unable to ascertain whether they were fined for playing cricket or for breaking the Sabbath—maybe it was a dual offence.

Legal or otherwise, cricket gradually became established by the year 1700. Old prints bearing that date show players in the field. The bowling is obviously underarm—the bats are curved—the wickets consist of two sticks (widely separated) with forks on the top and a long bail resting in the forks.

Apparently the Southern Counties, Kent, Sussex, Hampshire and Surrey, were the first to establish their prowess. Great glamour still surrounds the "Hambledon Men" who achieved fame in "Broad Halfpenny Down". The little "Bat and Ball" Inn and the old-fashioned monument on the corner still bear testimony to those grand days.

What tales could be told of Richard Nyren, "Silver Billy" Beldham, and other colourful players.

One of the loveliest things ever written comes down to us as an epitaph to Alfred Mynn. Any modern player would be proud to have such a one adapted to himself. Read it :—

> With his tall and stately presence, with his nobly moulded form,
> His broad hand was ever open, his brave heart was ever warm.
> All were proud of him, all loved him—as the changing seasons pass
> As our Champion lies a-sleeping underneath the Kentish grass.
> Proudly, sadly, we will name him—to forget him were a sin—
> Lightly lie the turf upon thee—kind and manly Alfred Mynn.

Four balls were enough to the over in those days, and how quaintly the laws read :—

> "If a striker nips a ball up just before him he may fall before his wicket, or pop down his Batt before she comes to it, to save it."

A most important landmark was the formation in 1782 of the White Conduit Club. History seems fairly clear that this club gradually went out of existence and its place was taken by the Marylebone Cricket Club in 1787. The latter name came from the suburb or district of Marylebone in which was the home ground.

Thomas Lord, a labourer, was an employee of the White Conduit Club until he started a new private ground called Lord's.

Circumstances forced Thomas Lord to leave his original ground and by 1809 he had a new one ready at St. John's Wood. Parliament decided to run Regent's Canal through this ground, so Lord once more removed his beloved turf to a third site which was first used in 1814. This remains today the headquarters of cricket.

I want very clearly to emphasise that the word Lord's has nothing whatever to do with the aristocracy or the peerage. It was the name of the founder—a working man. There is far too much misunderstanding on this point even now.

It is fascinating to trace the gradual evolution of the play itself, but that would provide a separate volume.

Briefly, there was a change in bowling from underarm to overarm, the implements were improved and the laws revised.

These alterations have not been so terribly drastic. The ball, for instance, must still weigh the same as it did in 1895 though its circumference has been reduced about a quarter of an inch. Both the height and the width of the stumps have been increased one inch, while the L.B.W. law has been altered to assist bowlers.

Thank goodness the manufacturers reduced the weight of bats. There is at Lord's a bat dated 1771 weighing 5 lbs. As a rule I used one weighing less than half of the old relic. Imagine batting all day with a 5-lb. waddy.

I discovered a most fascinating description of a match in Ireland in 1792. It is recounted below :—

EARLY CRICKET IN YE PHOENIX PARK
Taken from the "Freeman's Journal"
of the
9th August, 1792.

GRAND CRICKET MATCH
played on the Fifteen Acres, Phoenix Park.
THE GARRISON OF DUBLIN AGAINST ALL IRELAND

Yesterday, a Grand Cricket Match was decided on the Fifteen Acres, for the sum of one thousand guineas—five hundred each side—which took rise from an expression thrown out a few nights since, in a convivial party, by Lieutenant-Colonel Lennox, and immediately taken up by the Right Hon. Major Hobart—the Garrison of Dublin v. all Ireland. There appeared :—

For the Garrison ·	For All Ireland ·
Lieut.-Col. Lennox	Rt. Hon. Major Hobart, Secretary-at-War.
Ensign Tufton	
Ensign Vaughan	Hon. Captain Wesby
Lieutenant Reeves	Mr. Box
Lieutenant Brisbane	Mr. Morris
Lieutenant Abercromby	Mr. Hickson
Lieutenant Wiltshire	Mr. King
Corporal Battison	Mr. Emerson
Private Robertson	Captain Saunderson
Private Andrews	Mr. Simpson
	Mr. Poyle.

Captain Sandby, who was to have played on the side of the Garrison, and who is esteemed one of the first players in England, was rendered incapable of acting in the field, from the disagreeable accident of his shoulder having been dislocated the evening before, in bringing himself into practice.

About half-past one the Garrison set upon their first innings, and from the commencement the odds ran two to one in their favour, which did not tend to raise the expectations of those who had made even bets the day preceding. More skill, judgment, and activity were never perhaps exhibited on any similar occasion than were displayed by both parties.

At about four o'clock, the whole set, which consisted of eleven, was outed; and, so keen were the competitors, that, without waiting for refreshments, the side of Ireland proceeded upon their Inning. Less spirit did not distinguish this contest than the former, though it was attended with less success.

As there was a very great disparity in the number of notches made by the contending parties, the Garrison exceeding Ireland by much, the latter proceeded upon their second Inning, in order that a single day might determine the competition, or that there should be a reasonable prospect of a doubtfulness of fortune to render it necessary to proceed upon a second. An hour and a quarter determined the fate of the wager; for, notwithstanding the severest exertions of the Gentlemen on the part of Ireland, it went hollow in favour of the Garrison of Dublin.

The game stood in the following manner:—

		Notches
GARRISON OF DUBLIN	First Inning	240
ALL IRELAND	First Inning	76
ALL IRELAND	Second Inning	59
		135

Of course the Garrison were winners by 105,—a single innings against two of their antagonists, which is esteemed by players a complete beating.

Mr. Quinn acted as umpire on the part of Ireland; a military gentleman for the Garrison.

The game was kept by Mr. Burrowe.

Her Excellency the Countess of Westmoreland lost ten guineas by betting on Ireland.

Two handsome marquees were pitched, one in Mr. Hobart's shrubbery, for the reception of a brilliant circle of ladies of distinction, who graced the simplicity of the manly scene with their presence; the second for the accommodation of the cricket players, on the other side of the Ha Ha, in the Fifteen Acres.

The band of the 35th regiment attended, and played a variety of favourite airs during this pastime, which, contrasted with the enervated amusements of the present taste, must be acknowledged to be rational, salubrious and deserving of encouragement.

Colonel Lennox astonished the spectators with a display of agility and skill during the whole contest, which even the amateurs of the science admitted to have been without parallel in the course of their experience. His subtlety at bowling it was, that so soon caused the event of the day to determine in favour of the Garrison ; and his facility of catching the ball may be witnessed, but cannot be described.

Mr. Tufton also proved himself to be an excellent player. At the wicket he was invulnerable. He stood the whole inning, and was never in danger of being put out. We do not at present recollect the number of notches that he made, but they were numerous.

On the adverse side, Mr. Cooke was particularly distinguished for energy and skill ; Mr. Secretary Hobart was indefatigable in his exertions, and in point of scientific ability was next to Mr. Cooke. The Hon. Captain Wesby was also active, and remarked for a promising player. The remainder behaved with much zeal and adroitness ; but " 'tis not in mortals to command success," though they did more,— " endeavoured to deserve it ! "

Looking at things from the economic angle, I wondered what the One Thousand Guineas would mean in our depreciated currency. And how would our modern legislators frown on those side wagers.

They might be interested in the light of 1949 running costs and receipts to browse over these amusing items culled from the affairs of the Penicuik Cricket Club in Scotland, roughly 100 years ago. They are taken from the audited accounts :—

Amongst the receipts
Found in the Pavilion by J.C.   6d
Amongst the expenditure
Policeman—night attendance at ball   3/-
2 cwts. of coal and tip to the boy for bringing it up   1/9
Refreshment to Lothian Cricket Club who turned up
    but match cancelled owing to rain   3/-

The National Coal Board will be envious, though doubtless the high cost of the coal was in the tip—not the coal. He must have been a " broth of a boy " or perhaps he made several trips.

And what an example by J.C. !

The year 1859 marked the commencement of a new era. In that

season an English team toured Canada and the U.S.A., playing a series of matches.

Australia had the pleasure of a visit in 1861-2 when Messrs. Spiers and Pond organised a team which played twelve matches and was most successful.

Perhaps its financial result was not unconnected with the prompt repeat performance—Parr's team in 1863-4.

There is no chronological record of the development of cricket in Australia. The first public record of the scores in any match relates to a game in 1833 though there had been reference to cricket in 1810.

The aboriginals became proficient to such an extent that the first Australian team to visit England in 1868, consisted of aboriginals captained by a white man, Lawrence. Some of the Australian names are worth recording :—

> Peter
> Twopenny
> Mullagh
> Red Cap
> King Cole
> Tiger
> Dick-a-Dick
> Bullocky
> Jim Crow.

They wore coloured sashes as distinguishing marks.

The great W.G. took the Third English Team to Australia in 1873, though it was not until 1877 that matches of 11 a side were played between the two countries.

Thus began the marvellous series of Test Matches. The ninth, in 1882, was responsible for the origin of the term " The Ashes " which is so familiar to cricket lovers.

The Australian Cricket Council was formed in 1892 in an attempt to co-ordinate control in the hands of a federal governing body. Disagreements caused it to be disbanded in later years. In those days the Melbourne Cricket Club exercised enormous influence over cricket in Australia.

The Australian Board of Control was created in 1905. It survived a historic clash with the players in 1912 and now, as its title implies, controls International Cricket Matches in Australia through State Representatives on the Board.

One could scarcely give a shorter review of cricket beginnings.

Sir Frederick Toone it was who described cricket as a science—" the study of a lifetime in which you may exhaust yourself but never your subject."

How true. Tragically so for that lovable personality Andrew Ducat, who died, bat in hand, at Lord's during an innings.

Only the other day I was beseeched by a man over seventy years of age to select him a new bat because he felt there were still " a few runs left in him." There you have the spirit of cricket.

Eternal credit must go to the Marylebone Cricket Club for its painstaking watchfulness in preserving the best features of cricket, gradually altering the laws to keep pace with the game's changing technique ; never giving way to any panic-stricken legislation.

Throughout cricket's history the standard of play has fluctuated. One era was termed " The Golden Age ". Since then we have gone off the gold standard.

Cricket in England is at this very moment surrounded by great difficulties, not the least being of an economic character. Even so, great players still exist. They will continue to develop.

The heart of cricket is sound and still beats strongly as a symbol of British character and tradition.

The world badly needs such symbols right now.

Question Time

DURING THE TIME I CONDUCTED A CRICKET SESSION ON THE WIRELESS, it was quite a revelation to read the variety of questions which reached me in a never-ending stream.

I sometimes wish I had kept the letters because they covered so many possible but improbable happenings. They were almost the basis from which one could have evolved a set of laws.

Then there were questions of a general character dealing with individuals, events, wickets and so on. A large percentage dealt with the rules. I found them most interesting. Very often they would necessitate much delving into history which revealed unexpected happenings.

Perhaps a few questions could be dealt with here. It is fascinating to debate subjects upon which so many divergent views may be held. *What was the greatest Test Match ever played ?*

If such a question were asked at a cricket gathering, there would be many different answers, depending a good deal upon the ages of those present. Nobody can definitely answer the question. For me, I can only deal with those matches I have seen or played in. The greatest Tests I ever played in were :—

1. Leeds 1938
2. Melbourne 1932-3
3. Lord's 1930

4. Nottingham 1934
5. Sydney 1947
6. Leeds 1948.

The sequence may not be entirely accurate, though without hesitation Leeds 1938 was outstanding. Every phase of cricket was demonstrated at its highest peak.

Who could ever forget the bowling of O'Reilly? He bowled Hardstaff with a ball which left that fine batsman simply dumbfounded. Hassett's daring and brilliant 33 in our second innings. At a critical stage Merv. Waite took a catch at second slip which, to the spectators, may have appeared simple, yet it was made possible only by brilliant anticipation. The closing stages were breath-taking in their excitement.

Each of the other games mentioned produced extraordinary cricket. It should be noted that most of them were relatively low scoring matches—the exceptions Lord's 1930 and Leeds 1948.

I think the most exciting cricket is usually seen on wickets which do not rob the bowler of all hope.

Great batsmen enjoy their cricket when it is a battle against an intelligent bowler. There is no pleasure in getting a century on a feather-bed pitch against second-rate bowling.

Perhaps you will ask why these desirable wickets are not produced all the time. Here we are on difficult ground.

The groundsmen themselves differ a great deal on the weight of the roller which should be used, whether the pitch should be scythed or mown, when it should be watered. These factors vary on the same ground according to the weather, and I believe one can rightly claim that no groundsman could guarantee to produce a certain type of pitch. I have asked many of them how they thought the pitch would play. They were so often wrong that I came to the conclusion they did not know any more than the skipper.

This is particularly true in England, where a much more even balance is held between batsman and bowler.

Sometimes, of course, English wickets become very easy, though the coating of grass usually allows the bowler some assistance.

On hard Australian wickets from which all the grass has been scythed, leaving bare earth, little help can be obtained until there are signs of wear.

The Australian pitch can normally be distinguished from the pavilion as a brown strip in the centre of comparatively green grass. I have seen English pitches that were almost indiscernible from the pavilion.

Sometimes I wonder if Australian curators roll the wickets too much and remove too much grass.

I am fully aware of the difficulties. I endorse the perfectly flat surface and uniform grassing, but some life and spin are desirable for batsman and bowler alike.

Although Australian wickets are generally regarded as easier to bat on than those of England, I always preferred to play on the latter.

My style of play was such that back-play predominated. My small stature did not lend itself to the forward driving school. My reach was too short unless the ball was pitched well up. The English wickets, being slower, suited this style.

Moreover, I simply loved batting on a dull day without a cap. This was especially true in 1930. At that time I did not need to wear a cap to hide evidence of advancing years.

The soft light of England seemed ideal for picking up the flight of a ball quickly.

Elsewhere I have mentioned modern score-boards.

Another innovation which adds to the enjoyment of cricket by the spectators is the use of an amplifying system. I am sure this could be improved enormously. The intelligent use of loud-speakers could not fail to add enjoyment and enlightenment, especially during periods when play was not in progress.

Could the laws of cricket be improved ?

This question is a fruitful source of argument. Hundreds of times the suggestion has been put forward that tossing for innings should be abolished and the choice be taken alternately.

The luck of the toss is an essential element of cricket. Supposing Australia was to have a choice of innings by right and this fact was known in advance. By accident the groundsman produced a wicket entirely suitable for Australia's players. There would immediately be a storm of unwarranted criticism directed at the curator.

No, it would not work. The luck of the toss admittedly may decide the fate of a match, but I see no alternative without worse consequences.

In certain directions the laws may require to be gradually modified in the future. I would like to see an alteration in the L.B.W. law, but I see no drastic change on the horizon. Rather do I think they are a tribute to the wisdom of our forefathers.

In any case, I have continually claimed that the mental outlook of the individual transcends all rules and regulations. Any game can be ruined by a wrong interpretation of its character, irrespective of the perfection of its rules.

Why can Australia, with one-sixth of the population of England, hold her own at cricket ?

There is a poser. Our climate must be a factor. A far greater percentage of Australian youth is enabled to go out of doors all the year round. Even so, one would imagine this to be more than off-set by England's larger population.

Then the question of professionalism arises. Surely men who play every day should beat those who play more or less spasmodically. In billiards no amateur can live with a professional. It is the same in boxing.

Perhaps the answer here lies in a very salient point. On a perfect table a billiard ball will scientifically react in a uniform manner. Not so in cricket. Because one spins a cricket ball it does not necessarily turn when it hits the pitch.

Cricket in no sense evolves around mechanical accuracy. It continually calls for flexible judgment.

Sometimes, too, I think the physical demands upon a professional cricketer are so exacting that he becomes mentally tired of the game with a resultant decline in concentration. The player himself may not be aware of it but it can be there just the same.

This question of professionalism or payment to players is of major importance under modern economic conditions. England has straight-out professional cricket. There appears to be no alternative.

The amateur who can afford to play six days' cricket each week without payment has become almost extinct.

Quite a few counties are experiencing difficulty in obtaining even one amateur for their first eleven.

Australia with her small population could not possibly support professionalism. Yet the existing system presents many difficulties for those engaged in first-class games.

Until an Australian player reaches International standard or becomes a member of a touring side, financially he must be a bad loser. If one takes into account the time spent in practising, the cost of clothing and equipment, there can only be a debit balance. Transcending everything is the possible loss of promotion in business, or advancement in some sphere of professional life.

In most avenues of life a person may further his position without criticism. One might instance the singer who sells his talent to the highest bidder and is not expected to confine his attentions to one country to his own financial detriment.

Somehow, in sport, public sentiment is a little harder to please, and perhaps it would surprise to tell the opportunities which have been declined by sportsmen in order to remain patriotic. I know of some cases, and in my own career have refused big offers simply because I felt they were incompatible with my moral obligations.

At the close of the 1936-7 season I was offered £100 a week, plus fares for my wife and myself, to go to New Zealand where I would have been required to give two fifteen-minute talks daily on cricket. Several times I received pressing invitations to visit India on my own terms, but always declined. On numerous occasions I refused substantial invitations to write for the press because they would have prevented me from playing.

The best offer I ever received was £1,000 a week, plus fares for myself and family, to fulfil a proposed engagement in South Africa.

My experiences are not unique. All players have to decide their destinies according to circumstances and their own desires.

Within the framework of a system designed to benefit the game and the players, they should be as free as possible.

I strongly deprecate criticism of any cricketer who follows his inherent rights. If an Australian player chooses to go to the English League, that is his business.

By all means let us try to retain our players by making conditions attractive at home. But don't let us decry the desire of any individual to legitimately benefit from his own talents.

Do you get nervous playing cricket ?

This is a favourite query. It really should be divided into two parts—1. before a match ; 2. during a match.

I always felt anxiety prior to the start of a big game. Once action commenced I lost the earlier sensation. It was replaced by a sort of tense exhilaration which, at the conclusion of a match, often gave way to a severe reaction.

I seldom ate proper meals during Test Matches, especially after a hard day in the field or batting. Perhaps the nerves of the stomach revolted. Whatever the cause it was quite a definite and predictable effect.

The mental strain of Test cricket was the worst. Physical exhaustion without accompanying mental stress can usually be quickly rectified. Both together are a different proposition.

Should Tests be played out or have a time limit?

I originally favoured matches being played to a finish. It seemed incongruous for a team to travel 12,000 miles, play four drawn games, and then have the last one decided by the caprices of the weather.

England's experience in South Africa in 1939 when the last Test was abandoned on the tenth day because the players had to catch a boat home was exasperating. The Oval Test in 1938 between England and Australia was another unfortunate affair.

Since then a genuine effort has been made to limit the duration of Tests, and at the same time ensure a result (weather permitting). The experiment up to date has been promising. The public don't want matches to last ten days, and they dislike drawn games. Those facts are clear.

Both countries have given way on certain points to try and find a solution. Future experiments will decide whether 30 hours play is the ideal. It may yet prove to be a reasonable compromise.

Should wickets be covered ?

Here again English and Australian conditions differ considerably. M.C.C. has always preferred uncovered wickets. In England, wet wickets are not impossible to bat on. They quite frequently turn out relatively easy. Not so in Australia, where rain usually spells the doom of one side.

Those who favour uncovered wickets usually cry, "Let us have natural conditions." We can all remember breath-taking moments when the pitch was wet and wickets fell like ninepins. We can also look back on the harassed secretary whose loyalty was firstly to the exchequer.

The bowlers' footholds are generally covered even when the pitch is not. Why? I suppose the idea was conceived to expedite play after rain. The result has been to encourage the use of fast bowling on wet wickets with a resultant decline in the use of spinners. If we must have cricket on wet wickets, I would prefer to watch bowlers like Verity and Rhodes rather than Larwood or Farnes. And so, I am not convinced that covering the bowlers' footholds has been, on technical grounds, a good thing.

Finance must be considered. That is indisputable.

To be truthful, I would prefer to see all matches played on dry wickets. It would be a fairer test of skill for both sides.

There, briefly, we have a few of cricket's fireside questions. The more I consider them the less dogmatic I become about the answers, and the more I believe cricket's future well-being lies mainly in the spirit of the game.

"Drink deeply of the wisdom of your forefathers," said Lord Harris when commenting on the spirit of cricket. "You do well to love it, for it is more free from anything sordid, anything dishonourable, than any game in the world. To play it keenly, honourably, generously, self-sacrificingly is a moral lesson in itself, and the classroom is God's air and sunshine. Foster it, my brothers, so that it may attract all who can find the time to play it ; protect it from anything that would sully it, so that it may grow in favour with all men."

Those beautiful words I commend to all players as a glorious creed.

The L.B.W. Law

THE GAME OF CRICKET IS PLAYED ACCORDING TO CERTAIN LAWS.

The fundamental character of the game has remained constant, but certain modifications in the rules have been made from time to time.

Perhaps the most debated law of all has been that relating to " Leg before wicket ".

It has frequently been altered, but my view is that another change could well be made in the interests of cricket.

Law 39 now reads :—

" The Striker is out 'Leg Before Wicket'—If with any part of his person except his hand, which is in a straight line between wicket and wicket, even though the point of impact be above the level of the bails, he intercept a ball which has not first touched his bat or hand, and which, in the opinion of the Umpire, shall have, or would have, pitched on a straight line from the Bowler's wicket to the Striker's wicket, or shall have pitched on the off side of the Striker's wicket, provided always that the ball would have hit the wicket."

In theory it is simple enough to interpret.

Assuming that the ball has not first touched the Striker's bat or hand, the Umpire must be satisfied that :—

1. The ball would have hit the wicket.
2. It did not pitch outside the Striker's leg stump.
3. That part of the Striker's person which was struck by the ball was between wicket and wicket.

Unless the umpire is convinced on these three points, he must not give the striker out.

I suggest that the rule should be amended to read :—

" The Striker is out ' Leg Before Wicket ' if with any part of his person except his hand he intercept a ball which has not first touched his bat or hand, and which, in the opinion of the Umpire did not pitch on the leg side of the Striker's wicket and would have hit it."

This would eliminate consideration No. 3 outlined previously.

There is a general desire on all sides to assist the bowler and to brighten cricket.

To this end, R. W. V. Robins has suggested that the width of the bat be reduced. Douglas Jardine advocates a smaller ball. I do not favour either suggestion.

A smaller bat would, in my opinion, reduce the science of batsmanship.

The ball has already been reduced in size without any apparent effect. Jardine believes such a move would assist spin bowlers. Clarrie Grimmett should know more about this than Jardine, and Clarrie has often told me that the smaller ball is harder to flight. He thought the last move in this direction of no help to bowlers.

An experiment is at present being tried with a ball which has a slightly bigger seam. If it has any effect on the game at all I feel that it will be negligible and in any case it would only assist swing bowlers.

I believe my suggestion would assist all types of bowlers, brighten cricket and improve the science of batsmanship.

Let me trace the history of the L.B.W. law.

In the original laws of cricket no reference whatever was made to

L.B.W. It first came into being in 1774, and the cardinal feature of it was the provision : " If the striker puts his leg before the wicket with a design to stop the ball."

Here was a ready-made case for the legal mind. What does " before the wicket" mean ? Who is to say the striker's action was " by design " ? Obviously such a law could not work, but its wording gives a clue to its genesis.

When cricket was first played there was no need for an L.B.W. law. According to William Beldham the law of L.B.W. " was not made nor wanted till Ring . . . was shabby enough to get his leg in the way and take advantage of the bowlers. When Tom Taylor did the same the law was passed to make L.B.W. out." The quotation referred to is given by the Rev. James Pycroft in *The Cricket Field*.

Clearly then, the original intention of the law was to stop a batsman defending his wicket by the use of his legs instead of the bat itself. The striker's action is referred to as being shabby, which my modern dictionary defines as " mean in conduct or despicable." The striker had been guilty of an act designed to defeat the intention of the original spirit of cricket.

There can be little doubt whatever concerning the inconsistent interpretation of the old law. Some umpires thought it necessary for the ball to pitch between wicket and wicket. Others took the view that where the ball pitched was immaterial. The rules did not clearly define this vital point, although nine revisions were made between 1774 and 1831.

Eventually a disagreement occurred regarding the interpretation of the L.B.W. law between the two leading umpires of the day, Messrs. Dark and Caldecourt. The dispute was referred to M.C.C., whereupon it was incorporated in the law that the ball must pitch between wicket and wicket.

About the year 1887 Lord Bessborough (himself a good cricketer) expressed himself as being in favour of " a return to the old law of 50 years ago." Clearly then, Lord Bessborough believed that prior to the M.C.C. interpretation of about 1836 the question of where the ball pitched did not matter.

At the first meeting of the County Cricket Council in 1887 there was a general expression of opinion in favour of an alteration in the L.B.W. law.

At a special meeting of the County Cricket Council on February 8th, 1888, a resolution was carried by 11 votes to 3 recommending a change in the law so that a batsman would be given out " if with any part of his person being in a straight line between wicket and wicket he stop the ball which in the opinion of the umpire would have hit the wicket."

Upon the matter being considered by the M.C.C., that august body, whilst not agreeing to alter the law, did pass this resolution : " That the practice of deliberately defending the wicket with the person instead of the bat is contrary to the spirit of the game and inconsistent with strict fairness, and the M.C.C. will discountenance and prevent this practice with every means in their power."

Umpires were asked to report offending batsmen, and M.C.C. expressed the hope that with the co-operation of county authorities and players, the evil would be remedied.

Dissatisfaction must have continued, for in May 1901 a similar resolution to that of 1888 was brought before a special meeting of M.C.C. and carried by a majority of 71. This did not give the two-thirds majority required to alter the law, which remained as it was.

During the season 1902, the second-class counties at the request of M.C.C. gave a trial to the suggested change. The majority of them did not favour any alteration, but the reasons given for their views are rather extraordinary. I shall quote briefly :—

(a) Objection taken because of two unsatisfactory decisions during the season (we would be happy in these days with two only).

(b) I think it gives the umpire too large a scope.

(c) (By an umpire) It is much easier for an umpire, but the rule is not thoroughly understood.

(d) On good wickets the rule is absolutely innocuous. It only helps the bowler on bad wickets.

(e) Disapproved of using the rule in second-class matches and not in other games.

(f) I think it is a good rule, but do not consider it had a fair trial on account of the number of wet wickets.

(g) The new rule had the desired effect of stopping men playing with their legs and not the bat.

There you have a reasonable summary of the views expressed regarding the experiment. They are inconclusive.

May I stress a vital point : the experiment covered the leg-side as well as the off-side, which was probably too drastic.

So the game has gone along with a continual increase in the number of L.B.W. decisions. In 1870 they averaged 1 in 40—in 1926 they averaged 1 in 8. Today's ratio must be about the same.

The question of drawn matches brought about by the predominating success of bat over ball has for many years agitated the minds of legislators. Proof of their desire to assist the bowlers is to be found in a reduction in the size of the ball, increases in the size of the wickets, and an alteration in the L.B.W. law whereby a striker may be given out to a ball pitched outside the off-stump providing that part of his person struck by the ball is between wicket and wicket at the moment of impact.

Despite these changes, huge scores are still being made, and groundsmen are being counselled not to produce perfect wickets.

I have detailed the foregoing information as strong links in a chain of evidence to support my contention that a further change in the L.B.W. law is desirable.

Shortly after I entered big cricket, I discovered a measure of discontent amongst bowlers who could beat the batsmen with the ball only to be deprived of their just reward by diligent covering up with the pads.

I'm sure this was one of the indirect (if not direct) causes of body-line.

I am not proposing a new theory based upon my own retirement. As long ago as 1933 I suggested to M.C.C. that the law should be amended so that the striker would be given out providing he intercepted a ball which in the opinion of the umpire at the bowler's wicket was pitched on the off-side of the wicket and would have hit the striker's wicket.

One of the most unedifying sights in cricket is to watch a batsman cover his stumps with his pads, and, with the bat held over his shoulders, serenely watch the ball harmlessly cannon away.

Should a striker play forward to a ball which turns inside the bat and strikes him on the pad, umpires will rarely give him out. They interpret the rule very strictly. Some go so far as to claim you can't be out L.B.W. to a turning ball if playing forward.

If the protection on the off-side was completely removed I feel we would be returning to the original spirit of cricket.

Leg-guards were designed to prevent injury, not to enable protection of the stumps.

I believe my suggestion would bring about much more forward play—a reversion to the classical style of the golden age. Bowlers would constantly attack the off-stump, thereby reducing the incidence of on-side play which, though effective, is inelegant and unattractive compared with the glorious forward drives and cuts.

More slip catches would assuredly result. The off-break type would again take his rightful place amongst the attacking bowlers. Even the leg-spinner would gain an advantage (a) in the use of the googly, and (b) against the left-handers who are at present his particular nightmare.

I know there is much opposition to my suggestion. It comes from nearly all batsmen who see in it a threat to their dominance. Their opposition is numerically strong, but so many of them are prejudiced.

It comes from leg-break bowlers who see in it a lessening of their effectiveness as compared with off-spinners. They noticeably become much more sympathetic if one suggests bringing in the leg-side too—a sure sign of personal rather than general interest.

Lastly, the legislator, who thinks it would place too great a burden on the umpire and possibly affect the financial picture.

Frank Chester should know regarding umpiring, and he told me he thought it would be easier to interpret than the existing law.

Make the game as attractive as possible and the financial results are likely to improve. Drawn games are anathema to the public—not finished matches.

So in conclusion I express myself in favour of trying, as an experiment in the interests of cricket, a change in the L.B.W. law, so that no batsman gains any advantage by the use of his pads except in those cases where the ball pitches outside the leg stump.

I feel positive it would brighten the game and be of benefit in many directions, not the least of which would be its effect upon tactics.

Outstanding batsmen who regard cricket as a contest between bat and ball would find a larger gulf between themselves and the rabbits. So should it be.

I can do no more than give prominence to my views. History will tell whether I am justified or not.

Critics

IT IS INEVITABLE THAT A MAN WHO IS IN THE PUBLIC EYE SHOULD RECEIVE criticism. He expects it and does not resent it unless he becomes the victim of unwarranted and unfair accusations which extend beyond reasonable bounds.

The greater one's personal success, the more one becomes subject to the jealousy of rivals—or of those who like to think they may be rivals.

There is a Chinese proverb : " Just as tall trees are known by their shadows, so are good men known by their enemies." I should like to substitute the word " Successful " for the word " Good ". It would be nearer the mark.

At times jealousy can become an obsession and assume the character of positive hatred until the accuser reveals it so unmistakably that he becomes an object of pity. The flame he so carefully fans into a fire consumes him. The object of his wrath remains untarnished.

Considering all the circumstances of my rapid elevation from obscurity to the realm of Test cricket and viewing in retrospect my experiences, I claim to have been extremely fortunate in that I enjoyed what is commonly termed " a good press ". The great majority of journalists, specialist writers and broadcasters treated my career on its merits—criticised when they felt justified or praised if so inclined— though always without malice.

Nevertheless, it would be incorrect for me to say that I did not at times notice a particularly vicious and persistent criticism from certain quarters—not the type of comment which is based on facts but obviously of the kind which is inspired by an innermost desire to find fault whether it exists or not.

To suggest that I have not deserved criticism on many occasions would be absurd. I have always been first and foremost a human being— very much so—and therefore prone to error. Many of my greatest lessons have been learned through making mistakes. Indeed, if man did not learn in that fashion how else would he develop and mature ?

One cannot be expected, at twenty years of age, to have the depth of vision into character, the broad understanding or the tolerance which a man of forty might possess.

Opportunities for travel, acceptance of responsibility, experience of success and failure, even the very emotions of life which cause jubilation or despair, all enrich the human mind and character.

I make no apology for the fact that I started off without the advantages available to many. It is no disgrace to come from humble parents of modest means in a small and somewhat parochial country village. There are many simple qualities developed under such circumstances which are of noble virtue.

Nevertheless, when I first entered big cricket, it was a handicap that my education had been of a limited character and my experience of life comparatively negligible.

When I left for England in 1930, I was probably much less fitted in some respects to undertake the task allotted to me than many boys who have finished their secondary education would have been.

Possibly this lowly starting point was not unconnected with certain virulent criticism which gained in intensity as my own stature grew.

I propose to deal with this subject of critics and criticism under different headings. It can be related to general principles or to particular items.

Firstly, I would like to generalise on matters concerning my own career.

I was often accused of being unsociable, though I fear the charge was applied in a very loose sense. In substance it boiled down to my dislike of artificiality and publicity.

There were those who thought I was unsociable because at the end of the day I did not think it my duty to breast the bar and engage in a beer-drinking contest. At least I made no attempt to interfere with the habits of others, and if I thought my most important need was a meal and a cup of tea, I had as much right to complain of their late entry into the dining-room as they had to complain of my absence from the bar.

I well remember being accused of snobbery because in the evening, following my world's record Test score, I stayed in my own room listening to music. Was I expected to parade the streets of Leeds ?

Any exceptional performance makes great demands upon the physical and nervous resources of the performer. Some people try to overcome the resultant fatigue by the use of stimulants—others by seeking a counter-excitement. I always obtained best results by seeking quietness. Music is a tonic to jaded nerves. It may not be to a musician, but it is to me.

In any case, my preference for the more homely and peaceful side of life was a perfectly simple explanation of my reticence to make public or semi-public appearances.

Throughout my career I genuinely disliked the private lionising and feting with which people are afflicted only because they are temporarily in the headlines.

Public acclamation associated with one's performances is in another category. That is a natural and enjoyable manifestation of community interest and appreciation.

Conversely, I deeply valued the friendships which grew from cricket and were based on the more permanent foundations of mutual understanding and respect.

I feel that so long as people carry out their duties in a proper manner, their private lives should be their own affairs, not subject to the daily inquisitiveness of publicity agents. Surely that is a rational and reasonable viewpoint.

The ordinary citizen has not the remotest idea what it feels like to be a public figure, recognisable at sight in the trains of Melbourne, the buses in the Strand, or even in the shops at Port Said.

Another chap and I tried to go shopping one morning in Aberdeen. I had never been in Aberdeen before, yet I was stopped some twenty times in little more than half an hour by people of all ages, usually seeking autographs.

On one occasion a woman wheeling a baby in a pram asked me to sign an autograph because *he* would like it when *he* grew up. *He* wasn't interested. She had neither pencil nor paper. The sentimental folk will say, " What a compliment." That is probably so, but try it yourselves for twenty years and see what it does to your nervous system.

Remember, you can't turn this thing on or off like a tap. It goes on perpetually in trains, trams, buses and ships all over the world. If I tried to walk anywhere in London I was often followed by a crowd of small boys.

It is not much use trying to explain to people who crave publicity and can't get it, that one's greatest need may be quietness and privacy.

I have always had the utmost difficulty in getting certain people to understand the difference between one's public life as a player, and one's private life as a citizen. Some have been positively rude to me because I dared to refuse their entry into my private home to take photos or into my room at an hotel.

During the 1948 tour a card was one day sent up to our dressing room at Lord's with a message that an old friend wanted urgently to see me below. I looked at the card, did not recognise the name, but finally went down in case I might be wrong. The gentleman was most gushing in his desire to engage me in conversation and seemed taken aback at my reserve until in a valiant attempt to break the barrier, he claimed that I surely must remember having met him at the party the previous night. Rather an unfortunate remark. I was not at the party. Our conversation terminated somewhat abruptly, and no doubt another flame had been kindled to re-light the bonfire legend of unsociability.

This matter of publicity automatically brings up the question of professional men in that walk of life.

Some of my greatest friends are in the newspaper and radio field. I have the most profound admiration for the men themselves, their difficulties and problems.

Such eminent writers as Neville Cardus and Jim Swanton have at times been harsh critics of mine. Their constructive comments developed in me a greater appreciation of their qualities. Their writings contained no suggestion of base motives or jealousy, only a genuine attempt to write honest convictions.

The same could apply to dozens of men of the calibre of Johnnie Moyes, Arthur Mailey, Jack Hobbs, and so on.

How different from the bitter acid of the journalist who once wrote of me, "Twenty years of cricket do not seem to have taught Bradman the real British Empire meaning of the word." This same fellow also wrote a scathing article criticising my sportsmanship for not informing the opposing captain at the interval that I intended to bat on. Even schoolboys know that one only needs to tell if *closing* the innings.

In the broadcasting field, chaps like Arthur Gilligan and Alan McGilvray have been able to do a grand job for the public, telling the truth and giving the facts without finding it necessary to distort them or to alienate people's friendship.

I mention this very incomplete list of names as examples. My friends in the field of publicity are legion.

On the other hand I have no time for the type of journalism which lives by sensationalism. I deplore articles which by their innuendoes and half-truths can be most misleading.

I believed in treating all journalists as trustworthy men until I found out anything to the contrary, but if ever I formed the opinion that a confidence had been betrayed I seldom risked a second opportunity. This strict code sometimes created enemies, for it isn't always possible to prove a breach of trust, and genuine misunderstanding can arise.

As a Player. One's performances on the field are a legitimate subject for criticism—good or bad. I never had the slightest objection to a writer claiming that my stroke play was incorrect—my timing astray—placing inaccurate, or making any other charge as to my shortcomings.

Right or wrong, they were only matters of opinion and not grounds for objection.

Similarly, the merits or demerits of players could intelligently be argued without bias or rancour. The views expressed could be incorrect without in any way causing resentment.

Many an innings of mine has been praised when in my heart I knew it was far from satisfactory. This sort of thing counterbalances the adverse reaction to a really good knock.

As a Captain. Again a captain must expect to run the gauntlet of counter-opinions. Whether he used his bowlers in the right sequence or placed his field correctly may be open to question.

Under this heading perhaps I could bring in one or two matters which attracted my attention.

A captain may be accused (as I have been) of unfairly using the heavy roller to the disadvantage of his opponents.

If the laws clearly indicate what is allowable, it is scarcely right to attack the captain for observing the law.

Worse still is any insinuation of unworthy motives which may have no foundation in fact. The critic, if he doesn't agree with the law, should devote his energies to having it amended.

A captain must always make his decision *before* he knows what will happen. The critic usually bases his statements on what *has* happened and thus takes no risk.

Sometimes the critic takes a chance by making an advance condemnation of a captain's tactics and ends up by looking ridiculous.

I quote an outstanding example.

During the Second Test in Sydney in 1946 a morning paper came out with a big headline nearly seven inches long.

" BRADMAN'S MISTAKE

Lets Australia bat too long "

In the ensuing article the writer, an ex-Australian XI Captain, renowned for his condemnation of all other captains, said :—

" Bradman erred yesterday in continuing Australia's innings for nearly an hour and this may cost his team their second Test victory.

" England now have every chance of making the game a draw, and I think they will succeed.

" If they do, Bradman's over-confidence in the ability of his bowlers will be responsible.

IT WILL BE A VICTORY THROWN AWAY BY BAD TACTICS."

The forecast was conveniently forgotten when my judgment was vindicated to such an extent that we had a bare 33 runs to spare when the match ended with nearly three hours left for play.

The skipper usually has a finer appreciation of conditions and what can be accomplished, than have the people in the pavilion.

It is common for a captain to be criticised if he elects to bat and the wicket turns out nasty. Under such circumstances he is a " sitting shot ".

Sometimes a writer betrays his inconsistency by praising in one captain that which he deplores in another, thereby illustrating not his knowledge but his bias against an individual.

Compare the following two statements :—

1. " As Yardley continued to slow up the scoring rate, the afternoon's play developed into a battle of tactics. Yardley succeeded in taking Bradman and Hassett down to a snail's pace with defensive field placing to defensive leg-side bowling of Young and Laker.

   It would have been unpardonably bad captaincy if Yardley had not closed up the game."

2. " Defensive field-placing tactics are a deplorable feature of Test cricket. They ruin the game as a spectacle and reduce otherwise assertive bowlers to characterless pieces of politic machinery."

The first was a comment on Yardley's defensive tactics during the First Test in 1948, the second a comment on my defensive tactics during the Fourth Test 1948. They were both written by an ex-player who probably hoped his change of front would not be noticed by the stewards.

When Bill Woodfull was Australian XI Captain, he would not read comments during a game and he advised the players to follow his example. Human nature being what it is, very few have the strength of mind to abstain.

Too many players devour press comments and are sensitive to articles sometimes dealing with technical points and written by people who haven't a fraction of their own cricket knowledge.

As a Selector. In most cases the men chosen for Selection Committees have had wide experience and possess a good knowledge of the game. I have always found them keen to be scrupulously impartial and anxious to carry out their duties in a manner befitting the trust reposed in them.

Criticism of selections is inevitable and proper. Again, it is a matter of opinion.

I have not found any Selector who expressed hostility towards his critics unless they became personal.

Selectors are constantly blamed for failures, but seldom congratulated on the success of their judgment or foresight.

Here again, critics are usually careful in their comments beforehand, although occasionally we find indiscretions which are disastrous for the writer.

During the 1946-7 season against England, a Sydney writer who had, I think, played in one first-class match, aired his knowledge by having this to say on the selection of Arthur Morris for the Third Test :—

> " The Selectors apparently decided to retain Morris on the strength of his innings against England in Melbourne, but he failed in Brisbane and Sydney. There should be no place in a Test team for ' failures '.
>
> Test Matches are not trial matches to encourage promising youngsters."

Morris promptly showed who was right by making a century in Melbourne and a century in each innings at Adelaide. Altogether in the following eight Test Matches in which Morris played, he scored 6 centuries against England. No Australian player (other than myself) in the whole history of Tests has scored more throughout his whole career, not even Trumper. So much for the Selector's bad judgment in persevering with Morris !

There are some who pose all the time as experts—a stupid attitude to adopt. Somebody must fail from time to time in every team.

One prominent writer has recently been most condemnatory of selections, Australian or English.

When the 1948 team for England was about to be chosen he advocated three slow leg-spinners and said : " The whole success of the tour from the match-winning angle depends on the success of our spinners." We won a greater percentage of matches than any previous team. Of the 89 English wickets which fell in the Tests our leg-spinners got one. His error of judgment did not deter him from writing of England's Third Test team : " This astounding selection smacks violently of a mixture of panic, toughness and foolhardiness," and of England's Fifth Test team : " It is an ill-balanced, ill-equipped and definitely an illogical combination." His crowning effort came recently when a prominent Australian was not selected. The same critic gave full rein to his ego in this diatribe : " But the thing that hurts most of all is the knowledge that petty jealousies and Inter-state greed for representation in the touring team can bring about a position where one of Australia's greatest players must pay the penalty . . . *the Selectors are quite unfitted for their job.*" All because he didn't agree with them.

Such a statement far exceeds the bounds of reasonable comment. If a man feels so strongly about the Selectors, I can only suggest that he should try to serve cricket by aspiring to a seat on the Selection Committee.

My job as a Selector has been extremely pleasant. Apart from general criticism of selections, there has only been one aspect which perturbed me, namely, the tendency in some quarters to ascribe the responsibility for selections, good or bad, to me instead of to the Committee as a whole. I have never dominated, nor tried to dominate, a Selection Committee. Often I have given way to my colleagues. Sometimes they were right, sometimes not, but there is no other course.

Occasionally this business of blaming me for selections has been used to foster other grievances. Here is an illustration. It relates to a game at Scarborough in 1948 :—

"There has been an arrangement between the bodies governing cricket in England and Australia that Leveson-Gower should not include more than six Test players in his Festival Team. Bradman has certainly paid this agreement a back-handed compliment in using the full Test Team for the occasion."

The inference behind such a statement is unmistakable.

The facts ? Well, firstly, I was not responsible for the Australian Team. It was chosen by a Selection Committee, not by me alone. Secondly, no such " arrangement " existed. Leveson-Gower was perfectly free to choose whatever players he wished.

There are lighter moments even for Selectors. When an Australian player failed to gain selection on one occasion, a certain gentleman published the comment that it was " a disgrace ". He himself had been a member of the Committee which dropped me from the Australian XI. Not much wonder I smiled !

A happy feature of a Selector's job is that the players who are passed over seldom harbour a grudge. They fully understand the position and resolve to try harder. Occasionally one strikes a disgruntled person. It is the exception rather than the rule. Cricketers, generally speaking, are very fair-minded.

General. Coming round to more general criticism of my own career from a personal angle, there are one or two matters which I feel may be somewhat misunderstood.

I've often heard it said, for instance, that I relentlessly pursued big scores—other fellows did not. This particular claim was especially hammered out to find a reason why my batting average was better than other people's, but more often than not to excuse Trumper's comparatively low average.

One article bluntly put it : " When Trumper and Hobbs were great batsmen, it was customary for cricketers to try and get out when their scores went beyond, say, 150." Hobbs must have forgotten the rule in his 15 double centuries and especially his 316 not out against Middlesex.

I do not want to enter into a discussion about Trumper, but perhaps in fairness to myself I may say this. If the argument is used that big scores were responsible for my high average, then surely scores of up to 100 only would not come into it. In that regard Trumper's record in England disclosed 19 centuries in 193 innings, mine was 41 centuries in 120 innings. On a percentage basis, Trumper got one century for every 9·8 innings, whereas I obtained one century every 3·4.

Perhaps I should also mention that my highest score against an English County is 258 compared with 300 not out by Trumper against Sussex in 1899 on his first trip to England. These figures should successfully dispose of that contention. Further, I can find no merit in the action of any player who deliberately gets out when his side still requires runs. That is not playing for the team.

Another line often used against me was that I played the game "too hard". The exploiters of this parrot-cry always had the utmost difficulty in explaining what they meant because they hated to admit it meant "playing to win". Is there anyone in his right senses who thinks I should have done otherwise than play to win?

Ask the same critics whether they can find a single instance of my not playing cricket according to the spirit or letter of the law.

If I was a bit "hard" on isolated occasions it could not be wondered at. My baptism in Test Cricket was at Brisbane in 1928 when England was captained by the debonair, carefree, dashing Percy Chapman—the happy-go-lucky skipper who played cricket as a game. England led on the first innings by 399. Instead of enforcing the follow-on Chapman elected to bat again and set Australia 741 to get on one of the worst stickies I have ever seen. We made 66. Not only that but we were two men short, as Jack Gregory had broken down and Charlie Kelleway was ill and unable to bat.

I could also recall the Oval in 1938. What did we see there? England, winning the toss and batting on a perfect wicket, took nearly three days to make 903 for 7 wickets before declaring.

Some time before that I had broken a bone in my ankle, and it was known that neither Fingleton nor I could bat.

Wisden, referring to the game, said: "The whole of the batting seemed to be inspired by a desire to build up a stupendous total."

Cardus wrote: "I tremble to think what the crowd would have said if the Australians had stone-walled with their grand total, 520 for 2. The press would have been husky with letters about it tomorrow."

Of Hardstaff's batting, Cardus had this to say: "If a man will not play cricket when he has made 100 in a Test Match, and his side is 800 for 6, when on earth will he play cricket."

In case some reader trots out the theory that England was merely playing Australia at her own game or instituting reprisals, will you pardon me for referring to a Test between England and the West Indies, 1929-30.

England won the toss, batted and made 849. West Indies batted and made 286. They were 563 behind, but did England send her opponents in again? No. She batted once more. Australia can't be brought into that one! These were English tactics—not mine.

On the other hand, compare the types of cricket played by me and by teams under my control. The rate of scoring, especially in later years when I had some say in moulding the type of player, has often been so fast as to dwarf that of the opposition. The 1948 team holds the world's record score for one day in a first-class match.

I have constantly tried to play attacking cricket and encouraged other batsmen to do the same. It has not always been possible, for both captains must be imbued with the same idea.

I have never been guilty of starting slow cricket, but if my opponents felt that way inclined, I accepted the challenge as I thought fit. That was fair enough.

Test Cricket is not a light-hearted business, especially that between England and Australia.

Would you like a bowler's point of view? This is what O'Reilly says: "I am not prepared to waste time in listening to those who talk moonshine about the grand old game and all the poppycock which goes with that type of small talk when Tests are being played. Test matches are hard work and must be won. No side expects any quarter."

I played cricket according to my idea of how it should be played. I would do the same again.

I repeat my earlier appreciation of the very fair manner in which I was normally treated by the critics. The exceptions therefore stood out in bold relief.

Perhaps one of the most openly bitter articles about me was one which appeared in a London daily on the opening day of the First Test in 1948. It was written by an ex-cricketer, well known to both sides. The whole thing reeked of personal spleen, naked and unashamed. I had the unusual experience of opposing players and officials (as well as our own players) coming to me and expressing their disgust at what was obviously a personal tirade against me. They further went out of their way to assure me they entirely disagreed with the contents of the article. Their references to what they thought of this critic were better expressed verbally than in print.

This same fellow apparently made a special study of my alleged weaknesses, and whenever the opportunity arose, would labour my shortcomings (according to him) on wet wickets.

When it was announced that I would go to England again in 1948, he wrote an article and said, "If it is dry, he (Bradman) will go to his finish with a goodly run of centuries. But what if the English summer is wet ? There's the point—and on all three previous Bradman visits the English summer has been dry." He naturally thought his readers would accept that statement as true. They wouldn't remember what the weather was like in other tours.

Of my first and most successful trip in 1930, the editor of *Wisden* wrote : " The large proportion of drawn games was due to the fact that in most of them bad weather interfered. Indeed, the weather placed the Australians at a considerable disadvantage. Still, they triumphed in a remarkable fashion over the discomforts of a wet and cheerless English summer." He was there and saw the matches. The know-all critic was not.

I will end this chapter more or less where I began, by saying, I should not have been, and did not expect to be, immune from criticism—that I was not without faults—all because I was a fallible mortal. But I don't think many of the personal attacks made on me through jealousy or lack of knowledge were warranted.

I can honestly lay claim to a steadfastness of purpose—a genuine attempt to be implicitly fair and honest in all my dealings and decisions— to show no favouritism to men under my control—to play the game in its deepest and widest sense.

My reward comes in the certain knowledge that my own standing in the community today has not been debased, but rather enhanced by criticism, for the public are not slow to detect the difference between fact and fiction.

Very early in my career, a friend passed on a piece of advice. " You cannot make people love you," he said, " but you can make them respect you."

If I have been able to do the latter—and I believe I have—my efforts have not been in vain.

Has Cricket Improved

MY ANSWER TO THE ABOVE QUESTION IS THIS : " UNLESS WE BELIEVE that cricket has improved we do not believe in progress."

Every generation adds its quota of knowledge. This applies to any given subject and is more pronounced in science than in any other field.

I have studied the evolution of cricket and have endeavoured to trace its development up to the present day.

At first the implements used were primitive. Bats were shaped something like a hockey stick because bowling was all underarm.

Only two stumps were provided. Wickets were just reasonably leve patches of turf. They scarcely needed to be any better.

Our forefathers wore high hats, collars and ties. Wicket-keeping gloves were more like dress gloves. Pads were unknown.

It has been written that " Hayward Budd, one of the best amateur cricketers in the early part of the 19th century, stood up to the fastest bowling of his day without any further defence than an extra pair of stockings rolled down so as to prevent his ankles being hit."

They weren't nylons either.

My only commentary on that is :—

(1) The fastest bowling of his day couldn't have been fast, and
(2) Today it is not their ankles the batsmen worry about protecting.

There was a gradual improvement in grounds and wickets. Batsmen began to master the bowlers.

In the period from say 1830 to 1850 it appears that the leading bowlers depended mostly on their accuracy combined with a slight turn from leg—apparently an evolution from the under-arm period.

Up to this stage the hand could not be raised higher than the shoulder.

Finally, the law was changed to allow over-arm bowling.

This was probably the most significant advance ever made in cricket. It undoubtedly brought about further improvements in equipment, a need for truer wickets, and naturally the curved bat had to be changed to its present form.

I submit that bowling must have improved. Individual talent must blossom at certain intervals and one can only generalise.

People are always to be found who will decry the theory of advancement. As regards bowling, W. J. Hammersley, a cricket authority of his day, writing in the Sydney *Mail* 1884, said : " Is the bowling of the present day superior to that of thirty years ago ? My opinion is that it is not. There are a few good bowlers now, but as a rule the bowling of the present day I consider much inferior to that of the past."

According to the late Lord Harris it was Spofforth who first taught the bowling of medium-fast off-breaks. It would have been well-nigh impossible to bowl fast off-breaks keeping the hand below the level of the shoulder.

With this bowling change there must also have come an alteration in the tactics. Field placing and batting styles could not have remained the same.

No doubt the faster bowling set up an agitation which eventually brought sight-screens as well as pads which properly protected the legs.

Scoring was at first by notches on sticks—not scoring books. Newspapers would record the scores of matches in this form :—

Thomas Neap	6 bowled out by Rutter
Richard Warsop	8 catched out by Thompson
R. Barker	6 stumped out by Dennis

The first match in which printed cards were used showing the state of the game was the Sussex v. M.C.C. fixture at Lord's on June 26th, 1848.

Now we have in Australia the magnificent boards which give all the detailed information a spectator could desire. The operators even flash a coloured light against the name of the fieldsman handling the ball.

England has not yet decided on the change from score cards and old-fashioned score-boards, but the march of time will, in due course, force this improvement.

In bowling there was the natural field of swing or swerve to be explored. The theory or science of swing has been thoroughly understood for very many years. I doubt whether anything further can be discovered here although from time to time bowlers with some special aptitude will arise.

Similarly, I should think off-break bowling has reached its zenith, and I am quite prepared to concede that off-spinners of fifty years ago might have been just as good as any of the moderns.

The same would apply to medium pacers using variations in pace and such modifications.

Straight-out leg-break bowling of the over-arm variety must have been a decided improvement on the under-arm. Furthermore, it permitted the development of the " bosey " or " googly ". For the benefit of the uninitiated, a " bosey " consists of bowling an off-break with a leg-break action, by the simple expedient of turning the wrist over until the ball is actually delivered out of the back of the hand.

The bosey was a big scientific advancement in bowling, and when first introduced brought a temporary bowling superiority. Batsmen soon advanced their technique to cope with the new terror.

In support of my contention that modern bowling of the leg-break-bosey variety is an improvement upon the old-time technique, is the opinion of Capt. C. B. Fry.

He played in the " Golden Age " and then became one of our outstanding critics.

Fry commended the skill of earlier fast bowlers but then added : " Quite a few well-thought-of batsmen of my day would have been perpetually dead birds to the modern leg-break bowling."

I should think further improved methods by bowlers can only come from " freak " developments.

Bill O'Reilly outshone all his rivals by combining the essentials of accuracy, variations of flight, etc., with the googly and a leg-spinner delivered in a manner peculiarly his own.

The Australian Cecil Pepper, now in the Lancashire League, made the ball turn from the off by some unique method of delivery which even now remains a mystery to me.

There is a bowler in Victoria who has developed a special grip because of an unusually large hand, and it enables him to do extraordinary things.

We shall doubtless hear of other "freak" bowlers who by their thoughtfulness and ambition will evolve something fresh. They will need to do this whilst still retaining the important attributes of length, direction, stamina, vitality, perseverance and application.

Bowlers today seem inclined to regard practice as a form of exercise instead of an opportunity to work diligently along pre-determined lines for improvement. The great bowlers all had to practise long and hard. Future ones will have to do likewise.

In batting I am led to the conclusion that the principles which were considered orthodox when W. G. played, still remain the basis on which general play should be encouraged.

Apparently W.G. was an orthodox player of the old school whose success was due to indefinable factors such as eyesight, co-ordination of muscles, etc.

Ranji brought to the game a touch of genius which from all accounts was based on incredibly keen eyesight. It enabled him to leg-glance balls off the stumps, something no ordinary mortal had previously attempted.

Then Trumper carved for himself a special place in the game, not by results so much (there are many whose figures are an improvement on Trumper's) but by style and daring.

Similarly, who can say my own performances have contributed anything new to the art of batting? Other players could drive, cut, hook and play every shot in the game. Such intangible assets as concentration, judgment and application cannot very well be measured.

I incline to the view that the most significant change in batting since W. G. Grace has been from forward play to the modern preponderance of back play.

The latter is less elegant but undoubtedly gives the batsman greater control and a wider range of shots.

The above paragraph must be qualified by adding " on slow wickets " and here the trend has unquestionably encouraged back play.

Perhaps it was this which moved Sam Jones, doyen of Test players, to say recently that he disliked modern batsmanship, even deploring the methods of Hobbs and Hammond compared with Grace and Trumper. Fancy anyone casting aspersions on Hobbs' batting. It was well-nigh the perfect style.

W.G. was a disciple of forward play and the " firm right foot ". So was Clarrie Grimmett—the only similarity in their batting I should say.

Grace advised against moving the back foot across in front of the stumps. Practically all modern coaches do the reverse—as they must if batsmen are to learn correct back-defensive methods.

Back play brings in its train more on-side play but less driving, and frankly I think cricket would be all the better for a revival of the classical Archie MacLaren style of forward play—left shoulder down the wicket.

I fear we shall not see it unless (a) wickets become faster and (b) the L.B.W. law is altered so that a batsman can derive no advantage by playing back to a ball pitched outside the off-stump.

A great student of cricket in A. C. M. Croome predicted over thirty years ago that : " The next stage in the evolution of batting will be the perfecting of back play."

How true has this forecast proved !

In regard to wickets, the evidence is not completely reliable. The use of heavier rollers, top dressing and other things brought about a decided improvement.

At first the pitch was selected by the captain winning the toss. He would pick an area likely to suit his bowlers. Later on more time was devoted to the preparation of a special wicket for each match.

One reads a lot about shooters and bumpers in the old days. Yet I recently discovered a commentary of 1884 which referred to McAlpine, Curator of the Melbourne Cricket Ground, as the champion ground maker. It went on : " His wickets are perfection and his heart and soul are in his work, although his soul is at times sorely vexed at the tremendous wear and tear his beloved wickets have to sustain." No suggestion of shooters on those wickets.

A Sydney writer, sixty-five years ago, wrote a discourse on the standard of cricket in which he claimed more runs were being made because of better wickets. Here is what he wrote :—

" They get more runs now—how do you account for it ? My reply is in the first place grounds are better than they used to be, and *the billiard table wickets* and the absence of shooters enable a batsman to hit more than of yore."

The method of preparation plays an enormous part in the type of pitch produced, though other factors also enter the picture.

Australian wickets are, on the average, faster than English. Yet it is not axiomatic. One of the fastest I ever saw was at Cambridge in 1930, and I could quote other examples.

The Manchester and Oval Test pitches of 1938 were only doped imitations of the kind on which cricket should be played. The same stretches of turf in 1948 produced fair and equal opportunities for batsmen and bowlers.

Without any doubt whatever, the Sydney Cricket Ground wicket of 1926-1928 was much faster than of recent years.

I remember a long discussion in about 1936 with the late " Sep " Carter, in which he firmly declared : " Wickets prior to 1914 were very fast and in my opinion as good or even better than those of today."

At Lord's the authorities firmly refuse to allow marl top-dressing which has made a batsman's paradise out of the Nottingham pitch. This is certainly one of the reasons why Lord's usually provides a pitch in which a reasonable balance is struck between batsman and bowler. There have been exceptions as in 1930 when the wicket was a real beauty from the batsman's point of view, but in general Lord's sets an equitable standard.

Curators must be careful to see that batsmen can play strokes with reasonable confidence and that the ball does not fly dangerously. There should be sufficient pace not to blunt the edge of fast bowling and at the same time not to deprive the slow bowler of all spin. It can be done, and the matter is of sufficient importance to warrant the constant vigilance of administrators.

As for wicket-keeping, we may dispense with the subject quickly. Why, in 1843 a Cambridge undergraduate match was played in which 183 sundries were recorded. Such a happening today would be laughable.

Long-stop was at one time an important member of the fielding side. We would now regard it as absurd to employ one.

In all sports there has been an improvement in technique and in tactics. This can't always be easily proved.

Faster times in racing are generally attributed to better tracks.

I invariably fall back upon swimming, in which sport records have been smashed beyond recognition. The water has not changed over the years.

The champion of one era would have been the champion of any other, but he would have been called upon to vary his methods.

That is my view. I think it is the only logical conclusion.

On Grounds

HOW MANY TIMES IS THE QUESTION ASKED OF A PLAYER : " WHICH ground do you like best ? " The answer in most cases is probably a mixture of fact and sentiment. The most insignificant ground may conjure up happy memories.

Elsewhere I have mentioned Brockton Point Ground in Canada as the most beautiful of all. Few cricketers have been privileged to see it and in any case a questioner usually has in mind the grounds upon which first-class matches are played.

Under the latter heading I suppose Adelaide would gain top marks if one considered the natural beauty of its environment. The lovely park-lands and gardens adjacent to the oval—the stately cathedral which I sometimes feel has a beneficial effect on the spectators (at least those whose back are not towards it) and the delightful background of the Adelaide Hills.

From a player's point of view it is rather too long and too narrow. When a wicket is pitched on one side of the centre patch it brings the boundary too close. The pitch itself is usually slow and inclined to keep a fraction too low for attractive stroke making.

As a cricket ground pure and simple, excluding all considerations other than those inside the fence, I always have thought the Sydney Ground to be unsurpassed.

Its dimensions are almost uniform in every direction, the turf is so soft, and even the groundsman's method of mowing it in circles seems to enhance its attractiveness.

When I first played in Sydney the pitch was made of Bulli soil. It was black, hard as flint and very fast. One could scarcely mark the surface with sprigged boots. Today the soil is much more chocolate in colour; it wears more quickly; takes more spin, but is slower.

The light in Australia is rather harsh. In this respect I found Sydney the softest of our grounds.

Another point I liked was the architectural beauty of the score-board which could well be emulated elsewhere.

The hardest of our grounds, both to play on and in actual fact, was Melbourne. Very few players can stand a whole day on the Melbourne wicket or ground without noticing the extreme hardness of the surface.

Often it is slippery too.

Since the new public stand was built, the playing arena has been hemmed in like an amphitheatre. This eliminates the natural winds. It sets up fishtail eddies which are disconcerting to players. On a hot day the stillness becomes stifling.

Another difficulty in Melbourne is to see the ball when it gets up any height. The background of people in the stand has caused many players to lose sight of an outfield catch.

Yet somehow I always liked batting in Melbourne and was more successful there in Test cricket than on any other Australian ground. Perhaps the wicket suited me.

Even the Brisbane ground has its special virtues. At the moment it possesses a pitch of even height and pace which batsmen would probably say is the best in Australia. It is always a credit to the curator.

Then, too, the arrangement for players whose dressing rooms are in a separate building and enclosure is greatly appreciated. It is ideal in such a hot and humid climate, enabling the maximum rest to be gained during intervals.

Accommodation in Brisbane will improve as opportunity allows.

Despite the features of these grounds, none of them possesses the atmosphere of Lord's, which is unique and indescribable.

It is an education to play at Lord's—one's very experience and outlook seem to visibly benefit.

The relics of earlier days, photos of historic people, places and events, are an absorbing interest, even to the little bird which was killed by a cricket ball only to find immortality in a glass case in the long room.

The original " Ashes " urn is there too.

Don't imagine the ground to possess nothing but atmosphere. It is a delightful ground. The wicket is natural. It usually provides an even balance between bat and ball.

Cricket at Lord's seems to be a calm and peaceful game as our forefathers found it, and I think much of this delightful calm is missing on the bigger grounds.

Throughout England one finds charming spots such as the Canterbury Ground with its sacred tree in the outfield. The proximity of tents—spectators at the boundary's edge unhampered by a fence, all seem to bring an air of intimacy.

Take your choice. The ugliest ground has something to contribute.

No team could be more inspired by an enthusiastic audience than the Yorkshiremen at Bramall Lane, and nobody would ever describe such a setting in terms of ecstasy, especially when the smoke of nearby factories almost justifies an appeal against the light.

There is an old saying that the word goes round, " Stoke up the furnaces, lads—the Aussies are batting."

Perhaps that may be called Yorkshire's secret weapon.

Smoke or no smoke, cricket in Yorkshire is usually pregnant with vitality and courage, essential elements which are sometimes bred under difficult circumstances.

I suppose cricket can be made too pleasant.

On Correspondence

I HAVE ELSEWHERE GIVEN AN INDICATION OF THE TREMENDOUS MAIL which must be dealt with by an Australian XI Captain on an English tour.

Apart altogether from such special occasions I have for many years received a regular flow of what might be termed " Fan Mail ".

Much of it came from young cricket enthusiasts seeking autographs, photos, souvenirs and such like.

I have tried to be reasonable in the matter, but to cope with the demand for souvenirs would have taxed the resources of a second-hand dealer.

To me, however, this correspondence has shown how remarkable is the Empire-wide interest in Anglo-Australian cricket. Even from beyond the Empire, America, Holland and Denmark, inquiries have arrived.

One thing always intrigued me. That was the characteristic hand-writing or means of expression which instantly gave a clue to the writer's nationality.

There is a marked difference between the handwriting of English and Australian people. It not only applies to the children but also to the adults.

If you ever get the chance to compare a set of signatures—say an English team and an Australian team—take notice. Without doubt, the writing portrays many of the personal qualities of the people.

I once received the following letter. It was to thank me for an autograph.

" Dear Don Bradman,
    I thank you from the bottom of my heart for your kind reply.
    Oh how nice of you. How my heart is leaping for joy. Words refuse to come and I must needs stop here.
    I thank you once again. Many thanks—truly thanks. I beg to remain dear Don,

                       A lingering memory at least "

No Australian or English boy could possibly have written that letter. You don't need to see his signature—it is quite obvious he was from India.

A good deal of pleasure is gleaned from letters of goodwill.

One must be prepared for a small percentage of anonymous letters which are always abusive. They are invariably relegated post-haste to the W.P.B.

A person who hasn't the courage to sign his name to a letter is not worthy of a second thought and possesses a warped personality.

Occasionally there is pathos—obviously genuine requests for assis-tance. Sometimes humour and mostly of the unintentional variety.

On my last tour I could not help seeing the funny side of the follow-ing :—

"Dear Mr. Bradman,
  I am sending to ask you if you could do me a favour."

After referring to certain arrangements which had apparently been made for her to fly to Australia to get married, she added :—
"I am not quite sure if he is playing a straight game. I have been run off my feet trying to get over there and trying to find out what is going on. I am told he is going about with a woman in his car who is about 40 years of age—maybe less in years and he may take her over as a substitute in place of myself—try and do me.
  I am of course turned 60 years of age but am in splendid health.
  I would see you are well rewarded for your kindness if you can see to this and her.
  P.S. I have just received news this morning he is getting married at 3 o'clock today, Friday, to this other woman. Can flying arrangements be cancelled ?"

I fail to see how my cricketing knowledge could suggest any skill in the matter of matrimonial tangles.
  One of the most remarkable happenings in regard to correspondence was the receipt by me of a letter from Amsterdam.

I have had a photograph taken of the envelope which is reproduced here.

The letter was delivered to me at Lord's without delay—a tribute to the English postal authorities.

What chance has one of dodging recognition when his eyes are a sufficient address in a population of nearly 50 million people.

On Captaincy

WHEN THE RIVAL CAPTAINS GO OUT INTO THE MIDDLE TO TOSS IN A TEST Match what are they thinking ? What problems confront them ? I suppose thoughts like these constantly run through the minds of the spectators. But do they ever ponder over the apprenticeship these captains have served before being appointed to such responsible positions ?

The actual game itself is the moment of action. Years of thought and training have preceded it.

It was my good fortune to captain Australia in five Test series—four against England and one against India. During that period Australia did not lose a rubber, but I lost a great deal of sleep.

Not for a moment do I claim any special ability as a captain. I do claim to have learnt many lessons from my experiences, all of which emphasise the necessity of hard work and application. There is no short cut.

At school I had virtually no opportunity. The cricket was not competitive except on rare occasions. I did not have control of a team, broadly speaking, until I first captained a grade side. I was still far from confident when the task of handling a Test team came my way. My own consciousness that I was relatively inexperienced only increased my anxiety and may have caused me at first to move along strictly orthodox lines.

The first duty of a captain is to win the toss. This is pure luck, though some captains have been blessed with more than their share. I was not one of them.

In 1936 I lost the first two and won the last three.

In 1938 I lost all four.

In 1946-7 I won two and lost three.

Against India 1947-8 I won four out of five.

In England 1948 I lost three out of five.

The summary shows that I won 11 out of 24—just less than half. A rather interesting point is that Australia did not lose one Test Match in which I won the toss.

Winning the toss is not always an advantage. The winner has to make his decision, whereas the loser is sometimes spared such an embarrassment.

Sometimes the loss of the toss enables a win to be gained due to the time factor.

Take a case where A bats first and makes 400. B replies with 350. A then makes 300 for 5 declared and B is 9 for 170 when the match ends in a draw. Team A has a margin of 180 runs to get 1 wicket. Assuming the reverse batting order, team A might have won comfortably by 8 wickets.

I am certain we won the 1948 Nottingham Test because I lost the toss. It enabled our speed bowlers to break through quickly while there was still life in the pitch.

Wickets do not always play as anticipated. At Lord's in 1948 I won the toss, and decided to bat, fortified by the groundsman's forecast "slow and easy." It turned out to be a real "green top" and we struggled very hard to survive.

Unfortunately for a captain the spotlight of publicity beats very fiercely upon his every move. What he should or should not do is chronicled in advance by experienced and inexperienced critics. They have no responsibility. The skipper's decisions are minutely analysed, and the verdict given in the light of after events.

There lies the big difference. A captain must make every decision *before* he knows what its effect will be, and he must carry the full responsibility, not of whether his decision will be right or wrong, but whether it brings success. The margin between success or failure can be so slender.

Cast your minds back to Leeds in 1926. Arthur Carr, having won the toss for England, sent Australia in to bat. Bardsley was caught first ball. Off the fifth ball Carr himself had the mortification of dropping Macartney who showed his appreciation by making a century before lunch. Had Carr held that catch, his decision might have been hailed as a master-stroke—instead he was torn to shreds.

The captain's decision may be perfectly correct according to all available information—one mistake and he is undone.

Sometimes personal considerations intrude. Many a captain has sacrificed his own wicket to the detriment of his side because he feared the stigma of not attempting to set an example to his men. It is all very well to be gallant and heroic, but the captain's job embodies the welfare of the team, and if his own personal success is an integral part of victory, he should act accordingly.

On several occasions I was compelled to rearrange our batting order as a matter of tactics because of the state of the wicket. It almost invariably succeeded.

Some were unkind enough to suggest that my purpose was to avoid batting on a wet wicket. Of course it was ; but only because such avoidance was necessary in the interests of the team.

Cricket pitches behave in a variety of ways after rain. The man never lived whose judgment was infallible. Not the least difficulty is to decide how long a wicket will remain bad.

Under Australian conditions sufficient rain on a hard wicket, followed by a hot sun, will generally produce a glue pot. Some are worse than others. But will it remain sticky for an hour or all day ? One cannot tell.

In 1936-7 against Allen's team, we worked like beavers to try and get quick wickets. Then I found the pitch was drying more slowly than anticipated and had to tell my bowlers not to get England out.

The question of field placing is a captain's natural responsibility, though he will, if wise, work in harmony with his bowlers.

Decisions might have to be taken occasionally on matters where the captain's judgment must prevail over that of his men. For instance, I often had difficulty with slip fieldsmen who insisted on standing too deep. From my side view at cover, I thought the ball would not carry to them. They, in turn, said if they stood closer they would not be able to hold a catch. My reply was : " If the ball doesn't reach you, you can't catch it. Better to drop a catch than not be in a position to attempt it."

I was always very particular about the position of fieldsmen. I might even have been called fussy. But it is important. One might just as well miss a catch by ten feet as three inches, and if a captain anticipates the possibility of a catch going in a certain place, it is his job to put the fieldsman *exactly* in that spot—not somewhere near it. This applies more forcibly to positions near the wicket.

A constant problem is the task of deciding the right moment to make a bowling change. Your fast bowler is getting wickets but tiring rapidly. Shall he be used right up in the hope of achieving quick results or shall he be rested for a later effort ? Perhaps a bowler is doing well when a batsman comes in who is renowned for his weakness against some other bowler. Should a change be made at once ? These are typical problems which cannot be decided in advance.

The great captain is the man who can get the best out of his men and achieve results with a poor combination.

For instance, there was no skill shown by Armstrong in opening the bowling with Gregory and McDonald. To follow them was such an array as Hendry (medium pace), Macartney (slow left-hand), Mailey and Armstrong (slow right-hand). It was a tailor-made combination. What a difference to some of the later teams when the openers were really only medium pace change bowlers.

Generally speaking, it seems that a batsman is a better type for captain than a bowler. He is spared the unfortunate choice of whether to overbowl himself or not. Wasn't it George Giffen who acceded to the crowd's entreaties to "take yourself off" by going on the other end?

Also, I think the captain should be a player whose place in the team is indisputable. If a skipper has need to worry about his own position, it must detract from his ability to make untrammelled decisions.

I always liked playing under a captain who was firm but kindly. There is no joy in playing under a man who lets you wander around the field where you will, or who will hesitate when necessary to tell you what is required of you.

I think players react much better to the leader who sets them a high target.

Complete cricketers should constantly be seeking ways of assisting their captain. It is a fundamental duty so to do. A variety of temperaments does not always enable this perfection to be attained.

Sometimes a conflict may arise between the desire to please the public and the need to adopt an unattractive or unpopular policy. It can be most disconcerting if the public is clamouring for action and the captain feels it necessary to instruct his men to "dig in". Strongminded players will often succumb to these external influences.

If both captains are bent upon making the play attractive, there is little difficulty in providing entertaining cricket. Should one captain depart from this attitude, the game can be ruined as a spectacle. More than once I was criticised for unimaginative tactics when in fact I was only combating those of my opponents. I did not believe in initiating slow play, and only resorted to it in cases of necessity.

One thing all captains (and players) should do is to make themselves conversant with the rules governing the game. Apart from the value to be so gained, they are a fascinating study.

This has been a sketchy outline of some captaincy problems. They are very real. A great many of them on the field are obvious. Off the field they are not so obvious but perhaps more onerous.

If any young player aspires to the leadership of an Australian XI, let him do so only if imbued with the ideal of service. It isn't always pleasant trying to please 50,000 spectators, 50 journalists and 10 other players. Their interests often clash.

Sometimes I think the public would do well to ponder that captains are normal, sensitive human beings, striving so hard to do the right thing. They are not a race apart. Public support is a great tonic when the going is hard.

Umpires

When the great matches of cricket are discussed around the fireside, at the wayside inn or at any of those places where people foregather to debate the merits of their favourites, how often is a thought given to the umpires who are of such extreme importance to cricket?

Good umpires are vital enough to the success of any sport, but in cricket one decision can decide the fate of a Test Match.

In football and tennis an umpire can make several mistakes which may not alter the result of the match.

The mistakes themselves may cut both ways so that neither side is penalised.

There may be plenty of time for a team to recover the lost ground.

In cricket, if the umpire makes a wrong decision and gives a batsman out, he *is* out and that is the end of the matter. There is no second chance.

Thus the umpire is such a vital figure in cricket. By a decision involving but a fraction of an inch he can, in a moment, do irreparable damage to the chances of a team.

One of the first things a young cricketer should be taught is to accept the umpire's decision under all circumstances without quibble.

Anyone who has played much cricket will have been " out " to wrong decisions, and will have been given " not-out " when he should have been sent back to the pavilion. Over the years the right and wrong for individual players will usually balance out fairly accurately. In any case the batsman does not always know whether he is out, especially if it is a close L.B.W. decision. At other times he may be certain an error has been made.

I once went in to bat, for instance, against a new ball. I took a brand new white cricket bat. I received only one ball and walked back to the pavilion with a big red half-moon on the edge of the bat, having been given out L.B.W. first ball. That was positive proof. But it isn't always so easy.

I maintain that a batsman always knows whether he is caught behind the wicket. No matter how faint the " touch " may be, it can be felt through the bat handle. I have been caught behind and no appeal was made, either because the wicket-keeper did not hear it or because he thought the ball touched my pad.

These are only matters of detail. The great and important fact is the integrity of the umpires, and most certainly during my period in cricket that could not be questioned.

There was a time when it was considered the proper thing to have your own umpire. Happily, that is no longer a practice nor a necessity.

English umpires, generally speaking, are better than Australian. The reasons are not hard to find. Firstly, there are many more of them officiating throughout the season in first-class cricket. Secondly, the leading English umpires get as much experience in one summer as an Australian umpire would get in several years. Thirdly, I am sure the number of ex-cricketers who join the ranks of umpires in England has had a beneficial effect, because of the dove-tailing of theory and practice.

Even umpires, who were at one time players, change their minds. Bill Bestwick, English Test umpire and former county player, said, " I've found out since I've been umpiring that a lot of wickets I took myself when I was playing, were not out."

In both countries I would like to see more young men take on this arduous but important job. Their eyesight and hearing must naturally be keener, and all the cricket knowledge in the world won't help an umpire if he cannot hear a faint snick.

I once saw, officiating in a first-class match, an umpire who was wearing thick glasses. A wicket fell. He went to the stumps to re-make the wicket, borrowed a bat, tried to knock the stump in with the handle, but missed it altogether. From that moment I questioned his ability to see the edge of the popping crease from his position at square-leg.

Without hesitation I rank Frank Chester as the greatest umpire under whom I played.

In my four seasons' cricket in England, he stood for a large percentage of the matches and seldom made a mistake. On the other hand he gave some really wonderful and intricate decisions. Not only was his judgment sound, but Chester exercised a measure of control over the game which I think was desirable.

Not long ago I read an article which suggested that players were appealing too frequently and sometimes bluffed the umpire.

You couldn't bluff Chester. In fact in a Test Match at Leeds, Hedley Verity appealed for L.B.W. against one of our batsmen. Chester's reply was : " Not out, Hedley, and that was a very bad appeal."

I am not implying that umpires should constantly be making such remarks to bowlers, but I think an umpire is within his rights if he thinks the bowler is making a frivolous appeal.

Chester's case was unique. He gave promise of being a high-class batsman, but through a war injury had to desert the playing field at an age when most men are in their prime. Umpiring became his profession while all his faculties were keen. Chester was an ornament to the game and rendered great services to cricket.

Next to him I would rank the Australian George Hele. I think the Englishmen who played under Hele would agree that he was the best Australian umpire between the two wars. They had every confidence in him.

It makes a tremendous difference if batsmen can trust their own judgment and that of the umpire as well. Let me illustrate my meaning. With Chester umpiring I would have no hesitation whatever in trying to leg-glance a ball which, in my opinion, was pitched on the leg stump but was going away to the leg-side and would miss the stumps if allowed to pass. With a less competent umpire I would not attempt that shot. I would have to feel that the ball was pitched a couple of inches outside the leg stump. The alternative would be to play the ball with the full face of the bat to mid-on. This is one way in which competent umpiring helps to brighten cricket.

For a long time the Australian view was that the two best umpires should have charge of all Test Matches.

England rather held the idea that where there were say six umpires of relatively the same standard, it was only fair for each of them to get a match or two.

Both points of view have their merits, and the panel system certainly develops a wider range of umpires.

Under such a system, however, the greatest care must be exercised. No umpire should be placed on a panel just to obtain experience. He should first pass searching tests as to knowledge and temperament.

Test Matches are too important to allow relatively inexperienced umpires to use them for educational purposes. Other games can serve this purpose.

English umpires always impressed me as being a particularly fine and tolerant body of men.

I had the pleasure of addressing an umpires' gathering at Lord's in 1948 before the season started, and could not help noticing their obvious desire to co-operate with the players, and to be scrupulously fair.

There have been regrettable occasions when individual players delighted in trying to embarrass, rather than to assist, umpires. The tendency of a few to show openly their disgust when a decision goes against them, is deplorable. Not only should captains discipline players who cannot exercise better control over their feelings, but the umpires should report them.

Another notable trait of English umpires is the individualistic way in which they develop. Could, for instance, one imagine Bill Reeves having a double? Amongst today's ranks Alec Skelding is a real character. I never tired of hearing Alec's famous expression when stumps were drawn : " Well, gentlemen, that concludes the entertainment for today." It was the inflection in his voice as much as the words which used to intrigue me.

I want to conclude by emphasising as strongly as I can that it is the duty of every player to assist the umpire in his job.

It is not clever to obtain a decision under false pretences. If you do, the day will most assuredly come when the position will be reversed.

Reviewing the Stars

A REVIEW OF CRICKET HAPPENINGS DURING MY TEST MATCH YEARS WOULD scarcely be complete without reference to the men who were outstanding in their respective departments.

One of the glories of cricket is the way it lends itself to fireside reminiscences. Men can sit down and either amicably discuss or fiercely argue the merits of various players.

Opinions are vehemently and dogmatically expressed by lovers of the game who themselves are entirely without playing skill.

Such a person was associated with one of the clubs for which I played. He was passionately fond of cricket—worked night and day to help the club, and had an incredible memory for past records.

Yet one evening at practice we were short of a bowler and asked him to take a turn. He jumped at the opportunity but soon gave up, for only on rare occasions could he get the ball to the other end without first hitting the net at the side of the pitch.

This fascinating attraction which cricket has for incompetent players is something of an enigma. These same people are able on many occasions to discourse most intelligently on the finer points. In that regard cricket differs from other forms of entertainment such as music.

I can listen to and appreciate good music but certainly would not presume to argue the technical side of it with a competent musician.

There are intangible things about cricketers which make them great. I can remember two batsmen with whom I played district cricket. They had the most wonderful ability—could play every shot, had lovely wrists, beautiful timing, splendid physique. Indeed I was envious of their skill.

One of them played a few inter-state games—the other none.

Why is it that such gifted personalities do not go on to Test cricket? Perhaps temperament, perhaps faulty judgment; I don't know.

Maybe the difference between the mediocre and the great player is that the latter has either developed the knowledge of how to avoid errors or has an inborn intuition.

Most certainly it is not luck. Anyway for what they are worth, here are a few observations on the stars of recent years. I do not expect all my readers to agree with me, but after all, I have been in a rather favourable position to form my opinions.

Wicket-keepers. There are not many to consider when it comes to wicket-keeping. Australia has had barely half a dozen in the long history of cricket.

Once a wicket-keeper is established as the best in the country he is not usually supplanted until advancing years take the edge off his speed and the keenness from his eyesight.

In early days, wickets were undoubtedly less reliable than they are today. Wicket-keeper's gloves were akin to those worn with an evening-dress outfit. Leg-guards were of such dimensions that they might have been designed for the wearer to slip on under his pants—more like shin pads.

The presence of long-stop in the field and the importance placed on this position clearly indicate that the wicket-keeper was unable to stop a large percentage of the deliveries which passed the bat.

The favourite joke of Tom Hollway, Premier of Victoria, was that his chance of becoming an international cricketer was ruined by the abolition of long-stop.

I understand that Blackham was the first man to dispense with such a position. This was naturally a tribute to his skill, and to be dubbed the " Prince of 'keepers " illustrates the high repute in which Blackham was held by writers of his day.

I have seen a pair of the gloves he wore. He must have been a stoic to have " kept " in them. Without doubt a modern player would have his hands ruined if he were to use them for any length of time against fast bowling.

My own knowledge of Australian wicket-keepers from participation in matches with them is confined to three who were pre-eminent—Carter, Oldfield and Tallon.

" Sammy " Carter was at his best before the 1914-18 war. In the 1920-1 series of Tests, Oldfield, fresh from the A.I.F. matches, took Carter's place, but failed to hold it, for the Selectors brought Carter back for the Fourth and Fifth Tests of that series, despite his 42 years.

I saw Carter in that Fifth Test, and even now can picture his lovely work, especially when taking Gregory and McDonald.

Then in 1932, when he was 54, Carter went to America with Arthur Mailey's Team. Day in and day out on most indifferent wickets he performed wonderfully well.

Sammy had very definite theories. One was that a wicket-keeper should never go in front of the stumps to take a return from the field. Another was that he should stand at the stumps to take all kinds of bowling except the very fastest.

The latter theory had unfortunate results, because in New York he persisted in staying up at the stumps to Stan. McCabe when the ball was flying dangerously off a coir mat laid on a none-too-level earth pitch. He could not possibly have dodged the one which flew and caught him in the eye. He was taken to hospital and eventually lost the sight of the eye.

On that tour Fleetwood-Smith was very young but a potential Test Match player, and I well remember Carter telling me that he would love to have just one season in first-class cricket with Fleetwood. He said, " I could make him so good he would win a Test for Australia."

Those prophetic words nearly came true. Carter's wish to play a first-class season with him was never fulfilled, but if ever a man won a Test Match with one ball it was Fleetwood-Smith in Adelaide against England in 1937, when he bowled Hammond.

There have been fewer men possessing a kinder heart or greater cricketing knowledge than Sammy Carter.

Following him came Bert. Oldfield, who, for a few years was indisputably the greatest wicket-keeper of the day.

I played with Oldfield through a considerable portion of his career, and many times have marvelled at his skill. There was about his work a polish far transcending that of all others.

Never any suggestion of an ugly movement—feet always right— hands in perfect position, and remarkable speed when stumping— especially on the leg-side, off a medium pace bowler.

Oldfield achieved a reputation for sportsmanship, and it was said of him that he never appealed unless certain in his own mind that the man was out.

On occasions he adopted an air of apology. You could almost imagine him saying to the batsman, " Sorry old chap—I stumped you and you're out. I didn't like doing it but then it's in the rules you know."

How different from George Duckworth, whose raucous " Howzat ! " terrified many an unsuspecting victim !

There is a story that after frightening the life out of some young player by his noisy appeal, Duckworth completed it by telling the quaking batsman he was out. At this the batsman, visibly relieved, replied, " Is that all ? Thank God ! I thought for a minute I was sandbagged."

Until his retirement, I could not do otherwise than class Oldfield as the finest wicket-keeper I had seen.

Today I am inclined to hand that supremacy to Don Tallon.

There can be little to choose between them, but my reasoning is that Tallon makes fewer mistakes, and covers more ground on the leg-side to fast bowlers. In other respects they may be regarded as about equal.

Don Tallon is rather tall for a wicket-keeper, and for this reason alone does not move with quite the same grace as Oldfield. Nevertheless, he is attractive to watch, moves like lightning when required, and has uncanny anticipation on the leg-side.

In one respect Tallon and Oldfield were direct opposites. The former never apologises for appealing. He is positively belligerent in seeking the umpire's decision if there is any hope of gaining the verdict, and possibly errs a little in this direction.

Tallon is incomparably the finest batsman of all Australian wicket-keepers.

Opinions may vary as to the respective merits of players, but on one thing all will agree—Australia has been distinctly fortunate in that she has been so ably served by wicket-keepers in the international field, for the position is of cardinal importance.

My experience of English wicket-keepers is limited to Duckworth, Ames and Evans. There have been others during the period, but they did not quite come up to the class of the three mentioned.

When Geo. Duckworth first came to Australia, he was a great 'keeper. His work on the leg-side to medium-pace bowling was brilliant, and he covered so much ground that he forced our batsmen to avoid the fine-leg glance for fear of being caught.

Although he did not remain England's 'keeper very long, he was only supplanted because Les. Ames was such a fine batsman. The latter was not up to Duckworth's standard purely as a 'keeper.

Godfrey Evans did some wonderful work during the 1946-7 tour of Australia. Over 1,000 runs were scored by Australia in Tests before he conceded a sundry. He has remarkable agility and extremely hard hands which never seem to be affected by the worst knocks.

In England in 1948 Godfrey made some errors which told heavily against him, but at that time he was still the best 'keeper in the country.

Englishmen seem pretty united in their views that Strudwick was their finest 'keeper. They may be right. I am not in a position to say.

Bowlers. How many times in my life have I been asked : " Who is the greatest bowler you have ever played against ? " My answer has invariably been O'Reilly.

I will go further and say that of all the first-class batsmen I know and who played against O'Reilly in his prime, not one disagrees with this view.

But it is not reasonable to compare O'Reilly with, say, Larwood, because, under certain conditions and with a new ball, Larwood was much more likely to get wickets. Therefore, the only way to deal with bowlers is to divide them into types.

Fast. When I first entered big cricket Jack Gregory was Australia's speed bowler. My first Test Match was his last, for Gregory broke down in that game. Previously I had played with and against him in other matches.

England's fast bowler was Larwood, who had not then achieved the reputation he now enjoys.

I had in 1921 seen Ted McDonald, and was to play against him in England in 1930.

Later came Tim Wall, McCormick and Lindwall.

How do they compare ? This is a problem, for I saw them operating under widely differing conditions. The greatest bowler is at times reduced to mediocrity—a poor bowler becomes a giant—according to the state of the pitch.

The fastest bowling I ever faced for a few overs was by the Queensland aboriginal Eddie Gilbert, though one would not dream of classing him amongst the great. Moreover, his action was decidedly suspect.

On that day in Queensland we struck a green-top wicket. Whilst Gilbert was fresh he hurled them down like thunderbolts.

At the start of my brief innings one ball knocked the bat completely out of my hands, the only time I ever had such an experience.

I was eventually caught by the wicket-keeper who was standing almost half-way between the stumps and the boundary. He took the ball over his head.

Over a full season, under all sorts of conditions, I rank Larwood as the fastest bowler of all.

At times he attained exceptional speed.

There was the Melbourne Test in 1928 when Jack Ryder tried a hook but hit the ball on the edge of the bat. It went well over the fence for 6, right over the wicket-keeper's head.

In the same spell of bowling, Ryder tried for another hook but missed. He obscured Duckworth's vision. The ball hit Duckworth on the forehead, bounced off it and landed on the sight-screen.

Then I have seen McCormick bowl tremendously fast for about three overs, and Lindwall at Manchester in 1948 bowled a few overs at this same terrific pace. But it isn't only pace that counts, because a hot sun and a dead wicket soon take heavy toll, and then the bowler's stamina and brains must be brought into play to overcome the handicaps.

Tim Wall was the finest fast bowler I ever faced whilst the ball was new. He had a wonderful ability to make it swing late. I recall Archie Jackson in Adelaide one year trying to leg-glance a ball from Tim, and then in bewilderment looking round to see his off-bail on the ground.

After the ball became old, Tim did not have the same devastating pace as the others, though he was a great trier, and no more loyal player ever drew on a pair of boots.

Harold Larwood gained notoriety during the body-line season, which, I think, almost any of the leading fast bowlers could have done using similar methods. Apart from that one season he did not unduly trouble Australian batsmen. Indeed, for a great bowler he had some very unimpressive performances in Tests. For instance, Adelaide 1928-9, 1 for 152, Melbourne 1928-9, 1 for 168, Leeds 1930, 1 for 139, and the Oval 1930, 1 for 132. Those figures were recorded when Larwood was using the same field as Gregory, McDonald, and others used throughout their careers.

I, personally, found much more difficulty in handling Ken Farnes, who, though not as fast, moved the ball off the wicket and delivered it from a much greater height. His 8 for 43 in Gents. v. Players at Lord's 1938, 6 for 96 in a total of 604 at Melbourne 1937, and 10 wickets in his first Test against Australia, were all truly grand performances.

It is interesting to compare the Test records of Farnes and Larwood omitting the 1932-3 series of Tests. Here they are :—

| Farnes | 38 wkts. | 1,068 runs. | Average 28·10 |
| Larwood | 31 „ | 1,280 „ | „ 41·29 |

The tremendous success of the Gregory-McDonald combination always brings these two into the limelight together. Gregory was without doubt the greater player because of his superlative fielding and fine batting, but, purely as a bowler, McDonald was his superior.

This tall lean Victorian had a perfect rhythmic action, incredible stamina and real pace plus the ability to do things with the ball.

Taking everything into consideration he would probably win a cricket Gallup Poll—take the points for the best of all fast bowlers.

Very close behind him in my opinion (on his 1948 form) is Ray Lindwall.

Here we have the same smooth rhythm, splendid stamina and fighting spirit, magnificent control plus ability to swing the ball and vary the pace.

Ray lacks McDonald's great height and that is a disadvantage, for the bumper must be pitched so much shorter to make it lift.

It is a coincidence that McDonald on the first tour after the 1914-18 war took 27 Test wickets, Lindwall doing the same after the last war. They share this record of having taken the greatest number in a series by any fast bowlers.

A discussion on fast bowling would not be complete without reference to Constantine, the mercurial West Indian.

There was one day at Sydney when he bowled with a gale behind him and took 6 for 45 against N.S.W. Here was real speed bowling of high quality.

In addition to his bowling it was Constantine's cat-like agility in the field and his unorthodox but powerful hitting which made him such an attraction.

Whilst he could rightfully be classed as one of the world's great all-rounders, I would not rate him in McDonald's class purely as a bowler.

Fast bowling takes enormous toll of one's physical resources, and it is not surprising that so few really fast ones come to light.

They sometimes come in for criticism for they are usually somewhat volatile by nature. Under a hot Australian sun and on our hard wickets, the wonder is that the race exists at all.

Medium Pacers. Under this heading I class bowlers who are not of the slow spin type and who are not quick enough to be called fast, irrespective of their particular style.

There are only two of my time who merit discussion for the No. 1 place, namely Maurice Tate and Alec Bedser.

If we take figures only to decide the issue, then Tate stands supreme.

He first toured Australia in 1924-5 under the captaincy of Arthur Gilligan, and his wonderful bowling in that series, during which he took no less than 38 Test wickets, is still talked about. No other medium pace bowler has approached such a feat.

Tate was then a young man of twenty-nine summers.

He had a glorious action—in fact his shoulder swing was so perfect that it should be used as the film example for all young bowlers to see.

This beautiful shoulder swing, plus the combination of arm and wrist, enabled him to obtain tremendous speed off the pitch. In addition, he swung the ball well and varied his pace most intelligently.

The same attributes were present in 1928-9 when I first played against him, but it was generally conceded that by now a little of the nip had started to go out of his bowling.

Tate had good control of swing, making the new ball go either way. Later, when it was old, he made the ball come back into a right-hand batsman off the pitch.

One of his greatest performances was to bowl unchanged from the start of play until lunch time against the Australians at Hove in 1930, taking in that period 6 for 18. His victims were Ponsford, Jackson, McCabe, V. Richardson, Fairfax and a'Beckett.

Alec Bedser was a similar type of bowler. They were about the same pace, though Bedser had a slightly higher delivery which assisted him in getting lift from the pitch.

Bedser had that same quality " speed off the pitch ", and he could at times actually turn the ball from leg to off by cutting across the seam. It was this particular ball of his which always worried me and which beat so many batsmen.

I don't think Bedser bowled an outswinger nearly as well as Tate. On the other hand his inswinger was better in that it dipped later.

If Bedser had a fault it was his tendency to bowl just short of a length.

There is no doubt in my mind that I found Bedser harder to play (especially in England in 1948) than Tate. But my own advancing years doubtless caused my reactions to be slower.

Still, I think all Australian players of the modern generation think Bedser the best medium pace bowler they have met.

Had they faced Tate in 1924, it is probable they would have found him better still. Anyway, both were magnificent, both delightful personalities and ornaments to the game.

Had he not been such a wonderful batsman, I think Wally Hammond may easily have proved equal to Tate and Bedser with the ball, for on some occasions, particularly when he failed with the bat, I have known him bowl medium-paced stuff superbly.

Slow Bowlers. Here we have a very wide field because in it I suppose we must include slow leg-break bowlers like Grimmett and Mailey, the left-hand googlies such as Tribe and Fleetwood-Smith, the orthodox left-hand like Rhodes and Verity, right-hand off spin of the Blackie-Ian Johnson breed, and also O'Reilly, though I propose to let the latter have a niche of his own.

I would rate Grimmett as the greatest of these.

He was simply phenomenal in the way he could come on at any time and immediately drop into a perfect length.

Arthur Mailey had a vicious spin, far greater than Grimmett. He also had a " wrong-un " which was far better concealed, but to obtain these things he had to sacrifice accuracy.

It has been written that Mailey bowled like a millionaire and Grimmett like a miser. This description is very true, for Mailey never cared how many runs were scored off his bowling so long as he captured wickets, whereas Grimmett obviously begrudged every run, and I really think he enjoyed bowling a maiden just as much as getting a wicket.

Clarrie Grimmett was a genuine slow leg-spinner. He used variations in pace, cleverly exploited a breeze and was dynamite the way he would trap L.B.W. new players who attempted to play back to him. He did not bother much about the " wrong-un ", but preferred to rely on his accuracy coupled with a moderate turn from leg.

In later years he developed what came to be known amongst the players as his " flicker "—so called because of the way he flicked his fingers as he let the ball go.

It was delivered from the first and second fingers virtually squeezed out but a clever turn of the wrist made it appear to be a leg-break, whereas the ball went straight or turned very slightly from the off. He got many L.B.W.'s with this one.

No other leg-spinner of my time could be classed alongside Mailey or Grimmett.

H. V. Hordern was of the same mould. Some place him higher than either. They may be right. My limited experience with Dr. Hordern does not enable me to offer judgment.

Incidentally, Grimmett possesses one unique record. He is the only player from whose bowling over 1,000 runs have been scored in one Test series.

The best Englishman of recent years was Doug. Wright, though he was perhaps more akin to the O'Reilly type.

Little Tich Freeman was a fine bowler in England, so was Dick Tyldesley, but Freeman was never much trouble to Australian batsmen in Australia.

Of the left-hand googlies Fleetwood-Smith was outstanding. At his top he would deceive anybody as to which way the ball would turn, and his great spin and nip off the pitch were most disconcerting. This necessarily brought inaccuracy in its train, and many a time he became the despair of his captain because of his loss of control.

Of a very different type were Rhodes, Verity, Jack White and Bert Ironmonger.

They depended almost entirely on accuracy. There is very little spin to be obtained from the index finger when the wicket is firm, so this type of bowler must pit his wits against the batsman and force him into the mental state in which he commits errors.

The scene changes rapidly on a sticky wicket or when the wicket crumbles towards the end of a match.

Wilfred Rhodes had virtually ended his career before I started, although I did play against him. In that brief encounter I could tell what a wonderful bowler he must have been.

Even so, I doubt if he could have been superior to Hedley Verity who learned his cricket from Rhodes and combined all the same attributes.

It was the identical theory on good wickets of forcing the batsman onto the defensive, bowling to a field and pegging away until the exasperated batsman would commit an indiscretion.

When rain produced a sticky wicket these left-handers became a nightmare to batsmen because, while they retained their uncanny accuracy, they could now get turn and lift as well.

Until recent years English teams always included a left-hander in case of rain.

Things have changed somewhat because in modern cricket the bowlers' footholds are covered even when the pitch remains uncovered.

The result has been that fast bowlers have been increasingly used on wet wickets to the semi-exclusion of left-handers.

It is not a trend which I admire.

The fast bowler gets his wickets under such conditions by intimidation—not wilful intimidation, but simply because the fast-flying ball causes a reflex protective action by the batsman.

There was, I think, more joy in the old-fashioned type of contest, and I am rather inclined to think even now it would be better to have all the pitch and the ends uncovered, or else have the whole thing covered. The present method legislates entirely in favour of the fast bowler.

There have been some great bowlers of the right-hand off-spin type. Don Blackie was a marvel for his age. He was remarkably clever at flighting the ball into a suitable breeze, and he also produced plenty of spin.

Amongst the moderns, Ian Johnson is a good example of one who intelligently combines the essential elements of flight, spin and accuracy.

The Daddy of Them All.   William J. O'Reilly first played against me on a concrete wicket, on what is now called the Bradman Oval at Bowral, in a Saturday afternoon fixture.   I survived his first few overs more by good luck than good management and remained 234 not out at stumps.

We continued that match the following Saturday at Wingello, and in the first over he bowled me round my legs before I had added to my score.

I was amazed that a man could turn the ball from the leg at his pace with his grip.

That was in the year 1926.

Before many more years were past every leading batsman in the world was amazed at the same thing.

O'Reilly did not hold the ball in the fingers quite like the orthodox leg-spinner.   It was held more towards the palm of the hand.   He was advised by certain " experts " to change his grip, but fortunately refused to be advised.

This grip did not enable him to spin the ball very much, but it did enable him to achieve phenomenal accuracy plus *sufficient* spin.

His stock ball was the leg-break, but now and then he would bowl a very well concealed googly or an overspin with a delightfully delicate change of pace and for good measure an occasional fast one.

This slower ball would often be played uppishly by batsmen because in addition to the deceptive flight O'Reilly's great height gave it much lift from the pitch.

The particular type of bowling he exploited enabled him to adopt an attacking field embodying two short-leg fieldsmen and he would concentrate on the leg stump for hours at a time.

O'Reilly never gave the batsman any respite. He was always aggressive, had great stamina and courage.

To hit him for four would usually arouse a belligerent ferocity which made you sorry.   It was almost like disturbing a hive of bees.   He seemed to attack from all directions.

His record in Test cricket is amazing, for in the brief period from the 1932-3 to the 1938 series, he achieved the distinction of getting 102 wickets against England.

No other player can approach such a performance.

Some other figures of his should also prove illuminating.   In Sydney First Grade District Cricket we find that over a period of 45 years from 1895 to 1939-40, only seven players have had a bowling average of less than 10, for 30 or more wickets.

Not one of those players did it more than once.

O'Reilly had a bowling average of less than 10 (with a minimum of 31 wickets) *seven times.*

Those figures I think are a true reflex of his greatness, especially as they were made during a period when the batsmen's averages all advanced considerably.

From what I have read and from conversations with old players, there can be no doubt S. F. Barnes was a magnificent bowler.

He must have been very similar to O'Reilly though I imagine slightly faster and without the wrong-un or googly.

It is impossible accurately to compare the two men of different generations, but my enquiries lead me to the conclusion that Barnes and O'Reilly were the two greatest bowlers who ever lived, and that each was undoubtedly the greatest of his time.

Their respective Anglo-Australian Test Match figures were :—

> Barnes   106 wkts.   2,288 runs.   21·58 average
> O'Reilly   102 „   2,616 „   25·64   „

The late Sir Stanley Jackson once tried very hard to convince me that George Lohmann was a greater bowler than O'Reilly.

I listened intently.   On every count (but one) I gave in to Sir Stanley that Lohmann might have been as good as O'Reilly.

However, I claimed as my winning point that O'Reilly bowled a googly as against Lohmann's orthodox off-break and on technical grounds must have been more difficult to handle.

With the tenacity which characterised his batting, Sir Stanley (not having played against O'Reilly) refused to concede the argument.

I am in no doubt on the point.

Batsmen.   Where there are so many great players one feels most diffident about making a choice, but after all it is only an opinion.

I am not going to try to assess the merits of W. G. Grace or Victor Trumper.   That would be absurd.

They must have been great players, and would have been so, no matter in which era they had lived.

Their batting averages cannot be construed as a reliable guide for no doubt wickets have changed, the psychology and the technique of cricket have altered ; whilst the wickets have been made larger, the ball smaller and the L.B.W. law amended in favour of the bowler.

If we were to take averages alone, how ludicrous it would be, for Trumper's Test Match figures against England were :—

> 74 innings.   5 not-outs.   2,263 runs.   32·79 average.

Alan Fairfax of New South Wales had a batting average of over 53, but nobody would dream of mentioning his name by way of comparison with Trumper.

Recently, an enthusiast was questioning me on the merits of the 1948 cricket team as compared with 1902. In substance I replied that unless the 1948 team was better we had not progressed.

He countered me by saying that I must admit 1948 had no slow bowler to compare with Grimmett.

I said that whilst such a statement was true, we didn't need one. We were playing under a new law which allowed a new ball after 55 overs (6-ball). Our team was selected with this in mind, our tactics were based thereon, and any comparisons just simply had to be related to the rules under which the game was played.

It is impossible to concede, for instance, that bowling was better before the introduction of the googly, for the latter was a technical improvement or an additional hazard for batsmen to overcome.

Fast bowlers could have been better, but not slow bowlers who did not know what a googly was.

So I am going to limit myself to discussion on the players I have seen in action.

For England—I think the leading four would be Hammond, Hobbs, Compton and Hutton.

Their Test records v. Australia are :—

	Innings	N.O.'s	Runs	Average
Hammond	58	3	2,852	51·8
Hobbs	71	4	3,636	54·26
Compton	26	3	1,235	53·6
Hutton	21	1	1,232	61·6

Hammond's career virtually coincided with mine. He was a batsman of the classical, majestic school.

Of lovely athletic build, light as a ballet dancer on his feet, always beautifully balanced, Hammond was the outstanding batsman between 1918 and 1938.

His game was based on driving, and nobody was his peer when it came to the cover drive which he made with tremendous power and equal ease off either the front or back foot.

There were two weaknesses (if such they could be termed) in Hammond's game. He did not like being forced to hook and seldom essayed either the hook or the pull shot. Furthermore, he did not possess an attacking range of shots between square-leg and mid-on.

But it is important to note that he had no defensive weakness whatever, and whilst bowlers might curb his attacking powers by concentrating on his leg stump (as O'Reilly and Grimmett did) they did not necessarily obtain his wicket by so doing.

On the other hand, his enormous off-side strength counter-balanced the on-side, and nobody can deny his claim to be at least the equal of any English batsman since 1918.

Of Jack Hobbs I write with some hesitancy, for I knew him only when past his prime, and from personal experience know such comparisons can be dangerous.

He was the best equipped batsman of all, in the technical sense—English or Australian.

I could detect no flaw in attack or defence.

His footwork was always correct, stroke production sound, and he seemed to get out simply because he was a fallible mortal and made errors of judgment.

Naturally he was not very aggressive when I first played against him in 1928, for at that time Jack was about 46 years of age.

A movie film of Jack Hobbs as he was in 1912 should be the perfect batting example for coaching purposes.

Apart from his great skill, Jack's cricket demeanour was always an object lesson.

In a way I cannot help comparing Hobbs with Hutton.

Leonard is certainly the best technician amongst modern players, and his chief fault lies in his lack of aggression.

It is not sufficient for one to keep the ball out of the stumps and not give a catch—there is need to attack, take the initiative from the bowlers and thereby pave the way for your comrades.

I know it has been said that Hutton's arm injury is the reason, but I cannot altogether subscribe to such a viewpoint. Firstly, Hutton had the same failing before his arm was injured, and secondly, for brief periods since that injury, notably the Second Test at Sydney in 1946, I have seen him play the most gloriously aggressive cricket that one could imagine.

I think he is still capable of rising to probably the most superb heights, but believe the constant demands of professional cricket may have taken the edge off his enthusiasm. It is extremely difficult to maintain a light-hearted aggressive spirit of batsmanship for years on end when playing cricket almost every day. All the more so when the fierce spotlight demands runs in addition to style.

Hutton has no weaknesses. As it was with Hammond, he does not like being forced to hook, but he can if he wants to. He is more at home to slow than to fast bowling, but the difference seems psychological.

Incidentally, it also applies to Compton and to almost any modern English cricketer, for these fellows have not recently seen fast bowling in England except when there was a visit from an overseas team.

Denis Compton—a glorious natural cricketer. His left elbow does not always please the purists and in some respects his stroke production is not up to the standard of other masters. Denis plays the cover drive very well but does not make the shot with the same majesty or grace as Wally Hammond.

Despite these imperfections in style, Compton's record portrays his greatness. He does things that are unexpected and which nobody else can copy.

It is only when a player flashes out these individualistic shots that you notice he is so different and superior, perhaps, to his contemporaries.

Denis has one weakness he has not yet been able to overcome—his inability to handle the short ball off a fast bowler.

The reason is obvious. He seems unable to decide whether to get inside the line of flight or whether to play a pull shot by standing on the leg-side of the ball.

With this uncertainty in his mind there must always be some risk about his shots, but once he decides to get inside the ball and hook from there, this weakness should be conquered.

In any case it is a small point to mention in a great player and a grand sportsman.

There is no doubt the debonair, easy-mannered Denis has been England's post-war cricket idol, and how modestly he has accepted all the tributes showered upon him. They have not been without just cause.

Did he not in 1947 break that long-standing record of Tom Hayward's?

Tom in 1906 scored 3,518 runs at an average of 66·37, but his figures must now give way to Compton, 3,816 runs, average 90·85.

Great players usually give the impression of possessing a bat of rare quality and power. Such an impression is created by Compton more than most, especially when he makes a cover drive, probably his pet shot.

It is not only in his stroke-making one senses Compton's ability. Often have I seen our bowlers astonished when they sent down a specially good ball only to see it countered by his splendid defence.

Of the Australians I select two as being the finest of the period— Ponsford and Morris.

The choice of Morris may be risky, for he is still young enough to have many years of cricket ahead of him, but I have confidence that his wonderful beginning will be more than maintained.

Bill Ponsford burst into cricket and instantly began to tear the record book to shreds by making abnormal scores with great rapidity and consistency. He carried all before him.

When Victoria were to play New South Wales in Sydney big posters would announce : " Come and see Ponsford play."

He was the victim of much jealousy (until I began to take the load off his shoulders) and became a target for fast bowlers who would, in advance, organise an attack on him. I saw, and heard, it happen.

The public had the impression in 1928 that there was some enmity between Larwood and Ponsford. Perhaps this view was coloured by an incident in the Sydney Test of that series when a ball from Larwood broke Ponsford's hand.

From then on until the end of Ponsford's career in 1934 (a period which included body-line) he was always being "shot at". These tactics undoubtedly hastened his retirement. A pity, for Bill was still a magnificent player when he retired.

There were innuendoes against Ponsford that he was afraid of fast bowling. Pure rubbish. I've seen him take tremendous thrashings—have seen his body black and blue—covered with bruises.

He did take the view, and rightly so, that cricket was not supposed to be a game in which a batsman's superiority should cause him to be the subject of attack—whereby physical injury became a paramount consideration. This is quite a different story.

He could play fast bowling splendidly. Many can testify to that fact. I still visualise the way he pasted Gubby Allen at Lord's in 1930.

Against slow and medium pace bowlers his bat seemed exceptionally broad. Admittedly it did not always appear straight, but it was usually in the same place as the ball.

This bat, incidentally, was fondly termed "Big Bertha" because of its weight. Many people may have wondered why Bill got such power into his shots with a short back lift. The secret was in strong wrists, good timing and this heavy bat.

Ponsford was essentially a "front-of-the-wicket" player with on-side play predominating in a game which possessed no weakness. Driving was always a feature of his play and seldom have I seen finer square-cutting than Bill could turn on against a fast bowler when he was in the mood.

Some of his early figures were stupendous, and to this day I believe he remains the one player in history with 2 scores over 400 to his credit and with the record of scoring over 1,000 runs in 4 consecutive innings.

There were more beautiful players, but for absolute efficiency and results, where can one turn to equal him?

It is perhaps a big thing to classify Arthur Morris as one of Australia's two greatest modern batsmen when, at the time of writing he started his cricket career against England a bare three years ago.

Nevertheless, I am prepared to say that if he never played another innings he is without doubt the finest left-hand batsman since Clem Hill.

The devotees of Bardsley may already be preparing to attack. I suggest you wait and read on.

It took Bardsley 49 innings against England to make 3 Test centuries. Morris has already scored 6 centuries in 17 innings.

Bardsley never once made a Test century in Australia against England. Morris made three in his first season.

Readers may not remember, but it is true that in his last 15 Test innings Bardsley only once scored over 25. If you suggest he was then approaching the end of his career, here are his scores in Australia 1911-12 and England 1912 :—30, 12, 0, 16, 5, 63, 0, 3, 21, 30, 0, a total of 180 in 11 innings, average 16·3.

Bardsley was then 28 years of age. Morris was 26 on the 1948 English tour.

According to Tate, Arthur Morris is "streets ahead of Bardsley." As Tate bowled against Bardsley he should be well qualified to speak.

Arthur Morris is a player of individuality—of distinctive style. One would not hold him up as a copybook model, for he, too, is a genius and does things others could not, and should not, try to emulate.

The way he holds his bat is unusual. He plays with stiff forearms when driving on the off, but despite the lack of wristiness, gets the power just the same.

Often he will play with the bat well away from the pads when trying to cover drive. Technically, it is wrong, but he seldom makes an error.

I've seen him bowled round his legs by going too far across to the off-side. The bowlers, noticing it, concentrated on this weakness to such an extent that he has now largely overcome the habit.

You might think I am finding a number of faults in one I class so great, but it indicates the measure of his ability to have them and still be so superior.

Arthur possesses an ideal temperament. Quiet and unobtrusive in manner, no nerves, but just that degree of tenseness which is better than being either phlegmatic or jittery. His courage is outstanding and he has a great capacity to absorb lessons.

During the early part of the English tour of 1948 Arthur was often in trouble, but his play improved visibly day by day until towards the close of the tour his superb artistry only became really obvious when at the wickets with him, for he made the most difficult bowling look easy.

Finally his figures for the tour were the best for any player (other than myself) making his first trip, and they have only been bettered twice in history by players (other than myself) even on their later tours.

There is only one shot in cricket which Arthur does not now play with safety and freedom. That is the late cut, and it is his grip and style which militate against it. All other shots, drives, cuts, hooks, glances, come alike to him, and his lofty shots over the infield are a revelation in their certainty and ease of execution.

On his 1948 form I rank Morris ahead of Woolley and Leyland. Supporters of Woolley will lift their eyebrows but only until I point out that Morris in his first season in England made 3 Test centuries. Woolley never made a century in England in Tests against Australia despite his 25 innings. In fact, Woolley only made 2 Test centuries against Australia in his career totalling 51 innings.

With normal luck Morris is destined to play an enormous part in Australian cricket for years to come, and with such a modest and lovable disposition he should also be a great ambassador for the game.

Stan McCabe. Here was a lovely player. He, like myself, was a country lad but his cricket was all polish and grace, for he came to the city early and gained experience on turf before his style was set.

There are not many who would place McCabe on the highest pedestal, yet his figures are better than those of Ponsford in Tests against England, and his style unquestionably more pleasing to the eye.

Perhaps he failed at times in concentration, and we always tend to remember his comparatively lean figures in the latter stages of his career.

I would include McCabe in this book if for no other purpose than to refer to his innings of 232 at Nottingham in the First Test in 1938.

That was the greatest innings I ever saw or ever hope to see. Let me tell you about it.

England had batted first and made 658 for 8 wickets (declared). A win for Australia was then out of the question. But could we even draw the match?

That seemed impossible when we had lost 6 wickets for 194 runs. But we had reckoned without McCabe.

Even though we relied on Barnett, O'Reilly, McCormick and Fleetwood-Smith to hold the other end (and of them only Barnett had any pretensions to being a batsman) Stan set about the bowling as though this thing was only a matter of time.

McCabe scored 232 out of 300. Towards the end I could scarcely watch the play. My eyes were filled as I drank in the glory of his shots.

No less than 44 runs came off Wright in 3 overs and finally, with the boundary studded with fieldsmen, he scored 72 runs in 28 minutes out of the last wicket partnership with Fleetwood-Smith of 77.

Such cricket I shall never see again, nor shall I ever feel competent adequately to describe this elegant display.

Let me therefore quote what Neville Cardus wrote about it in *The Manchester Guardian* :—

" Today McCabe honoured the First Test with a great and noble innings. McCabe changed the gravest situation with the ease of a man using a master key. In an hour he smashed the bowling and decimated a field which for long had been a close, keen net.

The dear valiance of his play won our hearts.

McCabe demolished the English attack with aristocratic politeness, good taste and reserve. Claude Duval never took possession of a stage coach with more charm of manner than this ; his boundaries were jewels and trinkets which he accepted as though dangling them in his hands.

In half an hour after lunch he scored nearly 50, unhurried but trenchant. He cut and glanced and drove, upright and lissom ; his perfection of touch moved the aesthetic sense ; this was the cricket of felicity, power and no covetousness, strength and no brutality, opportunism and no meanness, assault and no battery, dazzling strokes and rhetoric ; lovely brave batsmanship giving joy to the connoisseur, and all done in a losing hour.

He blinded us with fours in an over from Wright ; his innings became incandescent. With consummate judgment he kept the bowling ; Fleetwood-Smith was almost as much a spectator as I was.

This gorgeous Siroces had a calm pivotal spot ; McCabe's mind controlled the whirlwind ; his shooting stars flashed safely according to an ordered law of gravitation.

One of the greatest innings ever seen anywhere in any period of the game's history. Moving cricket which swelled the heart. He is in the line of Trumper, and no other batsman today but McCabe has inherited Trumper's sword and cloak."

When Stan. returned to our dressing room at the conclusion of this epic performance, I was so moved by the superb majesty of his innings that I could scarcely speak.

However, I gripped his hand, wet with perspiration. He was trembling like a thoroughbred racehorse. I can recall saying to him after expressing my congratulations, " I would give a great deal to be able to play an innings like that." No skipper was ever more sincere in his adulation of another's skill.

McCabe played one other outstanding innings against England.

It was on the Sydney Cricket Ground in 1932 against Jardine's team— 187 not out in the First Test.

Australians who saw it rate that knock as a masterpiece. So it was, and yet compared with his Nottingham effort it was as a sapphire to a diamond.

We see few players who combine skill and artistry in such a high degree.

Reference to McCabe would scarcely be complete without mention of his 189 not out against South Africa at Johannesburg in 1935.

I did not see the innings. Those who did, were enraptured by his glittering strokes.

A remarkable feature of the innings was that it concluded in a light so bad that Wade, the fielding South African Captain, appealed. Is there another instance in Test history ? I doubt it.

Here are the relative Test Match performances against England of Ponsford, Morris and McCabe :—

	Innings	N.O.'s	Agg.	Average
Ponsford	35	2	1,558	47·21
McCabe	43	3	1,931	48·27
Morris	17	2	1,199	79·9

I have, in mentioning these players, only touched the fringe.

The game is greater than the individual. True. But is not cricket the sum of the greatness of its players ?

Say what you will, the public do pay homage to the individuals. Such is human nature. It will never change.

Farewell

LOOKING BACK OVER THE TWENTY YEARS SINCE I ENTERED INTERNATIONAL cricket, I have asked myself, in the broadest sense, a natural question. " Was it worth while—was my career of any benefit to mankind and of service to the Empire ? "

Maybe I am not the best judge. However, I can justly lay claim to certain things.

Only four years after my entry into Test cricket, the game passed through a crisis which caused grave misgivings even in high political circles.

I had no voice in those matters, but as Captain of Australia from 1936 until 1948, I worked unceasingly towards two paramount ends :

(1) To try and elevate the standard of play along sound and attractive lines.
(2) To foster international goodwill through the medium of cricket.

Whether I succeeded in the first objective is a matter of opinion. At least we had at my retirement a great team worthy of comparison with those of all ages.

With regard to the second objective, I quote the British Minister of State, who said in 1948, " No team has ever done so much to stimulate and to create good feeling."

Then I would like to quote from a leading article in the *Canberra Times* which, commenting on my retirement, said :—

" In all these years, he (Bradman) has given rise to cheers literally from millions of throats, but no cheer has been associated with any act of violence or ill will. If a computation were to be made, it is probable that as many cheers have been evoked spontaneously for Bradman as were organised or demanded by Hitler. The man of violence perished by his own hand, and millions died and suffered and are still dying and suffering through his deeds.

There is no man, woman or child, who has suffered aught but

302

inspiration or happiness from the career of Bradman. This is a greater test of celebrity in world history.

No violent passion, no harmful deed, no revengeful spirit and no harm to any fellow man can be ascribed to the life of Bradman.

This is an exemplification of the basic appeal of cricket and a justification of the place which it has earned in the minds of British peoples."

The game of cricket existed long before I was born. It will be played centuries after my demise. During my career I was privileged to give the public my interpretation of its character in the same way that a pianist might interpret the works of Beethoven.

It is a comforting thought that only happiness and inspiration to one's fellow men could result.

The world today is beset by doubts and uncertainties.

The men who shall guide our destinies in the future will need courage, enterprise, and calm judgment. They will need to be vigilant and far-seeing.

Without doubt the laws of cricket and the conduct of the game are a great example to the world. We should all be proud of this heritage which I trust may forever stand as a beacon light guiding man's footsteps to happy and peaceful days.

THE
END

SIR DONALD BRADMAN'S SCORES IN
FIRST-CLASS CRICKET

In Australia

Season	Innings	Not Out	Highest Score	Runs	Average	Centuries
1927–28	10	1	134	416	46·22	2
1928–29	24	6	340*	1,690(a)	93·88	7
1929–30	16	2	452*	1,586	113·28	5
1930–31	18	—	258	1,422	79·00	5
1931–32	13	1	299*	1,403	116·91	7
1932–33	21	2	238	1,171	61·63	3
1933–34	11	2	253	1,192	132·44	5
1934–35	Did not play.					
1935–36	9	—	369	1,173	130·33	4
1936–37	19	1	270	1,552	86·22	6
1937–38	18	2	246	1,437	89·81	7
1938–39	7	1	225	919	153·16	6
1939–40	15	3	267	1,475	122·91	5
1940–41	4	—	12	18	4·50	0
1945–46	3	1	112	232	116·00	1
1946–47	14	1	234	1,032	79·38	4
1947–48	12	2	201	1,296	129·60	8(b)
1948–49	4	—	123	216	54·00	1

In England

Season	Innings	Not Out	Highest Score	Runs	Average	Centuries
1930	36	6	334	2,960(c)	98·66	10
1934	27	3	304	2,020	84·16	7
1938	26	5	278	2,429	115·66	13(d)
1948	31	4	187	2,428	89·92	11
Total	338	43	452*	28,067	95·14	117

1,690(a)   Record aggregate for an Australian season.
     8(b)   Record number of centuries for an Australian season.
2,960(c)   Record aggregate for an Australian in England.
    13(d)   Record number of centuries by an Australian in an English season.

Opponents	Innings	Not Out	Highest Score	Runs	Average	Centuries
England	63	7	334	5,028	89·78	19
West Indies	6	—	223	447	74·50	2
South Africa	5	1	299*	806	201·50	4
India	6	2	201	715	178·75	4
TOTAL	80	10	334	6,996	99·94	29

STATISTICAL RECORD OF
SIR DONALD BRADMAN'S CAREER

	Innings	Not Outs	H.Score	Aggregate	Average
All Matches	669	107	452*	50,731	90·27
All First-class Matches ..	338	43	452*	28,067	95·1
All Second-class Matches	331	64	320*	22,664	84·8
All Test Cricket ..	80	10	334	6,996	99·9
Tests v. England ..	63	7	334	5,028	89·78
Sheffield Shield Matches	96	15	452*	8,926	110·19
Grade Cricket	93	17	303	6,598	86·8

Number of Centuries Scored

All Matches ..	..	211
All First-class Matches	..	117
All Test Matches ..	..	29
Tests v. England ..	..	19
Sheffield Shield Matches	..	36
Grade Matches ..	..	28

Of the 211 centuries, 41 were double centuries, 8 treble centuries and one a quadruple century.

Methods of Dismissal

Number of innings		..	669
Caught	..	.. ..	340
Bowled	..	.. ..	148
Not out	..	.. ..	107
L.B.W.	..	.. ..	37
Stumped	..	.. ..	22
Run out	..	.. ..	14
Hit wicket	..	.. ..	1

BRADMAN'S RECORD SEASON BY SEASON

1927-8 (In Australia)

Match	First Innings		Second Innings	
New South Wales v. South Australia	c. Williams b. Scott	118	b. Grimmett	33
New South Wales v. Victoria	l.b.w., b. Harkoph	31	b. Blackie	5
New South Wales v. Queensland	b. Gough	0	c. O'Connor, b. Nothling	13
New South Wales v. South Australia	c. and b. McKay	2	st. Hack, b. Grimmett	73
New South Wales v. Victoria	st. Ellis, b. Blackie	7	Not out	134

1928-9 (In Australia)

Match	First Innings		Second Innings	
New South Wales v. M.C.C.	b. Freeman	87	Not out	132
An Australian Eleven v. M.C.C.	not out	58	l.b.w., b. Tate	18
Australia v. England	l.b.w., b. Tate	18	c. Chapman, b. White	1
Australia v. England	b. Hammond	79	c. Duckworth, b. Geary	112
Australia v. England	c. Larwood, b. Tate	40	run out	58
Australia v. England	c. Tate, b. Geary	123	not out	37
New South Wales v. M.C.C.	c. Tyldesley, b. White	15		
The Rest v. Australia	c. Oldfield, b. Grimmett	14	b. Oxenham	5
New South Wales v. Queensland	c. O'Connor, b. Thurlow	131	not out	133
New South Wales v. Victoria	b. Hendry	1	not out	71
New South Wales v. South Australia	c. Grimmett, b. Wall	5	b. Wall	2
New South Wales v. Victoria	not out	340		
New South Wales v. South Australia	c.Walker, b. Grimmett	35	c. Walker, b. Carlton	175

1929-30 (In Australia)

Match	First Innings		Second Innings	
New South Wales v. M.C.C.	b. Worthington	157		
Trial Match	c. Jackson, b. Oxenham	124	l.b.w., b. Grimmett	225

New South Wales v. Queensland	run out	48	c. O'Connor, b. Brew . . 66
New South Wales v. South Australia	run out	2	l.b.w., b. Grimmett . . 84
New South Wales v. Victoria	b. Alexander	89	not out 26
New South Wales v. Queensland	c. Leeson, b. Hurwood	3	not out 452
New South Wales v. South Australia	c. Richardson, b. Whitfield	47	
New South Wales v. Victoria	c. Ellis, b. Ironmonger	77	
1930 Australian XI v. Tasmania	l.b.w., b. Nash.	20	
1930 Australian XI v. Tasmania	c. Rushforth, b. Atkinson	139	
1930 Australian XI v. Western Australia	c. R. Bryant, b. Evans	27	

1930 (IN ENGLAND)

Australians v. Worcester	c. Walters, b. Brook.	236	
Australians v. Leicester	not out	185	
Australians v. Yorkshire	c. and b. Macauley	78	
Australians v. Lancashire	b. McDonald	9	not out 48
Australians v. M.C.C.	b. Allom	66	l.b.w., b. Stevens . . 4
Australians v. Derby	c. Elliott, b. Worthington	44	
Australians v. Surrey	not out	252	
Australians v. Oxford University	b. Garland-Wells	32	
Australians v. Hampshire	c. Mead, b. Boyes	191	
Australians v. Middlesex	b. Hearne	35	b. Stevens . . . 18
Australians v. Cambridge University	c. Barnes, b. Human.	32	
Australia v. England	b. Tate	8	b. Robins . . . 131
Australians v. Surrey	c. Allom, b. Shepherd	5	
Australians v. Lancashire	c. Duckworth, b. Sibbles	38	not out 23
Australia v. England	c. Chapman, b. White	254	c. Chapman, b. Tate. . 1
Australians v. Yorkshire	l.b.w., b. Robinson	1	
Australia v. England	c. Duckworth, b. Tate	334	
Australia v. England	c. Duleepsinhji, b. Peebles	14	

Match	First Innings		Second Innings	
Australians v. Somerset	c. and b. Young	117	not out	19
Australians v. Glamorgan	b. Ryan	58		
Australians v. Northants	b. Jupp	22	c. Hawtin, b. Cox	35
Australia v. England	c. Duckworth, b. Larwood	232		
Australians v. Gloucester	c. Sinfield, b. Parker	42	b. Parker	14
Australians v. Kent	l.b.w., b. Freeman	18	not out	205
Australians v. An England XI	l.b.w., b. Allom	63		
Australians v. Leveson-Gower's XI	b. Parker	96		
1930–1 (In Australia)				
New South Wales v. West Indians	c. Barrow, b. Francis	73	c. Headley, b. Martin	22
New South Wales v. West Indians	b. Constantine	10	l.b.w., b. Griffith	73
Australia v. West Indies	c. Grant, b. Griffith	4		
Australia v. West Indies	c. Barrow, b. Francis	25		
Australia v. West Indies	c. Grant, b. Constantine	223		
Australia v. West Indies	c. Roach, b. Martin	152		
Australia v. West Indies	c. Francis, b. Martin	43	b. Griffith	0
New South Wales v. South Australia	c. Pritchard, b. Deverson	61	c. Waite, b. Deverson	121
New South Wales v. South Australia	b. Richardson	258		
New South Wales v. Victoria	c. Hendry, b. a'Beckett	2		
New South Wales v. Victoria	c. Barnett, b. Alexander	33	c. Rigg, b. Ironmonger	220
Woodfull's XI v. Ryder's XI	b. Mailey	73	c. and b. Mailey	29
1931–2 (In Australia)				
New South Wales v. South Africans	c. and b. McMillan	30	c. Bell, b. Morkel	135
New South Wales v. South Africans	c. Curnow, b. McMillan	219		
New South Wales v. Queensland	c. Waterman, b. Gilbert	0		
New South Wales v. Victoria	c. Smith, b. Ironmonger	23	b. Nagel	167
New South Wales v. South Australia	b. Carlton	23	b. Wall	0

Australia v. South Africa	l.b.w., b. Vincent	226	
Australia v. South Africa	c. Viljoen, b. Morkel	112	
Australia v. South Africa	c. Cameron, b. Quinn	2	l.b.w., b. Vincent . 167
Australia v. South Africa	not out	299	

1932–3 (In Australia)

Combined XI v. M.C.C.	c. Hammond, b. Verity	3	c. Pataudi, b. Allen . 10
An Australian XI v. M.C.C.	l.b.w., b. Larwood	36	b. Larwood . 13
New South Wales v. M.C.C.	l.b.w., b. Tate	18	b. Voce . 23
Australia v. England	b. Bowes	0	not out . 103
Australia v. England	c. Allen, b. Larwood	8	c. and b. Verity . 66
Australia v. England	b. Larwood	76	c. Mitchell, b. Larwood . 24
Australia v. England	b. Larwood	48	b. Verity . 71
New South Wales v. M.C.C.	b. Mitchell	1	c. Ames, b. Hammond . 71
New South Wales v. Victoria	c. O'Brien, b. Fleetwood-Smith	238	not out . 52
New South Wales v. Victoria	c. Bromley, b. Ironmonger	157	
New South Wales v. South Australia	c. Ryan, b. Wall	56	b. Lee . 97

1933–4 (In Australia)

New South Wales v. Queensland	c. Andrews, b. Levy	200	
New South Wales v. South Australia	b. Collins	1	st. Walker, b. Grimmett . 76
New South Wales v. Victoria	not out	187	not out . 77
New South Wales v. Queensland	b. Brew	253	
New South Wales v. Victoria	c. Darling, b. Fleetwood-Smith	128	
Testimonial Match	c. Woodfull, b. Wall	55	c. Darling, b. Blackie . 101
New South Wales v. The Rest	c. Walker, b. Chilvers	22	b. Ebeling . 92

1934 (In England)

Australians v. Worcester	b. Howarth	206
Australians v. Leicester	b. Geary	65
Australians v. Cambridge University	b. Davies	0

Match	First Innings		Second Innings	
Australians v. M.C.C.	c. and b. Brown	5		
Australians v. Oxford University	l.b.w., b. Dyson	37		
Australians v. Hampshire	c. Mead, b. Baring	0		
Australians v. Middlesex	c. Hulme, b. Peebles	160		
Australians v. Surrey	c. Squires, b. Gover	77		
Australia v. England	c. Hammond, b. Geary	29	c. Ames, b. Farnes	25
Australia v. England	c. and b. Verity	36	c. Ames, b. Verity	13
Australians v. Northants	c. Bakewell, b. Matthews	65	b. Matthews	25
Australians v. Somerset	c. Luckes, b. White	17		
Australians v. Surrey	c. Brooks, b. Holmes	27	not out	61
Australia v. England	c. Ames, b. Hammond	30		
Australians v. Derby	c. Elliott, b. Townsend	71	not out	6
Australians v. Yorkshire	b. Leyland	140		
Australia v. England	b. Bowes	304		
Australia v. England	c. Ames, b. Bowes	244	b. Bowes	77
Australians v. Essex	b. Pearce	19		
Australians v. An English XI	not out	149		
Australians v. Leveson-Gower's XI	st. Duckworth, b. Verity	132		
	1935-6 (In Australia)			
South Australia v. M.C.C.	l.b.w., b. Sims	15	l.b.w., b. Parks	50
South Australia v. New South Wales	c. and b. Robinson	117		
South Australia v. Queensland	c. Tallon, b. Levy	233		
South Australia v. Victoria	c. Quin, b. Bromley	357		
South Australia v. Queensland	c. Wyeth, b. Gilbert	31		
South Australia v. New South Wales	c. Little, b. Hynes	0		
South Australia v. Tasmania	c. and b. Townley	369		
South Australia v. Victoria	c. Ledward, b. Ebeling	1		

An Australian XI v. M.C.C.	b. Worthington	63		
Australia v. England	c. Worthington, b. Voce	38	c. Fagg, b. Allen	0
Australia v. England	c. Allen, b. Voce	0	b. Verity	82
Australia v. England	c. Robins, b. Verity	13	c. Allen, b. Verity	270
South Australia v. M.C.C.	c. Ames, b. Barnett	38		
Australia v. England	b. Allen	26	c. and b. Hammond	212
Australia v. England	b. Farnes	169		
South Australia v. Victoria	c. O'Brien, b. Gregory	192		
South Australia v. Queensland	st. Tallon, b. Wyeth	123		
South Australia v. New South Wales	l.b.w., b. O'Reilly	24	not out	38
South Australia v. Victoria	c. Ebeling, b. Fleetwood-Smith	31	c. Hassett, b. McCormick	8
Testimonial Match	c. O'Reilly, b. Grimmett	212	c. Fingleton, b. Grimmett	13

1937–8 (In Australia)

South Australia v. New South Wales	c. O'Brien, b. O'Reilly	91	c. Chipperfield, b. O'Reilly	62
South Australia v. Queensland	c. Baker, b. Dixon	246	not out	39
South Australia v. Victoria	c. Sievers, b. Gregory	54	c. Sievers, b. Gregory	35
South Australia v. Queensland	c. Tallon, b. Dixon	107	c. Hackett, b. Allen	113
South Australia v. New South Wales	c. McCabe, b. O'Brien	44	not out	104
South Australia v. Victoria	b. McCormick	3	c. Ledward, b. Thorn	85
Testimonial Match	b. Grimmett	17		
South Australia v. West Australia	c. Wilberforce, b. Eyres	101		
South Australia v. New Zealanders	c. Tindill, b. Cowie	11		
1938 Australian XI v. Tasmania	c. Sankey, b. Thomas	79		
1938 Australian XI v. Tasmania	b. Jeffrey	144		
1938 Australian XI v. Western Australia	st. Lovelock, b. Zimbulis	102		

Match	1938 (In England) First Innings		Second Innings
Australians v. Worcester	c. Martin, b. Howarth	258	
Australians v. Oxford University	l.b.w., b. Evans	58	
Australians v. Cambridge University	c. Mann, b. Wild	137	
Australians v. M.C.C.	c. Robins, b. Smith	278	
Australians v. Northants	c. James, b. Partridge	2	
Australians v. Surrey	c. Brooks, b. Watts	143	
Australians v. Hampshire	not out	145	
Australians v. Middlesex	c. Compton, b. Nevell	5	not out 30
Australia v. England	c. Ames, b. Sinfield	51	not out 144
Australians v. Gentlemen	c. Valentine, b. Meyer	104	
Australians v. Lancashire	c. Pollard, b. Phillipson	12	not out 101
Australia v. England	b. Verity	18	not out 102
Australians v. Yorkshire	st. Wood, b. Smailes	59	c. Barber, b. Smailes. 42
Australians v. Warwickshire	c. Wilmot, b. Mayer	135	
Australians v. Notts.	l.b.w., b. Jepson	56	c. Jepson, b. Marshall 144
Australia v. England	b. Bowes	103	c. Verity, b. Wright 16
Australians v. Somerset	b. Andrews	202	
Australians v. Glamorgan	st. H. Davies, b. Clay	17	
Australians v. Kent	c. Todd, b. Watt	67	
1938-9 (In Australia)			
M.C.C. Centenary Match	b. Nagel	118	
South Australia v. New South Wales	b. Murphy	143	
South Australia v. Queensland	c. Baker, b. Christ	225	
South Australia v. Victoria	c. Hassett, b. Sievers	107	
South Australia v. Queensland	c. Christ, b. W. Tallon	186	
South Australia v. New South Wales	not out	135	
South Australia v. Victoria	c. Fleetwood-Smith, b. Thorn	5	

Match	Dismissal	1st	2nd
1939–40 (In Australia)			
South Australia v. Victoria	run out	76	64
South Australia v. New South Wales	not out	251	90
South Australia v. Queensland	c. Hansen, b. Ellis	138	
South Australia v. Victoria	c. Johnson, b. Fleetwood-Smith	267	
South Australia v. Queensland	c. Dixon, b. Stackpoole	0	97
South Australia v. New South Wales	l.b.w., b. O'Reilly	39	40
South Australia v. West Australia	c. Lovelock, b. MacGill	42	209
South Australia v. West Australia	c. Zimbulis, b. Eyres	135	
Rest of Australia v. New South Wales	c. Saggers, b. O'Reilly	25	2
1940–1 (In Australia)			
South Australia v. Victoria	c. Sievers, b. Dudley	0	6
Patriotic Match	c. Tamblyn, b. Ellis	0	12
1945–6 (In Australia)			
South Australia v. Queensland	c. Tallon, b. McCool	68	52
South Australia v. Services Team	c. Carmody, b. Williams	112	
1946–7 (In Australia)			
South Australia v. M.C.C.	c. and b. Smith	76	3
An Australian XI v. M.C.C.	c. Pollard, b. Compton	106	
South Australia v. Victoria	st. Baker, b. Johnson	43	119
Australia v. England	b. Edrich	187	
Australia v. England	l.b.w., b. Yardley	234	
Australia v. England	b. Yardley	79	49
Australia v. England	b. Bedser	0	56
Australia v. England	b. Wright	12	63
South Australia v. M.C.C.	c. Langridge, b. Wright	5	

Match	First Innings		Second Innings	
1947–8 (In Australia)				
South Australia v. Indians	c. Sarwate, b. Mankad	156	st. Sen, b. Mankad	12
South Australia v. Victoria	l.b.w., b. Johnson	100		
An Australian XI v. Indians	c. Amarnath, b. Hazare	172	c. Sarwate, b. Mankad	36
Australia v. India	hit wicket, b. Amarnath	185		
Australia v. India	b. Hazare	13		
Australia v. India	l.b.w., b. Phadkar	132	not out	127
Australia v. India	b. Hazare	201		
Australia v. India	retired hurt	57		
1948 Australian XI v. Western Australia	c. Outridge, b. O'Dwyer	115		
1948 (In England)				
Australians v. Worcester	b. Jackson	107		
Australians v. Leicester	c. Corrall, b. Etherington	81		
Australians v. Surrey	b. Bedser	146		
Australians v. Essex	b. P. Smith	187		
Australians v. M.C.C.	c. Edrich, b. Deighton	98		
Australians v. Lancashire	b. Hilton	11	st. E. Edrich, b. Hilton	43
Australians v. Notts.	b. Woodhead	86		
Australians v. Sussex	b. Cornford	109		
Australia v. England	c. Hutton, b. Bedser	138	c. Hutton, b. Bedser	0
Australians v. Yorkshire	c. Yardley, b. Wardle	54	c. Hutton, b. Aspinall	86
Australia v. England	c. Hutton, b. Bedser	38	c. Edrich, b. Bedser	89
Australians v. Surrey	c. Barton, b. Squires	128		
Australia v. England	l.b.w., b. Pollard	7	not out	30
Australians v. Middlesex	c. Compton, b. Whitcombe	6		
Australia v. England	b. Pollard	33	not out	173
Australians v. Derby	b. Gothard	62		

Australians v. Warwickshire	b. Hollies	31 not out		13
Australians v. Lancashire	c. Wilson, b. Roberts	28 not out		133
Australia v. England	b. Hollies	0		
Australians v. Kent	c. Valentine, b. Crush	65		
Australians v. Gentlemen	c. Donnelly, b. Brown	150		
Australians v. South of England	c. Mann, b. Bailey	143		
Australians v. Leveson-Gower's XI	c. Hutton, b. Bedser	153		

1948–9 (IN AUSTRALIA)

Bradman Testimonial	c. Harvey, b. Dooland	123	c. Saggers, b. Johnston	10
Oldfield-Kippax Testimonial	c. Meuleman, b. Miller	53		
South Australia v. Victoria	b. W. Johnston	30		

NATURE OF BRADMAN'S DISMISSALS

Bowled	78
Caught by fieldsman	121
Caught and bowled	12
Caught by wicket-keeper	40
Stumped	12
Run out	4
Leg before wicket	27
Hit wicket	1
Not out	43
	338

INDEX

317

318

319

All books from the Pavilion Cricket Library are available from your local bookshop, price £12.95 hardback, £6.95 paperback new titles, £5.95 backlist, or they can be ordered direct from Pavilion Books Limited.

New Titles

Farewell to Cricket
Don Bradman

Jack Hobbs
Ronald Mason

End of an Innings
Denis Compton

Ranji
Alan Ross

Backlist

In Celebration of Cricket
Kenneth Gregory

The Best Loved Game
Geoffrey Moorhouse

Bowler's Turn
Ian Peebles

Lord's 1787–1945
Sir Pelham Warner

Lord's 1946–1970
Diana Rait Kerr and Ian Peebles

P.G.H. Fender
Richard Streeton

Through the Caribbean
Alan Ross

Hirst and Rhodes
A.A. Thomson

Two Summers at the Tests
John Arlott

Batter's Castle
Ian Peebles

The Ashes Crown the Year
Jack Fingleton

Life Worth Living
C.B. Fry

Cricket Crisis
Jack Fingleton

Brightly Fades The Don
Jack Fingleton

Cricket Country
Edmund Blunden

Odd Men In
A.A. Thomson

Crusoe on Cricket
R.C. Robertson-Glasgow

Benny Green's Cricket Archive

Please enclose cheque or postal order for the cover price, plus postage:

UK: 65p for first book; 30p for each additional book to a maximum of £2.00. Overseas: £1.20 for first book; 45p for each additional book to a maximum of £3.00

Pavilion Books reserve the right to show new retail prices on covers which may differ from those previously advertised in the text or elsewhere and to increase postal rates in accordance with the Post Office's charges.